the pitc

hfork500

OUR GUIDE TO THE GREATEST SONGS FROM PUNK TO THE PRESENT

Edited by Scott Plagenhoef and Ryan Schreiber

Deputy Editor: Chris Dahlen

Contributing Editors: Nitsuh Abebe, Catherine Lewis, and Mark Richardson

A Fireside Book

Published by Simon & Schuster

NEW YORK   LONDON   TORONTO   SYDNEY

Fireside
A Division of Simon & Schuster, Inc.
1230 Avenue of the Americas
New York, NY 10020

First Fireside trade paperback edition November 2008

FIRESIDE and colophon are registered trademarks of Simon & Schuster, Inc.

For information about special discounts for bulk purchases, please contact Simon & Schuster Special Sales at 1-800-456-6798 or business@simonandschuster.com.

Designed by Chris Capuozzo / Intergalactico LLC and Thea Kluge
Cover illustration by Chris Capuozzo / Intergalactico LLC

Manufactured in the United States of America

10 9 8 7 6 5 4 3 2 1

Library of Congress Cataloging-in-Publication Data

The Pitchfork 500 / edited by Scott Plagenhoef and Ryan Schreiber.
        p. cm.

"A Fireside book."

1. Popular music—History and criticism. 2. Rock music—History and criticism. 3. Popular music—Miscellanea. 4. Rock music—Miscellanea.

I. Schreiber, Ryan. II. Plagenhoef, Scott. III. Pitchfork (Firm). IV. Title: The Pitchfork five hundred.

ML3470.P57 2008
781.6609—dc22   200812831

ISBN-13: 978-1-4165-6202-3
ISBN-10: 1-4165-6202-8

Contents

Introduction

The Internet was still in its infancy when I started Pitchfork in 1995: The Web had hardly begun to connect people, e-mail was a novelty, and the only useful music resources were a few infrequently updated webzines, fan sites, and incomplete databases. Coverage of independent music was especially scarce: Primitive searches for "Feelies," "Meat Puppets," and "Ride" mostly returned porn links.

Those early frontier days of the Internet had the same kind of leveling effect on writers, critics, and publishers as self-released seven-inches had on the first wave of independent punk bands: Just as those groups realized it was possible to cut records and book tours on the cheap, the Web made it affordable—in fact, virtually free—to carve out a daily space where your thoughts, opinions, and insights could reach like-minded people. In my case, it allowed a non-college-educated nineteen-year-old with no writing experience and even less income to create the independent music publication I'd always wished existed—something that production and distribution costs would have made an impossibility in print.

Pitchfork was started as a means of drawing focus to burgeoning underground artists, but also to take shots at the corporate homogenization of alt-rock culture. In 1993, Beck could score a hit song with a tape loop and a four-track recorder, but just two years later, commercial alternative airwaves began ignoring deserving new talent—Built to Spill, Stereolab, Elliott Smith—in favor of disposable three-noun/one-hit grunge-pop bands like Primitive Radio Gods, Seven Mary Three, and Our Lady Peace. Independent rock music was thriving, but only a niche group of dedicated fans was paying attention.

As Pitchfork gained readers and contributors, its musical palette expanded: It began to explore new forms of electronic music (jungle, IDM, minimal), hip-hop (underground, dirty South, hyphy), avant-garde (ambient, noise, modern classical), roots (folk, alt-country), and, around the turn of the decade, pop music, which was experiencing a creative renaissance, as producers like Timbaland, the Neptunes, and Kanye West battled to outcrazy each other on the charts. The new philosophy was equal opportunity—great music of all forms, regardless of context.

In this book we dig into the 500 best songs of the past three decades, starting with the year that changed everything: 1977. It's famously the year that punk hit its stride, spawning the do-it-yourself mentality that would become an ideology and way of life for independent musicians. And that was just rock. Two other subcultures also came to prominence that year: Disco was taking over dance clubs, marking the rise of the DJ and North American cratedigger culture, while the seeds of hip-hop were being planted at dance parties in the Bronx.

As these quiet revolutions emerged, they would quickly change the face of music: Disco would influence new strains of electronic music throughout the 1980s and '90s before eventually merging with rock in the '00s. Hip-hop would spread its positive message during the '80s before refocusing on gritty realism a decade later, ascending as the dominant cultural and musical force. And punk would birth post-punk, hardcore, and indie rock, inspiring fans to form their own bands, release their own albums, and book their own tours, creating a parallel music industry that valued artistic freedom over platinum sales.

So much great music has emerged over the past three decades that compiling a definitive list of just 500 essential songs was nearly impossible. After all, the math averages out to only sixteen songs per year—a tiny fraction of our favorites. In many ways, choosing 500 albums would have been easier, yet many of the most significant artists of this period typically worked outside that format: In punk, hip-hop, dance, reggae, and pop music, singles were the primary focus, and many of the most influential and genre-defining tracks never materialized on proper LPs. This approach forced us to be even more selective: The overwhelming majority of artists in this book are represented by just one song, and only the truly exceptional are featured more than twice.

But ultimately, this project was about much more than simple song selection: This book is organized in chronological order, each chapter representing a distinct period and offering a loose narrative of how music itself progressed. It's an attempt to contextualize how the musical landscape of the day informed its artists—to bring into perspective the influences that shaped these songs, and how they, in turn, shaped those that followed.

This book encompasses just thirty years—less than half a lifetime—and as new technologies make new sounds possible, its evolution will continue to accelerate. The 500 essential songs of the next thirty years are already being written. We look forward to hearing and documenting what's coming.

Ryan Schreiber
Founder/President
Pitchfork

Editors and Contributors

Editors

Ryan Schreiber is a lifelong music obsessive living in Brooklyn with his wife, Elizabeth. He is the founder and president of Pitchfork, and he loves his job.

Scott Plagenhoef (SP) is the editor-in-chief of Pitchfork and the author of *If You're Feeling Sinister,* a 33⅓ series book published by Continuum. He is a former editor of numerous now-defunct sports magazines, and has contributed to *Time Out Chicago,* the *Chicago Tribune,* and the *Chicago Sun-Times,* among others. He lives in Chicago with his wife, Sarah, and his dog, Beckett, and he supports Arsenal.

Chris Dahlen (CD) writes about music, games, and technology for Pitchfork, *Paste* magazine, and *The Onion's* A. V. Club. He lives in Portsmouth, New Hampshire, with his wife, Teri, and his son, Nicholas.

Nitsuh Abebe (NA) is a writer of fiction and music criticism. He lives in New York and thinks you're great.

A chemical engineer by day, **Catherine Lewis** writes about music regularly for *The Washington Post.* Her photographs have appeared in *The Wire, Harp,* and *The Village Voice,* and on Ecstatic Peace's Nautical Almanac benefit compilation *Less Self Is More Self.*

Mark Richardson (MR) is the managing editor at Pitchfork, to which he has contributed since 1998. His column, "Resonant Frequency," appears monthly on the site. Mark's music criticism has appeared in *L.A. Weekly, Metro Times Detroit, Paste,* and *Washington City Paper,* and his 33⅓ series book *Zaireeka* is forthcoming from Continuum.

Contributors

Zach Baron (ZB) is a Pitchfork staff writer. He lives in New York.

Andy Battaglia (AB) lives in New York. He works as an editor for *The Onion's* A. V. Club and wanders an aesthetic world triangulated, more or less, by techno, Buster Keaton, and Donald Barthelme.

Stuart Berman (SB) is the senior editor of the Toronto arts and culture magazine *Eye Weekly,* and is the author of *This Book Is Broken: The Broken Social Scene Story,* due in fall 2008 from House of Anansi Press. Over the past ten years, his writing has also appeared in *Magnet, The Village Voice, CMJ New Music Monthly,* and NME.com.

Tom Breihan (TB) is an associate editor at *The Village Voice,* where he writes the daily "Status Ain't Hood" blog. He's also written for *Spin, Blender, King, Stuff, Seattle Weekly, Baltimore City Paper,* and any number of other music websites, magazines, and newspapers he can't remember now. He's been a Pitchfork contributor since 2004. He lives in Brooklyn with his wife, Bridget, and his dog, Finnegan.

Jason Crock (JC) has contributed to Pitchfork since 2005. He resides in Chicago, where he works as an editor at a publishing house. He has also written for *UR Chicago* and the *Chicago Reader.*

Grayson Currin (GC) is the only full-time employee of the *Independent Weekly* born after the central North Carolina alternative newspaper was founded. He serves as the newspaper's music editor and freelances for a variety of publications. He has been writing about good guitarists and bad drummers for Pitchfork since May 2006.

Drew Daniel (DD) lives in Baltimore with his boyfriend and musical partner, M. C. Schmidt. Together they are the electronic band Matmos. He teaches in the Department of English at Johns Hopkins University and has published a book on Throbbing Gristle's album *20 Jazz Funk Greats.*

Geeta Dayal (GD) is a freelance scientist-turned-journalist who divides her time between Boston, New York, and Berlin. She is currently based at the MIT Media Lab, where she is a researcher at the MIT Center for Future Civic Media.

Stephen M. Deusner (SD) is a Washington, D.C.–based freelance writer whose work has appeared in numerous print and online publications, including *Paste, Harp,* and the *Memphis Flyer*. He has been a Pitchfork staff writer since 2004.

In 1856, farmer Arcangelo DiCrescenzo married Letizia Sirolli. The twenty-two-year-old couple buried two of their infant children—Domenico and Domenica—on their Gessopalena plot. Their great-great-great-grandson, **Brent DiCrescenzo (BD)**, would grow up in places like Canton, Valparaiso, and Roswell, but not the famous ones. He was nearly killed by a treble-hook fishing lure jammed into his wrist (skateboarding accident, 1986) and an Audi (bicycle accident, 2004).

Ryan Dombal (RD) is a staff writer at *Blender* and lives in Manhattan.

Tom Ewing (TE) has had an unrequited crush on pop music since 1980. To express it, he founded the online community ILX and the pop culture zine freakytrigger.co.uk, where he writes regularly about music and anything else.

Sean Fennessey (SF) is the associate music editor at *VIBE* magazine. He lives in New York City with his girlfriend and the spirit of a dog he has not yet purchased. Sean has written about music and culture for *Spin, Blender,* and *Complex.*

Tim Finney (TF) is a freelance music journalist in Melbourne, Australia.

Jess Harvell (JH) is a writer living in Baltimore, where he drinks too much and is often tired.

Eric Harvey (EH) is a Ph.D. student at Indiana University, studying communication and Culture and Ethnomusicology. He has been published in *New Media and Society,* written for *The Arizona Republic,* and blogs at marathonpacks.com.

Marc Hogan (MH) is a music critic and business journalist living in New York. He has been a Pitchfork contributing writer since 2004. His work has also appeared in *Spin, The Village Voice,* BusinessWeek.com, the *Chicago Tribune,* Playboy.com, and *Paste,* as well as several trade publications owned by the *Financial Times.*

Brian Howe (BH) is a freelance writer living in Chapel Hill, North Carolina. Besides Pitchfork, his arts and entertainment journalism appears regularly in *Paste* magazine (where he is a contributing editor), *Independent Weekly,* TheFanzine.com, and the mp3 blog Moistworks.com.

Maura Johnston (MJ) is the editor of *Idolator.* She lives, works, and listens to her dusty collection of Sarah seven-inches in Astoria, New York.

Joshua Klein (JK) is a freelance writer based in Chicago. Along with Pitchfork, he writes regularly for the *Chicago Tribune* and *Time Out Chicago,* with bylines in the occasional book, magazine, newspaper, or other publications wherever music and movies are concerned.

Matt LeMay (ML) is a writer and musician living in New York. His band, Get Him Eat Him, has released two full-length albums on Absolutely Kosher Records. He is currently working on a book about Elliott Smith's *XO* for the 33$^1/_3$ series.

Dominique Leone (DL) is a musician, producer, and writer based in San Francisco. Besides Pitchfork, his writing has appeared in *Paste, Seattle Weekly,* All-Music Guide, and *Trouser Press.* His debut record is available on Strømland, and he's currently thinking about spending time playing in Switzerland. Or maybe Italy.

Marc Masters (MM) lives in Arlington, Virginia, and writes for Pitchfork, *The Wire, Paper Thin Walls, Signal to Noise,* and the *Baltimore City Paper.* His first book, *No Wave,* was released in 2008 by Black Dog Publishing.

Michaelangelo Matos (MiM) is a writer in Seattle.

Rob Mitchum (RM) has a Ph.D. in neurobiology. No, really. He also has written about music and science, and was a staff writer for Pitchfork for nearly six years. Rob is currently a reporter at the *Chicago Tribune,* under his grown-up name, Robert.

Matthew Murphy (MMu) lives in Minnesota with his wife, three young children, and an ever-dwindling number of brain cells.

Nate Patrin (NP) is a lifelong resident of St. Paul, Minnesota, and has been writing about music dating back to his review of the Ramones' *Acid Eaters* in 1994 for his high school newspaper. Since then, he's contributed to Minneapolis/St. Paul *City Pages, Spin, Blender, Seattle Weekly, Paper Thin Walls, eMusic,* and Pitchfork, as well as authoring the 2008 edition of Workman's *365 Tunes* Page-A-Day calendar.

Amanda Petrusich (AP) is the author of *Pink Moon.* Her second book, *It Still Moves: Lost Songs, Lost Highways, and the Search for the Next American Music,* is forthcoming from Faber and Faber. She has been writing for Pitchfork since early 2003. She lives and works in Brooklyn.

Amy Phillips (APh) is the senior news editor at Pitchfork. She has written for *The Village Voice,* the *Philadelphia Inquirer, Blender, Spin, Seventeen,* her long-lost teenage zine *Junkyard Rat* (no, you can't see a copy), and many other publications. She loves Fall Out Boy and Sonic Youth equally.

Canadian-born **Mark Pytlik (MP)** has written about music for *XLR8R,* the *National Post,* NME.com, and *Eye Toronto.* He is also the author of the Björk biography *Wow & Flutter.* He currently lives in London, England, where he works in film production and digital media.

After badmouthing the site on his proto-blog Popshots.org, **David Raposa (DR)** began contributing to Pitchfork in 2001, and officially joined the staff in 2003. He has been published by *The Village Voice,* the *Hartford Courant,* fakejazz.com, and notable music blog NYLPM (part of the Freaky Trigger web-media empire). When not upsetting Pitchfork editors, he contributes to both the satirical sports blog Yard Work and catch-all webzine *Cave 17.*

Barcelona-based journalist and critic **Philip Sherburne (PS)** has been writing about electronic and experimental music since the late 1990s and is one of the genre's most respected critical observers. He is the editor of *Earplug,* an electronic-music newsletter, and his columns

appear regularly in Pitchfork, *The Wire,* and *eMusic.* His writing has also appeared in *The New York Times, Slate, Interview, Parkett, Frieze, XLR8R, URB,* German magazines *Groove* and *De:Bug,* and other publications.

Julianne Escobedo Shepherd (JS) is a former dance teacher (Latin, hip-hop), current senior editor of *The FADER,* and blogs at urbanhonking.com/cowboyz. She has written about music, dance, politics, culture, and Mariah Carey for *The New York Times, VIBE,* MTV, and many more. People with Internet: Please read back episodes of her now-bodied column, "INTERROBANG," on Pitchfork. She lives in Boerum Hill, Brooklyn, and voted for Barack Obama.

Dave Stelfox (DS) is a music critic from London. In addition to Pitchfork, his work can be found in *The Wire, Uncut, The Guardian,* and *The Village Voice.*

Brandon Stosuy (BS) is a writer who lives in New York. *Up Is Up, But So Is Down,* his anthology of downtown New York literature, was a 2006 *Village Voice* book of the year.

Joe Tangari (JT) is a senior contributor to Pitchfork and has written for the site since 2000. He is a musical xenophile and plans to see and hear as much of the world as possible before he dies.

Stephen Troussé (ST) lives in London and has written for *Melody Maker, Freaky Trigger, Uncut,* Pitchfork, *Paste, Gay Times,* and *Loaded.* He also co-edited *The Message,* a book about pop lyrics.

Douglas Wolk (DW) writes about pop music, politics, and comics for *Rolling Stone, The New York Times, Blender,* the *Believer,* and elsewhere. He is the author of *Reading Comics: How Graphic Novels Work and What They Mean* and the 33$\frac{1}{3}$ series book *Live at the Apollo.*

Chapter One:
1977–1979

Rock critics have long romanticized 1976 as a Year Zero, a time when the tired modes and myths of classic rock were challenged by hungry young outsiders with a back-to-basics aesthetic. Too often, when this story is told, the punk music of the time is viewed as a one-off moment rather than a new beginning. In a sense, this myth has emphasized punk's combustible qualities, acknowledging its help in overthrowing a dying orthodoxy, but lazily failed to explain how it led to what happened next.

That's a shame and a mistake, because the thirty years following punk have seen pop splintered, democratized, rearranged, and delivered in ways much richer than the typical survey of post–baby boomer music—often reduced to signposts such as the Clash, U2, Public Enemy, Nirvana, and Radiohead— would lead listeners to believe. To reduce the legacy of punk to a handful of chords and a bit of attitude misses its most lasting contribution to the worlds of music: the philosophy that any kid with desire and some ideas can and should make music.

Before punk, there was a belief that rock music was something made by corporate-funded and well-practiced individuals in expensive studios. Not surprisingly, a lot of music fans found they couldn't relate to bearded millionaires performing in stadiums, and they set off to create their own sounds—and not just with the electric guitar. In the Bronx, urban youth reappropriated turntables and turned them into revolutionary noisemakers, forging hip-hop from the desperation to create music but the impossibility of getting "proper" instruments. Meanwhile, in industrial Northern England, garage bands formed around crude synthesizers that echoed the mechanics of the factories in cities like Sheffield and Manchester. A decade later, kids in Chicago and Detroit would manipulate machines and ape the factories in their own cities too, inventing house and techno music in the process.

The network of independent artists, labels, and promoters that emerged in the wake of punk in England created a nationwide DIY system that incorporated the nascent three-chord bands of 1976–77 and other adventurous sounds. In the U.S., punk took a slower road to kick-starting indie and college rock, but in the UK it quickly begat a series of ideas and songs that— more than those short, staccato blasts of nihilism— formed the seeds of the next thirty years of music. On both continents, the key figures of post-punk vociferously engaged with everything around them, looking as far afield as possible for their inspirations. Rather than boxing oneself into careerist tropes, artists on both continents—Talking Heads, Public Image Ltd., Blondie, the Clash, Suicide, Magazine—tuned in to disco, hip-hop, Jamaican music, electronic music, and krautrock, absorbing and regurgitating new music at alarming speeds.

Disco itself, too often dismissed as an opulent joke, served as a sort of R&B version of punk music, casting aside supper-club soul and, increasingly, acid-fried funk and returning soul music to a more crucial, popular sound. Giorgio Moroder gave it a sleek European sheen, while in New York underground DJs made it elastic and malleable, forging today's club culture in the process. Eventually, like punk, facets of it would coalesce into a rigid genre, fixing it in people's minds as a period piece.

But the real power of this era derived as much from punk as it did from the art-rock godfathers who kick off this chapter and set the tone and tenor for the next three decades: David Bowie, Lou Reed, Iggy Pop, Kraftwerk, and Brian Eno. That quintet of artists (both in those guises as well as with bands such as the Velvet Underground, the Stooges, and Roxy Music) laid the foundation for most of the restlessness, glamour, decadence, and potency in the pages to come— not just in rock, but in hip-hop, dance, and pop as well. Incredibly, as diverse as the descendants of punk would become, most of them can be traced back to at least one of these artists in sound or spirit.
—SP

David Bowie: "'Heroes'" 1977

David Bowie's multiple genre and fashion changes came not from some prescient, chameleonic ability but from sheer music geekdom.

Instead of settling for influence, Bowie assimilated—and collaborated with—his musical idols. And usually those collaborators emerged from the Bowie career track having produced their lives' great achievements. Young Bowie worshiped the Velvet Underground and the Stooges before throwing his arms around their singers, Lou Reed and Iggy Pop, in nightclub booths. Out came Reed's *Transformer* and Iggy's *Raw Power*. Soon, Bowie would tire of glam, too, and fly to Philadelphia to try his hand at American R&B.

Bowie's records during this period demonstrate the behavior of a hyperactive and ecstatic artist. But perhaps Bowie's greatest influence was cocaine. As his personae accelerated, so did his dependency. The drug etiolated his frame. By the mid-1970s, Bowie crashed in Europe. He began listening to the electronic music and rhythms coming from Germany and Brian Eno's tape loop experiments with guitarist Robert Fripp, which they dubbed "Frippertronics." Naturally, he rang up Eno, Fripp, and krautrock producer Conny Plank for his forthcoming recordings. Plank turned him down, but Eno and Fripp landed with Bowie in Berlin.

Bowie's Berlin Trilogy of albums—*Low, "Heroes,"* and *Lodger*—is a misnomer: *Low* came from sessions at the Château d'Hérouville, northwest of Paris, while *Lodger* formed in Switzerland. Responsibility for the Berlin Trilogy distinction lies with the overshadowing success of *"Heroes,"* recorded at Die Hansa Tonstudio, between Berlin's zoological park and dividing wall.

Bowie, longing for anonymity and regimentation, had absconded from his crippling chemical addictions to an apartment in Schöneberg. Eno and Fripp added to his Philly R&B band. The group's tracks were improvised and recorded, typically, in one take. "'Heroes,'" a marriage of the Beach Boys' "Marcella" to German motorik band Neu!'s "Hero," owes its legend to producer Tony Visconti. Bowie's lyrics came from witnessing Visconti's extramarital tryst with a background singer along the rampart. The song title's irony-emphasizing quotation marks underline the romance's futility.

By the *"Heroes"* album, Bowie had shed his theatricality. Decades later, on the topic of his Berlin era, he would confess, "Cut me and I bleed *Low*." But the lasting brilliance of "'Heroes'" suggests that art overtly tied only to a particular time, place, and mind-set can transcend its historical ties and become universal. Similarly, it was at his most raw and least mythological that Bowie would become most immortal and influential.
—BD

Iggy Pop: *"The Passenger"* 1977

If Iggy Pop was the passenger, then the driver was David Bowie. In 1977, Bowie might have been the only person crazy enough to see potential in the thirty-year-old institutionalized, chest-slashing junkie. Still reeling from the wounds he'd inflicted on himself as the frontman of rock's most infamous burnouts, the Stooges, Iggy welcomed Bowie's guidance, relocating to Berlin for detoxification and a fresh start. The resulting albums—*Lust for Life* and *The Idiot,* both produced and largely cowritten by Bowie—would grant a second life to an artist who should've been long dead. And for the first time in Iggy's career, his surname didn't feel like a punch line.

No song better captured this transitional period than *Lust for Life*'s "The Passenger," in which the streetwalking cheetah upgraded to a limousine (albeit one rented by the hour). Guitarist Ricky Gardiner's ceaseless chicken-scratch riff set the song in a constant circular motion, evoking Iggy's perpetual outsider status. "I stay under glass," he crooned, gazing out at a glamorous life that was closer in view but still out of reach—which could be why that "la la la" chorus felt less like an expression of celebration than tired resignation.
—SB

Lou Reed: *"Street Hassle"* 1978

Throughout the 1970s, Lou Reed wrote romantic ballads about the scum of New York—outsiders, transgressors, and users who grabbed moments of pleasure wherever they could find them—and the three-part "Street Hassle" caught all their highs and lows. In part one, two strangers put in a paid-for hookup where they use each other with no regrets. That's followed by a monologue from one man urging another to dump his lover's body in the street. The song is full-bore punk in its urge to take life only in extremes—from the body as a receptacle for a straight-from-God orgasm to the body as trash on the sidewalk.

A cello drives the nonjudgmental pulse that lasts the song's entire eleven minutes, while whispery production takes everybody down a peg—including Bruce Springsteen, who uses his cameo in the song's third movement to knock down one of his own best lines: "Tramps like us, we were born to pay." But the key to the appeal of "Street Hassle" is its gentleness. Such lines as "that bitch will never fuck again" still feel safe from Reed's lips. That voice could forgive anything. As so many punk romantics recognized, if you're going to swaddle yourself in nothingness, nobody gives you a cozier cradle than Reed.
—CD

Kraftwerk: *"Trans-Europe Express"* 1977

Given that the krautrock quartet Kraftwerk did so much to de-individualize the pop star—donning uniforms, foregrounding machines, and absorbing the performer within a technologically determined system—it's ironic that "Trans-Europe Express" would help give birth to hip-hop, arguably the most ego-driven genre in pop music. Afrika Bambaataa and coproducer Arthur Baker borrowed the song's main riff and fused it with a fidgety rhythm—reminiscent of Kraftwerk's 1981 song "Numbers"—to create Bambaataa's 1982 hit "Planet Rock," a cornerstone of hip-hop history.

One of Kraftwerk's most mechanistic songs, "Trans-Europe Express" is a portrait of continental rail travel, from its opening drum machine salvo, filtered to sound like the chug of a locomotive, to its train-whistle refrain, a series of spine-tingling ascending fourths. Even the song's rudimentary vocals, a mantra-like recitation of the title phrase, are dehumanized and run through a synthesizer. It was only one among many of the Düsseldorf group's songs paying homage to the trappings of technological society, from 1974's "Autobahn" to the 1975 sketches "Geiger Counter" and "Transistor" to 1981's "Pocket Calculator." Popular music's obsession with circuitry in the late twentieth century is inconceivable without this band's innovations. Oybotron, Yellow Magic Orchestra, Gary Numan, and Daft Punk, to name just a few, fashioned not only their music but their presentation from Kraftwerk's original motherboard.
—PS

Brian Eno: *"1/1"* 1978

In 1975, Brian Eno was walking home from a London studio when he slipped on some wet pavement and fell into the path of an oncoming taxi. The collision left him bedridden for months. One day, a friend came over to put some harp music on his stereo but left the volume too low. Unable to adjust it himself, Eno resignedly watched the rain fall on the window while straining to hear the tiny bits of music that permeated the room. In time, he recognized something: Rather than dominating the environment by demanding the full attention of its listener, this music was churning quietly in the background, and thus performing an entirely different purpose. The notion that sound could work on such delicate but functional terms intrigued Eno; he eventually dubbed it "ambient music."

In 1978, Eno launched the Ambient label, which he devoted to exploring the concept in greater depth. *Music for Airports* was the first of the label's four releases. Since ambient was ambiguous by definition, Eno decided that airports—"nothing spaces" defined by people's varied experiences within them, rather than any prescribed emotion—would serve as an ideal inspiration. The album's opening piece, the beautiful and mysterious "1/1," has neither a beginning, a middle, nor an end. In fact, over the course of its nearly seventeen minutes, it barely does much of anything at all. It consists of two main parts, played by acoustic and electric pianos, phased against each other at varying intervals. While these parts play off each other with a melodic sweetness, they never lead anywhere. The end effect is music that rejects traditional listener participation by being simultaneously enveloping and redundant, tinting its environment while barely changing it at all.
—MP

The Ramones: *"Rockaway Beach"* 1977

The Ramones—four skinny guys from Queens who adopted the same last name—played songs that were short, loud, and boorish, built on power chords, grunted choruses, and little else. The band released its eponymous debut LP on Sire Records in 1976. By 1977, the group, eternally wrapped in tight jeans and leather jackets, had inadvertently established punk rock as a viable, revolutionary movement—on two separate continents.

Still, when these lifelong New Yorkers decided to augment their punk roots by reinventing surf rock, they naturally looked not to the Pacific Ocean, but to the ten-mile stretch of sand where the dim, gray Atlantic hits Queens: Rockaway Beach.

Written by Dee Dee Ramone and recorded for the band's third LP, 1977's *Rocket to Russia,* "Rockaway Beach" embodies everything the Ramones did so stupidly well: a hollered opening countdown; minimal instrumentation; simple, spirited lyrics ("The sun is out and I want some!"); doltish drums; a perfect sing-along chorus; and a quick fade-out before the studio clock inched too far past two minutes. The Ramones were hardly virtuosos, but this song's desperate, propulsive punk rhythms still manage to make anyone within earshot crack a sloppy grin.
—AP

Talking Heads: *"Psycho Killer"* 1977

Witchy and weird, pointed and affecting—"Psycho Killer" helped define Talking Heads. Unlike their Lower East Side peers, the band members were art school preps best characterized by David Byrne's striking delivery: a nervous vocal grind in which he sounds unhinged but also divinely in control, whether seething through digressions in French or scatting staccato magic in a rousing command to "run, run, run, run, run, run, run away." It's advice, sure, but Byrne sounds like he's singing about himself as much as any trickily transgressive stand-in. The rest of the band remains mum on the subject, for the most part skulking over a primitive rhythm and flashing guitars that interlock in laconic patterns, and the mix of lazy riffs and Byrne's sour, soulful voice plays to haunting effect. Indeed, "Psycho Killer" exemplifies, early in Byrne's career, the tension between meaning and insignificance that he would spend his life exploring.
—AB

Television: *"Marquee Moon"* 1977

"Marquee Moon," from the album of the same name, lasts just more than ten minutes. Live, it often stretched even longer. But the song itself could have been relatively brief—only a few enigmatic verses delivered by singer Tom Verlaine—were it not for an epic guitar solo that found Verlaine and fellow guitarist Richard Lloyd twisting and turning against one another, their playing escalating in intensity.

It was the farthest thing anyone expected from a punk band. Then again, Television were only nominally punk. Formed in 1973 by boarding-school runaways Verlaine and Richard Hell (who would soon depart to form the Voidoids), the group quickly evolved into a complex and sometimes contradictory creative entity. On one hand, Television were nervy and agitated like many punk acts; on the other, they were in love with the space and rhythms of jazz, classical, and other more technically ambitious fields. The results were unlike anything anyone had heard before—punk played with a virtuoso edge—and Television's near-residency at the legendary CBGB club allowed the band the freedom to refine its unique sound.

Even so, "Marquee Moon" remains something else. It begins with a few tautly strummed riffs, countered by a tiny elegiac guitar trill, before the rhythm section of Billy Ficca and Fred Smith kicks in with an elastic pulse. Verlaine's blurted lyrics don't make a lot of narrative sense, but that doesn't matter much: It's the emotional impact of hearing how "the darkness doubled" or "lightning struck itself" that fuels the unbridled romanticism of the track, with the soloing its cathartic payoff.

The second half of the song is basically the Tom Verlaine show, as the guitarist calmly and precisely winds his way to a graceful epiphany. While some have decried the song's relative indulgence, time has been kind to the band's navel-gazing. Like a sunset, "Marquee Moon" is one of the rare things in life where too much turns out to be just enough.
—JK

Patti Smith: *"Rock n Roll Nigger"* 1978

Before sneering teen vegans took to touring each other's VFW halls on three chords and a scream, punk wasn't a genre but an attitude: It rejected artistic convention and mainstream success, whether by bastardizing pre-Beatles pop, like the Ramones did, or through the unfettered guitar heroism of Television. That's how Patti Smith, the missing link between Jim Morrison and poetry slams, could seize the role of "punk poet laureate."

In her lyrics and liner notes, Smith takes the word "nigger" as a rallying cry for artists and outsiders like herself. "Outside of society, that's where I want to be," she cries over a smear of guitar, writing in her liner notes that those who ditch "the classic form" to walk

in the "valley of pleasure" are commonly cast down and denigrated. With a backup rant by cowriter Lenny Kaye, it's as brash a slap in the face as she intended, and while her positive interpretation of the n-bomb never caught on, that doesn't flag this screed for a second.
—CD

The Sex Pistols:
"God Save the Queen" 1977

Now mythologized as epoch-making art, the Sex Pistols' debut single, "Anarchy in the UK," fizzled at the time, stalling at number 38 on the UK charts in November 1976. The band's second single, "God Save the Queen," delivered the riot they'd promised. Released in May 1977, as the UK was gearing up for the twenty-fifth Jubilee of Queen Elizabeth II, the song saw the group seize its perfect pop moment, crashing the state street party with a sense of urgency and political wit. It kicks off like an English speed-freak take on Alice Cooper's "School's Out," with Johnny Rotten railing against the "fascist regime [that] made you a moron, a potential H-bomb" with the sarcastic relish he'd learned from proto-punk Ian Dury. It was also the first song the Pistols recorded after the arrival of bassist Sid Vicious, and it actually benefits from his lunkhead performance rather than the ousted Glen Matlock's power-pop leanings.

Things take an uncanny turn midway through the song, with Rotten lurching into a kind of Gnostic poetry ("God save your mad parade"), and then prophesizing doom. Quickly banned by a cowed media, the single became a samizdat hit, ascending to number 2, where legend has it that a not-so-secret industry conspiracy ensured that it stalled in Jubilee week—appropriately enough, behind Rod Stewart's "I Don't Want to Talk About It."
—ST

The Clash:
"(White Man) In Hammersmith Palais" 1978

The Sex Pistols may have been the scabby, safety-pinned muscle behind the first wave of British punk, but the Clash supplied brains, marrying leftist politics and a social consciousness to thundering reggae- and ska-inspired tracks. It was a call for global

revision from a group wearing torn-up leather jackets, sneering, and slamming their guitars in all directions.

Considerably less riff-heavy and more ska-influenced than the band's earlier songs, "(White Man) In Hammersmith Palais" first appeared on a self-produced seven-inch single in June 1978. The song recounts a reggae showcase that frontman Joe Strummer attended at a jazz club in Shepherd's Bush, London. Disappointed that the pop-friendly concert featured so few "roots rock rebel[s]," he launches into a caustic indictment of contemporary Britain, from the commodification of punk rock to the unfair distribution of wealth. Up until this point, UK punk was more for misfits than musicians, and technical prowess wasn't celebrated within the community. But "(White Man) In Hammersmith Palais," with its instantly recognizable punk-rock intro gradually giving way to a more deliberate, reggae-influenced rhythm, helped the Clash transcend the confines of British punk.
—AP

Buzzcocks:
"Ever Fallen in Love?" 1978

Of punk rock's original UK foursomes, Buzzcocks were the subtlest revolutionaries. Let the Sex Pistols and the Clash turn garage rock's long-standing sexual aggression into punk's political fury; Buzzcocks were more interested in the politics of sex. The Manchester-based group played a key role in launching the British do-it-yourself movement, issuing the influential *Spiral Scratch* EP on its own New Hormones label in 1977. After the departure of early frontman (and Magazine founder) Howard Devoto, Buzzcocks signed to United Artists in the UK, releasing a series of seven-inches that would later be packaged together on the 1979 compilation *Singles Going Steady.* Chief among them was 1978's "Ever Fallen in Love?"

Buzzcocks weren't the first UK punks to sing about romantic angst—the Damned beat them to it with 1976's "New Rose"—but this bittersweet pairing of ennui and pop melody was unusual for a British punk band; most of the others traded on ugliness or confrontationalism. The Sex Pistols' Johnny Rotten purportedly dismissed sex as "two minutes of squelching," but here, Buzzcocks express misguided longing in two-and-a-half breathless minutes of restless guitars, wickedly tight drums,

and Pete Shelley's high, hiccupping vocals. In further contrast to the macho poses of punk and classic-rock artists alike, the song describes a homosexual or feminist relationship. "We are the same," Shelley observes, foreshadowing the fey sexual ambiguity of Orange Juice, the Smiths, Belle and Sebastian, and countless others.
—MH

Vic Godard and the Subway Sect:
"Parallel Lines" 1978

"We oppose all rock and roll," Vic Godard and the Subway Sect announced in 1978, echoing the Year Zero mentality of first-wave punk. Godard actually meant it, though, telling *Zigzag* magazine, "We wanted to change the reasons for playing rock music…we wanted it to be a medium for ideas rather than a release from boredom."

The original lineup of the Subway Sect, which toured throughout the UK in 1977 alongside the Sex Pistols, the Clash, and Buzzcocks, recorded one of the great unreleased albums in rock history; its power can be heard only on singles and radio sessions or recalled in breathless firsthand accounts of their live sets. "Ambition," the Sect's second single, ultimately became their most famous song, but "Parallel Lines" remains their most urgent and vital. "Oh God, we turn to you for the final word / Ask you, 'Is life absurd?'" Godard blurts the question over heavily layered guitar, as if he's already out of ideas at nineteen. The whole thing would simply sound like a harangue— a jostling reality check to beleaguered working-class UK youth—if it weren't so powerful. And it still wasn't enough: Godard abandoned punk for stabs at Northern Soul and cocktail jazz before taking a lengthy hiatus from music to work as a postman.
—SP

X-Ray Spex:
"Oh Bondage! Up Yours!" 1977

The audible sneer worn by singer Poly Styrene as she roars the opening salvo of X-Ray Spex's first single— "Some people think little girls should be seen and not heard…Well I think, Oh bondage, up yours! 1-2-3-4!"—not only set the template for the raucous two-minutes-and-change that followed, it laid out the framework for the female punk ideal. Of course, even

if Styrene had been placed in the world solely for ornamental purposes, she would have stuck out; her thick braces and neon-bright clothes immediately confirmed that she wasn't interested in societal standards of normalcy. But it's the joy underscoring her taunting of the audience that made "Bondage" so jarring. With its simple, shout-along lyrics and atonal saxophone blasts (courtesy of fellow icon Lora Logic), "Bondage" set the table for the next generations of girl punks because of one simple fact: It made defying the norms of gender sound like one of the most thrilling acts a woman could ever undertake.
—MJ

The Adverts: *"One Chord Wonders"* 1977

One of the most lasting musical contributions of punk's first wave was the addition of a thick coat of irony to the self-reflexivity that had been one of rock's major components since (at least) Chuck Berry's "Rock and Roll Music." Songs like the Voidoids' "Blank Generation," the Clash's "White Riot," and the Sex Pistols' "Pretty Vacant" struck the first blows against these bands' own perceived inadequacies before the cultural gatekeepers could—a crucial symbolic victory.

The Adverts were among the first to admit their own naïveté when it came to musicianship; their April 1977 single "One Chord Wonders" finds the band almost reveling in their lack of prowess, with singer T. V. Smith fearing that he'll "Look up and the audience has gone." By the end of the track, he's defiantly spitting the song's antiheroic refrain: "We don't give a damn!" And the music echoes that sentiment, building to a wash of stark, violent noise that overpowers Smith's acerbic tantrum altogether.
—EH

Wire: *"Ex–Lion Tamer"* 1977

There's a chicken-or-egg argument with Wire's debut, *Pink Flag:* Was punk shorthand for originality, or were Wire simply the most original band to be called punk? They shared the same indifference toward musicianship as peers like the Sex Pistols and thrived on punk's directness and economy. Even at their most minimal, their songs bristled with energy that countless post-punk and hardcore bands would soon pick up on—everyone from R.E.M. to Big Black has covered their songs.

But there was also a bemused art-school detachment to Wire's take on punk, and *Pink Flag*'s "Ex-Lion Tamer" is almost plebeian compared to where they'd end up three records (and three years) later, as they grew progressively more sparse and electronic. A barrel-chested chorus, a shout-along hook forged from just one disdainful line ("Stay glued to your TV set!"), on-target harmonies, and even a few oohs and ahhs—it was all a little too easy. A punk anthem was just another variation on a theme for them, a stylistic norm to break down and reconstruct.
—JC

Donna Summer: *"I Feel Love"* 1977

For all the software-driven sound on your favorite dance (or non-dance) hit and all the CPU processing that goes on during the average DJ set, it's easy to forget that once upon a time, disco + electronics = hardly a sure thing. Munich-based producers and songwriters Giorgio Moroder and Pete Bellotte had worked with transplanted American singer Donna Summer for several records before hitting on the notion that, hey, it makes more sense to construct endless disco epics using computers and synthesizers than to have a bunch of trumpet players and human drummers do the same. First came the massive seventeen-minute remix of Summer's 1975 hit "Love to Love You Baby"; by exploiting the proto-house 4/4 kick-drum pulse coming from their Roland 606, Moroder and Bellotte were able to turn a four-minute pop song into a disco dream-suite and keep people dancing with no hint of a break.

1977's "I Feel Love" went one better: But for Summer's voice, it was constructed entirely with synthesizers and drum machines. And while this may seem technically impressive—there's an oft-relayed tale of Brian Eno bursting into a Berlin studio proclaiming to David Bowie that this song was "the sound of the future"—more impressive is that this music still works. Unlike much of disco's 1977 class, "I Feel Love" stands up as functional, non-retro-night club music, utilizing most of the same tricks of the techno trade that still get folks sweating until four a.m.: strategically paced intro, gradual introduction of the track's basic elements (bass line, kick drum, melody, harmony, refrain), subtle movement into extended "development" sections where melody is faded out in favor of minor variations and rhythmic details, and eventually the surging climax. And then there

is Summer's vocal: No amount of digital sheen or efficiency could keep her angelic voice from resonating to the heavens.
—DL

Giorgio Moroder: *"The Chase"* 1978

Italian-born disco producer Giorgio Moroder's track "The Chase," recorded for the 1978 flick *Midnight Express,* was a big hit. But these days, it figures more prominently in the lives of young party people through its influence on indie dance: The synth melody, electro drums, and repeating bass pattern could all appear on a modern-day DFA twelve-inch without anyone batting an eye. (Not to mention the song's general impact on all things Italo disco, which the Dutch producer I-F exploited on his crucial 2000 electro-house set *Mixed Up in the Hague.*) Like Moroder's work on Donna Summer's "I Feel Love," the key to this song is the way its minimalist cycles and dreamy melodies overpower any resistance one might have to disco. It was always fun to imagine blasting "The Chase" while speeding down the open road—and now it's easy to do since Rockstar Games used it in their *Grand Theft Auto* video game series.
—DL

Chic: *"Good Times"* 1979

Exhibiting a kind of dymaxion principle of pop physics, Chic's "Good Times" demonstrates that funky music becomes even funkier when a deliberately stiff and affectless vocal performance is draped across it. Weighting each syllable in the lines "we want the best, we won't settle for less" with martinet severity, Chic's faintly ridiculous lyrical evocations of the good life (clams and roller-skates?) are delivered with an ice-cold, drop-dead seriousness.

Boasting Nile Rodgers's ticker-tape guitar and one of the most enduring bass lines in the disco canon, the album mix sails past the eight-minute mark, breaking down but never breaking character. (No solos, thanks.) It's somehow fitting that a formally tidy song about superabundance has repeatedly overspilled its own boundaries: The cool assurance of Bernard Edwards's bass line served as a launchpad for the Sugar Hill Gang's "Rapper's Delight," and the staccato string stabs already sound like the Grandmaster Flash crossfade they would become in his "Adventures on the Wheels of Steel." Truly the

From Here to Eternity: Italo Disco

What Giorgio Moroder started with his all-electronic production on Donna Summer's "I Feel Love" and his album *From Here to Eternity* was continued well into the early '80s by a host of other musicians across Europe. The best Italo disco is mostly synthesized, nebulously "futuristic," and, frequently, engagingly weird.

"Supernature," **Cerrone:** A year after the bacchanalian "Love in C Minor" made him one of disco's biggest names, the Parisian, Italo-by-proxy Cerrone had a new idea for a dance-floor anthem: a sci-fi tale about the threat of deadly genetically altered animals. Thanks to his synth arrangements, it works—in a foreboding, B-movie sort of way.

"I'm Left, You're Right, She's Gone," **Giorgio Moroder:** Maybe the catchiest song—no small feat—from Year Zero Italo album *From Here to Eternity,* this track finds Giorgio combining ABBA-caliber melodies and Kraftwerk-style digital warmth to create smooth disco-pop. In the process, he somehow manages to make a vocoder sound morose.

"Remember," **Vivien Vee:** This one's an acquired taste: As a singer, Vee is alternately chirpy, squawky, and Debbie Harry glamorous, while the production—arranged by Claudio Simonetti of prog-horror soundtrackers Goblin—sounds like the offspring of "Supernature" and "The Chase" on a high-speed sugar buzz. Completely bonkers.

"Dancer," **Gino Soccio:** Gino Soccio's brand of disco originated in Canada but passed for Italo, thanks to more than just his name. The song's gradual mutation from slap bass and horns to an electronic bass line and burbling keyboards makes this one of North America's most Euro-sounding disco hits.

"I'm Ready," **Kano:** In its original context, this track's berserk game-show melody, omnipresent vocoders, and heavily accented falsettos are fantastic. But if that's still more Italo than you can handle, you could always listen to Tag Team's "Whoomp! (There It Is)," which samples it liberally.

"Gloria," **Laura Branigan:** Two years after disco was left for dead in America, New York–born Laura Branigan took a passionate, endlessly hooky English-language rewrite of a 1979 Umberto Tozzi Italo hit all the way to number 2 on the Hot 100. (Pulp would later incorporate a bit of its melody into their "Disco 2000.")

"Plastic Doll," **Dharma:** Like many Italo tracks circa '82, you could just as easily call this electro, with its harsh, piercing drum machine and restlessly oscillating bass lines. At least, you could call the *instrumental* version electro—the enjoyably cheesy vocal version is a different thing entirely.

"Take a Chance," **Mr. Flagio:** By 1983, much of mainstream pop and R&B was cribbing significantly from Italo, and "Take a Chance"—first performed by Bill Laswell's group Material—didn't need to alter the original version's icy electro-funk very much to fit in.

"Robot Is Systematic," **'Lectric Workers:** A deadpan android voice intones, "Cranks Computers is glad to present you the new robot to give you hours of dancing and play: Robot Systematic." Imagine *Blade Runner* as envisioned by French computer geeks in neon body stockings. (Or Daft Punk—same thing, really.)

"Stranger in a Strange Land," **N.O.I.A.:** This Italo/synth-pop group released one of the more hypnotic and rhythm-centered singles to fall under the Italo disco umbrella, sounding like something Jan Hammer might write for a *Miami Vice* boat-chase sequence.
—NP

bass line that keeps on giving, "Good Times" also supplied the crucial DNA for Daft Punk's "Around the World," whose hook is a note-for-note inversion.
—DD

Thelma Houston:
"Don't Leave Me This Way" 1977

A 1975 Philly Soul hit for Harold Melvin and the Blue Notes, "Don't Leave Me This Way" became an international disco smash in the hands of vocalist Thelma Houston and producer Hal Davis. Reassembling the team of players who helped Davis turn "Love Hangover" into a number 1 for Diana Ross, the two kept the soul and gospel roots of the song intact but modernized it, adding a syncopated bass and tweaking the tempo. Houston gives a strong performance, working to secure her lover's dedication without the support of the singing group enjoyed by Melvin in the original. Houston charms more than pleads, eschewing the desperate, dramatic tone that weighs down too many jilted-lover songs—instead, she confidently inventories the reasons she's so damn irreplaceable. On the evidence here, he'd be a fool to turn her down.
—SP

Gloria Gaynor: *"I Will Survive"* 1978

With its glissando piano runs, brass stabs, and syrupy strings, "I Will Survive" was decadent even by Studio 54 standards. But despite being pummeled at the hands of boneheaded cover artists, parodists, and karaoke singers over the years, it still retains its spark. Part of that has to do with the simple economics of its subject matter: Great songs about love are a dime a dozen, but great songs about survival are rare—and almost never this universal.

It almost didn't happen; the song was first released as the B-side to the lesser "Substitute." Luckily for Gaynor, with disco came the rise of a more discerning DJ culture to rescue it from obscurity. In the context of New York's club circuit, it eventually took on a new meaning, serving as an anthem of strength for a gay community besieged by the AIDS epidemic. That all-purpose adaptability would become its hallmark; in the decades since, its tune and sentiment have been co-opted by everyone from feminists and soccer clubs to cereal brands and, um, the band Cake.
—MP

Michael Jackson:
"Don't Stop 'Til You Get Enough" 1979

It's hard to imagine a lull in young Michael Jackson's career, but that was precisely where he found himself at the end of the 1970s. Having split with Motown, he'd gained control of his family's troupe, the Jacksons, but lost the rights to use the Jackson 5 name and logo. Worse still, his 1975 solo album *Forever, Michael,* had failed to crack the Top 100.

But things began to turn around for Jackson when he landed his first starring role in a major motion picture, the high-profile musical *The Wiz.* Although a critical and commercial failure, the project brought together Jackson and producer Quincy Jones, who had served as the film's music supervisor. On the set, the two forged a partnership that would result in the complete reinvention of Jackson's sound, image, and legacy—and "Don't Stop 'Til You Get Enough" was the catalyst.

By now, the mental image that accompanies the song is unshakable, thanks to its video: Jackson, not quite twenty-one, spinning and smiling under the gleam of a mosaic of disco lights. With its warring symphonic arrangements and rat-a-tat percussion, "Don't Stop 'Til You Get Enough" brilliantly capitalized on the then-booming disco movement by utilizing the highest register of Jackson's elastic falsetto. It remains the perfect precursor for the decade to come: glitzy, glamorous, and gluttonous.
—SF

Parliament: *"Flash Light"* 1977

This song had its start with legendary Parliament bassist Bootsy Collins, who took a shot at recording it with his own Rubber Band; something must not have worked, because he kicked the tune over to George Clinton and the Parliament behemoth. That nonworking "something," interestingly enough, may have been the bass itself. Parliament's version is one of their earliest tracks with the bass line played on a synthesizer, in order to achieve the grainy wobble that would scream "funk" for decades to come.

It's a minor testament to the track's grandness that Parliament could actually sell thousands of branded flashlights to the fans at their shows. It's a *major* testament to watch old video of those thousands of fans—in the clubs and on the stage itself—dancing

joyously to this music. That's the way it goes with this kind of generous, all-embracing funk: Whatever description we could provide, and whatever arguments we could make for historical importance, are completely secondary to whether it brings actual people to their feet. And with "Flash Light," then and now, it invariably does.
—NA

Marvin Gaye: *"Got to Give It Up"* 1977

"Got to Give It Up" is a monster groove, with Gaye vamping in his feathery falsetto and an actual party going on—loudly—in the background. It's nominally a song about learning to dance, and that's what its subtext was, too: When disco went mainstream, Motown and the rest of the old guard of R&B found that they had to reconstruct their style from scratch.

Very few of those singers, who were used to delivering tight, three-minute performances, were willing or able to let the static disco beat rule a song, as pop conventions suddenly demanded. Diana Ross made the leap, and so did Michael Jackson. But Gaye went one better, becoming an actual disco auteur: He wrote, coproduced, and played most of the parts on this number 1 hit, which was a four-minute excerpt on the radio and a twelve-minute jam in the clubs. He had to abandon his previous approaches to singing and songwriting, but part of Gaye's artistry was knowing when to leave room for others—whether it was his duet partners in the 1960s or the new sounds he'd continue to adopt throughout the last years of his too-short life.
—DW

Public Image Ltd.: *"Public Image"* 1978

"Ever get the feeling you've been cheated?" Johnny Rotten famously sneered from the stage of San Francisco's Winterland, the site of the Sex Pistols' then-final show in 1978. He was addressing the unruly crowd drawn by the band's hype, but probably no one felt more cheated than Rotten himself, possibly the only member of the Pistols perceptive enough to see through manager Malcolm McLaren's smokescreen and recognize the band as a cynical sham. As if to prove he was his own man and no manufactured flash in the pan, Rotten, reverting to his given name of John Lydon, barely waited for the Sex Pistols to officially disband before forming

Public Image Ltd. with his old friend Jah Wobble and ex-Clash guitarist Keith Levene.

The group rushed out its debut single, "Public Image," at the end of 1978, retaining the slashing, primal power of punk while pointing in a different direction. Wobble's subterranean bass and the echoing drums hint at the band's dubby left turns, while the ringing guitars foreshadow New Wave's (and U2's) emphasis on texture over muscle. Running through it all is Lydon's distinctive caterwaul—even more adenoidal than usual—with the singer forcefully laying claim to his persona in defiance of all his critics and detractors.
—JK

Gang of Four: *"Damaged Goods"* 1978

Alienation and anger were par for the course when it came to '70s British punk. The movement was fueled by lingering postwar malaise and the aimless state of the nation. Gang of Four, however, aspired to something greater, consciously placing their disillusionment in the context of Karl Marx's takedown of capitalism.

The equivocations of "Damaged Goods" are strictly rhetorical, and it comes to a cynical conclusion: "Sometimes I'm thinking that I love you," begins the cold assessment, "but I know it's only lust." "Damaged Goods" offers a frightening depiction of free (but not fair) trade, the cost paid for an inability to connect on an emotional level. Like the rest of their *Entertainment!* LP, "Damaged Goods" encapsulates what it's like to be a restless cog in the machine. It's almost hopeful and anthemic despite its humorless assessment, if only because a society that's hit rock bottom has nowhere to go but up.
—JK

Magazine: *"Shot by Both Sides"* 1978

"You know me, I'm acting dumb-dumb," squawked Howard Devoto on "Boredom," the standout track on Buzzcocks' self-released debut EP, *Spiral Scratch.* It was an act he quickly tired of. Dismayed by punk's rapid descent into cliché, Devoto quit the band and put together Magazine, a more refined, brainier outfit—but not without carrying off one of bandmate Pete Shelley's most irresistibly epic and sinister riffs.

Its escalating upward spiral was practically tailor-made for Devoto, who was inspired to write the incisive "Shot by Both Sides": "I wormed my way into heart of the crowd / I was shocked to find what was allowed," he seethed, like some paranoid post-punk hybrid of Richard Hell and Dostoevsky. The song's classic rock structure found favor with audiences bewildered by punk, but its momentum was crushed by an infamously lifeless *Top of the Pops* performance that sent the single plummeting down the UK charts—an ignominy from which the group never commercially recovered.
—*ST*

The Cramps: *"Human Fly"* 1979

There are few forms of rock criticism as potent as starting a band. That's what the Cramps did, and their thrilling revisionist history—a vision of early rock and roll done up as the raunchy monster-movie menace trashy paperbacks always imagined—was enough to send a thousand bands riffing in their wake. Like an audio version of *Reefer Madness,* this is the sound of teenage comic-book readers being corrupted by the rockabilly band across the swamp; it's what happens when the beach party goes bad and the zombies come out.

"Human Fly" is their best moment—big, messy, and lumbering, riding on a two-note surf-guitar riff. Frontman Lux Interior, probably wearing his heels even in the studio, slinks through levels of debauchery that make Mick Jagger look like Mel Torme; by the midpoint, his "reborn maggot" is spending time just saying "bzzzz." They're scholars, too—this song knows its Wanda Jackson and drops in a sly reference to the 1960s hit "96 Tears"—but that's just the kind of clever it takes to turn out slime seductive enough to make your kids go bad.
—*NA*

The Misfits:
"Night of the Living Dead" 1979

A punk band wearing corpse paint and singing about collecting the heads of little girls sounds brutal, but the Misfits coated it in poppy harmonies and melodies. Even on their classic single "Mommy, Can I Go Out and Kill Tonight?" they're still willing to seek parental permission—what's subversive or dangerous about that?

With a deep vocal style rooted in such atypically punk styles as doo-wop and opera, singer Glenn Danzig provided a full-bodied base to the group's obsessions with camp and kitsch: B movies, pulp novels, late-night television, and other pop culture detritus. The Damned-like buzz-saw guitars and shouted sing-alongs of "Night of the Living Dead" betrayed those influences, showing how addictive they could make even their most Halloween-esque sounds. "This ain't no love-in / This ain't no happening," Danzig sings, trying his best to cast aside the feel-good '60s—but it's all so damn catchy and engaging that he winds up paying homage instead.
—*SP*

Wire: *"Outdoor Miner"* 1978

In three years and three albums, Wire underwent a career's worth of development and growth. *Pink Flag,* their brilliant 1977 punk debut, was a ragged, ferocious, and fractured affair, but its follow-up, 1978's post-punk-leaning *Chairs Missing,* was more melodically refined, with hints of synthesizer and a lot less shouting. That album's "Outdoor Miner" is one of the band's most memorable songs, with pillow-soft backing harmonies, melodic bass, and clear, almost watery guitar parts. Colin Newman's gentle lead vocal, oddly enough, hangs nearly the entire chorus on a single note—and yet it's incredibly catchy, the best illustration of how the band's minimalist approach to songwriting produced distinct and inviting music.
—*JT*

Joy Division: *"Disorder"* 1979

Formed in Manchester after a 1976 Sex Pistols show, the tribal post-punk quartet Joy Division initially called themselves Warsaw (after the song "Warszawa," from David Bowie's *Low*) before shifting their name to reference the prostitution wing of Nazi concentration camps. Steeped in the work of J. G. Ballard, Lou Reed, and Iggy Pop, the band's Martin Hannett–produced debut album, 1979's *Unknown Pleasures,* opens with the chilly anthem "Disorder," which pinpoints a divergence between Joy Division and those class-of-'76 punk forebearers: While Johnny Rotten sneered about "no future," Curtis peered inward, wrestling with the more existential "no feeling."

Curtis suffered from epilepsy, and much of Joy Division's music feels like it engages with a self-awareness and confusion about one's own body—Curtis wrote "She's Lost Control" for a girl with epilepsy, and "I Remember Nothing" examines weakness and gaps in memory. But the shamanistic "Disorder" offers the tightest, catchiest entrance into the band's sound. And despite easy-to-swallow hooks, shadowy spaciousness, and a tight, almost bubbly rhythm, it's also among their most harrowing songs, with Curtis's baritone vocals and lyrics expressing a desperate desire for warmth and human connection. "I've been waiting for a guide to come and take me by the hand / Could these sensations make me feel the pleasures of a normal man?"
—BS

Althea and Donna:
"Uptown Top Ranking" 1977

"Three Piece Suit," released in 1977 by a twenty-two-year-old dancehall DJ named Trinity, was a decent proto-bling track, but it was massively eclipsed by its answer song, "Uptown Top Ranking." Recorded by teenagers Althea Forrest and Donna Reid—and promoted by no less a tastemaking pair than Mikey Dread in Jamaica and John Peel in the UK—"Uptown" became a huge underground hit. The defining song of London's 1977 punky reggae party, it became a UK number 1 the following year.

Where Trinity swanked around in his finery, Althea and Donna detailed the essentials of the discerning girls cruising in their Benz: the heels, the pants, the khaki suit, and the "'alter back." But what's most charming isn't the Jamaican slang and patois as much as the limpid groove, the exotically cryptic wit, and the insouciant grace of two schoolgirls—distant sisters of X-Ray Spex's Poly Styrene and Lora Logic—casually claiming their own voice.
—ST

Lee Perry:
"Roast Fish and Cornbread" 1978

These days it's difficult to tell whether or not Lee "Scratch" Perry has finally crossed the line from willful eccentricity into all-out craziness. After all, this is a man who thought nothing of talking to trees while walking backward through Kingston and hitting the ground with a hammer, and who famously set fire to his own Black Ark studio while at the height of his creative powers.

Luckily, his workspace stood long enough for this complex and perplexing character to record 1978's innovative *Roast Fish, Collie Weed and Cornbread.* As the more-or-less title cut, "Roast Fish and Cornbread" is a crystallization of dub's studio-as-instrument ethos: It's spacious, entrancing, and deeply experimental. Most importantly, as much as its red-eyed reverb and time-stretched percussive counterpoints push the avant-garde envelope, Perry's mischievous sense of humor also shines through, thanks to the incongruous cow noises splattered all over these ghostly rhythms.
—DS

The Congos: "Fisherman" 1977

It's now widely regarded as one of the greatest reggae songs of all time, but the Congos' "Fisherman" took almost two decades to gain its rightful status. It was originally found on 1977's Lee Perry–produced *Heart of the Congos*—a beautiful, multilayered album that saw a very limited release in Jamaica, was turned down by Island Records in the U.S. and Europe, and didn't become widely available until 1996, when it was reissued on the UK's Blood and Fire label.

The song paints an unflinching illustration of working-class life in the Caribbean, while the biblical connotations of its title and central metaphor convey a powerful spiritual motivation. With the contrasting yet transcendent voices of Cedric Myton and Roydel "Ashanti" Johnson underpinned by a riddim as liquid as waves lapping against a wood-hulled boat, it's everything a sufferer's anthem should be. Celebrating the nobility of labor, underscoring the world's injustices, and reassuring the listener that with a little bit of faith (and ganja), better days will soon come, "Fisherman" is humble, proud, and ultimately triumphant.
—DS

Willie Williams: "Armagideon Time" 1979

With the exception of just about anything by Bob Marley and the Wailers, most canonical reggae songs gained recognition outside their original audience, thanks to the enthusiasm of the Clash. Like the early skinhead movement before them, the West London art-schoolers were key figures in the spread of

Jamaican music to a wider, whiter culture. Unlike the skins, though, they didn't just listen to reggae—they played the records to fans at concerts and laid down spiky rock interpretations of everything from Toots and the Maytals' "Pressure Drop" to Junior Murvin's "Police and Thieves." The best of all their reggae covers remains a stellar version of Willie Williams's "Armagideon Time."

Originally recorded as an echoing, dubbed-out voicing of Clement "Coxsone" Dodd's "Real Rock" riddim—the most employed reggae instrumental in the world to date—it's hardly surprising that this track found favor with reggae's punk constituency. Light and propulsive but still rebellious and apocalyptic, "Armagideon Time" is pure dread party music with lyrics ("A lotta people won't get no supper tonight") that don't so much address the issues of the poor as simply acknowledge their plight.
—DS

This Heat: *"24 Track Loop"* 1978

Like fellow visionaries Can, Kraftwerk, and Raymond Scott, This Heat found ways to use existing technologies to construct pieces so divorced from contemporary sounds it's a wonder they managed to obtain even a modest following. Yet despite the robotic funk of "24 Track Loop," This Heat were hardly dance prophets; witness the furious, boundless reach of their 1981 LP *Deceit* or the almost wholly undated electro-acoustic punk-prog hybrid of the 1978 self-titled debut on which "24 Track Loop" appears. Drummer/vocalist Charles Hayward's James Brown beat gets looped, pitch-shifted, phased, and otherwise manipulated in a manner more fitting for dub reggae or IDM than something made with cut-up tape in the late '70s. The studio-bound song construction of This Heat and their artistic kin Throbbing Gristle and Faust would become standard practice in the coming decades—especially among electronic music producers.
—DL

The Slits: *"Typical Girls"* 1979

The Slits' 1979 debut, *Cut,* fused post-punk rhythms with acidic social commentary, but its more lasting image might be its cover art. Like an uprooted *National Geographic* discovery, the female trio was photographed caked in mud and nude apart from loincloths. Far from being exploited, they were aiming to make a splash on their own terms, distilling their dual conceits of primitivist punk and confrontational feminism to a single image.

Their first single, "Typical Girls," fleshed it out more. The backdrop was a superficially naïve take on Jamaican dub, which they merged with what singer Ari Up called "skippy and light girl music," a symbolic protest against the more masculine mind-sets of punk and reggae. Atop this, they scraped out a catty catechism, besieging women who bought into prescribed roles. Seventeen-year-old Ari castigates predictable girls who "buy magazines" and "worry about spots, and fat, and natural smells." The Slits didn't disguise their desire for fame on their own terms—something Island Records still allowed at a time when it appeared that "third-world" music, especially when imagined by three women, could actually be the next big thing.
—EH

The Pop Group: *"She Is Beyond Good and Evil"* 1979

The Pop Group's mongrel mixture of funk bass lines, disco drums, dub production tricks, and slash-and-burn guitars epitomizes post-punk's free-for-all genre promiscuity. But where fellow travelers courted numbness with slow tempos, grayscale palettes, and emotional detachment, the Pop Group's "She Is Beyond Good and Evil" delivered a maniacally intense fire sermon.

After an opening swell of distortion that recalls Jimi Hendrix circa "Foxy Lady," the femme fatale of the title is invoked as a spiky Venus. The band struggles to catch up to her, diving into dubbed-out foxholes dug by reggae producer Dennis Bovell. Frontman Mark Stewart stops the show with a shrieked "I hold you like a *gunnnnnnn*" that triggers a cavernous clang, then landslides into an anti-guitar solo of fantastically rude physicality. Crooning that "Western values mean nothing to her," the Pop Group earn their Nietzschean name-dropping with music that is suitably Dionysian, ruthless, and ecstatic.
—DD

The Clash: *"The Guns of Brixton"* 1979

1943: British midget submarines creep across the North Sea to plant explosives on a German warship.

The Nazis dispatch the *Monte Rosa,* a cruise liner turned troop ship, for repairs.

1945: The British capture the ship and rechristen it the *Empire Windrush.*

1948: The *Windrush* sails from Jamaica, carrying the first wave of West Indian immigrants to the UK. Among those on board are calypso pioneers Lord Kitchener and Lord Beginner, who—along with throngs of other Caribbean-born immigrants—settled in and around Brixton, South London.

Born in Brixton in 1956, Clash bassist Paul Simonon grew up in an environment soaked in calypso and, eventually, reggae. The mythology of his band usually spotlights central songwriters Joe Strummer and Mick Jones, but without Simonon the group might not have outlived punk. He named the band and, influenced by sleeves on the Jamaican label Trojan Records, developed its visual aesthetic. During Clash practices, Simonon spun Jamaican vinyl, but the others initially rejected his ersatz reggae numbers.

By 1979, the Clash, bored with the parameters of punk, dove into their influences—including Jamaican music. Simonon unveiled "The Guns of Brixton," a call to arms and one of the few Clash tracks to feature his vocals. It predated the violent Brixton riots of 1980 and heralded an era of London youth soaking up the sounds of the Empire's receding fringes.
—*BD*

James Chance and the Contortions:
"Contort Yourself" 1979

No Wave, the post-punk movement that flashed through late-1970s New York, was known for nihilistic attitudes and impenetrable music. But one band turned its bitter aggression into songs that urged you to dance. Weaned on James Brown and free jazz, James Chance breathed fire with his spitting vocals and raging sax while his bandmates married funk rhythms to punk noise. Chance often physically attacked his audience, and his group's unofficial theme, "Contort Yourself," is itself an aural assault.

Chance spews misanthropic commands, an indoctrination disguised as a dance lesson: "Reduce yourself to a zero," he screamed. "Baby, then you'll fall right in place." As the tourniquet-tight beat threatens to snap, the dueling guitars of Jody Harris and Pat Place wrap around Chance like a blindfold.

Beneath the track's raging noise lay the roots of New York's burgeoning disco scene; the group actually made its own disco album as James White and the Blacks, remaking "Contort Yourself" as a sultry dance hit. Still, the Contortions' version remains the burning face of No Wave, influencing nearly all punk-funk music since.
—*MM*

Suicide: *"Dream Baby Dream"* 1980

Alternately spooky and smart-aleck, Suicide never quite fit into any specific genre. Their 1977 debut LP united a few proto-industrial heads and No Wavers, but when the band hooked up with the Cars' Ric Ocasek on their second record in 1980, they came *this* close to pop. In fact, "Dream Baby Dream"— a lush remake of the first record's "Keep Your Dreams"— was disarmingly pretty and distractingly catchy enough to find a fan in Bruce Springsteen, who has used it as a show closer.

Alan Vega's vocals sounded like Lou Reed doing Elvis Presley, but even considered as gothic kitsch, they're both sincere and haunting. Martin Rev's minimal bed of bells, organ, and pulsing drum-machine (doubtlessly given more than a little extra padding with Ocasek's populist supervision) straddles the line between the simplistic and the simply beautiful. If ever the post-punk era produced an anthem fit for peaceniks and punks alike, it was this.
—*DL*

Cabaret Voltaire: *"Nag Nag Nag"* 1979

One of Cabaret Voltaire's earliest singles, "Nag Nag Nag" could be mistaken for punk rock, with its gruff vocals, two-chord structure, and jagged guitars sounding like they were phoned-in to the studio through tin cans and string. But with a drum machine supplying its tambourine-laced beat, little else in punk sounded quite like it.

Cabaret Voltaire didn't linger for long on this modified garage-rock sound. Over a string of studio albums (1979's *Mix-Up,* 1980's *The Voice of America,* and 1981's *Red Mecca*), the Sheffield experimenters distinguished themselves with tape loops, effects boxes, and all manner of electronic sound manipulation as they helped to invent industrial music. By the end of the 1980s, they would work with both dub producer

Adrian Sherwood and Chicago house producer Marshall Jefferson.

But this debut single highlights the bristling immediacy at the heart of Cabaret Voltaire's best work. With bionic blues-rock soldered together from tarnished electronics, sampled vocals, and blasts of white noise, "Nag Nag Nag" is bracing and headlong, tumbling forward with every roll of the artificial toms. With its abrasive vocal harangue and nearly five-minute run time, it subjects the listener to psychological stress tactics that most two-minute guitar punks wouldn't dare attempt.
—PS

Throbbing Gristle:
"Hot on the Heels of Love" 1979

Formed in London in late 1975, Throbbing Gristle were renowned for provocative live performances and their seismic influence on industrial music—which continued when their members moved on to the equally revered bands Psychic TV and Coil. Listening to their earliest stuff (via *The Second Annual Report of Throbbing Gristle* and *D.O.A.,* both initially released as limited twelve-inch records on the band's own Industrial imprint), it's easy to imagine scores of listeners either running in terror at the noisy wall of distortion and then-alien use of recorded samples, or rushing off to form industrial bands of their own.

1979's ironically titled *20 Jazz Funk Greats* was hardly so menacing. In fact, its "Hot on the Heels of Love" arguably has more in common with Giorgio Moroder than experimental electronic music, featuring an insistent, proto-techno kick; percolating electronic bass parts; and robotic synth lines. Few would bat an eyelash if you dropped this in the middle of a house set, something techno innovator Carl Craig must have picked up on when he remixed in 2004. Even in the ever-churning arena of electronic dance music trends, it still sounds futuristic.
—DL

Devo: *"Mongoloid"* 1977

Devo's nervous take on post-punk was born with an outsider's perspective. The group cemented its New Wave science-geek image with the release of its Brian Eno–produced 1978 debut with an album title (*Q: Are We Not Men? A: We Are Devo!*) suggesting the members weren't just outcasts, but actually inhuman.

Over a mix of jittery rhythms, spazzy vocals, and techno-freak synths—all so high-strung they make even Talking Heads sound relaxed—"Mongoloid" embraces the eternal nerd fantasy of simply seeming normal, relating the tale of a mutant with "one chromosome too many" who disguises himself as an ordinary citizen in order to hide his true identity.

As the song marches to its repetitive climax, the vocals slowly recede into the mix, mimicking the protagonist's assimilation into society. Ironically, Devo's very visible geekdom eventually landed them in the Top 40, but their dorky angles never straightened out: The band remained lovably, eccentrically awkward long after achieving widespread popularity.
—MM

Candido: *"Jingo"* 1979

"Jin-Go-Lo-Ba" was originally composed by Nigerian drummer Babatunde Olatunji and released on his 1959 album *Drums of Passion*; Santana made it famous for the rock set as "Jingo" a decade later. But Havana-born Candido Camero—best known as one of the most in-demand Latin-jazz drummers of the 1950s—recorded the most preposterously funky rendition for Salsoul, New York's premier disco label.

Three things stick out about this version: First, session man Louis Small, previously employed as the pianist for late-1960s boogaloo outfit the Latinaires, goes berserk on a succession of keyboards, including a snarling, psychedelic ARP Odyssey and a choppy, hopped-up clavinet. Secondly, a choir of vocalists provides a ghostly, hypnotic refrain of the strictly rhythmic lyrics, occasionally punctuated with the gnarliest "hunh!" to ever ricochet through a late-'70s dance club's sound system. And finally, there's Candido himself, fifty-eight years old and still raising blisters with a forceful and flexible conga drum groove that runs slaloms through the 4/4 beat. The only thing more invigorating than the way the song begins—with a synthesizer that sounds like a turbine being switched on—is the way it ends: right on the fourth beat, with an exclamation point.
—NP

Industrial Revolution

The term "industrial music" was coined from Industrial Records, which the Throbbing Gristle opened in 1976 to support music that combined tape splicing, samplers, synthesizers, and electronics into an aggressively mechanistic and uncompromising sound. By the '80s, the genre had developed a more danceable strain and would soon rub shoulders with the mainstream as second-wave industrial acts Ministry and Nine Inch Nails merged its sampled machinery and brutal electronic beats with churning metal guitars.

"Zyklon B Zombie," **Throbbing Gristle:** Led by transgressive provocateur Genesis P-Orridge (who eventually got breast implants to match his second wife), Throbbing Gristle began in a London performance-arts collective. "Zyklon B," named for an insecticide notoriously used in Nazi Germany, is an oddly catchy clatter of fuzzy garage bass and P-Orridge's underwater vocals.

"This Is Entertainment," **Cabaret Voltaire:** From their Dada-derived name and early performance-art pieces to their clattering, expansive sound, Sheffield's Cabaret Voltaire offered another flavor of white noise, guitar, electro percussion, and synthesizing, over the years adding larger doses of dub, house, and acid.

"Blank Capsules of Embroidered Cellophane," **Nurse with Wound:** With a title taken from Lautréamont and cover art clipped from a porno mag, 1979's self-released three-track *Chance Meeting on a Dissecting Table of a Sewing Machine and an Umbrella* is as famous for the list of influences featured in its sleeve notes as for its epic industrial kraut-noise freakouts.

"Letztes Biest (am Himmel)," **Einstürzende Neubauten:** Einstürzende Neubauten is translated as "collapsing new buildings," appropriate for a band that often made its own instruments out of scrap metal and tools. The minimalist "Letztes Biest (am Himmel)," from the 1985 album *Halber Mensch*, opens with vocalist Blixa Bargeld in strangulated a capella; he conjures ominous whispers over metallic plucks and increasingly insistent tones, bass, and factory percussion, ending with agitated shouts.

"New Mind," **Swans:** Emerging from New York's No Wave and noise scenes, the Michael Gira–led Swans concocted a post-industrial fury. On their 1987 album *Children of God*, some of the brimstone was tempered by vocalist/keyboardist Jarboe's ethereal incantations. But when Gira took the lead with his deep baritone, as on the pummeling, group-shouted "New Mind" ("the sex in your soul will damn you to hell!"), the violence was palpable.

"Murderous," **Nitzer Ebb:** This Essex duo raised sweat levels in the leather clubs with their clean, danceable, but still factory-loud sounds. On 1987's "Murderous," singer Douglas McCarthy shouts like a drill instructor ("Where is the youth! Don't be lazy with the pleasure of sin"), entreating his troops to give it one more set of push-ups over speedy drum machines and synthesizers.

"Windowpane," **Coil:** Ex–Throbbing Gristle/Psychic TV member John Balance and his partner Peter Christopherson formed the ever-mutating Coil. The LSD-drenched "Windowpane" finds the duo in a bizarre love triangle with Happy Mondays and Current 93, mixing house, psychedelic synths, staccato rhythms, and Balance's distorted vocals.

"Who's Laughing Now?" **Skinny Puppy:** This mohawked and blood-soaked Vancouver crew blended a suicidal throb, baroque layers of noise, and confrontational political issues. Here, amid a constantly morphing background, singer Nivek Ogre goes through a stream-of-consciousness, multivoiced track about a woman named Broken Alice: "She whispered lizard kiss rhetoric bitch pass on answering psycho babble with no security power escapes to the toilet room." (And it goes on like that…)

"Flashback," **Ministry:** Fronted by leather cowboy Al Jourgensen, Ministry set a new industrial template by giving it a heavy pulse and blasting guitars. "Flashback," from 1988's *The Land of Rape and Honey*, sounds like an apocalyptic youth rally, with a distorted Jourgensen scowling, "I'm gonna crack his skull." Why? "Coz I hate her."

"Head Like a Hole," **Nine Inch Nails:** Molding Ministry's violence into something more universal, former janitor Trent Reznor wiped the floor with "Head Like a Hole." Cleaning up his forefathers' kitchen-sink distortion and electronics, NIN offered the mainstream a more digestible gateway into industrial music.
—*BS*

Dinosaur: *"Kiss Me Again"* 1978

Arthur Russell was a cellist who had worked at a multidiscipline Greenwich Village arts center and collaborated with Allen Ginsberg and Philip Glass by the time he attended one of Nicky Siano's DJ nights at disco club the Gallery. One year later, he and Siano were making disco history, corralling a unique combo of players—including Talking Heads' David Byrne on guitar—on the bedrock dance song "Kiss Me Again." It was Siano's first production (and Sire Records' first disco twelve-inch release). The genius of "Kiss Me Again" comes, in a large part, from its loose, sexy, unglued sound: It stretches out for more than twelve minutes, is dissonant in places, and meanders like long jam sessions tend to do. But despite the famous names involved in its construction, its legend is tied to Russell. Molding his music-school training to the ecstatic sound of crowd-pleasing disco, "Kiss Me Again" forged the sensibilities of a renewed downtown dance scene—one that Russell would also help articulate on subsequent underground disco classics under other aliases, from "Is It All Over My Face?" as Loose Joints to "Wax the Van" as Lola.
—*GD*

Machine: *"There but for the Grace of God Go I"* 1979

Prior to forming the 1980s Latin art-funk ensemble Kid Creole and the Coconuts, August Darnell (aka Kid Creole) took a few gigs writing and producing songs for fledgling dance bands in the New York area. Among them was Machine's "There but for the Grace of God Go I," a brilliant synthesis of high-energy dance music and social commentary.

Luring in listeners with a mournful, delicate piano intro, Machine quickly drops full force into a muscular disco beat and keyboardist/cowriter Kevin Nance's unmistakable synth riff. But it's the lyrics that really make this song: Between Clare Bathé's impassioned wails and Jay Stovall's sneers, a story unfolds of how the strict disciplinary measures enforced by a pair of conservative Latin immigrant parents drives their daughter to "popping pills and smoking weed." The song culminates in her mother's pained realization: "Too much love is worse than none at all."
—*NP*

Kate Bush: *"Wuthering Heights"* 1978

Kate Bush was eighteen years old when she wrote "Wuthering Heights" and nineteen when the song was released as a single in January 1978. And in many ways, it sounds like the work of a teenager. A rolling, grandiose ballad, the song tells a tale of inflamed passions and doomed love as it tracks the story of the nineteenth-century novel of the same name. Using books as inspiration for songs is nothing new—particularly in the progressive/art-rock nexus in which the eccentric young singer found herself. But Bush boasted a marked pop sensibility and, most of all, an almost frightening ability to personalize the material. Her immersion inside the world of the song is complete and total—she *is* Catherine Earnshaw, the novel's heroine, yearning for the love of her adopted brother, bad boy Heathcliff. Every syllable of her vocal performance is delivered from inside the story, and she brings the listener with her, turning everyone who hears the song into a true-believer drama student, seeing the world through a joyously melodramatic lens.
—*MR*

Goblin: *"Suspiria"* 1977

Jessica Harper, the protagonist of the 1977 film *Suspiria,* asks a psychiatrist: Does magic exist? Or can you explain it away as psychosis? The films of Dario Argento argue for magic, and *Suspiria*—a mature example of his *giallo* horror flicks—is haunted by garish colors and populated by a wooden cast who pace through the film as if in a dream. But the score by Goblin brings the madness. Young women fall into bales of barbed wire and blood runs red, while Goblin celebrates the bloodlust with frenzied percussion, wraithlike synths, and gutteral chants of "WITCH!"

Before they hooked up with Argento to score his 1975 film *Profondo Rosso,* Goblin had struggled as the prog-rock group Cherry Five. Led by composer Claudio Simonetti, they would enjoy a fruitful partnership with the filmmaker; the soundtrack album to *Profondo Rosso* was a hit, leading to work on *Suspiria* as well as George Romero's *Dawn of the Dead.* The theme to *Suspiria* is ecstatic with its bells and hypnotically repeating figures echoing Mike Oldfield's score to *The Exorcist,* but as the track grows manic, throaty chanting builds to howling

abandon on the backs of driving guitar and garish synths. Goblin gave Argento exactly what he needed: They feast on the brutality of his set pieces, leaving the cinematography to dwell on the magic.
—CD

Blue Öyster Cult:
"(Don't Fear) The Reaper" 1978

Blue Öyster Cult spent their career oscillating between the taste-defensible brand of heavy metal we now know as "stoner rock" and flights of Spinal Tappish embarrassment; they were, after all, the progenitors of the superfluous umlaut. But "(Don't Fear) The Reaper" ensnares even those who've merely skimmed the band's output: it's a gloomy bit of late-1970s rock that still sounds Tupperware-fresh, having predicted a particularly gloomy strain of mid-'80s alternative rock.

One could pin the song's everlasting flame on its hypnotic riff, or on a certain insistent percussion instrument that's become a favorite frat-boy punch-line thanks to *Saturday Night Live.* But the real strength of "Reaper" is its thick, pervasive mood, which lies somewhere between blissed-out and paranoid, and nicely complements the suicide-pact lyrics. It's psychedelia run dark, its soft-rock gloss interrupted by *Twilight Zone* noodling and a nightmarish guitar solo. The official story of 1978 is that punk rock slayed the bloated, pretentious dragon of bands like BÖC, but "(Don't Fear) The Reaper" was deathbed proof that excess has its charms.
—RM

AC/DC: *"Highway to Hell"* 1979

"Highway to Hell" is a song about drinking—or, more specifically, about driving to a bar to meet friends and drink. But its title and epically dumb lyrics hint at something a little tougher to unpack: an embrace of oblivion, a biblical death-drive, and a pride in damnation. One of rock critics' favorite fun facts about Australian stomp-rock deities AC/DC is that drummer Phil Rudd never played fills. His restraint gave the band's rhythm section a metronomic stomp-clap push that connected it, weirdly, to disco. Guitarist Angus Young's central riff is just as mechanistic, a melodically minimal crunch. Bon Scott's voice is a strangulated yowl, but he always stays completely in the song's pocket,

never overstepping his boundaries. So: "Highway to Hell" is a song about the pursuit of abandon that makes that abandon sound like an exercise in rigor. Less than a year after recording it, Bon Scott would drink himself to death, and the band would hire an English replacement, Brian Johnson, who sounded exactly like him. On *Back in Black,* the band's first album with Johnson, the group, apparently oblivious to their frontman's fate included a song called "Have a Drink on Me," and the road-tripping continued.
—TB

Van Halen: *"Runnin' with the Devil"* 1978

The first song on the first album by Van Halen, "Runnin' with the Devil" was inspired by the Ohio Players' 1974 funk anthem "Runnin' from the Devil." While the two titles differ by only one word, the distinction is important: Skyrocketed by Eddie Van Halen's Olympian fretwork and David Lee Roth's cartoon–Robert Plant showmanship, the band had no intention of evading the classic rock and roll vices. They were "with" it all: yellow spandex, revolving-door groupies, and destructive egos. "Got no love, no love you'd call real / Got nobody waiting at home," boasts Roth, turning what could be a woe-is-me sentiment into a fist-pumping mantra.

As the outlandish bridge between 1970s Led Zeppelin–style stadium rock and 1980s Aqua Net metal, this foursome was all for the notion of pop as world-beating spectacle. But while their visual excesses knew no bounds, their music rarely rambled on ad nauseam; though Eddie was more gifted than any of the prog wankers and metallurgists of his day, his group managed to bypass musical excess by putting songs ahead of solos.
—RD

Fleetwood Mac: *"The Chain"* 1977

When the L.A. folk-pop duo of Stevie Nicks and Lindsey Buckingham was absorbed into UK blues-rock machine Fleetwood Mac in the mid-1970s, the trajectories of all parties concerned changed forevermore. Not only did the band become a one-stop shop for flawless, infectious FM-radio pop, but it forged the greatest model of intra-band romantic entanglements west of ABBA. "The Chain" was the centerpiece of 1977's hugely popular *Rumours* LP and featured almost every crucial

element of Fleetwood Mac: a perfect mix of male and female vocal harmonies, subtle performances from each member of the band (see especially Buckingham's masterful guitar solo on the outro, featuring not more than five notes), and, most of all, starkly confessional—even confrontational—lyrics harmonized by the songwriting trio of Nicks, Buckingham, and Christine McVie. This song's perfect transition from bleak, bitter mysticism into flailing release serves as a microcosm of the entire Fleetwood Mac saga and nails the (melo)drama of their legendary romantic turmoil. "If you don't love me now, you will never love me again." Heavy shit.
—DL

Steely Dan: *"Deacon Blues"* 1977

Artistically the strongest of the 1970s' oft-parodied yacht-rock bands, Steely Dan hit a pinnacle with "Deacon Blues." Here the narrator fantasizes about the decadent L.A. good life, fueled by the best liquor and a line of women whose names don't stick, and concluding with a glamorous car crash—all the finest things in life feeding the worst, basest behavior. The all-star California session players to which the Dan were accustomed (including Lee Ritenour and Bernard "Pretty" Purdie) bring as lush a gloss to the lyrics, making the song poignant even though you know better. And, in fact, Steely Dan main men Donald Fagen and Walter Becker *did* know better: There's plenty of irony in the narrator's fear and loathing, leaving no doubt he's a schmuck and a wannabe. ("I'll learn to work the saxophone / And I'll play just what I feel.") But thanks to the bold and beautiful melody, the song achieved a suspension of disgust—and became a radio hit and classic-rock anthem for guys who *wish* they had something worth throwing away.
—CD

Electric Light Orchestra: *"Mr. Blue Sky"* 1977

The great thing about Electric Light Orchestra is that they really thought they were making the music of the future. Though based in the Beatles and Beethoven, the ELO sound was about pushing the limits of rock music without becoming detached from pop priorities. Jeff Lynne might have overestimated the use of synthesizers, orchestras, and every damn track on the mixing board, but on "Mr. Blue Sky" he

unintentionally predicted the vanguard of twenty-first-century indie pop. No surprise, then, that the song's inevitable use in a 2002 Volkswagen campaign prompted many to wonder who this hip new band could be. Its lyrics were pure *Sesame Street*—and the bouncy piano matched—but as Lynne piles on the harmonies, strings, vocoder, and choir, the song takes on the giddy ambitions that characterize the best experimental pop, enthusiastically testing the strength of traditional song structure. Okay, so maybe disco strings and multitracked falsetto didn't endure as long as Lynne had hoped, but prognostication is a low-percentage game, and "Mr. Blue Sky" is that rare piece of dead-on prophecy.
—RM

The Only Ones: *"Another Girl, Another Planet"* 1978

Punk in the U.S. was largely a refuge for weirdos and outcasts. You didn't choose it; it chose you. Punk in the UK, however, was more of a line in the sand. You had to pick a side: stick with the old or embrace the new. The Only Ones (their leader, Peter Perrett, pushing—gasp!—thirty when punk hit) wisely sided with the kids, as his band's brief but bright career attests. While the Only Ones were full of great songs that straddled power-pop and punk, they're rightly best known for their second single, "Another Girl, Another Planet," one of the most beloved tracks of the punk and New Wave era. "I always flirt with death," the lyric begins, and from there the song careens from one peak to the next like a junkie riding the rush. But when Perrett declares "I think I'm on another planet with you," it doesn't really matter whether it's the drugs or some girl that's sending him into orbit. We feel elated, too, spinning up into space along with him.
—JK

The Undertones: *"Teenage Kicks"* 1978

When the Undertones first released this song on their 1978 debut EP of the same name, punk's initial jolt was already giving way to post-punk's gloomy disillusionment. But the members of this Northern Ireland five-piece actually *were* teenagers at the time, and their greatest song still resonates with not just the revolutionary freedom that 1977 had supposedly signified, but also the schoolboy innocence of a bygone era, before dole queues and Sid Vicious.

Detroit proto-punks the MC5 were an inspiration with their song "Teenage Lust," but the Undertones had also covered Bobby Troup's R&B standard "(Get Your Kicks On) Route 66." Written by rhythm guitarist John O'Neill, "Teenage Kicks" is two and a half minutes of simple drums, buzzing guitars, handclaps, and singer Feargal Sharkey's shaky shouts, like the Ramones' no-nonsense bubblegum without the leather or the deadpan. The song tingles with imagined adolescent thrills and is just as short-lived. Its opening lyrics—"Teenage dreams, so hard to beat"—adorn the tombstone of the late BBC DJ John Peel, who championed the record. Few songs better epitomize punk's less-is-more ethos or rock's flickering youthful enthusiasm.
—MH

Plastic Bertrand: *"Ça plane pour moi"* 1977

For every guy out there who says "timeless" music is a matter of complexity, deep emotion, or talent, there's a radio somewhere blasting "Wipe Out" or "Wooly Bully." "Ça plane pour moi" is one of *those* timeless classics—a three-chord New Wave novelty with some brat chanting in French and singing exactly one hook ("Oo-wee-oo-oo!"). Plastic Bertrand didn't even come up with it: This is an alternate version of a song called "Jet Boy, Jet Girl" by some MC5-loving English punks he played drums with. Same backing track, even—only the lyrics were replaced, because "Jet Boy, Jet Girl" was about teenage boys having sex with one another. Plastic Bertrand didn't write the new lyrics, either.

Plastic Bertrand was Roger Jouret, a Belgian fop who looked like a TV personality, and his "Ça plane pour moi" was about being just as ditzy and fun as this music: The slangy title could mean "this works for me," or "getting high works for me," or "being a total lazy lowlife spacehead works for me." Singing along with "Jet Boy, Jet Girl" is fine, but pogoing around shouting "I AM THE KING OF THE DIVAN" in Bertrand's sneery-dork voice is a pleasure a three-year-old could understand. And if there were ever any question, notice how even when Serious Underground Punk Bands cover "Jet Boy, Jet Girl," they can't resist singing "oo-wee-oo-oo" the way Bertrand did it—four syllables that might make the difference between a punk obscurity and an international smash.
—NA

The Records: *"Starry Eyes"* 1979

Great power pop comes immaculately crafted, yet centers on failure—failure to escape a one-horse town, to reach a girl on the phone, or to even get a girl in the first place. Much of the best power pop failed on the charts as well, becoming should've-been smashes that provide tiny epiphanies when finally dug up and discovered.

"Starry Eyes" endures as the greatest single of power pop's late 1970s zenith. Flawlessly structured, the song transcends its humble jangle and lyrics that are essentially a grievance against the band's avaricious manager: "While you were off in France, we were stranded in the British Isles / Left to fall apart amongst your passports and your files." Virgin Records packaged the single, misleadingly, in a sleeve depicting a teased blonde. The record stalled at number 56 on the U.S. charts, another perfect power-pop failure.
—BD

Cheap Trick: *"Surrender"* 1978

Before Cheap Trick, Robin Zander sang under contract at an amusement park, impersonating pop stars at the recreational mecca of Wisconsin Dells. There, at the Picadilly Pub, he earned renown as "the man of a thousand voices." Meanwhile, just down the Rock River, guitarist Rick Nielsen and bassist Tom Petersson floundered in Fuse, who released a dud record on Epic in 1969.

Initially, Cheap Trick fared no better. Sales lagged, though the band was rich with hooks and character. Nielsen styled himself in a flipped cap and bow tie, after Huntz Hall of slapstick screen thugs the Bowery Boys. Drummer Bun Carlos dressed like a horse-track reporter. Zander and Petersson played blond and brunette pin-ups, respectively.

Until the live album *At Budokan,* "Surrender" was commercially unsuccessful, perfunctorily announced as "the first song on our new album." Though a boomer himself, Nielsen wrote with the alienated voice of the next generation, creeped out by their liberated parents talking about STDs and necking to Kiss LPs. Zander channeled an English sneer while Nielsen nicked riffs from the Who. Now, the band claims, it's mommy and daddy, not the kids, who are "alright" and that refrain—steeped in mimicking,

marketing, and nostalgia—became a mantra for navigating suburban sanity.
—BD

The Cars: *"Just What I Needed"* 1978

The Cars formed a bridge between 1970s FM rock and emergent New Wave, straddling both worlds—which didn't necessarily seem so compatible at the time—with an easy grace. Their music had a synthetic sheen, power pop with endless hooks and a healthy love for the Beatles in an era when that wasn't entirely fashionable, but they also seemed to be looking forward. No wonder their transition to MTV worked so well.

"Just What I Needed" was the Cars' first single, and it laid out everything they'd ever do well: A memorable opening riff both punchy and spacious; yearning keyboard swells that couldn't wait for the '80s; a guitar break that was a ticket to an eternity on classic rock radio; lyrics that sound perfect even when they read lousy ("When you're standing oh so near / I kinda lose my mind"—kinda?); and enough repetition to hammer it all home. "Just What I Needed" also demonstrated why the band was perfectly named: When it hits FM airwaves during a long drive, no one touches the dial.
—MR

Elvis Costello and the Attractions: *"Radio Radio"* 1978

Any artist who takes half his stage name from the King places a heavy burden on himself to deliver. Declan Patrick McManus became Elvis Costello, and he was up to his own challenge, emerging from Britain's mid-1970s pub-rock scene ready to join the vanguard of punk's big takeover. Musically, Costello and his band, the Attractions, didn't quite fit with either the punk or New Wave scenes they found themselves mixed up with, but they had the energy and conviction to make his subversive blend of cynical lyrics and anthemic rock stand out.

"Radio Radio" follows Costello's desire to "bite the hand that feeds me," tearing into both the commercialization of radio and the restrictions on broadcast content that shut out many of punk rock's most pointed songs. The song's crashing electric organ intro makes it impossible to tune out, and the attack only intensifies as Costello rails against the BBC, cryptically referencing the Sex Pistols' banned "God Save the Queen" single. This was bold stuff for an artist who needed radio to help spread his music, but Costello's own propensity for political outcry in his songs gave him a direct stake in the censorship battle.
—JT

The Cure: *"Boys Don't Cry"* 1979

Most music fans know the Cure as the epic, gloomy force they became by the late 1980s. In some ways, that grand, mysterious Cure was a long way from the band roots as a wiry, spooky post-punk trio. In other ways, it's not so far at all. The Cure were always at their best when they were shading different emotions together into more complex permutations—the points where depression wraps around into who-cares ecstasy, love verges on the horror of being consumed, or Christmas lights start to look like the saddest things in the world.

You can hear hints of that in the Cure's earliest singles. "Boys Don't Cry," for instance, is as simple and chipper as a pop song can get: just a few chords jangling happily along and a childlike, singsong melody. But it's also about a guy who's done something so horrible to his girlfriend that he's given up all hope of making it right, which leaves that happy melody sounding awfully sardonic. Worse still, the verses consist of all the grand gestures he'd make to get her back if he weren't so busy acting tough. Like all the best simple songs, this one has almost as many layers as it does hooks.
—NA

XTC: *"Making Plans for Nigel"* 1979

Frontman Andy Partridge, bouncing off the walls and splicing pop with dub, Brian Eno, and amphetamines, wrote the highs and lows of XTC's songbook. But slow-and-steady bassist Colin Moulding was the reliable hitmaker, and he authored "Making Plans for Nigel," one of the pivotal singles of the band's three-decade career. Here, title character Nigel is forced by his parent into safe servitude with a job at British Steel. His response is passive-aggressive, inspired by the time that Moulding was kicked out of school—not for acting out or making trouble, but for refusing to cut his hair. As the lead track from *Drums and Wires*, "Making Plans for Nigel" introduced the barbed guitars and gigantic drums alluded to in the album title with a bare-bones, brilliant hook to sell it. It also illustrates a tendency Partridge and Moulding both share, of retreating from the world—the touring grind, the record biz—instead of fighting it. Rather than burn down British Steel or take to the streets, Nigel says he's "happy in his work," and thus the hero of XTC's biggest song buckles without a peep. But it gave Moulding a chance to wonder: What if he'd gotten that haircut?

—CD

Blondie: *"Atomic"* 1979

For a band with roots in the garage rock of the 1960s, Blondie sure made good futurists. Having scored their breakthrough hit, "Heart of Glass," by locking New Wave and disco into a bedroom with a bottle of gin, they spent the rest of their first incarnation turning the dance music of the moment into the chart pop of the day after tomorrow. On their fourth album, *Eat to the Beat* (released simultaneously as an LP and a "video album," with a clip for every song), singer Debbie Harry became the sexy robot she'd been threatening to change into since the beginning of the band, making everything she sang sound meaningless yet lovely. The lyric to "Atomic" contains eleven words, five of which are its chorus: "Your hair is beautiful tonight." (The word "atomic" doesn't modify anything here—it's just in the song to signify futurism, power, and terror.) Chris Stein's guitar plays a four-note hook that echoes the title, while the rest of the band does its best impression of mechanical perfection. Listen carefully, and you can hear flesh-and-blood performers becoming obsolete.

—DW

Talking Heads: *"Memories Can't Wait"* 1979

When Talking Heads formed in the mid-1970s, David Byrne played the beleaguered middle-class man observing mundane things that took on frightening dimensions in a New York that seemed to be imploding—a world where buildings, H-bombs, TV dinners, and psycho killers were all on the same unreal level. And, as the 1977 blackout riot that set New York ablaze had proven just a few years earlier, recession-era repression inevitably sparks violence. The best of Talking Heads' early work plays on this dangerous tension.

"Memories Can't Wait," from 1979's *Fear of Music,* captures the band on the cusp of this first astringent phase, where their already stiff avant-funk is chilled until you can hear the joints starting to freeze, all thanks to producer Brian Eno's ambient touches. Byrne laments feeling trapped inside "a party in my mind" that he still knows is safer than the world outside, with its drugs, knives, riots— and other humans.

—JH

Chapter Two:
1980–1982

The previous chapter of this book talked about the "year zero" mentality of punk rock—the way its artists wanted to drop the baggage of rock's history and cut back to the raw basics of three chords and no tricks. The vigor and fire of their efforts got plenty of attention, but it shouldn't overshadow what came next. If the blackboard had been wiped clean, it fell to the next wave of rock bands to start marking it up again—inventing new tricks, new languages, and shading the piss and vinegar of punk into a wider range of sounds and emotions. A lot of bands during this period were inspired to pick up their instruments by the possibilities of punk—the sense that anyone could start a band, even a weird one. But they took that fire and scattered it in a lot of new directions.

Some, especially in the UK, aimed for chart-topping glamour, trying to take over the music industry by sheer wit and good makeup—hence New Pop and the New Romantics. Some fashioned the kind of modest, homespun pop songs that are eventually called "indie"— the smart, elegant jangle of bands like Orange Juice and R.E.M. Others, especially in the U.S., hopped in their vans and slept on fans' couches, spinning off toward something fiercer than the first wave of punk ever got. And some tried it all: When a group like Scritti Politti can go from playing knotty post-punk to making creamy R&B, and score minor hits along the way, is it any wonder some people felt like anything was possible?

But the rock bands of these years were just plain lucky: If they looked around for new sounds to chalk up on that metaphorical board, they found a world teeming with options. The big boom of disco may have ended, but it, too, had spun off in fascinating directions, with even bigger developments still to come. In New York, disco had a genuine underground, centered on the left-field "mutant" dance music in downtown clubs; you can hear echoes of that sound in everyone from the Clash to Yoko Ono. In Europe, disco had already bled its way into styles like Italo disco, with human session players replaced by synthesizers, sequencers, and other finicky computers. Those machines were just becoming cheap enough for upstart musicians to get their hands on them, and more people leapt into the new world they promised, with a lot of people dancing.

And more than any of those developments, there was an entirely new reason for dancing in these years: hip-hop. For years already, that sound had been fueling parties and nights out in one New York City borough—DJs cutting and scratching disco and funk records, MCs rapping along, and dancers helping transform the whole thing from the work of artists to the pastime of an actual community. Of all the new possibilities in music, this was the biggest one: a sound and culture springing out of black and Caribbean neighborhoods in the Bronx, full of enough potential that from here to the end of this book—a quarter of a decade, and still counting— it remains one of the two biggest threads in the story of the past thirty years.

It might actually be a good thing that years passed before anyone invested in recording and distributing this new music: By the time it started leaking out to the world beyond New York, it had already developed a sound and culture broad and sturdy enough to last. The "old-school" hip-hop sounds of these years are draped, for most people, in a rosy glow—the music starts with friendly live-band disco, not DJs abusing records, and the rappers trading cheerful boasts and good-time nonsense rhymes. That's not just a matter of nostalgia; it's a matter of marketing, and the first entrepreneurs to try to sell this stuff did their best to offer a smiling face to the public. As with all babies, it's easy to like. But this baby learned to walk very, very quickly, and within months of the leap from block parties to vinyl singles, artists were pushing hip-hop straight forward—rapidly introducing all the scratches, samples, electronics, street realism, and radical breaks from tradition that the genre would come to represent.
—*NA*

Kurtis Blow: *"The Breaks"* 1980

The first rapper ever signed to a major label was Kurtis Blow, whose name is commonly tossed around in discussion of "the old school"—a gentle term for the time when rap was feeling its way around the pop landscape and building tracks primarily from breaks found in funk, disco, and reggae. Blow's second single "The Breaks" is more dance workout than formal rap exercise, with instrumental breakdowns running the show in place of the gregarious MC's lyrics. But it *is* high-octane fun, built on an elastic bass line and a familiar funk riff. (No surprise, since Blow was a DJ before he began rapping at the urging of his manager—a young Russell Simmons, future founder of Def Jam Records.)

Despite the downcast idea behind the song, there's something laughably sweet in Blow's lyrics: "And the IRS says they want to chat / And you can't explain why you claimed your cat." His two homophone-packed verses bookend the nearly eight-minute song, as Blow's commanding voice—which mightily stretches the syllables of the chorus—leaves the impression that the muck we're all dealt is the best reason to celebrate yet.
—*SF*

Spoonie Gee Meets the Sequence: *"Monster Jam"* 1980

Rap existed as live underground party music in the Bronx for years before labels thought to sign rappers, so maybe it's no surprise that those contract-holders would warp the music into unrecognizable shapes as they tried to turn it into pop. Still, it's jarring just how completely Sugar Hill Records, the first indie label to profit big from rap, changed the music. Instead of scratched-up pieces of popular records, Sugar Hill hired a crack session band to replay those parts. Instead of gang shout-outs, the label's rappers kicked life-affirming babble and for-the-ladies loverman talk. And, at least in the beginning, the label was more interested in prefabricated combos like the Sugarhill Gang than in established crews like the Cold Crush Brothers.

But even if the music lost a lot of its desperate urgency on the way to the charts, the Sugar Hill approach to rap had considerable charms of its own.

"Monster Jam," an extended flirtation between Casanova rapper Spoonie Gee and all-girl trio Sequence (whose Angie B would later become R&B singer Angie Stone), is a great example. In the Sugar Hill days, rap was still considered an offshoot of disco, and the house band treats it as such, laying whistles, trap drums, and ecstatic horn stabs over a metronomic pulse and spreading it out to nearly nine minutes.
—*TB*

The Sugarhill Gang: *"8th Wonder"* 1980

With "Rapper's Delight" in 1979, the Sugarhill Gang became the first rap group to score an actual hit single, which rankled the hell out of virtually every other rap group in existence. The trio came into being when Sugar Hill Records founder Sylvia Robinson saw a market opportunity in rap, assembled three New Jersey teenagers into a group, and put them to work. Hip-hop was still a Bronx thing and a live phenomenon; barely any rap had been recorded by the time "Rapper's Delight" emerged. Famously, Sugarhill's Big Bank Hank stole his "Rapper's Delight" lyrics from Cold Crush Brothers frontman Grandmaster Caz, and Caz never saw a dime for his efforts; he's still pissed about it. And the genre's Bronx originators weren't too happy to see these no-cred-having kids making money from their innovations, either. But, dubious history or no, the dizzy joy in the Sugarhill Gang's singles can't be denied, and "8th Wonder" is a prime example. For seven and a half minutes, the label's house band works up a light but delirious groove, layering handclaps and whistles and party noise over their slaps and horn riffs while the three rappers chant ecstatic gibberish. Years later, both the Beastie Boys and Busta Rhymes would swipe Big Bank Hank's "Woo-hah! Got them all in check!" interjection, stealing from rap's original thief, and keeping the cycle intact.
—*TB*

The Treacherous Three: *"The New Rap Language"* 1980

Early hip-hop vocal combos aped the harmonious, egoless sounds of doo-wop and Motown groups; you could almost imagine, for example, the Treacherous Three performing under a street-corner lamppost.

Their debut single, "The New Rap Language," highlights this dynamic, with MCs Kool Moe Dee, Special K, and L.A. Sunshine (along with DJ Easy Lee) crafting a mellifluous, fast-talking song that pushes the voice out in front of the scratch. Over a rubbery beat, the trio highlight the way hip-hop is often more about a message's delivery than its content—rhymes about sexual prowess or Kool Moe Dee's favorite flavor (spoiler alert: it's cherry) don't look like much on paper, but these "fast-talkin' rhymes" crafted a new way of attacking a groove. The mold-breaking didn't end there, either: The group's second single, "The Body Rock," was among the first hip-hop songs to feature a guitar. And, eventually, Moe Dee went solo and practically invented both the battle rap (dissing Busy Bee Starski onstage) and the hip-hop beef (sparring with a young LL Cool J).
—SP

The Clash:
"The Magnificent Seven" 1980

A few years after rallying around the slogan "No Elvis, Beatles, or the Rolling Stones," the Clash went sonically conservative, retreating to pre–British Invasion Americanisms on their classic *London Calling*. It was a massive artistic success, and they would have been forgiven for repeating the formula with its follow-up. Instead, they spent their critical capital on the triple LP *Sandinista!*, a sprawling exploration of contemporary sounds like dub, roots reggae, disco, and—on "The Magnificent Seven"—hip-hop.

Recorded in New York City, "The Magnificent Seven" was released within two weeks of Blondie's more-famous dalliance with hip-hop, "Rapture"—and bests it. Inspired, like Blondie, by Grandmaster Flash and the other Bronx DJs and MCs who had recently begun performing in Manhattan, the song attacks consumerism and celebrity culture with a clumsy charm that could have been mere novelty were it not for the band's open-eared and open-armed approach to nonguitar music. Unlike most of their peers, the Clash never sounded touristic when incorporating textures and rhythms from outside of rock and, as a result, "The Magnificent Seven" and its extended mix ("The Magnificent Dance") were huge hits with the Big Apple's dance club cognoscenti.
—SP

Talking Heads: *"Born Under Punches (The Heat Goes On)"* 1980

Talking Heads frontman David Byrne and Brian Eno play a shell game on the opening track of the Talking Heads' *Remain in Light* LP. Under one cup there's signal—a funk-pop hook, rolling polyrhythms, and a strand of lyrical sense. Under the other there's noise—glitchy guitar, primitive electronics, and eerie backing vocals. They shuffle these cups incessantly, destabilizing the song and cutting up its meaning. Byrne says he's a government man but acts like a carny, telling us to watch his hands while the musicians behind him pull the real bait-and-switch, flipping between uptight New Wave and loose Afrobeat.

Flirtations with African music were a hallmark of intelligent 1980s pop, but many voyagers treated that sound as a treasure house of lost authenticity, making records smothered in respectfulness. Three minutes into "Born Under Punches," guest guitarist Adrian Belew forges a missing link between thumb piano, guitar, and a jammed modem, laying down a marker for a different approach to "world" music. Talking Heads took post-punk into a terrifying, confusing, urgent, and above all futuristic Africa: What they unearthed still astonishes.
—TE

Yoko Ono: *"Walking on Thin Ice"* (twelve-inch version) 1981

If *Rust Never Sleeps* was Neil Young's answer to punk, it's helpful to think of "Walking on Thin Ice" as Yoko Ono and John Lennon's answer to New Wave. Ono and Lennon also liked disco, and on "Thin Ice," they came up with a jittery disco-punk groove driven and interrupted by Lennon's noise-guitar charges, with which Ono's steely shrieks kept a nice pace. Mostly, though, she murmured a disarming melody with a fraught lyric about watching your every step. Ironically, Lennon's death came the night he and Ono finished mixing this track.

"Walking on Thin Ice" evokes hoofing it through Manhattan during rush hour. But that might be due to the record's combination of nerviness and sheen: It feels a lot like contemporary records by the art punks just downtown, only with a studio-cat slickness. It was an underground hit crafted by multimillionaires, the ultimate early-'80s record made by the ultimate late-'60s figures.
—MiM

Robot Rock: Ten Electro Anthems

Though the genre's roots stretch back further, Afrika Bambaataa's "Planet Rock" crystallized the guiding principal of electro: Take the polished machine pop and robotic pulse of Kraftwerk and amplify the funk. Early electro made judicious use of syncopation and synthesized hand-claps while leaving space around every sound to give each beat more impact. It was music for the club as well as the streets; without electro, it's possible that no break-dancer would have thought to do the robot. Electro also proved to be a highly adaptable template, as dance tracks leaning toward New Wave and R&B and away from hip-hop made use of its sleek rhythmic drive.

"Looking for the Perfect Beat," **Afrika Bambaataa & Soulsonic Force:** The follow-up to "Planet Rock" lacked its predecessor's expansive statement of purpose, but showed how to create a forceful club jam from a minimum of ingredients. It also provided a catch phrase for cratediggers and producers the world over.

"Alleys of Your Mind," **Cybotron:** Simultaneously hard as Detroit steel and delicate as a robin's egg, this eerie slab of mechanized soul by producer Juan Atkins served as a bridge between electro and the more fluid Detroit techno.

"I.O.U.," **Freeez:** With its "Planet Rock"–style synth stabs, brittle production, and bouncing bass line, this cut from the UK funk outfit Freeez fits comfortably into an electro mix, but its sing-along chorus is far more pop than anything else on this list (it topped the dance charts in the U.S.). Its warm, vibrant sound demonstrates the elasticity of the electro aesthetic.

"Scorpio," **Grandmaster Flash and the Furious Five:** Perhaps the thickest, rawest, most cylon-tronic use of vocoder in early hip-hop, and the Furious Five are rapping through it, taking everybody higher as a laser shootout rages in the recording studio.

"White Horse," **Laid Back:** Two Danes collaborate on a tune with a lurching groove that Prince wishes he'd written. And their advice is sound: "If you want to ride, don't ride the white horse" (cocaine). The alternative? "Ride the white pony," obviously. It makes a lot more sense when you're hearing this bass line.

"Hip Hop, Be Bop (Don't Stop)," **Man Parrish:** Just about every sound here is used as percussion— each metallic ping, push-button handclap, tom roll, and chanting voice is deployed to shape the beat. In fact, this tribute to rhythm is so proudly skeletal that when actual chords enter they seem like an embarrassing indulgence.

"Confusion," **New Order:** "Confusion" was recorded in New York with "Planet Rock" producer Arthur Baker, an association that continued for years. It's remarkable how easily the moody guitar-pop of New Order's early records translated to the realm of electro-inspired grooves, suggesting that dance music might one day fill arenas.

"Jam on It," **Newcleus:** Brooklyn's cosmic funk outfit Newcleus scored a hit with this single, which combines hypnotic bass, Latin percussion, and most notably, chipmunk voices going "wikiwikiwikiwiki." Be sure to track down the song's video, which finds the band clad in black and silver suits straight out of *Star Trek* in a room packed with break-dancing kids.

"Walking on Sunshine," **Rocker's Revenge:** Written by Eddy Grant of "Electric Avenue" fame, this Arthur Baker production draws heavily from Latin disco with its conga break, busy array of bells, and tambourine, but its insistent repetition and steady-state groove ground it firmly in the electro realm.

"Set It Off," **Strafe:** The hissy, drawn-out high-hat throughout this track beckons to the dance floor. Mixed by New York club legend Walter Gibbons and a staple during Larry Levan's sets at the Paradise Garage, "Set It Off" uses minimal electronics to conjure soulful elegance.
—MR

Klein + MBO: *"Dirty Talk"* 1982

Despite the Germanic undertones to their name, Klein + MBO were actually the result of an Italo-American partnership: Rome's Mario Boncaldo shared cowriting duties with New Yorker Tony Carrasco. Their first and biggest dance hit, "Dirty Talk," is in a similar stylistic (and geographical) gray area, somewhere between Kraftwerk's "Computer World"–era proto-electro, the synth-pop that the Human League and Gary Numan were pushing to the upper reaches of the UK charts, and Italo disco. As a result, it became a smash hit in two important focal points of post-disco dance music: New York's Paradise Garage, presided over by tastemaker and remix don Larry Levan, and Chicago's Warehouse, where Levan's former associate Frankie Knuckles built on its blend of disco and electro to birth house music. (On top of that, "Dirty Talk" in part inspired New Order's smash "Blue Monday.") Its influence is well deserved: Singer Rossana Casale has a bright, coy charm reminiscent of a young Madonna, and the song's production makes maximalism out of minimalism by layering syncopated bass lines that neatly offset one another with punchy, off-beat emphasis.
—*NP*

ESG: *"Moody"* 1981

Formed in the South Bronx at the peak of post-punk and old-school rap's funk- and disco-redefining phase, ESG encompassed just about everything important going on in NYC at the time: sharing bills with A Certain Ratio, getting their records played at Larry Levan's disco nexus Paradise Garage, and winding up in the crates of every hip-hop DJ worth his crossfader. (If you like rap in any capacity, there's a 95 percent chance you own a track that samples their 1981 song "UFO.") All of ESG's success came from an unpretentious desire just to go out and make good dance music, which the Scroggins sisters (vocalist/conga player Marie, guitarist/vocalist Renee, drummer Valerie, and bassist Deborah) pulled off with a tightness that belied their self-taught background.

The funkiest track from their self-titled debut EP, the Martin Hannett–produced "Moody," features a raw but limber backbeat, with Valerie's aggressive disco rhythm, Deborah's minimalist, insistent bass line, and the dueling congas of Maria and Tito Libran providing all the momentum any dance floor would ever need. And though lead singer Renee doesn't say a lot—after the first verse, most of the lyrics consist of the refrain "very moody, yeah yeah"—her sharp vibrancy sustains the song all the way to its fantastically abrupt end.
—*NP*

Grandmaster Flash and the Furious Five: *"The Adventures of Grandmaster Flash on the Wheels of Steel"* 1981

Hip-hop on record, to this point, consisted largely of party chants over well-known grooves replayed by studio bands. It yielded plenty of terrific singles, but it also misrepresented what the music sounded like in its original environment: other peoples' records manipulated and manhandled to do only what their listeners and dancers wanted them to. This record was a line in the sand in every way imaginable. In addition to constructing an unyielding monster of a groove, "Wheels of Steel" brutally and skillfully reduces recordings—Spoonie Gee, Blondie, Chic, Incredible Bongo Band, Queen, Flash's own group the Furious Five, a father talking to his kids, the Sugarhill Gang, and old-time radio ("The official adventures of Flash…")—from texts to signposts. In doing so, it presents hip-hop not simply as a variation on existing styles but a usurping of them. Unlike prior pop cut-up records, like Buchanan and Goodman's 1956 track "The Flying Saucer," Flash's emphasis was less on voices or timbres than on beats and riffs.

Grandmaster Flash wasn't the first DJ to approach music like this, but he was the first on record, and he made the most exuberant noise imaginable doing it. His first scratch, one minute and four seconds into the song, must have sounded like a mistake or an alien broadcast to anyone who hadn't already witnessed the founding hip-hop DJs working block parties or clubs. But as Flash kept utilizing those scratches to announce the next selection, their utility became apparent, as did their means of arrival. A year later, Flash and the Furious Five's "The Message" was where hip-hop lyrics' street realism was foregrounded forever—but the vocalists were merely catching up to a musical template their DJ had already established.
—*MiM*

Funky 4+1: *"That's the Joint"* 1980

Funky 4 + 1 were one of the original and greatest South Bronx party crews: K. K. Rockwell, Lil' Rodney Cee, Keith Keith, the non–Fresh Prince–affiliated Jazzy Jeff, pioneering female MC Sha Rock (the group's "+ 1"), and DJ Breakout. They were also one of the first to record, with 1979's "Rappin' and Rockin' the House," sixteen minutes of exuberant and slightly exhausting party rhymes. In 1980, they'd do it again, with the nine and a half minutes of "That's the Joint." The record oozes a confidence few musicians have touched. The rappers' individual verses are all buoyed by group-vocal interplay and musicians every bit as nimble, as quick, as bad, as slick, and as unforgettable as the rhymes. When Funky 4 + 1 trade lines, with a poise bordering on telepathy, they make it sound like the easiest thing in the world.
—*MiM*

Kraftwerk: *"Numbers/Computer World 2"* 1981

Kraftwerk are best known for their major albums of the 1970s—the unstoppable succession of *Autobahn, Radio-Activity, Trans-Europe Express,* and *The Man Machine*—but by the release of 1981's dopey "Pocket Calculator" single, some were starting to wonder if the group had lost the plot. Compared to everything else that was emerging at the time (electro! hip-hop! post-punk!), the band seemed less like cool future-shockers and more like nerdy uncles. The Detroit electro crew Cybotron, who claimed an explicit Kraftwerk influence, had just come out with their first single, "Alleys of Your Mind," which would lay the groundwork for the reconfiguration of electronic music, pointing the way toward techno and threatening to leave Kraftwerk in the dust.

The Germans bounced back, retaining their roles as sonic pacesetters on much of *Computer World*—especially "Numbers/Computer World 2," a tight piece of electro-funk that, along with the group's "Trans-Europe Express," became a hip-hop foundation text. "Numbers" was one of Kraftwerk's most danceable tracks, despite consisting of only a breakbeat and random strings of numbers. And by the time the synth strains of "Computer World 2" entered the mix, any rumors of their demise could be put to rest.
—*GD*

Afrika Bambaataa & Soulsonic Force: *"Planet Rock"* 1982

From Sun Ra's astral jazz to George Clinton's mothership connection, African-American music has enjoyed a long and storied fixation on outer space. But rarely has this theme coalesced as successfully as on Afrika Bambaataa & Soulsonic Force's "Planet Rock," whose inspiration was provided by the pared-down futurism of Kraftwerk's "Trans-Europe Express." Bambaataa was a former leader of the Bronx's Black Spades gang, but in the mid-1970s, this imposing figure gave up street fighting for breakdance battles—and his DJ sets marked a pivotal point in hip-hop's evolution.

As well as advancing a belief in music as a powerful force for social change and education, Bambaataa reinforced the genre's intertextual aesthetic by drawing upon sources ranging from 1960s girl groups to early German electronics. On "Planet Rock," Bambaataa and the MCs in Soulsonic Force preached booty globalism over a starkly dystopian yet highly infectious dance track; they also proved prophetic, taking b-boy culture from the streets of New York, across the universe, and into the charts.
—*DS*

Grandmaster Flash and the Furious Five: *"The Message"* 1982

His name is on the sleeve, but Grandmaster Flash didn't actually have anything to do with "The Message," and neither did most of his group, the Furious Five. The song was entirely the creation of Five frontman Melle Mel and Sugar Hill Records house band member Ed "Duke Bootee" Fletcher; no one else in the group was too interested. "The Message" was the first track to seriously acknowledge the urban decay that birthed hip-hop. Prior to that, what little social commentary it featured (welfare chants, gang shout-outs) was coded and mostly incidental. Here, Melle Mel's lyrics phase between disconnected images of degradation, confessions of personal desperation, and weird sidelong glints of hope. The music is as much a bleak departure as the lyrics, with Fletcher forgoing Sugar Hill's usual bass-popping euphoria for a stark synthscape, giving Melle Mel's burly growl and mirthless, stuttering laugh all the room they need to weave their magic. Rap started getting ugly here.
—*TB*

Glenn Branca:
"Lesson No. 1 for Electric Guitar" 1980

After blazing No Wave trails with his group Theoretical Girls, Glenn Branca merged rock and modern classical music on his solo debut, *Lesson No. 1,* the first release on New York's influential 99 Records. Jumping on the repetitive techniques he learned from guitarists Rhys Chatham and Jeffrey Lohn (and the minimalist influence of composers Philip Glass and Steve Reich), Branca injected rock's guttural thrust into high-minded composition by using a simple tool: loud electric guitar. Working with Chatham's discovery that electric guitars playing the same thing over and over produce dense overtones and morphing melodies, Branca begins the album's first track, "Lesson No. 1 for Electric Guitar," with a two-note guitar pattern that builds into a joyous cloud of shimmering noise. When bombastic drums enter, the guitars shine even brighter, like beams of light splitting into fractals. Calling this a "lesson" might have been audacious, but Branca's debut really was a musical big bang, spawning his larger guitar symphonies and the avant rock of groups like Sonic Youth and Swans. Still, "Lesson No. 1" is not merely a blueprint—all the power and entrancement of future noise-rock is right there in its chiming chords and crashing beat.
—*MM*

Laurie Anderson:
"O Superman (For Massenet)" 1981

Laurie Anderson grew up in the Chicago suburbs of the 1950s and went to art school in 1970s New York. There's something in that path—from the postwar Midwestern sensibility to a hotbed of the avant-garde—that you can feel in her surprise UK hit, "O Superman." Describing the track makes it sound more difficult than it actually is: eight minutes of a single syllable repeating ("ah ah ah ah"), over which Anderson sings and speaks through a vocoder—processing vocals through chords played on a synthesizer and giving them a ghostly, robotic sound. But Anderson's sound is spacious, warm, and inviting, and she weaves it through enough gorgeous embellishments—fluttering arpeggios, swelling chords, and subtle recordings of birdsong—that you can sit rapt for the length of it without noticing the time passing.

The text is every bit as striking as the sound, ranging from ominous ("Here come the planes") to funny (a subtle imitation of a mother's voice on an answering machine). It's also a deeply honest song about American force and industry; when love, justice, and force are all exhausted, Anderson says, "There's always mom." It was the dawn of the Reagan era, and from Illinois suburbs to downtown Manhattan lofts, this was what you got—the all-embracing bosom of fighter jets, oil companies, and new appliances.
—*NA*

Joy Division: *"Atmosphere"* 1980

You could construct entire narratives around Joy Division's career based solely on their song titles. Where their debut album, 1979's *Unknown Pleasures,* dwelled on space and confinement with titles like "Disorder," "Shadowplay," and "Wilderness" evoking singer Ian Curtis's fragile mental state and violent epileptic fits, their second and final studio album, 1980's *Closer,* ended on a time-obsessed trio of songs—"Twenty-Four Hours," "The Eternal," and "Decades"—which in hindsight, proved a chilling harbinger of Curtis's suicide.

But "Atmosphere" bounds out of time and space entirely, thanks in large part to producer Martin Hannett's truly atmospheric production and Bernard Sumner setting aside his guitar until the song's swelling climax, instead using synthesizers to create a radiant, weightless fog. Curtis, testing his baritone's range as he squeezes uncharacteristically high notes from behind the lump in his throat, paints a picture of static dread before unleashing a refrain that's not hard to connect to his failing marriage to teen sweetheart Deborah Curtis: "Don't walk away / In silence…"

A few months later, Curtis would be dead, and Joy Division would mutate overnight, into New Order. *Closer* and the classic single "Love Will Tear Us Apart" would become the band's posthumous swan songs, but "Atmosphere"—played by BBC radio DJ John Peel to commemorate the singer's passing—stands as the strongest reminder that Curtis didn't go silently.
—*PS*

Contort Yourself: No Wave

When a loose collective of artists and poets descended on New York in the late 1970s, the city was run-down and abandoned, and punk was already getting stale. Reacting to the bleakness of their surroundings, these untrained musicians created an art-rock movement known as No Wave, filled with anarchic noise and nihilistic ideas. The bands burned bright and flamed out fast, leaving few traces (besides producer Brian Eno's scene-defining *No New York* compilation) but influencing underground rock for decades to come.

"Helen Fordsdale," **Mars:** The first No Wave band was also the most challenging. Mars's dissonant guitars, lopsided beats, and psychotic vocals were sonic quicksand, making blasts like "Helen Fordsdale" a mix of Velvet Underground–inspired locomotion and uncompromising noise.

"You and You," **DNA:** Mars's brother band, led by Brazil-raised proto-geek Arto Lindsay, added complex rhythms to their comrades' dissonance. On "You and You," Lindsay's surreal yelps mimic his atonal guitar, while rigid drums and stomping keyboard sound like a train leaping off its tracks.

"Orphans," **Teenage Jesus and the Jerks:** Lydia Lunch's trio made short, harsh songs out of dogmatic beats and blaring slide guitar. "Orphans," a tale of injured children running through blood-covered snow, captures her horror-movie worldview with pummeling power.

"Dish It Out," **Contortions:** No Wave could get funky, too: James Chance's Contortions were equal parts James Brown and Albert Ayler, ripping out tight tunes under their front man's screaming sax and flaming voice. "Dish It Out" opens *No New York* with a bang, turning six raging musicians into a mushroom cloud of funk-punk.

"U.S. Millie," **Theoretical Girls:** There was also an intellectual side to No Wave, embodied by Soho-based groups who played galleries rather than rock clubs. Theoretical Girls were the art-rock brainchild of Glenn Branca and Jeffrey Lohn, and Lohn's "U.S. Millie" is equal parts goofy punk and arch structure, injecting No Wave abandon into brainier music.

"Not Bite," **Red Transistor:** Brooklyn's Red Transistor managed only one posthumous single, but it was as insane as their live shows, wherein mad geniuses Von Lmo and Rudolph Grey took power drills to their guitars and axes to their amps. "Not Bite" sounds like the band looked, with frantic guitars and ugly vocals spurting out punk-noise mayhem.

"Diddy Wah Diddy," **8-Eyed Spy:** After Teenage Jesus and the Contortions split, some of their members formed 8-Eyed Spy, applying No Wave edge to trad-rock forms like rockabilly and surf. On radical covers like a ripping take on Bo Diddley's "Diddy Wah Diddy," sax and guitar chops merge with Lydia Lunch's harrowing howl to create a singular noise-pop hybrid.

"Ampheta Speak," **Ut:** Women were involved in almost every No Wave group, but Ut was its first all-female band. The trio grabbed rhythmic aggression from Teenage Jesus and screeching dissonance from Mars, crafting dirgey rants like the churning "Ampheta Speak" and presaging the post–No Wave drone-rock of Sonic Youth and Swans.

"Guitar Trio," **Rhys Chatham:** Rhys Chatham served in many short-lived No Wave bands, but it was his solo work that pulled the movement into new realms. Based on minimalist classical ideas, "Guitar Trio" features multiple guitarists single-mindedly strumming one string to create dense overtones, as Chatham finds the desperate sound of the city in a single note.

"The Spectacular Commodity," **Glenn Branca:** Ex–Theoretical Girl Branca built on Chatham's innovations with his own multiple-guitar compositions, scoring an underground hit with his first solo album *The Ascension.* Its best track, "The Spectacular Commodity," is like a minimalist film score, moving from foreboding noise to chiming melodies and propelling Branca toward the huge guitar symphonies he would craft for the next three decades.
—MM

The Fall: *"Totally Wired"* 1980

Mark E. Smith looks at the world through vision so sharp it bends at the edges, which probably has to do with what's affecting his eyes and brain: "I drank a jar of coffee!" he bellows in his loud, proud Manchester accent, "And then I took some of these!" He's been leading the Fall since 1977—"the Fall" being defined as whomever Smith brings onstage with him. But here, at the punk-hangover moment of their most crazed single, it was practically a cult, an out-of-tune, on-the-slant crew that would riff ad-lib behind his bug-eyed rants.

Most of the Fall's songs during this period had small musical signposts and a catchphrase or two, but those were only frameworks for Smith to run his mouth. This one, a monomaniacal track about monomania, keeps barging back into something like a chorus just as Smith's mad-prophet babbling (on communism, interiority, irritation) circles around to its hook. Craig Scanlon and Marc Riley's sour, trebly guitar parts smash into each other in a perverse imitation of the rockabilly deep in their genetic code. But Smith remains front and center, his crabbed lurch inspiring his disciples to jitter his way.
—*DW*

Elvis Costello and the Attractions: *"Beyond Belief"* 1982

By 1982, twenty-eight-year-old Elvis Costello had shaped himself into a manic pop savant. And on that year's *Imperial Bedroom* LP, he came to a sobering realization: At some point along the way, he'd grown up. The album was Costello's most sonically ambitious undertaking yet. He booked a studio for twelve weeks, rotating dozens of musicians while *Sgt. Pepper's* alum Geoff Emerick reined in the chaos. Emotionally, "Beyond Belief" opens *Bedroom* by signaling that the cocky prodigy had, at least temporarily, paused for personal reflection. The song chronicles a cryptic, Lennonesque bout of self-evaluation, as Costello's eyes follow a mysterious woman moving across a barroom floor. Ever the academic, he calls himself on his own attraction, recognizing his own predictability. As the song builds from its cavernous, patient opening section into a swirling psychedelic melange of skittering drums, frantic bass, and undulating organ, Costello's croon turns to a shout—not one of anger, but one of shock. Indeed, "Beyond Belief" documents the moment that

Costello stepped outside of himself and, for the first time, failed to grasp what he saw.
—*EH*

The Pretenders: *"Back on the Chain Gang"* 1982

Chrissie Hynde's tough-gal rep never told the whole story; her snarl gave her historical weight at a time when prominent bandleaders with convincing scowls were almost never women, and the more emotive stuff that got her on the radio was every bit as steely as her male counterparts. "Back on the Chain Gang" is freighted with backstory: It's an explicit tribute to the guitarist (James Honeyman-Scott) and bassist (Pete Farndon) whose drug habits broke Hynde's group in half—and, eventually, led to each man's death. But you needn't know the first thing about who wrote that lilting guitar lead or why. Elegy or not, it's still one of the most heartbreaking records ever made: As Hynde's delicate vocal progresses, it edges closer to audibly cracking without quite making it there, and by the time she finally lets out the hardest truth of all—"Those were the happiest days of my life"— it's almost too much.
—*MiM*

The B-52's: *"Private Idaho"* 1980

Athens, Georgia's B-52's were an improbable band, bringing together more strange talents than you'd ever expect a single group to combine. It's one thing to have three terrific voices; it's another when they can all belt and chirp like they come from the same Day-Glo alien planet. It's another still to have a guitarist whose Morse-code surf riffs are so thrilling, or a drummer strong enough to carry the whole thing on his shoulders. The B-52's had all of this, plus one simple, remarkable idea: What if a dance band, instead of yelling things like "move your feet!" or "get down!" shouted stuff like "get out of the state!" and "I'm not no limburger!" Plus impersonations of sea creatures! How could that not be better?

Of all the lovable dance rave-ups on the first few B-52's albums, "Private Idaho" is the most sinister and energetic. The keyboards stay mostly clear of Ricky Wilson's riffing, which rattles and spits as dangerously as anything in his short career. Fred Schneider's signature hectoring shoots for the point where it passes camp and verges into nervy, red-faced insanity.

Kate Pierson and Cindy Wilson belt and holler like glee-struck banshees. And those who dismiss the B-52's as silly or kitschy should live in fear of the frenzied last half-minute, which sounds like it's out to track those people down, lock them up in cages, and make them go-go dance until they cry for mercy.
—NA

Dexys Midnight Runners:
"There There My Dear" 1980

In the U.S., the British band Dexys Midnight Runners is remembered as the one-hit wonder behind "Come on Eileen"—a tremendous love letter to the power and possibility of youth. That's a mistake. From the soulboy rave-ups at the start of their career to their brave, awkward flameout (spoken-word asides, Brooks Brothers clothing, and lyrics that served as penetratingly honest and sometimes painful self-examinations), Kevin Rowland and his rotating group of players carved one of the more curious and stimulating catalogs of the 1980s.

"There There My Dear" was one of their earliest triumphs, an acerbic letter bomb to hipsterdom. Rowland's vitriol against poseurs overwhelms his ability to enunciate; Marcel Duchamp, J. G. Ballard, and Frank Sinatra join a slurred roll call of artists misused as badges of intellectual honor. Pushed and prodded by then-obsolete Stax horns and rhythms, Rowland argues passionately for truth and honesty in both pop music and politics, making each seem like a life-or-death decision. To a guy who put his band through exercise regimens and banned them from drinking, and who here sings "the only way to change things is to shoot men who arrange things," they probably were.
—SP

Young Marble Giants: "Final Day" 1980

If you don't listen carefully, "Final Day" sounds like one of the slightest songs ever released as a single: scarcely a hundred seconds long, Stuart Moxham barely flicking at his guitar, Alison Statton singing as if she's trying not to wake somebody up over a mosquito-high keyboard drone. But the subject of "Final Day" is nothing less than the Eschaton that Europe was bracing for in the Thatcher era—it frames the total destruction of life on earth as a long-overdue social leveling.

Formed in Cardiff, Wales, in the shocked silence after the first wave of punk rock, Young Marble Giants figured out that whispers communicate urgency at least as well as shouts. Their sole studio album, Colossal Youth—and this follow-up single—made quietness, understatement, and negative space do the same sort of work as the in-your-face assault of punk. They became one of the flagship bands of Geoff Travis's label, Rough Trade, which initially specialized in the aesthetically radical bands that sprang up around the same time—and "Final Day" was one of the anchors of Wanna Buy a Bridge?, a compilation of circa-1980 Rough Trade singles that has become one of post-punk's most crucial documents.
—DW

Altered Images: "Happy Birthday" 1981

Two months after the murder of John Lennon, the Scottish band Altered Images released its debut single, "Dead Pop Stars," to disappointing sales: number 67 on the UK charts, with a bullet. Six months later, they went into damage-control mode, switching from ironic, blustery post-punk to galloping New Wave and issuing the sweetly named LP Happy Birthday. Who could find fault with that?

Not many in the UK, it seemed: The record's title track went to number 2 on the back of spritely production from the Banshees' Steve Severin and singer Clare Grogan's charming vocal affectations. You can practically hear Grogan pout her lips, stick out her tongue, and bat her lashes in her coy, childlike reading of the song, almost single-handedly inventing twee pop in the process. Her dramatic chops translated to film as well: In 1981 she played a key role in Gregory's Girl, a coming-of-age movie hardwired into the DNA of Scottish groups like Belle and Sebastian and the Pastels.
—SP

The Specials: "Ghost Town" 1981

Living in Coventry, a run-down industrial town in the British Midlands, Specials mastermind Jerry Dammers felt the catastrophic effects on the working class after years of failing government and destructive social and economic policy. In the late 1970s, with unemployment rampant and racial tensions reaching flashpoint levels, Dammers created a new youth movement, fusing the energy of punk with reggae's rousing rebel spirit. This jagged, politicized take on ska coalesced, via his 2 Tone record label, into a vibrant and cohesive polyracial scene, a loud and proud embodiment of positive multiculturalism.

Of course, with such idealism came friction. By the time "Ghost Town"—an eerie, cavernous, and infectious picture of decaying inner-city life—was released, the band's members were barely speaking to one another. Given the circumstances, its sad, nostalgic lyrics proved prescient in more ways than one: As "Ghost Town" hit number 1 on the UK charts, the nation erupted in racially tinged riots and the band itself dissolved.
—DS

Robert Wyatt: *"Shipbuilding"* 1982

In 1982 in the north of England, Thatcherism had spelled the death of industry. Then came the Falklands War, and a rumor ran through one town that the shipyards were reopening, which would mean jobs. But it would also mean that the ships the men built would sail their sons across the Atlantic, to fight and maybe to die. "Shipbuilding" opens wondering: Is it worth it?

Elvis Costello wrote the words, and their text alone is terrific. Music has the potential to say Big Things, but it's not exactly common for anyone to write so eloquently and simply about the needs and the conscience of common people. Amazingly enough, Clive Langer's music is just as gripping—a slow stroll of fluent jazz chord changes, lilting in unexpected directions. And then there's the performance of one-time prog musician Robert Wyatt, whose small, quavering voice is double-tracked into harmonies worth more than some entire careers. It's the ideal voice for a character weighing big, important things—like war and death—against small, equally important things, like money for "a bicycle on the boy's birthday." It's that line that hits hardest, embodying the pressure of everyday people trying to take care of each other.
—NA

Bauhaus: *"Third Uncle"* 1982

Bauhaus's status as the godfathers of goth always gets them a bum rap: It's as if memories of bad haircuts and fake vampires are just too titillating for anyone to remember all the incredible things this band actually did. But there are a lot of those incredible things—including the surprising amount of time they spent being a dub band and the keen way they brought arty, glam-rock drama into a world of punks who didn't have much time for fantasy. Add in their way around guitar textures and studio techniques, and the sheer creative energy of their best music is just too valuable to waste much time on the g word: These guys delivered all the things other post-punk bands get congratulated for, and probably more.

Their cover of Brian Eno's "Third Uncle" brings together almost all those things: It takes a spare, art-rock oddity and sets it on fire, kicking off at breakneck speed and then letting every member claw for the ceiling. Daniel Ash's guitar is a marvel, alternating among spacy zooms, nailed-down rhythms, and psychedelic scrawls. But it's Peter Murphy's double-tracked vocal that does the trick: It starts off in a monotone chant, but by the halfway point it's frenzied and yelping, as the bug-eyed Murphy in the background shouts punctuation to the commanding one up front. If this isn't impressive enough, just consider that it was what the band considered fit to be B-side material—on a single with a cover of David Bowie's "Ziggy Stardust" on the A-side. After years of punk's down-to-earth ethos, these flashes of beastly, glammy romance couldn't help but resonate.
—NA

Adam and the Ants: *"Kings of the Wild Frontier"* 1980

As a punk latecomer, Adam Ant's dabblings in S&M chic and Weimar poses barely registered critically, let alone commercially. Ambitious and pragmatic, he sought advice from Sex Pistols impresario Malcolm McLaren, who kindly tossed the intense Ant an idea or two—then promptly stole his entire band to form Bow Wow Wow.

Ant might have given up at that point, but he shared McLaren's hunch that the massed drums of traditional music from Burundi could be alchemized into thrilling—and lucrative—pop, and he recruited a new set of Ants. These included two drummers and guitarist Marco Pirroni, whose hooks were the secret ingredient that turned Adam Ant into Britain's first real 1980s star.

"Kings of the Wild Frontier"—one of the band's six Top 5 UK singles in 1980–81—finds Ant trying on the new sound and feeling out where its double-drummed force might take him. There's little to it beyond scuzzy guitar, sloganeering, and those huge, uncoiling rhythms, but their power and his conviction possess a poise and danger he never recaptured.
—TE

Scritti Politti: *"The 'Sweetest Girl'"* 1981

Green Gartside's long-running band began in 1978 as a DIY art-student project so arch that their name was a reference to Marxist theorist Antonio Gramsci. But the kind of art that affected Green most deeply is pop art—particularly hit R&B—and over the course of the subsequent three decades, he's gone on to slip highbrow theory into international dance hits like "Perfect Way" and collaborations with Mos Def, Shabba Ranks, and Kylie Minogue. This makeout song about deconstruction marked the group's about-face toward the candied tones of American radio. The quotation marks in the title—"The 'Sweetest Girl'"—are telling: The girl Green's crooning about has been made into an ideal by received language just as the formal elements of the song (its gently skanking rhythm, its wispy synthesizers, its hissing Sly Stone drum machine, Green's singing style) are all quotations in their own way. And Robert Wyatt's rippling piano part is another loaded gesture: a link to an earlier wave of leftist-intellectual yet popular music.
—DW

The Human League: *"Don't You Want Me"* 1981

The Human League ranked "Don't You Want Me" as one of the weakest tracks on their New Pop breakthrough *Dare*. The band had just grown from an arty, all-boy quartet into a sextet with two attractive teen girl singers—but while they sought fame, they still had their pride. For example, frontman Philip Oakey claims that sticking with synth-pop was a risk: "The idea was that although pure synthesizer records weren't widely popular they had a fanatical following and there wasn't much competition. And I loved them."

Today, it's hard to find a more iconic moment of '80s synth-pop. Oakey's lyrics, a he-said/she-said between a big shot who discovers a girl who insists she made it on her own, are painfully blunt. Oakey and Susanne Sulley enact each role in duet, and Sulley has long maintained it's a song about sexual politics, rather than the desperate love anthem its title and chorus suggest. Ironically, what Oakey called a "poor-quality filler track" became, at the insistence of Virgin exec Simon Draper, the fourth single from the album—and the band's biggest hit, threatening to erase their past accomplishments in the popular mind. As the ex–cocktail waitress in the song could've told them, fame has its price.
—CD

Soft Cell: *"Tainted Love"* 1981

Originally recorded in 1964 by singer (and, later, lover to T. Rex's Marc Bolan) Gloria Jones, "Tainted Love" began its long, evolving journey through pop history as a brisk Northern Soul romp. Still regarded by cratediggers as a classic of the genre, that version was sufficiently dust-covered when Soft Cell's Marc Almond and David Ball, desperate for a hit, seized upon it as cover fodder in 1981. It turned out to be the most significant move of their career; under their watch, "Tainted Love" transformed from a soulful but straightforward lament of love gone wrong to something confrontationally seedy and perverse. A lot of that had to do with the simple genius of recontextualization: In the hands of an act already renowned for singing dryly about transexualism and erotica, the song's meaning changed, and suddenly the word "tainted" was carrying a lot more significance. But had the production not been so alluring, none of that would have mattered. With its electrocardiogram beep-beeps, plasticky drums, and haunting backing vocals, Soft Cell's version of "Tainted Love" was one of electronic music's first great pop songs.
—MP

The Associates: *"Party Fears Two"* 1982

Even in the high-cheekboned world of early-'80s New Pop, where a comically heightened sense of theater was a basic prerequisite, Scotland's the Associates were often dismissed as fatally overblown. Most of that had to do with the late Billy Mackenzie, their mercurial lead singer, who possessed an uncanny vocal range and a disarming affinity for flexing it midnote. The band's biggest hit, the stately "Party Fears Two," balances a set of nimble,

interweaving guitar and piano melodies against Mackenzie's scarily unhinged vocals. By the time he delivers the song's inscrutable punch line ("What's wrong's the wrong that's always in wrong"), his tremulous delivery has turned into a piercing shriek, and then a ghostly wail. At first, it feels a little like watching a child scribble over an old painting; the pairing of Mackenzie's lacerating vocals with such nimble, galloping pop isn't a natural one. In the end, though, that's exactly what makes "Party Fears Two" so exhilarating.
—MP

ABC: *"All of My Heart"* 1982

Following "Poison Arrow" and "The Look of Love," "All of My Heart" was ABC's third UK Top 10 hit from their matchless New Pop album *The Lexicon of Love*. Where those previous singles were arch conceits, dissections of romance and the lover's discourse, with "All of My Heart" they "skip the hearts and flowers, skip the ivory towers," cutting instead to the chase, to the heart of the ache.

It's the wee small hours following the Saturday night fever: Martin Fry is alone with a Fairlight symphony orchestra and his stardust memories. "I gave you my heart—the story ends." That's just the start— the song proceeds to swoon through five minutes of epic melodrama. But the real romance is provided by the extravagant cornball genius of producer Trevor Horn's Technicolor orchestration. In Fry and Horn's collaboration, you can hear the Art of Noise and ZTT label being born, and the next chapter of New Pop beginning.
—ST

New Order: *"Temptation"* 1982

After the suicide of singer Ian Curtis, the other members of Joy Division continued as New Order, and there's a level on which not much changed: They still sounded like they were rumbling away in a freezing-cold warehouse, and they even recorded songs they'd been playing live before Curtis's death. On another level, though, everything changed: After the addition of Gillian Gilbert on keyboards, New Order started soaking up new sounds from all around them. If Joy Division was a quintessential Manchester band—the sound of the grim English

north—then New Order was an international one, a crew stepping confidently out into the whole wide world.

What turned out to be most important, for this band, was the dance music coming out of New York and Europe—pulsing, euphoric, and full of new tones and textures. Soon enough, these four were wrestling with the unreliable, user-unfriendly boxes and panels and disk drives that once made the stuff. Not many years later, it'd be taken as a truism that rock and electronic dance music just don't mix, or at least that it took some kind of genius to pull off both at the same time. Here in the early days, New Order had no such worries and could leap into their sequences with a lack of self-consciousness that leaves their best singles still sounding fresh.

"Temptation" is one of the first and best of them, and there's a ramshackle, human quality to it that's absolutely key: You can hear the same people, seemingly still in that freezing-cold warehouse, shouldering their way into something ecstatic. Even back in the days of Joy Division, they'd learned to play to Stephen Morris's spare, mechanical drumming; here, they're doing the same with their sequencers, slashing excitedly at their guitars and pushing their way forward, as if they're discovering the beauty of what they're doing at the same time as you are.

Most important of all is Bernard Sumner's presence as frontman. Ian Curtis was always the kind of singer you watched, someone removed from you, different. Sumner—with his clumsy rhymes, average-guy voice, and starry-eyed earnestness—is, well, one of us, a fact that did a whole lot to sell dance music to the United Kingdom. On "Temptation," he's subsumed by the music, and he seems like he's listening to it and feeling it just like you are on your headphones. It's just that *his* happy coos and repeating chants— "Oh, you've got green eyes / Oh, you've got gray eyes"—actually wind up on the track.
—NA

The Jam: *"Town Called Malice"* 1982

The Jam peaked at a time when many UK punk musicians were looking to black music for new avenues of expression. But where the Clash absorbed contemporary reggae and disco and others probed into the avant-garde realms of free

Sailing the Seas of Cheese: Yacht Rock

Many musicians, when hitting the big time, drop their fat royalty checks on luxurious leisure craft. Only a chosen few, however, dedicate their songwriting to the sailing arts, showing no prejudice among catboats, cutters, or ketches. In the late 1970s through the early '80s, soft-rock acts wrapped in beards, sunglasses, and terry cloth smoothed their sound to a breeze. Aside from a swinging boom to the face, these blue-eyed, sweet soul numbers are the only link between the harbor and the dentist's office. The genre pushed off with the Beach Boys' "Sail On, Sailor" and beached itself with the Beach Boys' appearance on *Full House*. In between it was filled with 80 percent Michael McDonald. But for the sake of variety…

"What a Fool Believes," **the Doobie Brothers:** Like a fat mummy made of fabric softener, Michael McDonald smoothed up whatever group he joined, from the funky Dixieland of the Doobs to the, well, already smooth Steely Dan.

"What a Fool Believes," **Kenny Loggins:** True yacht rock aficionados claim three favorite bands: 1) Kenny Loggins, 2) Jim Messina, and 3) Loggins and Messina.

"Make Believe," **Toto:** Though seemingly a peaceful scene, the yacht rock wars boiled over in 1982, split into "What a Fool Believes" and "Make Believe" camps.

"Lady Luck," **Kenny Loggins:** Is the title referring to a boat or a woman? Both, as Kenny Loggins painted his hull to resemble a vagina. Possibly.

"Sailing," **Christopher Cross:** Pink Floyd may have lost to "Sailing" at the 1980 Grammys, but the band found redemption when NSYNC covered "Waiting for the Worms" alongside Cross's classic on the boy band's 1998 debut.

"Peg," **Steely Dan:** Referencing *Naked Lunch* has long been a secret handshake of nautical enthusiasts in rock, from paddle-boat fanatics Joy Division ("Interzone") to Sonic Youth ("Dr. Benway's House"), who for two years lived together in a dry-docked cigarette boat.

"The Things We Do For Love," **10cc:** England's lone yacht rock band, 10cc faced an uphill battle back home, where "yacht" means "sanitary napkin."

"Love Will Find a Way," **Pablo Cruise:** After this song's success, Pablo Cruise pioneered a method of navigation solely based on love. Sailors would hold hands and wish. The band disappeared off Baja in 1983.

"Biggest Part of Me," **Ambrosia:** Listeners used to phallus-obsessed heavy metal always assume the "penis" bit in the chorus of "Biggest Part of Me" to be an immature boast of manhood. Actually, the word is an old seaman's term for "mast."

"Reminiscing," **Little River Band:** Barely making the list due to poor navigating skills, these "Australians" started out in California before misdirecting their forty-footer in a storm.
—BD

jazz and dub, the Jam replicated vintage '60s soul. As one of the few bands in the punk and post-punk era to retreat to the past for inspiration, they helped forge one of the first revivals of the era (the late '70s reinterest in mod) and one of the most prominent: In the mid-'90s, Paul Weller would become known as "the Godfather of Britpop."

"Stop dreamin' of the quiet life / 'Cause it's the one we'll never know," go the opening lines of "Town Called Malice." The song isn't just vocalist Paul Weller's lament for small-town, working-class life but also a love letter to Motown and the northern soul dance scene that, earlier in the '70s, enlivened many of England's most hopeless cities. Bruce Foxton's bass line is picked from the Funk Brothers' James Jamerson's pocket, and drummer Rick Buckler smuggles in the beat from "You Can't Hurry Love" as the band, born as part of Britain's 1977 punk explosion, brings its deep R&B roots to the fore.
—JT

Duran Duran: *"The Chauffeur"* 1982

Like club kids accessorizing crosses and ankhs to suggest depth beneath their flash, Duran Duran loaded the back half of their monster hit vehicle *Rio* with songs about the spiritual and the immaterial. But even after the brooding of "New Religion" and "Save a Prayer," the album's closer, "The Chauffeur," comes as a shock. One of the band's most austere art-pop numbers—and a lesson well learned from their heroes and fellow New Romantics Japan— "The Chauffeur" features an icy synth arching over low-end rumbles. Over this brittleness, Simon LeBon's vocals are sure and crystalline, nailing the soaring non sequitur "Sing blue silver."

The song seeps high-class lust, while a pan flute suggests satyrs and mythical decadence. (The sapphic lingerie dance in the uncensored video seals the deal.) The style trumps any substance—yet it's also minimal enough to sound avant-garde in the context of the hit-spawning album it closes. "The Chauffeur" almost reads as a secret message for fans—among whom it's still a favorite—revealing a sinister edge to the band that gave us "The Reflex."
—CD

The (English) Beat: *"Save It for Later"* 1982

The lyrics to "Save It for Later" are the angry retorts and jerky mood swings of a grubby teenage lad doubting his friends and baiting his girl with crude puns for oral sex. (Try hearing the chorus the same way after you read "save it fellator" in the liner notes.) Pete Townshend, the song's most famous booster, said it's about "sex, drugs, and the apocalypse," and the chorus is a shove and a fall: "Don't run away and let me down / You let me down." But pretend you don't know English, and it's a song about fierce, fist-tight passion. Dave Wakeling's yearning snarl, the heartbreaking hook that never stops, reaching a state of rapture. The title phrase promises there will be a next time—and it'll feel even better marking the end of the second wave of ska and planting the seeds of Britpop. The messy emotions of "Save It for Later" are quintessentially adolescent—and so is its hope. Everyone hears in it what hits them the hardest.
—CD

The Go-Go's: *"Our Lips Are Sealed"* 1981

Miles from the *Billboard* charts on which they wound up, the Go-Go's formed in an L.A. punk scene during the late 1970s that elevated hopeless junkies into romantic heroes. And naturally—as five young women out for more traditional good times and with a love for classic American bubblegum and surfer girl harmonies— they got called lightweights when they played Sunset Strip rat holes. But when they coupled those same obsessions with spare, glossy arrangements that bounced like ponytails, they wound up the teen pop queens they were fated to be, painting images of a gum-snapping Mary Weiss or Ronnie Spector in zip-up boots and ripped, off-the-shoulder sweatshirts.

"Our Lips Are Sealed" is the bridge between the scrappy, bad girl New Wave that got them noticed and the locker-slam drums and pep rally cheers of their mid-'80s crossover smashes. The song's doe-eyed bass vamp and chiming trade-off between rhythm guitar and keyboard was cooked up by guitarist Jane Wiedlin and her beau, Specials vocalist Terry Hall. But it's the sugar cookie harmonies— especially the shivery bridge where singer Belinda Carlisle's pitchy coo evokes an endless, painless California summer of puppy love—that bump

This Is Hardcore

Photographs (invariably black and white) of hardcore bands show the singer (invariably shirtless) holding the microphone in one of three positions:

1. Clasped to his chest.
2. Clenched before his shouting mouth.
3. Extended outward, clutched before the open mouth of an audience member.

Because, naturally, these guys speak from the heart and bare themselves, loudly, for the people. Amidst all this intensity one element goes overlooked: humor. In some pockets, notably New York and Boston, hardcore grew aggressive and athletic. Those weight-room rants haven't endured like these more multifaceted blasts, from the Teen Idles' bratty anthem of boredom to Born Against's baiting of those meatheaded East Coast hardcore thugs.

"Teen Idles," **the Teen Idles:** The slower version from the *100* EP allowed Minor Threat's Ian MacKaye to capture the snotty, bored suburban youth parodied in the band's name, which they chant in the chorus like cheerleaders of detention.

"Filler," **Minor Threat:** After each chorus, Jeff Nelson attempts sloppy guitar solos that reveal these punks weren't against classic rock maneuvers. When Minor Threat disbanded, bassist Brian Baker formed a hair metal band, Junkyard, with a song called "Blooze."

"Out of Touch," **7 Seconds:** When in doubt. Whoa oh! Just shout. Whoa oh! After every line. Whoa oh!

"Sailin' On," **Bad Brains:** The title could pass as yacht rock, and indeed, despite the blitzkrieg pace, Beach Boys–like harmonies of "oooh"s float over the chorus.

"Wasted," **Black Flag:** This sentence lasts longer than the song, but in that brief time Keith Morris claims to have been a hippie, a skater, and a burnout. It could pass as satire, but this is a band that wrote an ode to beer.

"Lexicon Devil," **the Germs:** The impossibility of shouting "gimme gimme" like a tough guy ensures that this song somehow veers closer to "I Want Candy" than a political rant.

"Nazi Punks Fuck Off," **Dead Kennedys:** In the album version, Jello Biafra counts off the song with "Overproduced by Martin Hannett, take 4," in reference to the eccentric Joy Division producer. Also, his name is "Jello."

"Reagan Youth," **Reagan Youth:** This album's cover proclaimed "pop classics," while showing KKK members holding instruments. Some of this humor was kind of dark.

"Born Against Are Fucking Dead," **Born Against:** An answering machine threat from a heavily accented Noo Yawk hardcore singer warns Born Against to be "extremely fuckin' cautious who talk shit about." In a throat-shredding scream, the song kicks in with "Born Against are fucking dead! That's what the answering machine said!"
—*BD*

"Our Lips Are Sealed" from period piece to the top girl-group tier, the students joining the masters with no male Svengalis necessary.

—JH

Tom Tom Club: *"Genius of Love"* 1981

While David Byrne and Brian Eno continued their musical romance outside of Talking Heads, dreaming up and piecing together the ethnological collage of *My Life in the Bush of Ghosts,* the group's rhythm section, Tina Weymouth and Chris Frantz, were not to be outflanked. Retreating to the Bahamas, they took the rolling, looping funk they'd developed on 1980's *Remain in Light* and reimagined it as performed by a suburban girl group.

"Wordy Rappinghood," their first single, led the way with ditzy novelty funk and a lyric that felt like a parody of Byrne's pseudosemiotics. But the follow-up, "Genius of Love," was the group's masterstroke. Over a chirruping, rock-steady, featherlight track that was to become a heavily sampled hip-hop institution, Weymouth and her sister Laura harmonized a dreamy white-bread love song to the godfathers and funny uncles of "funk mutation," from James Brown to Bootsy Collins, from Sly and Robbie to Kurtis Blow. Initially only available as an import from the UK, the track wound up outselling any of their main band's singles up to that time, a taste of success that Frantz has credited with convincing Byrne to soldier on with Talking Heads.

—ST

Prince: *"Dirty Mind"* 1980

The opening beats of "Dirty Mind" hang alone in the air for a reason: Prince is letting us catch our breath before he upsets everything in his path. After issuing two records of sharp bubblegum R&B, Prince made one of the most audacious moves in pop history, stripping down to black underwear and a raincoat for the cover of his third album. Here, when he sings, "in my daddy's car, it's you I really wanna drive," the coy way he arches his voice shows that he isn't just a shameless tease pretending to be shocked at his own audacity, but that he refuses to grasp the meaning of the phrase "too much." And over the next decade, he would mostly get away with everything he tried. The tension of "Dirty Mind" comes from Prince's high-wire sonics: Though Rick James proclaimed himself "the

king of punk-funk," few R&B performers dove into New Wave's speedy beats and raw keyboards as thoroughly as Prince. The song's liberation is that he pulls it off—and in doing so, he pulled so far ahead of his contemporaries that for the rest of the 1980s, only hip-hop could pass him by.

—MiM

Daryl Hall & John Oates: *"I Can't Go for That (No Can Do)"* 1981

Hall & Oates' 1980 album *Voices* shot the duo back into the popular consciousness after the years of relative silence following their soft-rock hits "Sara Smile" and "Rich Girl." "Kiss on My List" and "You Make My Dreams" were signs of a slight but highly effective reinvention: soul-pop with New Wave sheen. That formula was perfected on 1981's *Private Eyes,* especially in the slick, unnerving electro-soul of "I Can't Go for That (No Can Do)." Essentially an after-hours creation, the album's second number 1 hit sounded like nothing the duo had done before—and nothing else on the radio at the time. The studio engineer pressed "Record" as Hall tinkered with adding a Korg bass line to an icy Roland CompuRhythm box preset. On top of that accidental funk futurism, Hall offered a hesitant, digitally polished romanticism, which reached its fruition on what he called the "Al Green bridge," as those eerie synthesized harmonies flash behind him. "I Can't Go for That" was as uniquely crossbred as the other electronic hits from its era— "Tainted Love" and "Don't You Want Me"—but its biggest compliment came from its most obvious musical legacy: Michael Jackson's "Billie Jean."

—EH

Michael Jackson: *"Billie Jean"* 1982

"PYT" is funkier and "Thriller" is freakier, but "Billie Jean" has better hooks and a juicier narrative throughline. A cautionary tale about a pop star accused of sexual impropriety with a fan, "Billie Jean" is Michael Jackson singing about being Michael Jackson when that prospect was still larger-than-life exciting rather than scary and depressing. It's a telling, stadium-sized irony that Jackson's entry into independent adulthood should commence with a tense announcement of his essential and embattled innocence, and in that stance—soon to be habitual for MJ—it looks back to 1972's "Ben" as much as it looks forward to future court dates. What

makes it work is not the certainty but the glancing shadows of doubt, the finger-wagging admonition to "remember to always think twice" that immediately triggers a lusty, funky "*Don't* think twice." The fear (guilt?) at the center of this spooky paternity-suit fable trickles through the gasps and coos of Michael's performance like James Brown's "Cold Sweat" turning sticky, but the scything shakers and lockstep snare keep things bottled tight, riding a chase-sequence bass line timeless enough to unite the Residents and Eminem, among others, in acts of creative reuse. The first single from Jackson's finest hour, this is a bulletproof pop-funk masterpiece.
—*DD*

ABBA: *"The Day Before You Came"* 1981

"Dancing Queen" freeze-framed ABBA as 1970s kitsch icons, but they were a pop fixture for another five years as members divorced and their sound darkened. By their final album, 1981's *The Visitors,* the Swedish pop group was singing about Soviet occupation, soldiers, loss, and death.

That year's "The Day Before You Came" seems less high-concept—a mundane sketch of a daily routine that now feels charmingly anachronistic (she leaves work at five!). Something's not right, though. The mood is numb and confused and the rhythm is a muted, midpaced pulse. The lyrics are shaky on detail, as if seeing the past down the wrong end of a telescope. Strangest of all, there's no chorus—ABBA had abandoned the skill that brought them fame, ripped out the heart of their popcraft. They replace it with banks of synthesized voices, rising in wordless dread whenever Agnetha Fältskog sings about the coming "You."

There's little question that the You is a lover. The song is about the disruptive terror of love, the way it can pry open a settled life like an oyster, never to shut again. It's beautiful and enigmatic, but its grandeur is paralyzed. It would be ABBA's final recording.
—*TE*

Roxy Music: *"More Than This"* 1982

In the early 1970s, Roxy Music toyed with glamour and decadence, as singer Bryan Ferry created an oversized persona built on high-class charm and a jet-setter's sense of boutique-bought style stuff that was, at the time, out of his financial reach. A decade later, Ferry actually *was* a star, and a wealthy one at that. After a few years of creative bankruptcy, he and his group embraced not only the look but the *sound* of luxury on 1982's *Avalon* and its two silky-smooth singles, the title track and "More Than This."

They were right on cue. The UK's clubs were bursting with New Romantics and its charts with New Pop, each valuing elements of fashion, ambition, and wealth—lessons learned by applying the DIY approach of punk to the boardroom as well as the rehearsal room. The exquisitely sculpted "More Than This" fit that mood; it initially seems cold and unapproachable, with a sound that's almost too smooth and fussed-over. But the polished façade hides Ferry's yearning and cushions his realization that "there is nothing more than" his unnamed "this."
—*SP*

Queen [ft. David Bowie]: *"Under Pressure"* 1981

How did this pairing not happen five years earlier? By 1981, both Queen and David Bowie had seen their best days, though not so long ago that they couldn't still come up with a great big 1980s single. And make no mistake, this song has it all: finger snaps, cabaret interludes and Who breakdowns, a big climax, and the requisite (for Queen, anyway) operatic chorus. It's a true anthem, and even though Bowie wisely doesn't attempt to compete with Freddie Mercury's high range, the two play off each other like old pros. "Under Pressure" was a beacon of light for all the young dudes whose penchants for theatrical confession hadn't been completely curbed by punk. And notice we don't mention the bass line once.
—*DL*

Bruce Springsteen: *"Atlantic City"* 1982

Given Bruce Springsteen's then-recent pop success—between 1977 and 1980, his "Hungry Heart" hit the Top 10, as did covers of his compositions "Fire" (by the Pointer Sisters) and "Blinded by the Light" (by Manfred Mann's Earth Band)—1982's *Nebraska* was a serious detour down a very bleak country road. The album was originally just a demo: Springsteen cut *Nebraska*'s songs at home on a four-track recorder, with just guitar, voice, and harmonica, and he expected them to be fleshed out later with the E Street Band. Eventually, though, the singer decided the songs were most effective in their stark, unadorned original forms.

"Atlantic City" neatly encapsulates *Nebraska*'s dark thematic concerns. The protagonist's emotional emptiness, desperation, and spiritual implosion are connected to the economic collapse of the Jersey Shore, and the stark production enhances the narrative in unexpected ways—a chiming acoustic guitar overdub, for instance, evokes the twinkling lights of an empty boardwalk. "I'm tired of coming out on this losing end," Springsteen sings in the last line, "So honey, last night I met this guy and I'm going to do a little favor for him." The story—its violent ending unstated but inevitable—is completed in our heads even after the guitar strum and harmonica fade out.
—MR

Journey: *"Don't Stop Believing"* 1981

You can tell something about a person's relationship to popular music as a whole by how they feel about this song. Generally, people fall into two camps. If they have at one time considered it a "guilty pleasure," a dim-witted power ballad made by guys with bad haircuts to be enjoyed despite its inherent cheesiness, they probably identify most with indie music of some stripe. If they just plain like it and always have, then they've probably spent their lives enjoying whatever was on the radio. You'll notice no consideration of those who don't care for the song at all, because, well—are there people like that? Like the Ronettes' "Be My Baby," or David Bowie's "'Heroes,'" "Don't Stop Believing" is unhinged melodrama at its finest; unlike those two songs, its makers have not ever been considered geniuses or, for that matter, even marginally "cool."

Journey, from the Bay Area, began as a proggy, Santana-like jam band. With the addition of singer Steve Perry in 1977, they became a corporate-rock hit machine for people who found Foreigner too edgy. They had a dozen or so good songs, but this was their only great one: Building from its iconic piano opening, the music in each verse becomes progressively more intense, as vague images about the search for connection and meaning pile on. And then, finally, the lone chorus comes at the very end, imploring the listener to keep the faith. Resistance is futile.
—MR

Bad Brains: *"Pay to Cum"* 1980

Mind Power were a jazz-fusion quartet from Washington, D.C., who, in 1979, changed their name to Bad Brains. They'd discovered the Sex Pistols and the Ramones, and soon after, learned that black men playing punk rock—considered offensive even when it came from white kids—weren't welcome in D.C.'s rock clubs. What sounded anarchic to fearful promoters was anything but; in the hands of more proficient musicians, ragged three-chord punk rock became faster and more compact, with more energy and more sharp edges. With this sound, they kicked off a genre—hardcore punk, soon to be just "hardcore." "Pay to Cum" was the band's first single, tougher than tough-guy hardcore (est. 1982), more sincere than emo (est. 1984), more melodic than melodic hardcore (est. 1985), faster than grindcore (est. 1994). But the bands that followed them would be first to admit that whatever Bad Brains started, they effectively finished as well: Bad Brains are still the best musicians ever to play in the style they invented.
—ZB

Minor Threat: *"Minor Threat"* 1981

In their three years of existence, D.C. bashers Minor Threat helped start one of hardcore's most fertile and lasting regional scenes, inadvertently launched the punk/puritan straight-edge sub-subculture, and developed an indie-label empire—so it's easy to forget that they were just teenagers for most (or, in Brian Baker's case, all) of the band's lifespan. The no-drink/no-drugs straight-edge ethos, later perverted and formalized by moralist thugs like Youth of Today and Earth Crisis, started out as a slap against D.C. promoters who refused to book all-ages shows.

"Minor Threat," the band's eponymous anthem, is a song about being kids and being proud of being kids: "Go to college, be a man, what's the fucking deal / It's not how old I am, it's how old I feel." Still, with his rigid blurt, Ian MacKaye never sounds like a kid dicking around in a garage. Instead, he's a budding autodidact, and there's zero mirth in the chuckle that ends the song. The other members streamline the hammering mess of Black Flag and Bad Brains into a convulsive but efficient machine: a whole song's worth of riffs and hooks and structure, over in 1:27, no fat on its bones.
—TB

Dead Kennedys:
"Holiday in Cambodia" 1980

In March 1980, Dead Kennedys were on the verge of releasing their debut, *Fresh Fruit for Rotting Vegetables,* when they were invited to a local industry showcase, the Bay Area Music Awards. They were to play their first single, "California Über Alles," and they did—for a few chords—before their singer, Jello Biafra, stopped the proceedings in order to clarify their presence at the event. "We are not a punk rock band," he said, for the benefit of the assembled industry legmen. And as he did so, all four Dead Kennedys pulled down hidden black ties from their collars, which, when crossed with the letter "S" each wore, formed dollar signs. They were never invited back.

Though Biafra's targets were most often capitalists and the brutal right wing of the 1980s, he was an equal-opportunity offender—as hinted by his band's name—and he found liberal pieties just as contemptible. *Fresh Fruit*'s "Holiday in Cambodia" is ostensibly an ironic take on the Khmer Rouge in Cambodia—a genocidal regime headed by Pol Pot and propped up by the U.S. government—but it fantasizes about sending a young liberal elite there. "Well, you'll work harder / With a gun in your back," sang Biafra, turning the protest music of a mostly white middle class against itself.
—*ZB*

Black Flag: *"Rise Above"* 1981

Black Flag had been together for five years when, in 1981, they invited an undersized, twenty-year-old groupie from D.C. named Henry Rollins to become their full-time vocalist. The band's guitarist and songwriter, Greg Ginn, had already burned through three other frontmen (including Keith Morris, soon to found the Circle Jerks), in part because of his grueling—and, for a punk band, bizarre—band-practice and tour slate. It paid off, though: As part of hardcore's first wave, Black Flag were already heroes to hundreds of burgeoning kids by the time they made their official debut.

On the steroidal *Damaged,* otherwise about alcohol abuse, greed, TV, and getting slugged by cops, "Rise Above" was a departure. Over Ginn's iconic descending riff, Rollins ticked off the victories of rebellion, shouting gang choruses against "society" and jealous cowards. "We are born with a chance"

was the idea—rare optimism, in the context of the Sex Pistols–birthed nihilism pervasive in punk at the time. This attitudinal leap—Bad Brains called it "Positive Mental Attitude"—finished off punk, though Black Flag would continue to be so filled with residual hate that nobody would notice what they'd done until years after they'd done it.
—*ZB*

Wipers: *"Youth of America"* 1981

Like his bookish peers in Mission of Burma, Greg Sage was liberated by punk's rage and minimalism but had little interest in its ripped-T-shirt fashionista poses. Aside from Oregon's deep garage rock roots, the refusenik music he made with Wipers was without peer in the Pacific Northwest of the late 1970s and early '80s—though it would be passed down to the area's next generation, which linked punk and metal and helped create alt-rock and grunge. Like the embattled stance of those pissed-off, postpubescent garage rockers, Sage articulated the defensive rage of an army of one. And "Youth of America," a sardonic anthem for that perpetually disenfranchised demographic, is Wipers at their rawest and most desperate. Sage's ropy riffs snarl like a starved dog chained to a post, the rhythm section a soundtrack to a white-knuckle chase through pitch-black pine barrens. It's smarter and fiercer than many of its antitotalitarian punk peers, too, even if it likewise failed to instigate mass liberation for those kids pinned under the bootheel of Reaganomics.
—*JH*

Flipper: *"Sex Bomb"* 1982

Born comedians who heard "no future" as the best possible excuse to take a dump on punk rock's pretensions, San Francisco's Flipper belched into life in the early 1980s with a sleazy sound that married Black Sabbath's sluggish tempos, California hardcore's sneer, and rock's delinquent sexuality. What most didn't have was Flipper's humanism, hidden like a rotten Easter egg under all the hate; happy couples kissing in the springtime made them want to retch, but they still claimed "life is the only thing worth living for." Catchy, compared to their usual raunch, "Sex Bomb" is the history of '60s garage rock mashed into one mongoloid line—"She's a sex bomb baby, yeah!"—delivered like a

taunt over a rhythm that suggests the horny rutting of large, greasy mammals. And just to prove they weren't fucking around, they brought in the kind of horn section that used to rock frat houses back when LBJ was president. Fools at the time took them as a bad joke, but where many of their contemporaries have aged worse than the 1980s pop they were desperate to supplant, Flipper's hilarious sludge remains as timeless as teenage frustration.
—JH

Motörhead: *"Ace of Spades"* 1980

Warts-and-all hard rockers Motörhead were formed in 1975 by ex-Hawkwind member Lemmy, who gave his band the name of the last song he wrote for the '70s space-rockers before being kicked out after his arrest for possession at the Canadian border. (He's joked that it was for doing the wrong kind of drugs—a motorhead is a user of amphetamines, not a typical vice for hippie-leaning groups like Hawkwind.) Motörhead were among the early progenitors of the New Wave of British Heavy Metal (NWOBHM), a late-'70s/early-'80s aesthetic that combined sludgy influences like Deep Purple, Black Sabbath, and Thin Lizzy with technical (and fast) chops, volume, power chords, and often melodic vocals, offering an alternative to L.A.'s glammier scene.

One of few late-'70s artists with links to both punk and prog, Lemmy also briefly played bass with garage-y Brit punks the Damned. That punk background is evidenced in "Ace of Spades," a high-octane guitar rocker that set the templates for speed- and thrash-metal. The taut, muscular song glorifies a live-fast, die-young ethos. It was seen as both a call to arms and a calling card: The first lines established Lemmy as a take-no-shit rock icon ("If you like to gamble, I tell you I'm your man / You win some, lose some, it's all the same to me") who, unlike other NWOBHM crews, didn't need fancy literary motifs or mythological references to get his point across. Much like their music, Motörhead's lyrics were blunt like a blow to the back of the skull: sex, drugs, and rock and roll.
—BS

Iron Maiden: *"Run to the Hills"* 1982

To outsiders, Iron Maiden—with their Derek Riggs–drawn skeleton mascot Eddie and torture-device band name—bordered on Spinal Tap cliché. Yet this New Wave of British Heavy Metal quintet had plenty of depth beneath their questionable surface, combining technical chops, melodic vocals, and heavy amplification with heady references to myth, fantasy, history, and the occult. Their longtime frontman Bruce Dickinson is even something of a metallic renaissance man, known for his skills as a fencer, pilot, and writer.

Maiden's first album with Dickinson at the helm—1982's *The Number of the Beast*—topped the UK charts, in part due to lead single "Run to the Hills," which details the bloody colonization of North America through the eyes of both a Native American and a white European soldier. Certifiably funky drums and midtempo riffs open as Dickinson details the plight of a Cree ("White Man came across the sea / He brought us pain and misery") until the song gallops into a high-pitched sing-along and shifts to the soldier's point of view, eventually alternating perspectives until Dickinson's metal-operatic peal gives the song its historically accurate punctuation.
—BS

Orange Juice: *"Blue Boy"* 1980

Orange Juice thought of their hometown of Glasgow as a kind of metaphysical sixth New York City borough—a place where CBGB bands were heralded as heroes, inaugurating a Scotland/NYC musical dialogue that would last for decades. Formed in 1976 as the Nu-Sonics, and later galvanized into Orange Juice by impresario Alan Horne, they were assiduous pop students, besotted equally by Buzzcocks and Buffalo Springfield, the Velvet Underground and the Subway Sect, Chic and Creedence Clearwater Revival.

"Blue Boy" was their second single on the nascent Glasgow indie label Postcard, and it was released in August 1980, a couple of months after the suicide of Joy Division's Ian Curtis and a couple of weeks after sprinter Allan Wells struck rare Olympic gold for Scotland in Moscow. After a martial drum intro, the song leaps out of the blocks, unleashing a choppy, chunky strum that would typify a strain of indie rock that ran through followers from the Wedding Present to Franz Ferdinand. Frontman Edwyn Collins, mean-while, having learned the language of love from Buzzcocks' Pete Shelley, croons that real romance lies not between boy and girl—but between the romantic pop fan and singer…and in the process he inadvertently invents Morrissey.
—ST

While there's no straight path through the heavy metal maze, the innumerable offshoots and subgenres— whether the New Wave of British Heavy Metal, thrash, grindcore, death, black, blackened thrash, melodic death, U.S. black metal, speed, symphonic black, or pop—are generally at least connected by their volume. And sometimes the hair length of those making it.

"(We Are) The Road Crew," **Motörhead:** The British hard rock trio are known best for the proto-thrash anthem "Ace of Spades" from their 1980 album of the same name, but the band's fourth album blasted through any number of gems, including the life-on-the-road anthem "(We Are) The Road Crew"—all swaggering riffs, bleeding ears, a chick in every city, and a final flanging guitar solo that bursts against its own feedback.

"Raining Blood," **Slayer:** "Raining Blood," from Slayer's third album, their Rick Rubin–produced major label debut *Reign in Blood,* opens with ambient guitar and deep percussion cast against the sound of rain and, yup, a lacerated sky, before speeding into double bass, buzz-saw guitars, Tom Araya's burly apocalyptic shout, and, eventually, a rollicking, dynamic "mosh part."

"Master of Puppets," **Metallica:** The almost nine-minute title track of Bay Area thrashers Metallica's *Master of Puppets* continues the album's theme of submission and control. As with Metallica's best songs, there are innumerable parts and flourishes: It dissolves into a soaring dual guitar instrumental interlude before shifting into a new variation on the song's opening riff.

"You Suffer," **Napalm Death:** The importance of "You Suffer," from British grindcore band Napalm Death's essential 1987 album *Scum,* goes beyond its brevity. Yes, it's 1.316 seconds long, but it packs in an entire musical philosophy. The only lyrics—a mere four words— are incomprehensible even when you know the context.

"Immortal Rites," **Morbid Angel:** The super-technical Florida death metal band Morbid Angel formed in 1984 and debuted years later with *Altars of Madness.* The album's first track, "Immortal Rites," finds guitarist Trey Azagthoth, drummer Pete Sandoval, and the rest of the crew in typically raw but precise form, opening with bass-playing vocalist David Vincent's "Lords of death, I summon you…" and blasting into dozens of ascending and descending parts.

"The Usurper," **Celtic Frost:** Swiss avant-garde trio Celtic Frost influenced black, thrash, goth, and doom, lacing their über-heavy attack with classical swells and vocalist Tom G. Warrior's deep vocals—it's pure Wagnarian bombast, while maintaining a heavy, hardcore edge. "The Usurper," from *To Mega Therion,* blended into the preceding track "Innocence and Wrath," encompassing a sword-clashing battle, a throne-ascending anthem, an oddly placed falsetto, and a massive hook.

"Battles in the North," **Immortal:** The title track from the Norwegian black metal duo's third album, *Battles in the North,* offers a wintry blast of Demonaz's buzzing guitar and Abbath's manic drumming and croaky voice. It's also about Blashyrkh, a fictional, raven-god-ruled land lorded over by Mighty Ravendark, "the Oath of Frost, who sits on the elder raven throne." No, really.

"Through Silver in Blood," **Neurosis:** This long-standing Oakland experimental metal band has moved through various styles: Neurosis started steeped in crusty hardcore but moved into their own unique, super-slow death hybrid. The title track of their fifth album, *Through Silver in Blood,* careens across twelve minutes of tribal drumming, sludge guitars, and double-tracked vocals.

"Jerusalem," **Sleep:** The San Jose trio hit their massive stride on their third album, originally called *Dopesmoker,* a sixty-three-minute long stoner rock classic that opens with the lines "Drop out of life with bong in hand / Follow the smoke toward the riff-filled land." The band's vocalist/guitarist, Matt Pike, went on to form High on Fire, while the slow, hypnotic rhythm section of vocalist/bassist Al Cisneros and drummer Chris Hakius created Om.

"Pretty in Casts," **Pig Destroyer:** The William Burroughs–quoting, post-grindcore crew Pig Destroyer don't have a bassist and don't really need one: Vocalist and gory storyteller J. R. Hayes, guitarist/producer Scott Hull, and drummer Brian Harvey are one blistering machine. Their conceptual double album *Terrifyer* includes one disc of the band's heady, kinetic grind and one thirty-seven-minute horror-drenched doom track. "Pretty in Casts" deals with a *Crash*-like fetish of obsessing over a girl's injuries, the glass of a shattered windshield making her all the more beautiful.
—*BS*

The Television Personalities:
"This Angry Silence" 1980

Punks are supposed to be tough, loud, and cynical, right? Not so, says Dan Treacy, the strange, troubled leader of the Television Personalities—a man whose voice will always sound like a vulnerable kid's. In late-1970s London, Treacy was one of the first to pick up punk's reckless, do-it-yourself attitude and point it somewhere else entirely: This band knocked out singsong pop nuggets with all the wide-eyed earnestness, impish humor, and unchecked enthusiasm of preteen schoolboys.

They may have sounded, at first, like an adolescent garage band, but they approach "This Angry Silence" like adolescents who think they're the Who—it's all big windmill chords on cheap guitars, complete with breakdowns sporting ambitions that well surpass the recording budget. It's the scrappy stadium rock of ordinary, boyish concerns: The angry silence of the title is just the family home, with Dad yelling at drunken Mom, an anorexic brother no one talks about, a barmaid sister, and our singer holed up in his bedroom, nursing a crush that even *he* knows is ridiculous.

People have been doing this for decades now—indie bands stumbling through songs about being shy, weird, ordinary, or uncool. Sometimes they come off self-pitying and boring; sometimes they're funny, comforting, righteous, or charming. This is one of the originals, and it's as pure and lovable as any underdog can hope to be—something you hear even more in the recording than in the words.
—*NA*

The Fall: *"The Classical"* 1982

By 1982, the Fall were firmly entrenched as outsiders looking in and scorning all they saw. "The Classical" did little to change that: Two drummers provide the teeth-rattling rhythm, the guitars grind away like scouring pads, and Steve Hanley's bass motors along high in the mix. In the middle of it all stands Mark E. Smith, the post-punk court jester and a nonplussed fountain of sarcasm, deadpanning and screaming as if he can't decide whether he's bored or outraged. The onslaught of racial slurs in the opening lines, followed immediately by shouts of "Hey there, fuckface!" purportedly scuttled a deal with Motown.

The label probably wasn't a good fit anyway. Smith had no time or desire to be the Next Big Thing. He lambastes the synth-pop hordes then taking over the charts, crying, "I destroy romantics! Actors! Kill it! Kill it!" Smith and Hanley launch dual spitballs at punk culture. "The Classical" is the Fall growing sharper, limbering up for their mid-1980s run of brilliance.
—*JT*

The Clean: *"Tally Ho!"* 1981

Though home-recorded on a $60 machine and released on the fledgling Flying Nun label, the Clean's debut single "Tally Ho!" somehow hit the New Zealand Top 20. But that's not what made the song and the group influential in indie rock circles worldwide. "Tally Ho!" provided a blueprint for catchy rock created with primitive tools. The crackling keyboard melody (provided by guest Martin Phillipps, of equally seminal Flying Nun group the Chills), David Kilgour's ebullient off-key singing, and his brother Hamish's shuffling drums are all infectious precisely because they're rough, loose, and polish-free, burning with a primal energy only $60 can buy. The vague lyrics—centered on repetitions of the phrase "I don't know"—only add to the glee, the group seemingly giddy from his own bubbling momentum. American bands like Pavement and Yo La Tengo would pick up the Clean's homespun vigor and run with it, but the original electricity of "Tally Ho!" has never quite been duplicated.
—*MM*

The Feelies: *"The Boy with the Perpetual Nervousness"* 1980

New Jersey's the Feelies arrived on the New York music scene amid the tumult of the late 1970s, bringing with them a sound aptly described by the title of their 1980 debut album: *Crazy Rhythms*. Borrowing the elemental beat of the Modern Lovers and the primal thunder of the Velvet Underground, they also sported a look and demeanor that presaged the nerd chic of the personal computing age.

On "The Boy with the Perpetual Nervousness," the Feelies managed to make an anthem out of a song that has almost no melody and begins with over a minute of barely audible percussion. Bill Million and Glenn Mercer strum their guitars frantically, and the sung-spoken vocals choke out lines recognizable to every socially awkward kid who lives in his own head

in order to escape abuse at school: "The boy next door is into bigger things / The boy next door is me." The key, though, is Anton Fier's ferocious drumming, which pushes the song along on a twitching, spastic beat—a headlong rhythmic intensity that gave the Feelies a distinct, pulse-racing edge over their many dinky-sounding DIY peers.
—JT

R.E.M.: "Radio Free Europe" 1981

In the two years between releasing the excitable, muddled debut single "Radio Free Europe" on Hib-Tone and issuing the version of the song that opened their debut album, *Murmur,* everything about R.E.M.'s sound fell into place. Its slashing chords may have had roots in punk, but the band replaced all the bile and angst with jangle, mystery, and inscrutability. What did R.E.M. learn in those two years? What Southern Gothic talisman did they consult to launch college rock as we would come to know it? They aimed for a kind of danceable folk-punk with *Murmur,* and the result was a little left of the mark, but it still sounded like little else around at the time. True, some of their contemporaries wrote abstract lyrics, but R.E.M. went one step further and wrote an anthem about absolutely nothing. And yet "Radio Free Europe" altered the face of underground rock: it was the mumble heard 'round the world.
—JC

Violent Femmes: "Blister in the Sun" 1982

"Blister in the Sun" started life in the early 1980s as a charming novelty—a boatload of teenage frustration poured out into a simple, chipper, ramshackle tune. By the turn of that decade, it had become a touchstone— a key alternateen text, a pop classic for weirdos. A few years later, Ethan Hawke would sing Violent Femmes songs in the major motion picture *Reality Bites,* and by the twenty-first century, "Blister in the Sun" was being used to sell hamburgers. This is one of the slowest, steadiest creeps into popular consciousness of any song in the rock era.

All of which can make it hard these days to hear "Blister" for how it was when it emerged. The best thing on offer is the way it operated during those touchstone days, when it formed a common bond between outcasts of all stripes. Still, even then,

connecting over this tune didn't mark people out as cool, in-the-know kids—for most of America, it marked them out as exactly the kind of awkward, maladjusted, swirly-worthy freaks who listened to songs about masturbation played by fidgety guys who sounded a little like they were banging on pots and pans. Hamburgers or not, that first Femmes album *still* feels like a proud moment for teenage misfit geeks, as sung by the nervous kid in the back of your homeroom class—the one who's still living down that day he smelled like pee.
—NA

Mission of Burma: "That's When I Reach for My Revolver" 1981

Bassist/singer Clint Conley cribbed this song's title from a Henry Miller essay without knowing it was attributed to various Nazi party members, and in much the same way, Mission of Burma grabbed volatile ideas from nearly anywhere and applied them with the vigor and naïveté of true punks. By moving beyond punk's black-and-white politics and primitive-by-necessity musicianship, the band pushed its lyrics toward more abstract notions and the music to more ambivalent, avant-garde horizons.

"That's When I Reach for My Revolver" is their strongest anthem and made the biggest impact, but even this song has quiet, stately verses and an almost pleading tone in its middle eight, making its desperate chorus all the more indelible. Some of the group's grander ambitions may have come from its classically trained musical backgrounds, but it still prized common themes like alienation and loss, as well as punk's economy. "Revolver" uses just a few chords that go quiet to loud and back again, simply because it's the shortest distance between the band and what they wanted to say. Mission of Burma's legendary status is manifest now, but they did it without reward, without radio play, and often without even an audience—just the desire to play something new and something loud.
—JC

Chapter Three:
1983–1986

The independent rock music that Pitchfork is best known for covering starts this book as a scrappy new thing— a cadre of do-it-yourself bands piecing together the tools to get their music out to whatever public will have them. But in the present day it's a defined genre, with its own sound, audience, history, press, and sacred cows— even middle-of-the-road practitioners whose albums debut on the *Billboard* charts. Between 1983 and 1986, the music world starts to look a lot more like today's, and not just because U2 and Madonna grow into perennial hitmakers. It's during these years that "indie" becomes…well, something that can be named.

The word itself comes from the UK, mostly, and this chapter can't help circling back and back again to one of England's indie flagships: the Smiths. They may not always have had much in common with the new wave of scrappy indie bands surrounding them, but they did as much as anyone to define indie's ethos and audience. Bookish and introverted, moody and romantic, sometimes stylish and sometimes uncool, this stuff pitched itself as pop music for outsiders, and it did so successfully enough for plenty of kids to take up "indie" as a badge of pride. (Literally, in fact: The one-inch badge pin remains one of indie rock's longest-running fashion statements.) Once that audience had been called forth and organized around a system of labels, stores, and magazines, it could support a lot of new sounds—stylish mopes like Echo and the Bunnymen, exotic dreamers like the Cocteau Twins, and sullen noise-blasters like the Jesus and Mary Chain. The U.S. also saw the beginnings of an independent rock establishment, with the new *CMJ* magazine following what college-radio DJs were playing and the SST label starting to unify the country's punk underground. But things shaped up differently here, partly thanks to geography: While British bands found it easy to infiltrate the national press of a smallish island, American groups were still fighting across a big continent in small, crappy vans. The scenes and bands that made big marks in the American canon tended to be rougher, dirtier, boozier, and far less interested in keyboards. There's an important divide here, one that's waxed and waned across the history of this indie audience: For the devoted punk,

the mopey glamour of UK bands and the cheery jangle of "college rock" were just as much The Enemy as the pop music on the radio.

Except that pop music wasn't just on the radio anymore. By this point, MTV had exploded from a cable upstart to a kingmaker. This end-run around the radio introduced America to a lot of oddball bands and terrific one-hit wonders—get together a catchy tune, some midgets, and a video camera, and a generation could be humming your "Safety Dance" forever. It also nurtured the first wave of pop stars for a truly visual era: Duran Duran, Prince, Madonna. If independent rock was for outsiders, MTV was taking on the role of the "inside." Lucky for us, years down the road, there's no cognitive dissonance involved in enjoying great pop like Cyndi Lauper's right alongside the punk rock that set itself up as an alternative.

MTV would also, eventually, turn out to be one of the conduits that brought hip-hop to the mainstream. Early detractors had pegged this music for a novelty or a fad. But you'll find this chapter returning time and again to the artists who proved them wrong—including Run-D.M.C., who served as the early public face of rap. This group helped set the stage for how the music could go forward: not on reconstituted disco grooves, but with bursts of samples and mechanical drum-machines that put the world of sound right in the hands of the producer.

Meanwhile, halfway across the country, a similar collision of computers and black Americans was birthing a genre that would prove almost as momentous and world-conquering as hip-hop: Detroit techno. It's easy to point to the influences that went into this music—Kraftwerk, funk, synth-pop, Italo disco, jazz—but adding them up doesn't begin to explain the mind-boggling leaps the first techno pioneers made. It's surprising enough that they could coax their pulsing, singing machines into such radically new shapes and patterns. But more shocking still is that they could invest their tracks with a sense of mysticism and spirituality so strong that adherents still talk about them like religious texts.
—*NA*

The Smiths: *"This Charming Man"* 1983

For all Morrissey's extravagant talk of the Smiths' debut single "Hand in Glove" as a pop landmark—and despite considerable press acclaim—it stalled on the charts, failing to reach the UK Top 40. They made no mistake with the follow-up. Released in October 1983, "This Charming Man" still managed to get only to number 25, but it secured the group its first appearance on *Top of the Pops,* and the performance—with Morrissey wielding and waving a bunch of gladioli—cemented them in the British pop pantheon.

Opening with one of Johnny Marr's most scintillating intros (the first fruits of his work with producer and one-time Roxy Music bassist John Porter), the song initially seems like a jangling Postcard Records take on Motown—an impression soon skewed by Morrissey's romantic intrigue of desolate moors, hillside seductions, handsome suitors, and thwarted desires. If Orange Juice's Edwyn Collins had defined a wittily effete romanticism, Morrissey made it plain that he was hungry for seduction on the smooth leather of the passenger seat (if a little conflicted about going through with it). It was a wholly original equation, and one that would define "indie" for a generation.
—ST

Sonic Youth: *"Death Valley '69"* 1984

"Death Valley '69" begins and ends with a scream. The first is Thurston Moore's, a shout of excitement, of plunging into cold water on a hot day. The last is downtown NYC scene queen Lydia Lunch's, a protracted shriek of terror, a horror film's leading lady being disemboweled by a serial killer. And fittingly, in between is a roller-coaster ride careening between the two extremes.

Sonic Youth's abstract rumination on the Charles Manson murders was first released as a single in 1984 and then became the final track on the band's 1985 American death-trip album *Bad Moon Rising.* Moore's shouts are echoed by Lunch's haunted mewling, which evokes something terrible happening out in the desert. As Kim Gordon's bass prods like the tip of a knife against a throat, Bob Bert's propulsive drumming moves faster and faster, and Moore's and Lee Ranaldo's guitars whip up a squall, the vocalists scream "HIT IT!" over and over, more desperate each time, squeezing every bit of violence—both physical and sexual—out of the phrase.

Along with "Expressway to Yr Skull," "Death Valley '69" marked the high point of Sonic Youth's early years. Its shotgun wedding of balls-out rawk riffage and wind-tunnel noize kicked open the door for the marriage of pop and avant-garde that the band has spent the rest of its long, fruitful career perfecting.
—APh

Hüsker Dü: *"Pink Turns to Blue"* 1984

It's a stretch to call Hüsker Dü "the Beatles of punk," but they at least had their own mini-versions of John Lennon and Paul McCartney. Guitarist Bob Mould was the former, writing the more complicated and powerful songs, while drummer Grant Hart shared McCartney's knack for infusing simpler tunes with wistful emotion. The best example of Hart's work is the bruising "Pink Turns to Blue," from the sprawling 1984 double LP *Zen Arcade,* a record that proved punk was capable of every mood and color. Over Mould's thick, burning guitar, Hart moans the sickly-sad tale of a girlfriend whose drug addiction turns her skin from the bright hue of life to the dark pallor of death. The surrounding maelstrom transforms Hart's falsetto chorus and sentimental conclusion ("She's lying on the bed / Angels pacing, gently placing roses 'round her head") into chilling swoons. Mould's guitar presages the melancholy fuzz of Dinosaur Jr., but the track's combination of noise, melody, and angst even more strongly predicts the fiery hooks of the Pixies and the bittersweet grunge of Nirvana. But no one has actually replicated the aching bliss of the still-resonant "Pink Turns to Blue."
—MM

Meat Puppets: *"Plateau"* 1984

Of the famed indie-rock class of 1984, Meat Puppets were the farthest out—geographically and metaphysically. Classmates Hüsker Dü and the Replacements hailed from Minneapolis, and Minutemen from San Diego, but the Puppets originated in seemingly sceneless Phoenix, Arizona. Their warped psychedelic country music was the sound of two brothers and a friend cobbling together their own rock mythologies, setting fever dreams and off-the-map prognostications to skewed takes on traditional music.

"Plateau" is a tricky, ambiguous metaphor about consumerism, or religion, or the afterlife. If you buy into the last of those, then all that awaits you once you die are, allegedly, "a bucket and a mop and an illustrated book about birds." Sisyphus and Audubon aside, the Puppets sound spookily controlled on "Plateau," despite their hardcore origins and their punk label, the famed SST Records. You might mistake that control for being stoned—even the psychedelic guitar solo refuses to freak out—but that sense of reservation actually makes the song sound weirder, even decades on.
—SD

The Replacements: *"I Will Dare"* 1984

The Replacements may have started as a punk band, but they weren't an especially good one. In America, at least, punk works best when tied to an extra-musical ideal—a political stance, a community, or an aesthetic critique. Early on, the Replacements were committed only to playing rock and roll, having a laugh, and drinking as much booze as possible. Forget the fashion statements and the glorification of DIY; these were average suburban screwups with a surprising softer side. *Let It Be*'s "I Will Dare" reinforced the notion that the Minneapolis band was most interesting when it seemed most vulnerable. Lead singer and songwriter Paul Westerberg addressed the song to a girl, but the words were understood as the band's message to the world: Let's do this, let's give it a shot, even though we'll probably never get anywhere. With Peter Buck on loan from R.E.M. for a quick solo (the bands played a number of shows together in the early 1980s), the Replacements officially aligned themselves with what was then called "college rock," an indication that they aspired to more than their regional independent scene.
—MR

Minutemen: *"History Lesson (Part II)"* 1984

Credit the frills-free production, the fast-and-loose style, or the way guitarist D. Boon sang like he'd just scrawled the lyrics on his forearm, but the Minutemen sounded like best friends breaking in their first rehearsal space—talented guys who took risks, toured their hearts out, and gave a shit about current events, but first and foremost were pals. When Boon reminisces on "History Lesson (Part II)"

about how he and Watt learned punk—"We'd go drink and pogo"—you get the sense that not much had changed between the learning and the playing. And when they tack themselves onto the end of a lineage of punk idols (Joe Strummer, Richard Hell), they don't sound presumptuous.

This gentle memoir comes as a breather halfway through their double album *Double Nickels on the Dime,* a magnum opus that cost just over a grand to record. Far from the only punk song to oppose the 1970s dream of Pink Floyd–sized fame, it makes its point with low-key grace: Success doesn't make a band as much as commitment, loyalty, and love do. The song's key line, "Our band could be your life," still resonates. A year later, Boon's life would be taken long before its time in a highway collision—not the fall of the tragic rock god, just a dumb, awful accident.
—CD

R.E.M.: *"So. Central Rain (I'm Sorry)"* 1984

This is one of R.E.M.'s most cryptic songs: Not only did its title change every time it was written or uttered ("So. Central Rain" originally, but then "Southern Central Rain" inside the LP flap and "So. Central Rain (I'm Sorry)" for radio stations), but it also features opaque lyrics about "rivers of suggestion" breaking their banks and Michael Stipe apologizing for who knows what, while the band plays a ballad at double time. And yet, the song, with its peculiar vibe and elegant hook, was also a modest hit and a calling card for the Georgians early in their career, when they were still making obscurity a virtue.

Assaying curious arpeggios against Mike Mills's honky-tonk piano (which is so low in the mix it sounds like an echo rather than the real thing), Peter Buck brings the jangle with his Byrds-like guitar. But "So. Central Rain" proves that the band's signature sound came as much from its rhythm section as anything else. With a high-hat in Memphis soul and a snare in Nashville country, Bill Berry's punchy rhythms seem about twice as fast as the song itself, have little use for fills, and place accents on unexpected beats; and his interplay with Mills's bass sets a pace as steady as the Mississippi. "So. Central Rain" works itself into a tense culvert tangle of *Psycho* piano chords, echoing low-ends, and Stipe's reverb howl, setting up the band's larger mythology as Georgian eccentrics and Athens rainmakers.
—SD

Echo and the Bunnymen:
"The Killing Moon" 1984

Many post-punk acts were smarter, more popular—hell, just plain better—than Echo and the Bunnymen, but few sounded as exotic, and no Bunnymen song epitomizes this like "The Killing Moon." Over a brushed-snare shuffle and a lurking bass line, Will Sergeant's guitar echoes Middle Eastern tones and rhythms, equating those sounds with a sort of pop mysticism that gives the song gravity. Meanwhile, Ian McCulloch pitches his voice somewhere between self-absorbed and seductive, but sounds increasingly impassioned as the song progresses—almost, but not quite, hysterical.

This is the highest of high-goth drama: a combination of post-punk claustrophobia and bubblegum synth-pop that fades out with some of the most exquisitely pained la-la-las ever cut to vinyl. "The Killing Moon" pinpoints the darkest and most natural teenage conceit: Misery builds character, and it's better savored than bemoaned. Maybe that's why so many emo upstarts have adopted the Bunnymen's sound and style—even if few have matched their emotional exoticism.
—*SD*

The Cure: *"Close to Me"* 1985

If you were an unhappy high school student in the mid-1980s, you were practically required to have a Cure cassette in your locker. The band's first five albums had been one long mood divebomb, culminating in 1982's *Pornography,* on which Robert Smith prepared for suicide before desperately grasping for hope in the record's final moments: "I must fight this sickness / Find a cure."

By 1985's *The Head on the Door,* he'd lightened up a bit, and the lipstick he smeared across his face finally stood a chance of winding up on someone else. "Close to Me" is a hop-skipping love song with existential dread in its heart: Smith finds himself swooning and skin-to-skin, but he's not sure whether his happiness is an illusion or an atrocity.

The real breakthrough, though, is the music itself. The band replaces the murky, cobwebbed guitar of its early records with a slinky groove, some innocent-sounding keyboards, and finally, hilariously, a New Orleans brass section that busts in and starts ripping it up until they notice they're the only ones still playing.
—*DW*

Siouxsie and the Banshees:
"Cities in Dust" 1985

The Sex Pistols' concerts were, legendarily, the meeting place for many future icons of the UK's post-punk scene. Siouxsie and the Banshees were one of those bands.

Assembled from a crew of rabid Sex Pistols fans, the group's first incarnation actually featured John Simon Ritchie, soon to be immortalized as Sid Vicious. But the band quickly moved away from punk's ragged three-chord fare, developing its sound within the space of just a few albums—from the apocalyptic clang of *The Scream* into a buzzing, thrumming, psychedelic swirl.

For all of their fright-wigged, kohl-eyed aspect, Siouxsie and the Banshees never contented themselves with standard goth imagery; instead, Siouxsie's lyrics included the unnervingly concrete ("Nicotine Stain") and the character-driven ("Christine"). "Cities in Dust," a tidy set piece dedicated to the victims of Pompeii, was the highlight of 1986's *Tinderbox*—the group's eighth studio album and the first to hit the upper half of the U.S. charts. In the song's stadium-sized reverb and unabashed grandeur, you can hear the results of years of playing to increasingly larger halls; but demure touches of Latin percussion, pushed high in the mix, ensure a prevailing sense of intimacy, which only serves to highlight the drama of Siouxsie's controlled wail.
—*PS*

Run-D.M.C.: *"It's Like That"* 1983

The first thing that hits you is the naked audacity of it: no lip service to soul, no rock crossover, no cooed R&B chorus, no attempt to make a drum machine sound like anything other than a drum machine—just beats and rhymes, period. Stripped to the bone, Jam Master Jay's programming makes every detail count: White noise ramps up to get beat down by outsized kicks, while militant snares and descending tom patterns add tension to a staunch clap on the two and the four. All that space in the mix puts maximum pressure on Darryl "D.M.C." McDaniels and DJ Run's search for an exit out of poverty and despair. Indeed, the progression of the lyrics to "It's Like That" models, in miniature, the contradictory arc of their entire career: They climbed from bitter realism to a bedrock of faith while making unstoppable

party music about everyday struggles. Life on the street in Hollis is depicted as a maze of self-destructive traps, but Queens never binds their globally ambitious imagination, which extends both "across the sea" and past the Last Judgment, darkly indicated in the line "we're all written down on the same list."
—DD

Crash Crew: *"On the Radio"* 1983

The transition from the lengthy, disco-inflected jams of old-school rap to the stripped-down toughness of Run-D.M.C. was abrupt enough to startle the young hip-hop movement into a completely different direction, but it wasn't without warning. One missing link between the two phases of rap is this underrated jam from Harlem's Crash Crew, originally released on Sugar Hill imprint Bay City. The five-MC operation had a bit of old-school style, bringing their fair share of turn-the-party-out rhymes and touches of early-'80s R&B vocalization in their close-harmony melodic hooks—notably in the memorable "rockin' on the radiooo" refrain (later referenced in De La Soul's 1991 track "Oodles of O's"). But the production's hard-hitting electro-funk, disguised under a cheerful melody, is a forerunner of what the majority of rap would sound like two years later, and there's a power in the MCing that was more prevalent in their successors than their contemporaries: Listen to the way Reggie Reg or EK Mike C or any of the other members spits his verses, and you'll hear the supreme confidence of the earliest battle rappers.
—NP

Rammelzee vs. K-Rob: *"Beat Bop"* 1983

When the tweaked art-rap of "Beat Bop" arrived in 1983, it came sleeved in a black-and-white graffiti schematic designed by New York Afro-bohemia poster boy Jean-Michel Basquiat, who also produced the track. Hip-hop had already scratched avant ideas onto community center dance floors—and at the time nearly all rap was still "underground" by dint of being released on tiny regional record labels catering to a pre-crossover fan base. Yet even then "Beat Bop" was a bugged-out artifact, tweaking a hardcore audience already willing to throw down on some weird shit.

At its start, "Beat Bop" sounds close to old-school disco rap with a long, dusted chicken-scratch groove.

But Rammelzee—a sci-fi-obsessed graffiti pioneer and downtown New York fixture who had already achieved infamy by appearing in Charlie Ahearn's hip-hop documentary *Wild Style*—and partner K-Rob trade rhymes that melt into acidic madness and threaten to fizz right off the tape. Disappearing into heavy reverb—the track's strange percussive noises drop arrhythmic shadows on the beat—the two kick knowledge about life in the early-1980s inner city before shipping into the cartoon jive and gnostic nonsense that indie rappers have spent the past twenty-five years trying to decode. After ten minutes it fades out, as if Ram and K-Rob are still jousting in their own special world, goading each other into taking each rhyme further out than the last.
—JH

Boogie Down Productions: *"South Bronx"* 1986

Forged in the fire of rap's first beef, "South Bronx" was a scintillating, surprising response to MC Shan's "The Bridge." That song, which erroneously claimed the Queensbridge Housing Projects as the place where "it all got started way back when," was taken as a slight by Kris Parker, aka KRS-One, a burgeoning Trinidadian-Nigerian MC and graffiti writer born and raised in the eponymous borough. Shocking in his candor, KRS raps with an impassioned, severe tone. Of Shan, he sneers, "Ya got dropped off MCA 'cause the rhymes you wrote was wack." He then outlines, almost moment by moment, the evolution of hip-hop from Cedar Park jam sessions to "crazy dreads" in Brooklyn. No Queensbridge in that history lesson. The production, originally credited to KRS and a fellow BDP member, the late DJ Scott La Rock, was later revealed to be an early work of Ced Gee, better known as a member of seminal NYC rap crew Ultramagnetic MCs. Flipping James Brown staples like "Get Up Offa That Thing," Ced's raucous, almost dissonant creation is shockingly spare, wide open enough for KRS to own the track but menacing enough to knock out the competition with a mere horn stab. Shan never recovered from the blow.
—SF

New Order: *"Blue Monday"* 1983

As legend had it, Factory Records in-house designer Peter Saville, after hearing New Order's "Blue Monday" for the first time, asked the band if he could bring a 5 ¼" floppy disc home with him for inspiration. The band assented, but only on the condition that Saville return the disc when he was done, since it contained much of the programming for the song itself. "Blue Monday" was confidently composed with drum machines and sequencers rather than "traditional" rock instruments, and a clear and formal break from the band's punk roots. The band nods to such precursors as Donna Summer's "Our Love," Sylvester's "You Make Me Feel (Mighty Real)," and Klein + MBO's proto-techno club classic "Dirty Talk," but as with most Frankenstein's monsters, the whole is much greater than the sum of its parts.

Another legend has it that "Blue Monday," the best-selling twelve-inch single of all time, actually lost money due to its elaborate packaging: Saville's design was a large-scale re-creation of the very floppy he'd borrowed, with a complex, die-cut sleeve and the vinyl itself as the data disc inside. But there's no question that New Order got a lot back in return for their initial investment. Those disaffected vocals, that stuttering bass drum intro, and the immortal sequencer progression not only immediately earned the group an entrée into the American dance scene it had admired from afar, but it also ensured that New Order's rapidly expanding fan base—not to mention the band itself—would remain interested in bpms as well as guitars from this point on.
—JK

Prince and the Revolution:
"When Doves Cry" 1984

Prince wears gold lamé leggings. Prince plants his Gibson in his groin and shakes his glittering glutes for ABC's zooming camera. Prince finishes miming the guitar solo to "I Wanna Be Your Lover" and leans against guitarist Dez Dickerson like David Bowie leaning on Mick Ronson. The sync track fades as Dick Clark jogs up with his Geiger-counter microphone.

"Where'd you learn to do this in Minneapolis!?" Clark guffaws. Prince rolls back his eyes before leveling them at Clark in belittling disbelief. Clark pushes: "This is not the kind of music that comes from Minneapolis!" Prince sheepishly mumbles, "No."

The interview proceeds awkwardly as Clark's mundane questions crash against Prince's laconic elusiveness. Is Prince coy or stupid? Prince knows that this mystery, the absence of words, draws the

viewers of his *American Bandstand* premiere to lean to the screen. Prince is just as precocious in marketing and myth building as in musicianship. Which is why the twenty one-year-old Prince tells Clark he's nineteen.

Four years later, the "semi-autobiographical" *Purple Rain*, the ultimate keystone in Prince's myth building, inflated the dichotomies of Prince's persona astronomically. Prince's mother was black, yet the movie cast a Greek actress. The routine Hollywood fairy tale is proudly set in the Twin Cities. Teenage Prince passed on four early record deals, demanding artistic autonomy, yet he wrote "When Doves Cry" overnight, at the behest of a film director—*Purple Rain*'s soundtrack was complete, but the director required a song to match a montage of domestic discord.

As per Prince's persona, the song is stripped for complexity. Four simple components—drum machine, keyboard, guitar, and vocals—mix with demo-like simplicity. Famously, Prince removed the bass line. Debussy noted, "Music is the space between notes." Space that, pre-MTV and *Purple Rain*, our imaginations filled. Space that Prince spackled with lavender and dove wranglers. Prince, the word "slave" etched into his facial hair, would later celebrate his freedom from Warner Bros. Yet his genius reached its pinnacle at its most steered and calculated.
—BD

Talking Heads:
"This Must Be the Place (Naïve Melody)" [*Stop Making Sense* version] 1983

A tour rider reading "Soft White Lightbulbs" likely struck concert promoters as quirky and indulgent, but on each night of the 1983 *Speaking in Tongues* tour, David Byrne shattered at least one of three bulbs in the traditional floor lamp he teetered and tipped in a dance during "This Must Be the Place (Naïve Melody)."

The transformation of a mundane domestic appliance into an object of wonder perfectly suited the song of domestic romance. The fumbles were unintended. But that December, as Jonathan Demme captured the performance for his concert film *Stop Making Sense*, Byrne nimbly executed the dance. Freeze the frame as Byrne catches the brass stand in the crooks of his elbows and finds a tender hug. His eyes and arms lock shut in unfeigned bliss. As the lamp swings back erect, Byrne steps back, eyes a-goggle in awe,

wonderfully stunned that sometimes things work out perfectly. "(Naïve Melody)" describes the repetitive musical bed, according to Byrne. The syncopated rhythm imagines the music of an unended colonial Congo, where Kraftwerk and soukous mix. Talking Heads dutifully craft the musical furniture of Byrne's design, and though it has the grace and curves of an Eames, it's as comfortable as a rocking chair.
—BD

Kate Bush: *"Running Up That Hill (A Deal with God)"* 1985

Chimerical pop auteur Kate Bush has always stayed within view of the mainstream, even as she paddles in its tributaries. At disco's peak, she made her name with the Victorian melodrama of "Wuthering Heights" and then began expanding her musical vocabulary beyond her British heritage. By 1985's "Running Up That Hill," she'd traded Emily Brontë for surrealist ellipses and pianos for synthesizers, English folk for pan-global synthesis.

Addressing a lover, Bush seeks divine intervention to swap their consciousnesses so they might understand one another. The original title, "A Deal With God," emphasized Bush's mystical yearnings; deemed potentially too scandalous for U.S. radio, it was changed to "Running Up That Hill." The song's "thunder in our hearts" is audible in the cavernous drums tumbling through billowing clouds of synthesizers. A weaker singer would've drowned in the squelchy digital dollops, bombastic mechanical fills, and buried flashes of funk, but Bush's panorama of aching leads and melismatic harmonies is impregnable.
—BH

U2: *"New Year's Day"* 1983

Early post-punk often placed emphasis on personal politics and academia; artists like Scritti Politti's Green Gartside or Gang of Four's Andy Gill were as likely to cite Derrida or Marx in interviews as Iggy or Bowie. And when post-punk spawned New Pop, it became even more solipsistic, associating the political with the pocketbook. None of that introspection and subtlety for Bono and U2, thanks. After a few solid records of jagged guitars and miserabilism, U2 kicked off their 1983 breakthrough *War* with a militaristic drumbeat, and the Big Statements continued from there. For a quarter of a century.

War's lead single, "New Year's Day" was so anthemic it literally waved flags—the band hoisted banners in its video as well as at shows. The potent symbol even graced the cover of their breakthrough live album, *Wide Awake in America*. The song's earnest, direct lyrics ("We can break through / Though torn in two, we can be one") were inspired by Lech Walesa's Solidarity movement, while its chest-beating sound was a welcome antidote to years of timid, inward-looking rock music. What followed was a mid-'80s scramble toward the MOR or the ponderous—Dire Straits, Sting, Midnight Oil, none of whom were able to repeat U2's most enduring trick: making Important Rock Music feel urgent and alive, something that swells the heart as well as the head.
—SP

Simple Minds: *"Don't You (Forget About Me)"* 1985

As pop scholars will already know, there's a case to be made for Simple Minds' highbrow credibility and a half decade of very arty LPs to back it up. But the tune that eventually made the band famous, "Don't You (Forget About Me)," is the big, melodramatic pop song from *The Breakfast Club*. It's also a good introduction to one of the grand achievements of 1980s pop, something that probably started with Roxy Music and ABBA and hit a peak right before Steve Perry's departure from Journey—how songs could put their goopy, unctuous hearts on their sleeves and wind up with something huge and impassioned, stirring and bombastic. Like all good pop, it requires the suspension of disbelief: in the whipcrack fanfares of the intro; in Jim Kerr's slick, squinting, practically Gothic vocal; in the way the chorus accents are played on the drippiest keyboard setting possible. Kerr didn't like this song, the band's only U.S. number 1. But that's precisely the point: Someone had to embarrass himself to offer us something this great. And we've been thanking him, in karaoke bars across the nation, by embarrassing ourselves right back.
—NA

The Replacements: *"Bastards of Young"* 1985

More concerned with the next round of drinks than the next president, the Replacements never waved

The Art of Noise

Noise can be traced to classical and academic exercises in atonality, but in its more streetwise industrial guise it owes plenty to the Theater of Eternal Music's 1960s drone and duration and Lou Reed's feedback-drenched *Metal Machine Music*. The sound started to gel into a subset of experimental music in the UK in the late '70s, then expanded its formless wings, enveloping transgressive literature, punk attitudes, and factory-sized energy, and pealing into strains of sonic terrorism that remain a force decades later.

"Dedicated to Peter Kurten," **Whitehouse:** The UK's Whitehouse began concocting brutal power electronics around the same time that industrial acts like Throbbing Gristle were reigning in some of their noise. 1981 was a good year for the band: Following *Erector*—whose cover art featured a disembodied penis—came *Dedicated to Peter Kurten: Sadist and Mass Slayer*. The German serial killer's theme song is a fingers-on-the-chalkboard glob of high-pitched electronics.

"Rainbow Electronics II," **Merzbow:** Dark ambient musician Masami Akita grabbed his moniker from Kurt Schwitters's junk-collage building and got started soundtracking bondage performances. The Japanese noise master has since issued hundreds of records; a good entry point is the mid-period *Rainbow Electronics II*, more than seventy-five minutes of processed, abusive electronics.

"Max Harris," **the Dead C:** The New Zealand noise scene delivered homegrown melancholy, with a number of its bands using rock instruments to rattle out improvisational psychedelics. "Max Harris"—the first song on the Dead C's 1988 debut *DR503*—is a section of a larger jam and opens in midswing: Over a clamoring lo-fi background, guitarist/vocalist Michael Morley slowly enunciates amid buzzing feedback and tribal drums.

Untitled (Live II), **Fushitsusha:** Sporting a distinctive pair of dark sunglasses and long, jet-black hair with blunt bangs, Keiji Haino started his blend of powerful guitar and vocal noise in the early '70s, both on his own and with power trio Fushitsusha. That band recorded two untitled live documents, each printed in black and released on the seminal PSF label. On the second one, he blends 150 minutes of free-form, nihilistic garage-y jazz-rock.

"The Rose Wallpaper," **Skullflower:** Formed in 1985, the London industrial-associated act Skullflower collaborated with Whitehouse, but were less outwardly confrontational, letting the music do the barking. "The Rose Wallpaper," a thirteen-minute slice of transcendent clamor, features horns, clanging, trebly metalwork, and tribal percussion.

"I Don't Care About Sleep Anymore," **Harry Pussy:** This pummeling Miami crew combined cheeky punk rock with their raging guitar/vocal/drum and dual yowling. "I Don't Care" takes a while to power up before hitting its stride—and then it's all detuned, anguished guitar craziness.

"Dead Hills," **Wolf Eyes:** Ann Arbor, Michigan's Wolf Eyes peppered their hardcore with damp dub and howling vocals. They made a huge splash when they signed to well-known indie label Sub Pop in 2004, but before that, in 2002, the title track from *Dead Hills* impressively harnessed backward tape loops and high-pitched rattling. Absolutely rabid.

"90 Chops," **John Wiese:** The king of cut-and-paste, John Wiese is a prolific laptop-wielding white-noise sculptor who's collaborated with Sunn O))), Merzbow, and Wolf Eyes, among dozens of others. He's able to get most obsessive on his own, though, as evidenced by "90 Chop," on which he howls for nearly seven minutes.

"I Trust My Guitar, Etc.," **Magik Markers:** Over a series of CD-Rs and other small-issue releases, Magik Markers were known largely for live performances—especially the whip-smart, at times bloody, actions of frontwoman/guitarist Elisa Ambrogio. With *I Trust My Guitar, Etc.,* the band moved into relatively tighter songs, but the album's twenty-two-minute title track rails like Keiji Haino's locked grooves.

"Apple Tree Victim," **Prurient:** Decorating records in erotica and images of women bound in S&M gear, one-man band Dominick Fernow runs the Hospital label (and Manhattan basement record store) when not brandishing mics. Like a strange hybrid of icy trance, noise, black metal, and masochistic vulnerability, "Apple Tree Victim" tempers scowling power electronics with strange ideas about love—he's asking a partner if they can kill each other while fucking.
—*BS*

(or burned) any flags. So it's only fitting that their most political song—their generational anthem—was a frustrated, shambling shrug. Paul Westerberg and co. weren't satisfied with living in the Greatest Generation's all-encompassing shadow, but when Westerberg howls at the top of "Bastards of Young," it sounds like he's waking up to the pounding result of a weeklong bender.

Perfecting the paradox that would define them, Minneapolis's scruffy sons breathe the passion of a thousand protest songs into their National Anthem of Indifference. "The ones who love us least are the ones we'll die to please," sings Westerberg, facing an uncrossable generation gap with peerless barstool poetry. The song even benefits from some loose articulation; though its climactic line was originally written as "ya got no warrant to name us," its more common interpretation drops the second syllable from "warrant" and picks up potent meaning in the process—just another moment of stumbling brilliance from a band that turned happy accidents into high art.
—RD

The Mekons: *"Last Dance"* 1985

It's nearly closing time, and Tom Greenhalgh spots a girl across the room: "So beautiful, you were waltzing / Little frozen rivers all covered with snow." He needs her like he needs a future—which is the way the Mekons probably felt when they recorded this song soon after their reunion. The punk band—self-described "nonaligned lefties"—had gotten back together for benefit shows to support the UK miners' strikes of 1984 and '85. Thatcher would put down the strike; the Mekons would stay together past their thirtieth anniversary. But that backdrop brings poignancy to this love song, recorded "one fine spring day" along with the rest of the protest material that makes up the back half of the band's *Fear and Whiskey* LP. Like the strikers, Greenhalgh's dancehall crooner does his best, as Susie Honeyman's high, hopeful violin eggs him on in the Oxfam hand-me-down style of "Come On Eileen." Also like the strikers, he walks out empty-handed—but from the howls at the end of the song, it's clear he'll live to fail another day.
—CD

Big Black: *"Kerosene"* 1986

Melding punk with proto–industrial rock, Big Black played ear-shattering guitars tweaked to trebly perfection by Steve Albini. The famed audio engineer was also the group's focal point, an outspoken vocalist/guitarist who wrote cynical and comically biting screeds for *Forced Exposure* and other zines, and gave smart, darkly humorous onstage speeches.

Big Black's subject matter itself was often tongue-in-cheek: Albini was fascinated with the violent, destructive underbelly of America, exploring child abuse, molestation, and police brutality, among other sorts of shrouded violence. "Kerosene," from the band's 1986 debut album *Atomizer,* looks at small-town boredom—places where, Albini wrote, "there are few forms of amusement, two prominent ones are easy sex and arson." Set to a chugging, slicing rhythm buttressed by a mechanistic drum machine, the song is a first-person narration by a stir-crazy type, looking for a release and finding it in highly flammable kerosene. When the fires are set and folks burned, the song's repetitive build also ignites, with Albini screaming and the guitars hitting like shrapnel, damaging everything in their path.
—BS

Scratch Acid: *"The Greatest Gift"* 1984

When not mentioned simply as one of Nirvana leader Kurt Cobain's favorite bands, Scratch Acid are often brushed off as the first, formative group of Rapeman/Jesus Lizard guitarist David William Sims, Rapeman drummer Rey Washam, and Jesus Lizard vocalist David Yow. That's a shame because this Austin noise-rock band created a compellingly sloppy and singed blend of discordant punk rockabilly and sexy, glass-shattering grooves. "The Greatest Gift" twists blues-punk and a countrified twang with Yow's howling vocals. The singer's more playful with his voice here than in his future projects, offering almost silly enunciations rather than the monster howl he'd later establish in the Jesus Lizard. The song's subject matter—the "greatest gift" is that, six feet under, we're food for worms—is darkly comedic, but it's standard fare from the band that also wrote "Mary Had a Little Drug Problem" and "Big Bone Lick."
—BS

The Jesus and Mary Chain:
"Just Like Honey" 1985

Dum. Dum dum—bam! Dum. Dum dum—bam! The heartbeat of rock and roll, first bashed by Hal Blaine to open the Ronettes' "Be My Baby," has supported entire genres upon its frame. Phil Spector's reverb-rich wizardry transfigured Blaine's drumsticks into Adam's ribs, and ever since, those four beats have served as a statement of intent from bands weaned on girl-group harmonies and walls of sound.

In the mid-1980s, two bands, Poison and the Jesus and Mary Chain, opened their debuts by aping Blaine's legendary spark. Ostensibly, the groups seemed opposed in principle. Embodying and embracing Hollywood sleaze, Poison kick-started the heart of hair metal with "Cry Tough," an anthem of going from gutter to glamour. Meanwhile, in Glasgow, the JAMC slathered buzzing distortion over 1960s pop candy on their mission statement, "Just Like Honey." The band loved their idea so much, it recycled it ten tracks later on "Sowing Seeds." In its white-noise wake followed noise pop and shoegazing.

Onstage, Poison sprayed confetti over Harley parts. The leather-clad Chain faced walls and boiled over with contempt. Their brief gigs ended in bloody fisticuffs. Both groups loved hairspray, the ideals of pop art, and Kenneth Anger. Both demonstrated the power of adding one novel twist to classic ingredients. Yet JAMC prove that history judges more on fruits than roots. In short, the Jesus and Mary Chain were cool.
—*BD*

The Smiths: *"How Soon Is Now?"* 1984

"I am human and I need to be loved," moans singer Morrissey, risking self-parody amid a dense, caco-phonous wall of sound. With its instantly recognizable intro—the muscular, echo-laden work of guitarist Johnny Marr—and lyrics dramatically lamenting the fruitlessness of nightlife and the loneliness it can bring, "How Soon Is Now?" is anthemic wallflower music, a stark opposition to the relatively soulless and whitewashed indie pop that would develop in its immediate wake. Incredibly, it was originally issued as a mere B-side.

As on many of the best Smiths songs, Marr and Morrissey stand in opposition here, playing their respective roles as the rocker and the poet, each taking his indulgences to extremes—Marr copped moves from Bo Diddley and Morrissey nicked part of his lyric from George Elliot's *Middlemarch*. It worked: This was the song that made them indie stars in America, with their U.S. label boss, Sire's Seymour Stein, calling it "The 'Stairway to Heaven' of the '80s"; geez, it's much better than *that*.
—*SP*

Cocteau Twins: *"Lorelei"* 1984

Throughout their lengthy career, Cocteau Twins created the kind of total universe rarely achieved in pop music. Record covers showcased abstract graphics that might have been Martian landscapes or electron-microscope enlargements. Amniotic production values suffused everything in a liquid haze, as instrumentalists Robin Guthrie and Simon Raymonde (and, until 1983, Will Heggie) smudged the signature sounds of guitars, basses, and keyboards. And Liz Fraser's vocals—which on early records ran the gamut from indistinct to indecipherable—plunged ever further into a world of her own making, a hodgepodge of collaged phrases, Scottish dialect, and made-up words.

Treasure, the band's third album, found Cocteau Twins testing their own limits and proving that they could be both beatific ("Pandora," "Aloysius") and darkly, almost abrasively forceful ("Persephone"). "Lorelei" stands out as both a singular piece of songwriting and a lesson in studio craft. Like the Smiths' "How Soon Is Now?" it features an easily identifiable intro—a high-pitched, bells-and-buzzsaws drone that persists almost uninterrupted for the course of the song. Alternating between verse and chorus in a way that moots the definition of each, the song finds its center of gravity in a sixteen-bar passage far too weighty to be a bridge. Multitracked bass lines work circles in the ground, and Fraser, chanting what might be a playground rhyme, seems to crouch down into herself, primal and unrelenting. A thundering Roland TR-808 drum machine keeps violent time, but the song is somehow neither tough nor tender, neither dark nor light—rather, it forges a middle path to a far stranger and more special place.
—*PS*

New Order: *"Bizarre Love Triangle"* 1986

For all the love that "Bizarre Love Triangle" garners from both dance and indie factions, it'd be natural to assume that it was a massive success upon its release. Yet its high standing in the eyes of listeners has been the result of a gradual, decades-long reevaluation, spurred by countless compilations, remixes, and a hugely popular cover, courtesy of Australia's Frente!. While that version reduced the song's spiky synths and juddering drum machines to an acoustic soup, it subtly underlined how one of the most likeable things about New Order was the way they convincingly folded an entire palette of electronic sounds into their music while still retaining the aura of a rock band. Whatever they were, they were cannily attuned to everything that went on around them; although the shiny, happy, anything-goes aesthetic of Balearic House was only just starting to make itself felt in Ibiza, you could already hear traces of its influence here, particularly in the bongo bits that dominate the rhythmic breakdown.
—MP

Billy Bragg: *"A New England"* 1983

The personal, as feminists used to say, is political. But Billy Bragg, England's foremost punk folk singer, is usually at his best when he sets the two pulling and nagging at each other. He wrote "A New England" in his very early twenties, when he was just a skinny kid, fresh from a stint in the army. It's a breakup song set against the social politics that complicate real relationships—and against the political ambition of Bragg's other songs. After two minutes, and not too many words, the song leaves us with large, heavy questions. "I'm not looking for a new England / I'm just looking for another girl"—but if the personal is political, couldn't it all be the same thing?

The sound of the recording is just as powerful. There's only one instrument; Bragg pulls a Fender electric guitar into a deep, gritty rumble, which echoes like it's bouncing off the brick wall behind a very small stage. He delivers his lyrics like a proclamation, in a series of hard-clipped consonants and broad, working-class vowels; he's the kind of guy whose songs you can't sing without impersonating his voice. Those with a soft spot for earnest eloquence and righteous young men will find that voice the perfect match for a world like Bragg's, where the shooting stars of romance always turn out to be spy satellites.
—NA

Metallica: *"Battery"* 1986

Metallica began in Los Angeles in 1981, when James Hetfield met Lars Ulrich, a Dane who'd relocated to the States at seventeen to pursue a tennis career. Another early member was Dave Mustaine who left on bad terms, going on to form Megadeth. Metallica's classic lineup was established when Hetfield and Ulrich relocated to the Bay Area, joining with ex-Exodus guitarist Kirk Hammett and bassist Cliff Burton. From the start, the quartet's aggressive, smart, and at times surprisingly delicate metal placed them squarely within the Bay Area thrash scene (Exodus, Testament, Death Angel) and well outside the commercial glam metal of Mötley Crüe and Ratt.

Metallica's third full-length, 1986's *Master of Puppets*—their final record with Burton, who died that year when the band's van flipped over during a tour in Sweden—opens with "Battery." The song, which begins with clean, interlocking guitars, deals with the human obsession with violence and power. The fragile, pastoral introduction disappears beneath distorted speed riffs and violent lyrics as the track is transformed into a technically tight swarm, which goes a long way toward establishing the early thrash template and the band's dominance over 1980s hard rock.
—BS

Slayer: *"Angel of Death"* 1986

Southern California thrash band Slayer came to be defined by Dave Lombardo's fast double-bass drumming, Kerry King and Jeff Hanneman's hyper-buzzing guitars, the shouts of bassist/vocalist Tom Araya, their dark, horror-tinged subject matter (serial killers, Satanism, Nazism), and live shows and artwork involving pentagrams, fake blood, and inverted crosses. Like Metallica, their inspiration came from both British heavy metal and punk—they'd go on to cover Minor Threat and TSOL, among others. The quartet's third album, 1986's *Reign in Blood,* was their major-label debut, recorded and produced by Rick Rubin for his (and Russell Simmons's) Def Jam—it was the label's first metal release. Rubin gave the band a cleaner sound, stripping their attack to its barest essentials and infusing it with an almost NYC-hardcore intensity. (At Rubin's suggestion, King played the famous guitar solo on the Beastie Boys' "No Sleep Till Brooklyn.")

Reign in Blood's most controversial track, opener "Angel of Death," is also its longest. Written by Hanneman, it details the atrocities of war criminal Dr. Josef Mengele, the physical and psychological human experiments he performed during World War II—gassing, performing surgery without anesthesia, hacking limbs, water burial, burning skin—and the "mutants" he created. This extreme subject material delayed *Reign in Blood*'s release when Def Jam distributor Columbia Records balked at the lyrics, along with the album's Satan-friendly graphic artwork. Geffen ended up distributing it without officially listing it on a release schedule.
—*BS*

Saint Vitus: *"Clear Windowpane"* 1986

Formed (under the name Tyrant) in Los Angeles in 1979, the doom crew Saint Vitus released their eponymous 1984 debut on SST, the seminal independent label founded in 1978 by Black Flag guitarist Greg Ginn to put out his own band's work. Expanding the roster beyond Black Flag, SST paved the way for indie labels and provided a home for a disparate cast of scruffy, ambitious underground American rockers—an early core that included the complex punk trio the Minutemen; the snotty, sophomoric pop-punks the Descendents; and major underground acts Sonic Youth, Meat Puppets, Hüsker Dü, and Dinosaur Jr.

Saint Vitus's dirge-like stoner rock stood out amongst the speedier stable: From 1984 to 1988, Saint Vitus released four records on SST, but their key period began three albums in with *Born Too Late* and its "Clear Windowpane." A lone drum kick starts the track as sludgy, phased guitars crunch, solo, and wail. "Clear Windowpane" deals with drug-fueled paranoia and psychedelia, conjuring images like "purple dragons" and a fear of "coming down." It was also, unwittingly, a prophetic vision of singer Scott Weinrich's life. The Saint Vitus frontman would spend time as a homeless speed addict in L.A. before cleaning up and reconstituting his musical career.
—*BS*

Einstürzende Neubauten: *"Halber Mensch"* 1985

The "Bohemian Rhapsody" of German industrial music, "Halber Mensch" exhibits the same operatic chutzpah and once-and-never-again singularity of its English cock-rock-cousin, but it's made of stronger stuff. Built out of layers of male and female choirs and the gutter cries of singer Blixa Bargeld—alternately multitracked into a battalion and cut back to a tin-can whisper—"Halber Mensch" sets a grim meditation on dehumanized abjection to a minimalist structure.

The track begins with a simple figure that repeats and builds as elements expand upon the endlessly cycling central motif. Deploying the canon form of Bach chorales and school-yard sing-alongs to a perverted and disturbing purpose, the anonymous singers lyrically invoke an ominous and malevolent "we," against which the hapless Blixa can only offer "Schönen Gruss vom Schnitter" ("Kind regards from the Reaper"). As a work of vocal bricolage, "Halber Mensch" expertly mines the German language for musical and rhythmic effects: Filtered male vowels become bass melodies, and sharp consonant phrases ("mir nichts dir nichts") crack like snares. Neubauten were previously pegged as little more than a junkyard drum circle, but this song revealed the group's wide-screen compositional chops.
—*DD*

Art of Noise: *"Beat Box (Diversion One)"* 1984

Hired by Malcolm McLaren in 1982 on the back of his lavish production of ABC's *The Lexicon of Love,* Trevor Horn was tasked with stitching together the field recordings for the pan-global hip-hop of *Duck Rock.* To assist him, Horn convened a studio band comprising Anne Dudley and Gary Langan (who had engineered and orchestrated *Lexicon*) and programmer J. J. Jeczalik. The project was so successful that Horn took the crew along to his next assignment, producing Yes's *90125*—a decidedly less rewarding project. Studio boredom led to Langan and Jeczalik goofing around with their latest gadget, the fantastically expensive Fairlight CMI, sampling, warping, and looping a booming Yes drum track—and inadvertently reinventing the hip-hop breakbeat. These studio experiments became the first draft of "Beat Box," the debut single from Art of Noise, who were christened by press provocateur Paul Morley and signed to the militant British pop label ZTT.

An unlikely hit, "Beat Box" is part stern European modernist epic (a high-tech collage of orchestral bursts, car ignition and disfigured human bleats), part daft surrealist folly, part twanging instrumental novelty. But the bombast of the beats ensured its success, and like Kraftwerk's visionary techno, the track's futurism touched a nerve in the hip-hop community. Along with its stunning B-side "Moments in Love," the song remains a triumph of conceptual pop.
—ST

Frankie Goes to Hollywood:
"Relax" 1983

After the avant-garde clarion call of the Art of Noise's "Beat Box" single, Frankie Goes to Hollywood's "Relax" was the heavy artillery of the ZTT label's British pop campaign. The original song—a rudimentary S&M anthem—was, as producer Trevor Horn was first to admit, more of a jingle than a pop song. (Indeed, it's become a kind of jingle for its whole decade.) This gave Horn the creative license he needed to compose his staggering, Fellini-esque vision of high-energy heavy metal, reworked over six months in a trio of remixes, including a sixteen-minute "sex mix" that sounded like a prog dream of the Paradise Garage.

But it might never have achieved its epic success (almost two million in sales in the UK alone) had it not been for *NME*-journalist-turned-pomo-impresario Paul Morley's tactical exploitation of controversy, hyping up the image of rampant gay hedonism under the nose of the nannyish British media at the height of Thatcherism. Its eventual ban from Radio 1 was precisely what was needed to kick-start the Frankie phenomenon—culminating in a historic UK chart one-two with the similarly sensational "Two Tribes" in the summer of 1984.
—ST

Liquid Liquid: *"Optimo"* 1983

The pop-culture boneyard is littered with the remains of pioneering bands that never got their due. On the flipside, however, sometimes a nominally obscure group leaves behind a legacy that far outstrips its original stature. Liquid Liquid—who specialized in the kind of uprooted funk that came to define the New York underground disco era—falls into the latter category. Both spiky and densely polyrhythmic, their sound went on to rock the floors of the Paradise Garage and underpin foundational hip-hop tracks—the bass lick from "Cavern," for example, was replayed by the Sugar Hill house band as the backing track to Grandmaster Flash and Melle Mel's "White Lines (Don't Do It)."

"Optimo," taken from a limited-run EP of the same name, offers a classic snapshot of the post-punk era, an absorbing picture of myriad influences and possibilities—lessons learned by such mid-'00s indie-dance forces as LCD Soundsystem, Hot Chip, and Scottish DJ duo Optimo. Applying garage rock's DIY approach to the libidinal pulse of R&B, then filtering the results through a gauze of dub reggae reverb, this is a propulsive and instantly affecting piece of music.
—DS

Alexander Robotnick:
"Problèmes d'Amour" 1983

Italo disco was an early-1980s variant of a popular dance-music sound, often putting synthesizers and drum machines in place of Philadelphia Soul's string orchestras. With electronics wizard Giorgio Moroder as its often-somber godfather, the genre found its quirkiest expression in "Problèmes d'Amour," a French-language song produced by Italy's Maurizio Dami under the futuristic name Alexander Robotnick.

An underground hit in American dance clubs, the song prominently featured the Roland TR-808 drum machine and TB-303 bass synthesizer, two instruments that would soon become staples in the arsenals of Chicago's house-music producers. The seven-minute electro-disco epic just keeps on giving, building from a metronomic skip and scat-inspired vocal trills into a complex construction brimming with synth counterpoints, tag-teamed male and

Grindcore: Ten Skatepunk Greats

The first skaters might've listened to Led Zeppelin and Black Sabbath, but as skateboarding gradually developed its own subculture in early-1980s Southern California, it became inextricably tied to the second-wave hardcore all around it. Skatepunk is an inexact genre tag, but these bands swiped the galloping sneer from close ancestors like Black Flag and the Circle Jerks, adding sugar-rush hooks as they surged onward and upward.

"Amoeba," **the Adolescents:** Tony Cadena snottily compares teenage life to that of a single-celled organism under a microscope slide, while half the population of Orange County howls the title's three syllables in drunken, sing-along defiance. The Cali hardcore orthodoxy starts here.

"Bloodstains," **Agent Orange:** The Dogtown skating subculture overlapped with surfing, so it follows that one of the earliest skatepunk bands would cover Dick Dale's "Miserlou" and take musical cues from the trebly school of early-'60s surf-guitar instrumentalists. On "Bloodstains," Agent Orange combined that pocket-epic sensibility with the misanthropic ranting of three antisocial kids, and the result is one of the great scream-along choruses of all time.

"Mommy's Little Monster," **Social Distortion:** If Agent Orange took their cues from surf-guitar, Social D's Mike Ness found solace in the meat-and-potatoes formalism of rockabilly, which somehow led him to sound like a punked-up John Cougar Mellencamp. No matter; "Mommy's Little Monster" is a thrillingly heartfelt plea on behalf of bad kids everywhere, and Ness's compassion must've made him look like an alien among his contemporaries.

"Code Blue," **TSOL:** True Sounds of Liberty might've polished and tightened the hooks of hardcore's first wave, but they kept the transgressive streak gleefully intact. On "Code Blue," Jack Grisham swipes Jello Biafra's theatrically nasal honk to praise necrophilia—because, you know, none of the girls at his school will talk to him.

"Hope," **Descendents:** A spurned lover's proto-emo plea turns into something creepier: "And I'll have my way / You won't have a say anyway." It's not hard to hate the nasty pseudo-joke, even when it comes attached to an adrenalized hook as fiery as this one.

"We're Only Gonna Die," **Bad Religion:** The fifty-cent words, the indie-label empire, and the Ph.D.s would come later, but even as fresh-faced high-school kids, Bad Religion were barking ambitious political laments over burly popcore churns like this one. The weird connection to protest folk only strengthens when the pianos and acoustic guitars enter on the second verse. Fifteen years later, half the bands in Southern California would sound exactly like this.

"We Got Your Money," **Big Boys:** These Texas jokers dressed up in tutus and faithfully covered Kool and the Gang, unwittingly paving the way for thousands of unbearable punk-funk pranksters. But the Big Boys' sense of fun was ecstatic, not oppressive, and dizzy garage-rock anthems like this one absolve them of all blame for the Red Hot Chili Peppers.

"Institutionalized," **Suicidal Tendencies:** The King Kong of anti-parent rants. Enormous bruiser Mike Muir just wants a Pepsi, and his mom won't give it to him, so he's left with no recourse but to splenetically rail against the Kafkaesque nightmare that is his life while his crew of Venice gang bangers thrash away behind him. Life-affirming.

"The Five Year Plan," **DRI:** By the late '80s, in part thanks to bands like Suicidal Tendencies, skaters were spending as much time with speed-metal bands such as Overkill and Exodus as they were with hardcore. Houston's Dirty Rotten Imbeciles brought those sounds together with the 1987 album *Crossover,* fusing thrash's power-fantasy wheeling with hardcore's hyperspeed chug and proving that the two were made for each other.

"Sound System," **Operation Ivy:** While their contemporaries were bringing the metal, Berkeley's Op Ivy, half of whom would later found Rancid, borrowed from the herky-jerk rhythms of Britain's late-'70s ska revival, playing it fast, slippery, and grimy. "Sound System" is an inspirational hymn to the healing powers of music, and it swings even harder than its limey ancestors.
—*TB*

female vocals, chicken-scratch funk guitar, and even a muted soprano saxophone solo. But its most thrilling moment, repeated throughout the track, is undoubtedly its pitch-bent lead riff: One of the most arresting *portamento glissandi* in pop music, it takes hold of the listener and bends him this way and that, as fluid as the arc of a disco ball.
—*PS*

Shannon: *"Let the Music Play"* 1983

Shannon's "Let the Music Play" manages that rare trick of evoking its place and time and slipping past it entirely—more a distillation than a relic. For freestyle—a form of 1980s hip-hop-flavored Latin pop, often sung by female teenagers with one-word names (even if Shannon was in her mid-twenties while setting the standard)—"Let the Music Play" is Year Zero. For the rest of us, it still sounds that way.

The singer's name is on the sleeve, but its producer and cowriter is Chris Barbosa, whose keyboards turn hard arcade pings into riffs and whose concussive high-hats contract against digital-bell motifs. Together with a lyric about dancing as courtship, it's hard not to picture the action taking place at a disco inside a pinball machine. It's a shame the song title "Pac-Man Fever" was already taken.
—*MiM*

Section 25: *"Looking from a Hilltop (Restructure)"* 1984

The Factory label's Section 25 may have been post-punk B-listers compared to labelmates Joy Division, New Order, or A Certain Ratio, but they exemplify the way that sounds and styles remained fluid in the early 1980s, as a generation of mostly self-taught musicians moved beyond power chords and rudimentary structures to embrace the rhythms of funk and disco and the studio science of dub and krautrock.

Their second album, 1982's *The Key of Dreams,* found them experimenting with electronics and tape edits, submerging an already bleak sound in even bleaker atmospherics. But 1984's *From the Hip* saw Section 25 emerge as a new band with a new mandate, as half the album's songs prominently featured electro-funk drum machines and brightly hued synthesizer leads. (The latter may be the mark

of the album's producer, New Order's Bernard Sumner.) "Looking from a Hilltop" smuggles in a spiky machine rhythm from Kraftwerk under billowing layers of keyboards. Other aspects of the song now seem prescient: In "Looking from a Hilltop (Restructure)," a minimally reworked single version of the album cut, a squelchy, resonant bass line lies wriggling deep in the mix. A year later, Chicago's disco scene would be reborn as acid house thanks to this technique's telltale squirm.
—*PS*

Madonna: *"Holiday"* 1983

Disco went cold in the 1980s as endless percolations of robotic synthesizer tones chilled Italo, electro, and later techno. Yet Madonna's first massive hit, "Holiday," reveals just how warm and winsome the synthetic aesthetic could be: Its simple bass line, synth-string flairs, and rinky-dink guitar feel like a welcome mat for dancers' feet. On this song—as with the equally charming "Lucky Star"—underground disco's most expansive, otherworldly qualities are secreted within the folds of a pop song's simpler charms.

At the heart of "Holiday" is Madonna herself—her lighthearted performance as yet uncomplicated by her megacelebrity status. Her voice also rarely sounded as good as it does here: light, airy, unforced, and charming, the high scrape of her plea to "bring back all of those happy days" is filled with a sense of yearning. Later, the star would try her hand at a succession of big statements and grand gestures, but it's the simplicity of her request here that makes it impossible to refuse.
—*TF*

Cyndi Lauper: *"Girls Just Want to Have Fun"* 1984

Cyndi Lauper's first single—an unabashed ode to staying out late and getting phone calls at all hours while living with your parents and dreaming of one day being free—is sometimes cited as a sort of feminist anthem. Blame the cultural hangover after the 1982 failure of the Equal Rights Amendment, because while "Girls Just Want to Have Fun" sounds anthemic, it's certainly not about any heavy issues that hairy-legged, frowny-faced ladies wanted to push on the world.

The track was penned by the Hooters' Robert Hazard, who allowed Lauper to change a few pronouns here and there so she could turn the titular females into a group that included her instead of one she was trying to get with. If there's anything feminist about the song, it stems from Lauper's larger-than-life persona; her Technicolor hair and outsized Noo Yawk personality were flashing red signs that she was defining her womanhood on her own terms. (OK, a few were dictated by the racks at Screaming Mimi's, the infamous NYC thrift store that once employed Lauper.) And her voice, all hiccupy ebullience, was what really made her version of "Girls," well, fun, and worthy of sing-alongs across the U.S.
—MJ

Prince: *"Kiss"* 1986

Toward the end of *Parade,* an album of neopsychedelic rock and theatrical flourishes like cabaret pianos and steel drums, Prince slipped in a skeletal, sensual song that stuck out like a thorn on a perfumed rosebush. Compared to the overripe 1960s pop pastiche he'd been chasing for a year or two, "Kiss" sounds like pop from a sexy dystopian future where producers line up to receive a ration of only three sounds per song.

Under a lustful falsetto that doesn't so much follow a standard melody as suggest what musical masturbation might sound like—from the ridiculously fey opening "uh!" to the multitracked self-love of the chorus to the ecstatic squeals that bring things to a climax—Prince's rhythm track swishes to jerking high-hats and snares, threaded with a chicken-scratch guitar as stark as white neon. At a precarious point in Prince's already storied career—and in a 1986 radio season where everyone was Wang Chunging to the booming sound of canned pop-funk—the spare, streamlined modernism of "Kiss" felt louder than bombs.
—JH

Run-D.M.C.: *"Rock Box"* 1984

However much time and reality television have blunted Run-D.M.C.'s music with cheery old-school nostalgia, their hardcore early singles were a stark sonic boom, a dividing line for most people not immersed in early underground rap—which is to say, just about everyone who didn't live in New York City during the early 1980s. The Hollis, Queens, group may not have been the first hip-hop act to slam their voices against implacable digital beats; they may not have been the first to shift from the rubbery rhymes of crews like the Funky 4 + 1 to the concussive back-and-forth that toughened hip-hop's flow like their black leather jackets; they may not have been the first middle-class kids to affect the mean-mugging street swagger of a b-boy stance. But for 99 percent of humanity, they were the pioneers of what would coalesce into modern rap. They also sounded like they were having way too much fun lobbing rhymes back and forth, which is how their rough-and-tumble formalism crossed over in the first place. Musically, most of the trio's 1984 debut album is all about those tarmac drum machines, battering bass, and not much else. But "Rock Box" looks ahead to their smash success with the metallic grind of 1985's *King of Rock* and their strutting cock-rock duet with Aerosmith by adding an endless, grimacing guitar solo made all the funnier by how their beatbox still sounds harder than anything else.
—JH

LL Cool J: *"I Can't Live Without My Radio"* 1985

Armed with a massive JVC ghetto blaster, seventeen-year-old Queens native LL Cool J offered an irresistible pitch both for his portable speaker system and for hip-hop as a burgeoning cultural force on this relentless opening salvo from his debut LP, *Radio.* Like any good salesman, he's emphatic ("my bass is so loud, it could rip your clothes") and practical ("get fresh batteries if it won't rewind"). With producer and Def Jam cofounder Rick Rubin providing the hollow-shell beat and mass-appeal foresight, LL set out to make hip-hop as catchy and undeniable as anything on commercial radio.

Released a year before Run-D.M.C.'s Aerosmith collaboration "Walk This Way" and the Beastie Boys' suburban crossover *Licensed to Ill,* LL's first album featured its share of chest-heaving boasts. But with guileless romance raps "I Want You" and "I Can Give You More," Ladies Love Cool James also seized upon a neglected hip-hop demographic: women. Of course, "I Can't Live Without My Radio" isn't just

for the ladies—it's for everyone who's ever tried to tune in to just the right frequency in the hopes of hearing something unequivocally urgent.
—RD

Beastie Boys:
"No Sleep Till Brooklyn" 1986

The Beastie Boys weren't dumb, they just played it on record. In their video for "No Sleep Till Brooklyn," the trio—spurned by a club promoter after showing up for a gig as rappers—return clad in hair-metal finery and are hurriedly shoved onstage. They were essentially reenacting what their boss Rick Rubin, the cofounder of Def Jam records, had done with his Run-D.M.C./Aerosmith collaboration "Walk This Way" earlier that year. His realization was one of the more profound business moves of the era: The breakbeats that Bronx DJs had been using for a decade were often copped from classic-rock records—so why not smuggle the Bronx on to the radio by pushing a rap group as a metal band?

With the Beasties' multiplatinum *Licensed to Ill,* it worked. Consider the track's components: Its title was adopted from a Motörhead live album, its lyrics were a Spinal Tap send-up of life on the road (dealing with managers, shows, groupies, and trashed hotels), and its classic riff came courtesy of Slayer's Kerry King. And that unforgettable anthemic shouting? A holdover from the group's roots within that other milieu for white juvenile delinquency: hardcore punk. On their follow-up, *Paul's Boutique,* the Beasties disowned the *Licensed* schtick before it got tired, proving that, despite evidence to the contrary, they knew exactly what they were doing.
—EH

Mantronix: *"Needle to the Groove"* 1985

The son of Syrian and Jamaican parents, Kurtis Khaleel moved to New York as a teenager in the late 1970s. It wasn't long before he found himself immersed in the city's booming rap scene, and by 1984, he'd reinvented himself as a dance-minded hip-hop DJ called Kurtis Mantronik. Not being from New York made it easier for him to stray from the blueprint; where other producers sourced most of their core samples from old-school funk and soul breaks, Mantronik instead looked to more continental sounds like electronic music and disco.

He soon found a creative anchor in Brooklyn-based rapper MC Tee, and together the duo founded Mantronix. The pair's flagrantly dance-friendly take on the genre wasn't initially well received by hip-hop's hardcore contingent, but the pinging electronic drum sounds, meaty synth hits, and vocodered refrain of early single "Needle to the Groove" now exemplify electro-tinged hip-hop.
—MP

The Go-Betweens: *"Cattle and Cane"* 1983

Coming relatively early in the Go-Betweens' career, 1983's "Cattle and Cane" was an evocative statement of place from a songwriter raised in rural Queensland, Australia—the middle of nowhere in a country that still consists largely of vast stretches of nothing. The duo of Grant McLennan (chief author of "Cattle and Cane") and Robert Forster initially developed a reputation for literary rock, which was another way of calling them too smart for their own good. In fact, McLennan and Forster first connected over films, so it's little surprise that their songs often packed in as much vivid detail and economical action as a good screenplay.

Music would be their ticket out of Australia, but the subtext of the sentimental "Cattle and Cane" is one of return, a portrait of the artist as a young man getting his first tastes of life and culture without forgetting where he came from. "Through fields of cane / To a house of tin and timber," McLennan's schoolboy trods over a simple but wistful guitar strum and deceptively quirky drumbeat. Many songs stir the imagination, and just as many stir the heart, but few stir both in equal measure. "Cattle and Cane" manages that by transporting listeners to the same time and place as its author—the literal divide between country and city, but also the more mysterious, fleeting gap separating youth from adulthood and innocence from experience.
—JK

The Chills: *"Pink Frost"* 1984

As with most seminal indie labels, New Zealand's Flying Nun Records featured a roster of bands in the early 1980s that shared a common aesthetic: scrappy guitar riffs, post-punky bass lines, rickety rhythms, and an eccentricity borne of being outsiders in a country that's remote. But on the Chills' 1984 single

"Pink Frost," frontman Martin Phillipps redirected those qualities into a much more ominous space. Literally, in fact: For its first twenty seconds, the song skips merrily along on a chiming guitar hook before the sky suddenly goes black.

In that darkness, we find Phillipps meditating over the body of a girl whose death he has seemingly caused. However, the song's tension lies in the mystery of whether the act was accidental or intentional—Phillipps's remorse seems genuine, but his unnervingly calm tenor suggests he's in no hurry to call the cops. The guitars, once so sprightly, become muffled and conspiratorial, while in the second verse, the song's steady drumbeat threatens to roll off-course, echoing Phillipps's loosening grip on his own sanity. As the band's first New Zealand chart entry, "Pink Frost" is not only the song on which the Chills made their name, but in its unrelenting air of coldhearted dread, the one where they earned it, too.
—SB

Felt [ft. Elizabeth Fraser]: *"Primitive Painters"* 1985

This UK post-punk band was led by the inscrutable singer Lawrence, a mysterious English eccentric who, three decades into his career, has never revealed his last name (it's widely believed to be Hayward) and who once fired a drummer for having curly hair. The sound of the band, however, was primarily determined by its key players—first by Maurice Deebank, a classically trained guitarist who shared Lawrence's obsession with the flanged guitar work of Television's Tom Verlaine, and in later years, by future Primal Scream member Martin Duffy and his Hammond organ.

"Primitive Painters" comes from the Deebank era. It's a slice of glistening, reverb-heavy pop that stood in stark contrast to the dark, rhythmic post-punk then dominating the UK underground. "I just wish my life could be as strange as a conspiracy / I hold out hope but there's no way of being what I want to be," Lawrence confesses, one of his frequent attacks on normalcy and common sense. Cocteau Twins' Elizabeth Fraser guests here, and her soaring vocals provide the otherwordly and out-of-reach counterpoint to Lawrence's relatively flat, clenched pipes.
—SP

The Smiths: *"There Is a Light That Never Goes Out"* 1986

If "How Soon Is Now" is how the public remembers the Smiths, "There Is a Light That Never Goes Out" is the diehard's anthem. An obvious lead single from their third album, *The Queen Is Dead,* it was reportedly vetoed because Johnny Marr felt other choices better showed off his guitar playing. He had a point: "There Is a Light" is Morrissey's, a death-wish road song that shows the singer at both his most preposterous and most seductive.

The Queen Is Dead is an album made by a band under severe strain from label unreliability, drug addiction, and reverent expectations. It's no surprise then that Morrissey keeps returning to ideas of escape. "There Is a Light" finds him with bridges burned, begging a beloved other to drive him away.

But once he's in the car, his true intentions become apparent. "If a double-decker bus crashes into us, to die by your side is such a heavenly way to die." Morrissey's pathological horror of taking any action is so complete that even suicide is beyond him. And yet, however absurd it is, the way Morrissey performs it makes it terribly beautiful. The dolorous, hollowed-out quality of his voice is perfect for this song, and he sings it with both care and grace and desperation and spite. The relief in his voice when the double-decker bus comes 'round the bend is wholly convincing. Morrissey has always made great lyrical play of being pop's loneliest man, to often tiresome effect. On "There Is a Light," that claim rings strikingly true.
—TE

Tom Waits: *"Jockey Full of Bourbon"* 1985

The centerpiece of 1985's *Rain Dogs*—Tom Waits's eleventh studio LP—"Jockey Full of Bourbon" is characteristic of the "junkyard orchestra" aesthetic Waits forged and embraced with 1983's *Swordfishtrombones.* By halfway through the 1980s, Waits had ditched the (relatively) straightforward piano balladry of his early career in favor of carny squawking and bizarre, otherworldly instrumentation—an artistic shift that cemented Waits's position as a cult icon and sent hundreds of critics scrambling for new adjectives for "weird."

Still, compare the vocals here to those of Waits's later career and his pipes sound downright staid. Lyrically, Waits has always memorialized outcasts and outlaws, packing his songs with shady, lurking men. On "Jockey Full of Bourbon," it's the kind of guy who swills his liquor from a broken cup, owns two pairs of pants and a mohair vest, and ends up on the lawn with someone else's wife. Waits layers his vocals over electric guitar swirls (churned out by longtime partner Marc Ribot), congas, bass sax, various percussive stutters, and double bass, and while he normally boasts a considerable vocal range, he holds back here, muttering and chanting quietly, submerging his voice in the rhythmic hum of his backing players.
—AP

Bruce Springsteen and the E Street Band: *"I'm on Fire"* 1984

Bruce Springsteen: the Boss, New Jersey poet laureate, man of the people, social activist…sex symbol? "I'm on Fire" isn't about the plight of factory workers or the lasting effects of the Vietnam War or whatever. It's a sliver of quiet lust that snuck into the middle of *Born in the U.S.A.*'s bombast. Lasting only two and a half minutes, without verses or a chorus, "I'm on Fire" finds the thunder of the E Street Band replaced by a gentle, insistent climbing-and-descending rhythm and prodding synth swells. Bruce moans like Elvis in heat: "Can he do to you the things that I do," "At night I wake up with the sheets soaking wet…" Before "I'm on Fire," the men knew. Now the little girls understood, too.
—APh

Scott Walker: *"Rawhide"* 1984

"This is how you disappear": The opening lyric to Scott Walker's "Rawhide" encapsulates the unexpected (and some would say unlistenable) third act in the enigmatic artist's career.

Walker was a 1960s pinup while fronting the Walker Brothers, who, despite being neither siblings nor English, were successfully packaged as part of the British Invasion: The expat trio had a few number 1s in the UK and some hits in the U.S. as well. But in 1967, Walker went solo, taking a detour into left field and recording gorgeous existentialist ballads populated by such unlikely pop-song figures as Stalin, prostitutes, and characters from *The Seventh Seal.* When these offbeat artistic triumphs cost him much of his fan base, he slumped back to the middle of the road and eventually reunited with his former bandmates the following decade.

Walker eventually regained the resolve to go it alone, and his music became even more uncompromising. 1984's "Rawhide" opens with the ominous clatter of a cowbell, and things remain cloudy and off-kilter from there, the singer's operatic, avant-crooner voice piecing together references to cattle and slaughters in a cavernous soundscape. Over the next twenty-three years, Walker would issue only two more proper albums, each more unique and puzzling than the last.
—SP

U2: *"Bad"* 1984

Those with inclinations toward modest indie rock find it easier to rep for early U2: "Well, *Boy* was a good album," they'll say, pointing out that the band's third single, "11 O'Clock Tick Tock," was produced by Factory Records founder and Joy Division associate Martin Hannett. But if you're going to talk about a U2 song, you might as well talk about the U2-iest of them all, and the epic, almost operatic "Bad" fits the bill. It's ostensibly about drug addiction, which might explain its marked structural similarity to the Velvet Underground's "Heroin." But it's really about U2 wanting to become the grandest, most emotionally over-the-top band in the world.

Matching ringing, treatment-heavy production by Brian Eno and Daniel Lanois with the soaring crescendos the band had featured on its previous album, *War,* "Bad" is baldly manipulative but undeniably powerful rock at its zenith. Track down video of the band performing "Bad" at 1985's Live Aid for the clincher; they extend the song to twelve minutes and insert bits of songs from Lou Reed ("Satellite of Love" and "Walk on the Wild Side") and the Rolling Stones ("Sympathy for the Devil" and "Ruby Tuesday"), as if to say, "These are our peers." Soon enough, they'd find lots of people who agreed.
—MR

Don Henley: *"The Boys of Summer"* 1985

Maybe it was a yearning for 1960s idealism that made nostalgia so appealing to baby boomers—or maybe it was just the vast marketing potential. Either way, Don Henley was creeping toward the magic age of forty when he hooked up with Tom Petty guitarist Mike Campbell and wrote "The Boys of Summer." Over a bed of de rigueur synthesizers and primitive drum machines—supposedly an attempt to retain the rough quality of the original demo—Henley reflects on a lost love, but it may as well be a lost era.

"Out on the road today I saw a Deadhead sticker on a Cadillac," he sings. "A little voice inside my head said don't look back, you can never look back." But of course he does. That the song resonates across generational lines testifies to its enduring melancholia and, more practically, Campbell's precisely calibrated anti–guitar heroics, which in some ways refer back to Petty's restless "American Girl." She was optimistic, "raised on promises"; Henley's first-person protagonist, however, is the reverse. He doesn't dare look back because he knows, deep down, that those promises of youth were lies.
—JK

Paul Simon: *"Graceland"* 1986

"The Mississippi Delta was shining like a National guitar." The opening image of "Graceland" shimmers like the steel guitar phrases that precede it. Paul Simon's song is rooted in the symbolic home of his rock and roll roots—complete with the Everly Brothers singing backup—but his backing band is, literally, thousands of miles away, in Johannesburg, South Africa. Simon had traveled there the previous year to record with African musicians after falling in love with their music through cassettes given to him by friends.

At the time, South Africa was still living under the apartheid system and was cut off from the world, but Simon skirted the cultural boycott to expose the sounds of local musicians to an international audience. And so "Graceland" mixes its themes of love, loss, and musical pilgrimage with an *actual* musical pilgrimage, and emerges with a cross between two traditions. The township jive bass, drums, and guitar give Simon a mellifluous, elastic backing as he plays with song form, altering the choruses as he goes, and twisting the verses in unexpected directions. All cross-cultural dialogue should be this effortless.
—JT

Wayne Smith: *"Under Me Sleng Teng"* 1985

One man's novelty can be a whole genre's wellspring—especially in Jamaican music. An engineer runs off a test pressing without a vocal, and dub is born; a keyboardist calling himself Augustus Pablo picks up a plastic toy at a session, and the melodica becomes one of roots reggae's signature sounds. So when producer Prince Jammy miked up a preset rock rhythm on a Casio keyboard for a new record by young dancehall up-and-comer Wayne Smith, he shifted the entirety of Jamaican pop's foundation. Synthesizers were nothing new to the island's dance halls, but after this, everything went digital.

Thing is, Smith doesn't especially sound like he was auguring a new day; he sings "Under Me Sleng Teng" so easily that the blips surrounding him sound like they've always been there. Well, of course: "Sleng Teng" is an ode to weed that's as hypnotized as it is hypnotic; if he sounds slightly robotic, it's for different reasons than the music. In global terms, the major achievement of the song is that it pushed Jamaican music further in the direction of synth-driven black music and dance pop—not to mention mainstream rock at its mid-'80s synthiest. By the early '90s, dancehall and ragga were regularly and casually fusing with hip-hop and R&B. It's hard to imagine that happening without this track.
—MiM

Anthony "Red" Rose: *"Tempo"* 1985

Anthony "Red" Rose began his musical career at an early age, acting as an altar boy in his local parish. After this ecclesiastical introduction to melody, the youngster began to take a more secular path, leading him to spend much of his youth hanging out and learning the tricks of the mic trade with Jamaica's Sir Duncan sound system. Rose cut a number of tracks with his friend Bunny Lee, and the door to dub progenitor King Tubby's studio opened; it was here that he would lay down his biggest hit.

With reggae going through a digital revolution, mid-1980s Jamaica was awash with computerized riddims and the emerging dancehall style. Thus was Rose called on to offer a voicing for "Tempo," a synthesized instrumental that, like Prince Jammy's watershed "Sleng Teng" and "Punnany" riddims, harked back to earlier times. Dub-influenced and adorned with ghostly keys, it provides an ideal backdrop for his relaxed vocal style—Rose calmly confident of his crew's ability to rain murderation down on other "eediat" selectors. Delivered in his soft singjay style, this packs greater menace than shouting ever could.
—*DS*

Model 500: *"No UFO's"* 1985

The most popular DJ on Detroit's most popular radio station, the Electrifying Mojo played a unique blend of '70s funk, Philly Soul, Teutonic rock, and electro-pop. The combination thrilled his audience, and none more famously than the Belleville Three (Juan Atkins, Kevin Saunderson, and Derrick May), a trio of black suburbanites who fetishized and philosophized about the music they heard until they were compelled to make their own. What they created—futuristic music that combined their Europhile fantasies with the tech-driven motorik of industrial Detroit—became known as techno transforming dance music. Saunderson was the commercial, disco-leaning member of the trio and May the master of heart-tugging melancholy—but Juan Atkins, aka Model 500, was the brains, and his influence on techno's evolution cannot be overstated. The Detroit producer started Cybotron in 1980 with his friend Rick "3070" Davis and released proto-techno classics including "Clear," "Alleys of Your Mind," and "Cosmic Cars." Model 500 was an alias that Atkins began using in 1985, the same year that he would launch the key Detroit techno label Metroplex with the single "No UFO's." On this pivotal track, Atkins continued the skeletal electro blueprint established by Cybotron but filled in some of the blanks, increasing both its speed and intensity. Complete with creepy lyrics, Atari 2600–style spaceship sounds, and an apocalyptic bass line, "No UFO's" would become a huge underground hit that made waves worldwide—particularly in Chicago, where the Belleville Three's records would help jump-start dance's other revolutionary post-disco sound, house music.
—*GD*

Chapter Four:
1987–1990

As the 1980s faded, rock went through a mixture of progression, maturity, retreat, and retrenchment. Ronald Reagan and Margaret Thatcher both left office; underground rock in the U.S., which was heard partly as a reaction to the conservative political climate those figures represented, had steadily grown in stature through the decade. Stalwarts like the Replacements and R.E.M. were building a national profile, releasing more commercial-sounding records and making inroads with MTV via *120 Minutes,* the alternative video show launched in 1986.

Indeed, for many fans who came of age during this period, *120 Minutes* was how they heard about new, weird bands that they wouldn't find on the radio—especially if they lived far from a college station. An entire wave of British rock and guitar pop as diverse as My Bloody Valentine, the Cure, the Jesus and Mary Chain, and the Primitives was exploring new textures and finding a new audience. Some of this stuff made its way to a young man named Kurt Cobain from Aberdeen, Washington. He was expanding his musical horizons beyond punk by digging the arty, dynamic soft/loud rock of the Pixies along with the childlike guitar pop of the Vaselines and Beat Happening. His band would record their first album in 1989, but their big break came a little later.

Hip-hop, after a decade in the national consciousness, was quickly maturing as an art form and cultural phenomenon. America's inner cities were beset with a crack cocaine–induced crisis—both the effects of the drug itself and the demographic shifts that came with the ballooning post–"War on Drugs" prison population. New York's Public Enemy and Los Angeles's N.W.A., the two most important rap groups of the time, addressed the situation differently. P.E., styling themselves after the militant black nationalists of the 1960s and '70s,

sought a leadership role, hoping that rap could serve as a conduit for information and activism—as the group's Chuck D termed it, the "black CNN." N.W.A., on the other hand, played both sides of the fence, protesting police brutality one minute and playing off thuggish gangster stereotypes for entertainment value the next. Rap also expanded its sound dramatically; more sophisticated recording technology and fuzzy rules about how the music of the past could be sampled resulted in dense, highly referential collages from producers like the Bomb Squad (P.E.), Prince Paul (De La Soul), and the Dust Brothers (the Beastie Boys).

A different use of technology was finding its footing in clubs. In the first half of the decade, advances in dance music played out in hit records like New Order's "Blue Monday" and Art of Noise's "Beat Box"; by the late '80s, unusual electronic sounds were coming from unknown artists who had internalized those styles and now, thanks to cheaper, more available gear, sought to do something new with them. The epicenter of this music was the Midwest, specifically Detroit and Chicago, home of a more elastic, disco-informed variant of techno that came to be called house. The obscure twelve-inches recorded there, way below the radar, would have a massive impact in the UK and throughout Europe as they mutated into acid house and fueled the burgeoning rave scene.
—*MR*

Mr. Fingers: *"Can You Feel It"* 1987

Bare-bones, rootless, and raw, early house music was created by mostly black and gay Chicagoans who grew up in the home of the Disco Sucks movement. Just as young New Yorkers a decade earlier had repurposed the turntable and transformed the breakbeat into a musical science—creating hip-hop in the process—enthusiastic and mostly untrained Chicagoans, in love with a combo of European synth-pop, Philly Soul, funk, and Italo disco, democratized the music-making process, misusing the TB-303 to create the roots of modern dance music.

In 1986, the labels Trax and DJ International were the major players in Chicago's burgeoning underground house music scene. Trax, in particular, was key in introducing both the minimal sound of track-oriented house and the more soulful, song-oriented house—each grounded by the four-to-the-floor beat that still characterizes the genre today. Among the label's stars was the prolific Larry Heard, also known as Mr. Fingers, who released several classics in the mid–1980s, including "Washing Machine," "Bring Down the Walls," and "Can You Feel It."

That last single was the track that lay the template for an entire house-music movement. Both in its all-encompassing sonic warmth and its uplifting lyrics, it was a rallying cry, an inspiration for the thousands of producers (and imitators) who would follow in Heard's footsteps. And while this song was minimal by economic necessity, the skeletal production had the happy side effect of ensuring the music's longevity. In contrast to much of the overproduced rock and pop music released during the mid-'80s, early Chicago house tracks like "Can You Feel It" still feel timeless and futuristic.
—GD

Rhythim Is Rhythim: *"Strings of Life"* 1987

"Strings of Life" stands as a musical high point for techno. It was an anthem at the time it came out, early in Detroit's reign as a locus for the whole techno world, and it remains the sort of classic that makes dance-music devotees turn sentimental whenever it spins. It's easy to hear why: Opening with an instantly recognizable piano roll, "Strings of Life" marries intense, driving rhythm to seemingly naturalistic flourishes of musicality that grow more and more emotive as the beat builds. The strings are only "seemingly" naturalistic because they're synthesized—sampled from the Detroit Symphony Orchestra—but Derrick May, the Detroit producer behind Rhythim Is Rhythim, owes his legendary status to the case he made for synthesizers as tools with untapped powers to move more than just bodies. One of the wonders of "Strings of Life" is the way it wanders from sets of banging beats to crafty interludes—including one in which the piano pauses to collect itself in a manic fit of contemplation. Then there are the "strings," which play by way of sudden swells and stabs. They sound eerie, euphoric, exalted, and a little bit sad—"Strings of Life," indeed.
—AB

A Guy Called Gerald: *"Voodoo Ray"* 1988

Gerald Simpson was a flat-topped, high-topped Manchester b-boy pop-locking to German synthesizer music and American electro when he joined forces with the duo 808 State. The new trio released its first records just when acid house—a bass-heavy, squelchy, and more psychedelic form of dance music—was staging a loved-up coup on the UK pop charts in 1988. Quickly falling out with the other members over business bullshit, Simpson would rise again a few years later with a gangsta-leaning grudge against whitewashed dance music and a string of genre-defining drum 'n' bass releases. But the anthem that still hypnotizes dancers from Delhi to Dubuque is his first single as a solo artist, "Voodoo Ray," a humid, polypercussive acid-house tune.

Full of snaking, otherworldly synthesizer noises—and yet as comfortingly cool to rave kids as early video-game sound effects—it's as catchy as acid house ever got, with one of the sexiest wordless vocal hooks in all of pop, a giggling girl who coos a shiver-inducing "ooh hoo…uh huh." For one moment, Gerald managed to merge underground dance with pop fun, and England loved it and its acid-house contemporaries enough to make it a sound that challenged the most rooted ideas behind how and why people made or engaged with contemporary music.
—JH

M/A/R/R/S: *"Pump Up the Volume"* 1987

There is no M/A/R/R/S album: They barely existed long enough to make their one and only single, a collaboration between the members of arty British indie bands Colourbox and AR Kane, who'd decided to take a stab at the new school of syncopated club music that was drifting over from the U.S. They released the record under a pseudonym, a nod to the ideal that the heaving mass on the floor was more important than the artist, and that a sort of utopia was within reach there—with the uniformity of house's familiar 4/4 beat serving as both a great leveler and shared foundation.

"Pump Up the Volume" was the first significant house record incorporating the materials of hip-hop—not just the title hook, lifted from Eric B. & Rakim's "I Know You Got Soul," but a pile of snippets from whatever else happened to be lying around: James Brown, the Bar-Kays, the *Wattstax* soundtrack, Public Enemy. The rhythm track is pretty much the doctrinaire house that hip-hop producers had been sampling and scratching for years, and the found-sound effect of a sample of Israeli folk singer Ofra Haza had been anticipated by Brian Eno and David Byrne's *My Life in the Bush of Ghosts*. But "Pump Up the Volume" brought all those ideas together and kept the original and appropriated hooks flying so fast that it sounded like a pop radio hit—which it proceeded to become. For the next few years, most of dance music was in this song's debt.
—*DW*

My Bloody Valentine: *"You Made Me Realise"* 1988

By 1987, after releasing a half-dozen EPs and cycling through a pair of vocalists, My Bloody Valentine were spinning their wheels. The group had been experimenting with combinations of sheets of guitar noise and lilting melodies, but, hamstrung by singer Dave Conway's ill-fitting pipes and a lack of finances, it had failed to translate those dynamics into something special.

Conway soon departed, forcing the band to hand vocal duties over to guitarists Kevin Shields and Bilinda Butcher, whose vocals drew out the group's ethereal qualities. Creation Records boss Alan McGee offered to bankroll MBV's studio dalliances, resulting in the *You Made Me Realise* EP. The first full fruit of what would become known as shoegaze, the EP's title track proved guitar music could engage with, rather than run from, the emerging sounds of acid house and techno. Its pummeling white noise, blended with glimmering melodies, immediately changed guitar rock, placing value on texture and volume rather than melody or riffs. On record, the song is a mere 3:36, with almost a third of it taken up by two sustained snarls of guitar; live, the song could stretch to up to twenty minutes of confrontational noise. Like Public Image Ltd. almost a decade earlier, My Bloody Valentine would merge creativity and emerging technology with the financial backing of a patient record executive and wind up crystallizing an entirely new and distinct sound.
—*SP*

Spacemen 3: *"Walking with Jesus"* 1987

First cut for Spacemen 3's 1984 demos recorded in Rugby, England, "Walking with Jesus" finds singer Jason Pierce trading the prospect of eternal life for the earthbound bliss of drugs and debauchery. Above a well-dosed haze of drums, guitars, and harmonicas, Pierce lands his kiss-off with narcotic vocals as the song ties the buckling drone of the Velvet Underground to the punch-drunk swagger of the Rolling Stones. The 1986 single for Glass Records improved on the demo, thickening the guitars and letting them swirl and smother.

The track's musical obstinacy parallels its protagonist's drug addiction. Jesus has warned Pierce that his sins will cost him in the afterlife, but Pierce considers the advice only when he realizes Heaven may mirror his life on earth: forever getting high and hanging with friends. Still, he needs another hit for now, and he hopes Jesus will understand and grant him that feeling for eternity anyway: "These wings are going to fail me / And I could have done you worse."
—*GC*

Ride: *"Dreams Burn Down"* 1990

Ride's music swirled with the effects-heavy washes of guitar that characterized the nascent shoegaze genre, and they had a more developed sense of songcraft than many of their counterparts. Their secret weapon was guitarist and lead singer Mark Gardener's voice—calm, almost drowsy—which floated and glided even amidst squeals of feedback and overdriven guitar.

"Dreams Burn Down," the slow-burning centerpiece of their first album, *Nowhere,* captures the mix of melodic grace and squalling guitar noise that made Ride so special. The deliberate drumbeat and Gardener's sedate vocals, sometimes joined in close harmony by fellow guitarist Andy Bell, are tossed on a gorgeous ocean of sound. Melodic phrases trickle from the fretboards; the tone of the lead guitar sounds like brushed stainless steel looks. As shoegaze died in the mid-'90s, Ride moved toward more traditional rock with a psychedelic tinge, but it was the band's early albums and EPs that truly cemented its legacy.

—*JT*

Galaxie 500: *"Blue Thunder"* 1989

Galaxie 500 were formed in 1986 by three students at Harvard who shared a love of all sorts of rock that could be traced back to the Velvet Underground (the Feelies, Television, Joy Division, Young Marble Giants), but G500 took the hushed, lyrical side of the band as a starting point and prettified it further by drenching everything in atmospheric reverb. Lyrically, Galaxie 500 drew from the simplicity and childlike outlook of fellow VU acolyte and Massachusetts native Jonathan Richman, whose "Don't Let Our Youth Go to Waste" became the band's most frequently covered song.

"Blue Thunder" can be heard as a dreamy, drugged version of "Roadrunner," Richman's classic ode to the joy that comes from combining a car, a radio, and an open road. In both songs, Massachusetts's Route 128 is mentioned by name, but where Richman sounds heavily caffeinated, escaping loneliness by distracting himself with kinetic motion, Galaxie 500 ride it out it in the backseat, leaning gently on the headrest, bottle of cough syrup cradled loosely in their open fingers. "I'll drive so far away…" Dean Wareham sings in the last line before letting a typically melodic solo seep from his guitar. He doesn't sound like he's escaping anything particularly unpleasant, more that he's looking forward to watching the up-and-down waves of the power lines passing outside the window. Like their heroes, Galaxie 500 knew how to imbue the mundane with a sense of wonder.

—*MR*

Happy Mondays: *"Kinky Afro"* 1990

Happy Mondays were a band of Manchester lads playing grubby funk-pop cut with psych guitar, with frontman Shaun Ryder's voice a slurred dredge across the top. Ryder's lyrics coagulated slang, chat, playground rhymes, poetry, and threats into a bleary stream of half-consciousness. They were a rough, unlikely proposition who nevertheless, at the start of the 1990s, became one of the most fashionable bands in Britain.

The key was acid house, which flipped the magnetic poles of British pop: "There's always been a dance element to our music" became a sheepish interview mantra for indie bands grabbing at the rhythmic brass ring. For the Mondays, it was the simple truth.

"Kinky Afro" is the band in wide-screen—overripe disco strings, sky-kissing guitars, and a chorus line pinched from "Lady Marmalade." It sounds like a group celebrating its success—but then in comes Ryder with one of the great opening lines in pop history. "Son," he leers, "I'm thirty / I only went with your mother 'cause she's dirty." On paper, it's a joke; heard, it's lacerating, a pit of regret. Ryder sings like a man telling the truth for the first time and daring anyone to call him on it.

—*TE*

The Stone Roses: *"She Bangs the Drums"* 1989

Despite a fierce rhythm section, claims of this band's influence on dance music are greatly exaggerated; fellow Madchester group Happy Mondays could groove rings around the Stone Roses. The Roses' hold on UK guitar music, however, can't be overstated: The band hot-wired the classicism of 1960s pop to the adventurism of the post–acid house 1980s, but perhaps their greatest gift was scale and ambition, a willingness to cast off the misconception of indie being equated with failure.

Indeed, while their peers were shoegazing and hiding behind effects pedals, the Roses aimed to be heroes to every last kid in the world, kicking off their self-titled debut album with a song called "I Wanna Be Adored" and closing it with the almost comical boast "I Am the Resurrection." The single "She Bangs the Drums" seemingly shines the spotlight on someone else for a change, but it's

Alleys of the Mind: Techno

A catchall term that means something very specific in context, techno originated as an idea in dystopian Detroit and went on to signal a particular kind of dance music the world over. The semantics of "techno" are less exhilarating than the sound: moody, driving, tense, and robotic.

"Sharevari," **A Number of Names:** Consided by some to be the first techno song, "Sharevari" was made in Detroit in the early 1980s, when a city in economic disrepair turned to fantasies of European fashion and sounds from what would seem to be outer space. The title alludes to the chain of clothing boutiques known as Charivari (the spelling was changed), and the synthesizers seethe with a vintage air of mystery and sadness.

"Clear," **Cybotron:** A mechanistic mood piece with synthetic drums and a monolithic sense of rhythm inspired by Kraftwerk, "Clear" was an early manifesto by Juan Atkins, one of the famed trio of techno inventors known as the Belleville Three.

"Elimination," **Underground Resistance:** The enigmatic Underground Resistance gave Detroit techno a serious makeover with hard, determined sounds and a line of aggressive rhetoric that was both militant and high-minded.

"Sonic Destroyer," **X-101:** A manic track given to speed and the sound of emergency sirens, "Sonic Destroyer" is exactly that—as well as the first single by an act from Detroit to be released on Tresor, the label that built a timely bond between Detroit and Berlin in the early '90s.

"The Bells," **Jeff Mills:** A founding member of Underground Resistance before he ventured out on his own, Jeff Mills made one of techno's most enduring anthems in "The Bells," a contemplative track with a measured mood and a resilient synth riff that proves both haunting and uplifting.

"Energy Flash," **Joey Beltram:** "Energy Flash" was produced by an expansionist producer from New York, but its pummeling beat and whip-crack breaks played into the post-geographical realm of the burgeoning rave scene.

"Losing Control," **DBX:** One of the roots of minimal techno, this spacious banger by Detroit offshoot Daniel Bell distilled an already formalist genre to a series of dashes and dots. A mantric vocal loop intones "I'm losing control," but the track underneath follows its marching orders with austerity and restraint.

"Phylyps Trak II," **Basic Channel:** This cryptically credited track from the German label/stable known as Basic Channel showcases the studious nature of Berlin techno. The beat is minimal and mesmerizing, but the prize is in the touch of dub and the meticulous sound design that would become a touchstone in the age of hard drives and sound files.

"Zu Dicht Dran," **Reinhard Voigt:** Cologne, the small German city that gave rise to such epochal techno labels as Kompakt, was as integral to techno's development as Berlin. This track from 2000 typifies the formative Kompakt sound, with ecstatic fits of energy shooting out over disciplined beats.

"Dog Days," **Matthew Dear:** Among the few Americans to hold sway in a contemporary techno scene gone wildly international, Matthew Dear started out near Detroit and resurrected the idea of the city as something more than a museum. "Dog Days" traffics in skittering beats as accomplished as those made overseas, and Dear's ashy vocals give it a sense of songcraft still uncommon in a realm devoted mainly to functionality.
—AB

a smoke screen. "The past was yours / But the future's mine," Ian Brown sings. And in the late '80s, the Stone Roses did seem to point the way toward a new future for guitar rock—a powerful combination of heart-soaring futurism and spiritual nourishment that helped nudge the underground toward the mainstream in both the UK and U.S.
—SP

Sonic Youth: *"Teen Age Riot"* 1988

It was neither their first major-label album nor a total reinvention. Sonic Youth's shift from free-form noise to gnarly noise-pop had in fact already happened, slowly, over the course of five albums and six years. But 1988's *Daydream Nation* was still the record on which Sonic Youth blew a small subset of young American minds by tangling up their slanted avant-garde past with the enchanted power of pure rock and roll. Sonic Youth bricolaged rock history like cut-and-paste fanzine graphics, until they reached a full-on double album with room for improbable fusions like seven-minute bubblegum pop songs that still came out sounding like ornery combine harvesters in need of an oil change. Or three-minute hardcore tunes with freaky feedback bridges that still should have been hit singles. It was music at home in suburban strip-mall parking lots and abandoned skate parks, whereas their previous music felt best-suited to the death valleys of downtown New York—if not an expressway to hell itself.

With "Teen Age Riot" they even came up with something that people still occasionally try to call an "anthem." The band may even have designed the song as an anthem, at least if you go by the interviews. Except "Teen Age Riot" is far too sardonic, pretty, and poignant to really fit any of the standard definitions of the word. (Plus, anthems tend to have actual choruses.) The funny thing is how you always remember "Riot" as being *slower* than it actually is—maybe it's that dreamy intro where Kim Gordon references the Stooges and the guitars swim in pools of reverb, or the infamous line where Thurston Moore claims it will take the titular riot to get him out of bed, evoking images of sleepy slackers spinning records on a lazy afternoon. But the song is as much of a shit-kicker as anything by the band's more punk-identified contemporaries. Steve Shelley's snares and cymbals fire at hardcore pace, and Moore and Lee

Ranaldo's guitars rev like the Ramones even as they chime like the Byrds. "Teen Age Riot" was the band's daydream—an army of marching, charging feet shouting for the reins of radio to be given over to the indie rockers—made audible.
—JH

Dinosaur Jr.: *"Freak Scene"* 1988

With its roots in hardcore, indie rock earned a rep for being unschooled, but the idea that it spurned guitar heroes was always something of a canard cooked up by critics. Even from its earliest days, indie enjoyed a fair number of virtuosos in its ranks, and none was rougher or more dazzling than a Massachusetts kid with a terminal hangdog expression named J Mascis. Formed in the mid-1980s, Dinosaur Jr. quickly mutated from a rangy grab bag of indie rock styles into a shaggy power trio with a distorted take on classic rock once it became clear that doleful slacker Mascis was actually a guitar god without a stadium.

The fuck-up's lament "Freak Scene," the breakthrough that made them one of alternative rock's advance guard, features Mascis running through every flashy trick in his fakebook—from a splayed version of New Order's glossy jangle, to thunderclap power chords, to shredding that would do a fleet young Eddie Van Halen proud. And that's all in the same solo. But rather than just a showcase for Mascis's chops, "Freak Scene" also perfects the mumbly, adorably introverted quality that was Dinosaur's other gift to indie rock (and a curse in the hands of those using it to hide a lack of tunes behind walls of hair and noise): a life philosophy that could be summed up with a shrug and a goofy smile.
—JH

Butthole Surfers: *"Human Cannonball"* 1987

The deranged Texan tribe called Butthole Surfers was like a psychedelic circus in concert. Skinny hick Gibby Haynes tore out a warbling drawl, spaced-out guitarist Paul Leary shook demons from his skull, and a (supposed) brother-sister drum duo pounded out robotic beats, while a maelstrom of fire and nudity engulfed them all. The absurd antics sometimes obscured the Surfers' singular music, much the way

the sex-change operation films they projected onstage made audiences avert their eyes. Too bad, because the band's early albums fuse drugged-out rock, tranced rhythms, and tales of giddy psychosis into a sound that hypnotizes, with or without visual hijinks. "Human Cannonball" strings all of the primal Surfers elements into séance: Opening with the siblings' tribal/industrial thud, it marries Leary's whining, brain-burrowing guitar perfectly to Haynes's desperate, LSD-addled cry. "Pardon me, I'm only bleeding / But you cut me to the bone," he screams as he melts into the surrounding noise, turning an elegy to spurned affection into a hallucinatory nightmare. The Surfers' brain-damaged flame burned too bright to last, but "Human Cannonball" still singes.
—MM

Pixies: *"Where Is My Mind?"* 1988

When they first emerged, the Pixies came on like total weirdos, but their soft verse/loud chorus dynamic, looping riffs, succulent tunes drenched in violent sonics, and stream-of-fucked-up-consciousness lyrics would set the template for 1990s alternative rock.

The hidden genius behind "Where Is My Mind?"—and the Pixies' first full album, *Surfer Rosa*—was audio engineer Steve Albini. At the time, he was mostly known as the frontman for the hyper-abrasive, recently dissolved Chicago trio Big Black, but 4AD Records boss Ivo Watts-Russell paired him with the Pixies, and guitar bands have lined up ever since to get *that* sound. Formally, "Where Is My Mind?" is a pretty straightforward pop song, but Albini recorded it as a mix of brutal audio verité and psychedelic fever dream. David Lovering's drum kit sounds inches away from your face, the rusty electric guitar part keeps lunging forward and dropping out of range, and Black Francis's raw whine is so precisely captured you can almost feel the veins straining inside his throat.
—DW

Fugazi: *"Waiting Room"* 1988

On Halloween 1981, *Saturday Night Live* hoped to convince alumnus John Belushi to cameo and deliver the signature "Live from New York" line from a urinal. Belushi conditionally agreed—if L.A. punks Fear played the show and NBC bused in authentic slam dancers. To gather this fan pit, Belushi turned to punk documentarian Penelope Spheeris, who suggested Ian MacKaye, teenage frontman of Washington, D.C.'s Minor Threat. MacKaye wrangled a troupe of moshers to Manhattan. To pass Rockefeller Center security, the punks whispered a code phrase: "Ian MacKaye." For millions, that broadcast was their first exposure to hardcore. Across the Studio 8H stage, as Fear bashed "Beef Bologna," Ian MacKaye and John Belushi stomped in a textbook Huntington Beach strut. See? Ian MacKaye, progenitor of the straight-edge movement, *does* have a sense of humor. Yet for some, the barrier to enjoying MacKaye's music remains its perceived bureaucratic asceticism. Young MacKaye screamed of "seeing red" while preaching abstinence and sobriety. Overlooking the sarcasm in songs like "Cashing In," legions of teens converted to the dogma. Head shorn and shirtless, MacKaye looked like a crusty monk.

MacKaye made efforts to change his image, along with the rest of the D.C. scene. In the summer of 1985, dubbed "Revolution Summer," the close-knit musical community devoted itself to mellower, more melodic projects and positive activism, in response to rising skinhead thuggery and tightening Reaganomics. MacKaye emerged with the New Wave–inflected Embrace. He also recorded the debut LP by Rites of Spring, featuring Guy Picciotto, who melded poetic romanticism with cathartic performances. Picciotto eschewed practicing, saving energy and instruments for fourteen total performances. Typical of the D.C. scene, both bands imploded.

For his next project, Fugazi, MacKaye set out to make it last. "Waiting Room" served as the mission statement, demolishing any notion that the band would be just another project with "the guy from Minor Threat" and random remoras. The motivational-speaker lyrics promise, "I won't make the same mistakes." Musically, "Waiting Room" sounds like an exaggerated compromise between Revolution Summer and straight-edge. The rhythm section plays loose, double-time reggae while MacKaye's guitar grits like teeth and screams through the chorus. Picciotto, who joined the group late, hoped to become a toaster or hype man in the tradition of Public Enemy's Flavor Flav. "Come on and get up!" he cries. Picciotto wearing a clock: In hindsight, that seems pretty funny, too.
—BD

Audio Two: *"Top Billin'"* 1987

Not that any record featuring the line "I stole your girl while you were in prison" needs further justification, but "Top Billin'" would be a classic for its beat alone. Audio Two MC Milk Dee put that beat together with a Roland drum machine, a guitar pedal that only sampled two seconds of sound, and a copy of the Honeydrippers' 1973 breakbeat masterpiece "Impeach the President." He also claimed that Stetsasonic's Daddy O added "his final touch," which is pretty astonishing, given that the record has nothing on it except rapping, drums, and some echo—maybe that last part was Daddy O's touch.

If it was, Daddy O was right: This song's Run-D.M.C.-meets-Eric-B sound makes it the quintessential b-boy anthem. Its reconstituted rhythm track would power hits by everyone from Mary J. Blige to 50 Cent, and Milk's gleeful boasts are a font of countless samples to come.
—*MiM*

Eric B & Rakim: *"I Know You Got Soul"* 1987

The original rapper's rapper, Rakim growled slyly like the world's smoothest linguistics professor. While contemporaries partied and bragged, he was ruthlessly analytical about his rhymes—their forms, their patterns, their meanings. With a poet's mind, a jazzbo's subtlety, and a hip-hop heart, the MC didn't need to yell to make his point. And with Eric B distilling the essence of funk with a strutting, cutting Bobby Byrd break, Rakim could freely contemplate without compromise.

The man commonly referred to as God MC gives a thinking mic fiend's tutorial to rapping on "I Know You Got Soul," a song that would inform the careers of countless disciples, including Jay-Z and Nas. The key was a savvy combination of lyrical depth and rope-chain swagger. "I'm not bold just 'cause I rock gold / Rakim is on the mic and you know I got soul." Precious metals can be bought, sold, faked, and pilfered, but soul—from James Brown down—isn't as easy to come by.
—*RD*

Public Enemy: *"Rebel Without a Pause"* 1988

"Some say no to the album, the show / *Bum Rush,* the sound I made a year ago." What Chuck D means is that *Yo! Bum Rush the Show,* Public Enemy's first album, released a few months before this terrifying single—and an album that altered the way people thought of hip-hop as music—is now ancient history, a mere rehearsal for what he has in store for us. This is classic musician hype: The next one is going to be really different; we've reinvented our sound. But Chuck D meant it. P.E.'s producers, the Bomb Squad (Hank and Keith Shocklee, Eric "Vietnam" Sadler, and Chuck D), transformed sampled horns from James Brown and Miles Davis into something that sounds like a cat being murdered over the beat from JB's "Funky Drummer," EQed for maximum clatter.

On their early records, Public Enemy's politics were as ad hoc as everything else they did, and on "Rebel" they're hit-and-run signifiers whose impact is amplified by their speed, agility, and dead seriousness. (Even Flavor Flav is relatively somber here. That's *relatively.*) In the middle of a song whose ostensible subject is what a badass lyricist Chuck D is, name-dropping imprisoned activist Joanne Chesimard (aka Assata Shakur, Tupac's aunt) might have jarred—but because the rest of the record jarred, too, it fit right in. "Rebel Without a Pause" is a declaration of war on the status quo, which at that time in rap was changing constantly. No matter: Chuck D thought Public Enemy could do more with the form than anyone else, even Eric B & Rakim, whom Chuck later cited as the primary inspiration for this song.

Public Enemy made four great albums in as many years, based on the idea that noise and rhetoric are as important as beats and rhymes. Only the Wu-Tang Clan has attempted anything like what P.E. accomplished on as large a scale—the enlarged posse with each member a specialist—and they kept politics out of it. But the directness, insistence, and squealing, constant hook of "Rebel Without a Pause" still makes most of P.E.'s peers sound like an afterthought.
—*MiM*

N.W.A.: *"Straight Outta Compton"* 1988

The snarling attitudes and chopped funk of "Straight Outta Compton" are old hat now, but at the time of its release the sound of a furious black quintet from Los Angeles was terrifying to America's prissiest constituents. For rap fans, it was a hosanna from the nation's most notorious hood. Then-unknown producer Dr. Dre opened the track with the ominous proclamation "You are now about to witness the strength of street knowledge." But what followed was filled not just with knowledge but with passion and violence, humor and technical prowess.

Ice Cube, the chief articulator of modern urban discontent, makes his debut; crew member MC Ren offers a crude, methodical diatribe after Cube's boiling blasts; and group founder, financial backer, and bon vivant Eazy-E delivers an allegedly ghost-written verse that is neither artful nor pithy, but rather gleefully decadent ("Eazy is a brother that'll smother your mother") and full of the manic enthusiasm that made N.W.A. more than just the "World's Most Dangerous Group." Later, West Coast brethren like MC Eiht, Spice 1, and even an Ice Cube–less incarnation of N.W.A. would take the group's formula to even more intense extremes.
—*SF*

Nick Cave and the Bad Seeds: *"The Mercy Seat"* 1988

By the time of 1988's *Tender Prey,* Nick Cave's fifth album with the Bad Seeds, the theatrical depravity of his earlier group, the Birthday Party, had given way to a considerably more refined and nuanced style. That's not to say that Cave had mellowed, exactly. For evidence, one need look no further than "The Mercy Seat," the harrowing death-row confessional that has since become his signature track.

Embodied by Cave with characteristic *Night of the Hunter* authority, the narrator of "The Mercy Seat" is a spellbinding force of righteous conviction and garbled theology. He forcefully proclaims his innocence and truthfulness, and then casually reveals that his "kill-hand is called E-V-I-L." To his mind, the electric chair that awaits him is the same biblical Mercy Seat that once adorned the Ark of the Covenant and will—guilty or not—provide his passage to salvation.
—*MMu*

Ministry: *"Stigmata"* 1988

Ministry frontman Al Jourgensen started his career as the kind of makeup wearing, New Romantic synth-popper that plenty of his later fans would have laughed at. Through the mid-1980s, though, he spent his time drawing everything grim and nasty out of his sound and, increasingly, shoving it in your face. Amazingly enough, by the beginning of the next decade, Ministry would stand next to fellow travelers Nine Inch Nails as the pop figureheads of industrial music: a dark, aggressive, and mechanistic clanging that, at its most accessible, would soundtrack the brooding of pissed-off, mall-haunting middle-American teenagers for years to come.

"Stigmata" is the propulsive terror that started Ministry's rise, and it's built on precisely the trick that's sustained industrial, goth, and metal forever: Who'd have guessed that music this curdled and antisocial would be so *fun*? The drum track is built to sound like it's beating you in the kidneys. When Jourgensen's voice enters fully—screaming—it's so distorted and trebly that it sounds like a chainsaw being started (as does nearly everything else in this song), and that's still less unsettling than his later goblin whine about eating his own fingers. These people are going way over the top to convince you they're the sickest trolls on the dance floor, and all you want to do is grab some power tools and join them.
—*NA*

The Jesus and Mary Chain: *"Head On"* 1989

The Jesus and Mary Chain's William and Jim Reid had trouble holding onto bassists and drummers, so here they enlisted drum machines and synth bass in the service of fist-pumping rock. "Head On" keeps ascending until it can't reach any higher, and by the time it gets to the line about blowing the stars from the sky, it sounds as if it might do just that.

The emotional ambiguity of the lyrics is important. "Head On" could be about love, freedom, happiness, anger, a chemically induced state, or any other feeling, but the fact is that it sounds like it's written for your current state of mind no matter how you're feeling. It was the opening shot in a sort of second act for the band, proving that the Reid brothers had

more than just one great noise/pop trick up their sleeves and setting the stage for the band's 1990s output, which varied from crushingly loud, feedback-drenched rock to melodic, largely acoustic road music.
—JT

The Sugarcubes: *"Birthday"* 1987

Where the hell did this come from? Once listeners collected their jaws from the floor and did a bit of hunting, the answer turned out to be Iceland; on first listen it may as well have been Neptune. With hindsight, we now know "Birthday" sprang forth from Björk, one of most enigmatic and singular artists of the post-punk era. But equally important here are her former bandmates, the Sugarcubes, whose skewed, playful take on the Anglo-American underground had precedent in the beauty of Cocteau Twins and the ugliness of Public Image Ltd., though the neck-turning "Birthday" certainly leans toward the former.

Percolating with echoing chimes, deep booming percussion, and a woozy, Theremin-like glide, this glistening single is still at its most magical during a wordless chorus from *that* voice. Originally released in 1986 as "Ammæli," the group re-recorded it with English-language lyrics, and it swept through the UK and U.S., helping the band make unlikely mainstream inroads via *Saturday Night Live* and a full concert broadcast on MTV—introducing millions to the pixieish, playful singer with a siren's call for a voice.
—SP

The Cure: *"Just Like Heaven"* 1987

You never quite recover from the breathless way Robert Smith sprints into the opening lyric of "Just Like Heaven." But the real trick is how this anthemic pop song remains true to the Cure's high-contrast approach (Smith's guttural wails scrawled across clean, strong guitar hooks) while replacing the band's usual gothic dread with gleeful, ecstatic reverie.

Fittingly, the song's lyrics are Romanticism 101: In the final lines, Smith's dialogue with his muse is revealed to be a solitary cliffside daydream, leaving him staring down at the waters "that stole the only girl I loved / And drowned her deep inside of me."

The intimate opening exchanges may only have been a hallucination, but the sunset glow of the song's cascading guitar and keyboard parts set the scene with such tangible clarity it felt real. Whether rendered as wobbly psych-rock by Dinosaur Jr., plucked at an adult-contemporary crawl by Katie Melua, or piously cloned by AFI, the original recording has withstood its well-deserved barrage of worshipful covers with stoic indifference.
—DD

Morrissey: *"Everyday Is Like Sunday"* 1988

After the Smiths broke up in 1987, Morrissey needed to prove he could go on without guitarist Johnny Marr. In 1988, the flamboyant singer's first post-Smiths single, "Suedehead," did just that. With its follow-up, "Everyday Is Like Sunday," the Pope of Mope consummated in a single track so much of what had already come to endear him to his cultlike fan base—theatrical misery, yes, but also self-mockery, soaring melody, and a delightfully ambiguous chorus.

The song describes an English resort town, probably during the off season, but Moz has remained characteristically coy about further details. Whether the town is Mablethorpe, which the Nazis really "forgot to bomb," or whether Moz was influenced by poet John Betjeman's similarly themed "Slough," what's most affecting is our narrator's loathing for the silent, gray everyday—and, as he pleads for nuclear Armageddon, himself. Like the Smiths' earlier "Heaven Knows I'm Miserable Now," the song is also an example of Moz toying with his sad-sack reputation, presaging the (accurate, irrelevant) charges of self-parody he would continue to face. Aptly windswept production by Stephen Street and guitar flourishes by Durutti Column mastermind Vini Reilly achieve a lonely grandeur unmatched by Morrissey's later backing bands.
—MH

The Pogues [ft. Kirsty MacColl]: *"Fairytale of New York"* 1987

The Pogues are a study in excess: The tempos were too fast, the lyrics too dense, the drink and drugs too copious. Not that principal songwriter Shane MacGowan ever gave a shit what anyone else thought, which doubtlessly lent him the confidence to conjure up a ballad (with bandmate Jem Finer) as enduring as

"Fairytale of New York." The group had convened with noted producer Steve Lillywhite, who helped them piece together *If I Should Fall from Grace with God,* and it was his then-wife, Kirsty MacColl, who eventually handled covocals as a substitute for recently departed Pogues bassist Cait O'Riordan.

MacColl proved the perfect foil for MacGowan, her sass a great match for his slurring. "You're an old slut on junk," snarls MacGowan, one half of a bickering couple on Christmas Eve. "You scumbag, you maggot," chirps MacColl in response. This is where, in the movies, the fighting couple would fall into each other's arms. "Fairytale," the song, remains unresolved, but you can't help suspecting these two bitter but sentimental souls will reconnect before the night is through. After all, better to be stuck with someone you no longer like on Christmas Eve than to be left with no one at all.
—JK

The Wedding Present:
"My Favourite Dress" 1987

The Wedding Present weren't just a 1980s British band—they *were* 1980s British indie, pared down to its everyday essence and constantly releasing singles. The high-speed jangle of their electric guitars made punk sound smarter and more celebratory; their casual tunefulness had the self-deprecating joy that collegiate indie kids demand. And the everyman singing of bandleader David Gedge—the clenched-teeth grumbling of a guy who's too pent up to shout—has remained captivating for decades. He sounds live-wire frustrated, eternally annoyed with himself, and more than clever enough to get you grumbling with him.

But the women of the world should give thanks that every man is not David Gedge, who fills his songs with the petty, craven thoughts left unsaid in the minds of lovers. "My Favourite Dress" is less hyper and buoyant than most early Weddoes singles, and the lyrics sink to match. "Jealousy is an essential part of love," announces Gedge in the third line. And then the song seethes, just barely repressing a tantrum, until he explains why: He's seen his girlfriend out with another man, "a stranger's hand on my favorite dress."
—NA

The Field Mice: *"Emma's House"* 1988

Heart meet sleeve: The Field Mice were the flagship act on Sarah Records, the UK indie label that defined the tiny, bedroom songcraft beloved by legions of indie-pop kids. Detractors called the Sarah bands shambling, amateurish, and fragile, but those qualities made them seem even more human and real to their legions of devotees.

In innumerable delicate songs about falling in love, breaking up, pining, courting, yearning, and just plain hurting, the Field Mice took a painter's eye to young love, examining familiar emotions and sights from every possible angle. "Emma's House," their debut single and an early Sarah release, is a jangly tale about memory and loss. "Emma's house is empty / So why do I call it Emma's house?" Bobby Wratten wondered it aloud, and thousands of heartsick kids filled in their own answers.
—SP

Another Sunny Day:
"You Should All Be Murdered" 1989

"Twee" was once exclusively an insult: It meant tacky, childlike, much too cute. But every slur eventually finds someone to wear it with pride, and in the late 1980s, a group of mostly British bands discovered that donning barrettes—figuratively and sometimes literally—was a way to rebel against the oppressive machismo of rock, and often a way to make anger and despair more interesting. Sarah Records was the epicenter and epitome of twee: a tiny (or at least modest) British independent label built around a handful of bands who specialized in seven-inch singles with gently chiming arrangements; the gauzy, monochromatic imagery of English scenes; and blinding rage in the guise of tender little songs about aching hearts. The act that embraced the Sarah aesthetic most fully was Another Sunny Day, aka Harvey Williams, who also had a hand in a bunch of other Sarah bands (including the better-known Field Mice). Williams sings here in a breathy murmur about every class of person who's hurt him—and how he plans to slay them all one of these days—until, halfway through the song, he trails off his list of grievances and lets his guitar express his repressed fury more boldly.
—DW

The Dead Milkmen: *"Punk Rock Girl"* 1988

A sometime novelty act with a topical range that extended about as far as a Philadelphia front yard, the Dead Milkmen were as much a rite of punk-rock passage as they were a functioning rock band. Understanding their irreverence and opposite-of-sex-appeal was the first step toward grasping punk itself for many suburban skaters, who from 1983 on would learn how to slag off various midlevel authority figures (like parents and bullies) from Milkmen songs like "Takin' Retards to the Zoo" and "The Thing That Only Eats Hippies." The band's crowning achievements included the college-radio conquering "Bitchin' Camaro," a jazz/hardcore/spoken-word ode that mocked the Doors, AIDS, and every local boy's favorite roadster—and "Punk Rock Girl," a day-in-the-life portrait of an underfunded punk courtship that takes place in the record shops and cafés of downtown Philadelphia.

This strident localism—not to mention the off-key, regionally accented singing, the insistent plugging of punk peer Mojo Nixon, and a Beach Boys interpolation—was unlikely material for success. But "Punk Rock Girl" was beloved in odd corners: MTV, where it was mocked by early-1990s cultural arbiters Beavis and Butthead; and Major League Baseball, whose Jim Walewander, then a Detroit Tigers infielder, was so attached to the group that the "obscure punk-rock band" was name-checked on the back of his baseball card.
—*ZB*

The Primitives: *"Crash"* 1988

By the late 1980s, scrappy, shambling indie bands had infiltrated the tape decks of a whole lot of English kids—but so had a much more polished version of the same sound. The Primitives, like a lot of their peers, were still riding on the brash energy and noise of New Wave punk. But like Blondie and the Ramones before them, they filtered that energy into a shiny, cartoon vision of pop music's early-1960s heyday, full of handclaps and na-na-nas: Between their striped shirts, leather jackets, Wayfarer shades, and singer Tracy Tracy's bottle-blonde haircut, they may as well have stepped straight out of an Archie comic. These were the Monkees of indie, the fake greasers with the badges on their lapels.

And "Crash" is their one masterpiece: exactly two minutes and thirty seconds long, full of big hooks and zoomy New Wave guitars, burnished to a high studio shine. It has the energy of a puppy and some of the same ungainly, big-eyed charm—except that the Primitives are so cutesy cool, laying back behind their shades and singing, "Shut your mouth / 'Cause I'm not listening anyhow." It cuts back to the basics of guitar pop until you can imagine nearly anyone playing it: Buzzcocks or the Jesus and Mary Chain, Debbie Gibson or Avril Lavigne, the Fonz and Pinkie Tuscadero or Frenchie from *Grease*.
—*NA*

The La's: *"There She Goes"* 1990

The La's' sole hit single is best appreciated in the context of their self-titled debut album. Amid the Liverpool quartet's scuffed-up skiffle and frontman Lee Mavers's Merseyside Morrisseyisms, its gilded glow and simple structure—no verse, all chorus—sound like the product of another band entirely. The song's luminous refrain places it squarely in the jangle-pop pantheon, alongside the Byrds' "Turn Turn Turn" and Big Star's "September Gurls." But its shimmering surface belies the song's true antecedent: the Only Ones' 1979 signature "Another Girl, Another Planet," another track that quantifies passion with images of blood and veins, raising the question of whether love is the drug or the drug is love. Similarly, the heroin subtext of "There She Goes" can be read two ways: as either black humor or an ominous harbinger of perfectionist (and rumored drug addict) Mavers's retreat from the music industry.
—*SB*

They Might Be Giants: *"Birdhouse in Your Soul"* 1990

Nowadays, synthesizers have renovated their image enough to be seen as instruments of cool, a sly nod to a fashionable retro-futurist past. Yet this redrafting of history washes away the subset of synth culture where the instrument was the musical symbol of nerdishness—Casio enthusiasts as demographic overlap with physics majors and Trekkies. "Birdhouse in Your Soul" portrays the forgotten world where synth players were more Bill Gates than Brandon Flowers, basement experimentalists toying with MIDI patches and build-it-yourself Moogs. Sure, there's also a mathy

Are You Scared to Get Happy?: Twee Pop

Does rock music need to be cool? Or tough? Or sexy? From the first amateurish blasts of UK indie pop to the "twee" subculture of the 1990s, there's always been a streak of bands who had fun answering "no" to that question—and making homemade pop as defiantly sweet, childish, or vulnerable as they wanted.

"I Don't Want to Be Friends with You," **Shop Assistants:** For some people, it's easy to forget that the UK's twee and indie pop bands descended directly from the uncute world of punk. If you run into any of those people, play them this amateurish little fuzz-bomb—a three-chord, hand-clapping race that has "RAMONES" written all over it, from the title on in.

"My Broken Heart," **Tiger Trap:** It's hard to think of a better way to describe this Sacramento band than "rebelliously girly." Songs like "My Broken Heart" bring glitter-covered notebooks and sweet melodies together with a DIY punk rumble that's flat-out tough.

"Three Star Compartment," **Heavenly:** Here, the best songwriters (and most popular crushes) of UK twee launch into what they do best: bouncy, singsong guitar pop with a verve that's anything but amateurish and a lyric sheet that's anything but innocent. Peter Momtchiloff's guitar work beats out a lot of bands who take themselves far more seriously.

"Bewitched," **Beat Happening:** Twee isn't all cute, especially when you're dealing with the primitive pop of Beat Happening. "Bewitched" is sinister: big blurts of fuzzy guitar, the stomp of the tom drum, and Calvin Johnson blaring "I've got a crush on you" in a way that kind of makes you wish he didn't.

"Your New Boyfriend," **Rocketship:** Rocketship's Dustin Reske was the twee kid who thought most about production, always carefully kicking up new tricks in sound. "Your New Boyfriend" is peppy sweetheart pop, but buried in layers of fizzy organs and overexcited guitar strumming—no surprise this was released on the same label as some early Stereolab singles.

"Yoga," **the Pastels:** A later track from Scotland's indie-pop kingpins the Pastels, who stumble through songs with a lazy grace that's always a treat. "Yoga" is a homespun drone, and the Pastels' peculiar way of singing—a kind of stoned Scottish drawl—fits it perfectly.

"Coach Station Reunion," **the Field Mice:** The most staunchly wimpy band in the UK twee world—they dressed like librarians and wrote songs about being sensitive—turn in a dreamy, smiling slice of the '60s: Chiming and sighing, "Coach Station Reunion" seems like it should be a cover of an unreleased Monkees song, shelved on grounds that it "lacks edge." The Field Mice make that the whole point.

"Boys Don't Matter," **Blueboy:** They're as defiantly fey as the Field Mice, but with an elegance fit for a cabaret and lyrics that poke in more adult directions—a group for the coziest wine bar in the world. "Boys Don't Matter" is so gentle it makes songs with drums seem cruel.

"100,000 Fireflies," **the Magnetic Fields:** Back in the Magnetic Fields' early days, this track was a staple for twee mixtapes. As usual, Stephin Merritt's lyric writing grabs the spotlight, even from Susan Anway's lips: "You won't be happy with me / But give me one more chance."

"Pristine Christine," **the Sea Urchins:** This slice of happy retro turns out to be one of the gems of '80s British indie. Never mind being fancy or looking forward: These guys sort out the core definition of "guitar pop" and gleefully race through it.
—*NA*

guitar in there, but the rest of the song is a pure slice of early keyboard tech: a tone that approximates an organ like Pong approximated tennis; a stiff, metallic drum machine; and–yikes, is that supposed to be a trumpet during the bridge? Even the lyrics, focused as they are on Argonauts and the Longines Symphonette (a name for old Texas Instruments calculators), are every bit as dweeby as the song's creators, who are always at their best when they let their geek flag fly. Maybe "Birdhouse in Your Soul" is the high school yearbook photo the synthesizer would rather forget, but for the rest of us it's a welcome reminder of the instrument's awkward phase.
—RM

Superchunk: *"Slack Motherfucker"* 1990

Prospective employers should be thankful Superchunk frontman Mac McCaughan became his own boss at Merge Records, the label he cofounded with bandmate Laura Ballance in 1989. Who could feel comfortable hiring the kid who wrote *the* refrain of the indie-rock service industry: "I'm workin' / But I'm not workin' for you"?

This track excelled for two reasons. First, McCaughan has a history degree from Columbia University. This isn't about art-class apathy or idealism or escapism; it's ultimately about the takeover, the coup of the clever. It's pragmatic, understandable resentment for a stopgap job and the inept manager who considers smoking strenuous. And second: In just under three minutes, two coiled guitars and an unrelenting rhythm section give that eager annoyance a razor-sharp gleam. Your boss may hate this song, but he will crank it.
—GC

Fugazi: *"Merchandise"* 1990

From anyone else, "Merchandise" would be unbearably heavy-handed and hypocritical. But Fugazi weren't any other band, and lyrics like "merchandise keeps us in line" and "you are not what you own" make a lot more sense coming from a band who famously refused to sell T-shirts at its concerts. The relentlessly anticommercial lyrics of "Merchandise" (and the album *Repeater* as a whole) can be overwhelming, but Fugazi's uncompromising approach pays off in the music.

Repeater shows them delving deep into their hardcore roots while expanding on the dynamic post-punk of their first two EPs. On "Merchandise," Ian MacKaye and Guy Picciotto's guitars trade off percussive stabs, providing an angular counterpoint to Joe Lally's round and melodic bass line. This sophisticated, high-contrast musical interplay would inspire legions of second-rate imitators, but the bands who were truly paying attention understood that it was Fugazi's originality that was worth emulating, not their exact sound or ideology.
—ML

The Jesus Lizard: *"Mouth Breather"* 1990

Formed in Chicago from the ashes of Scratch Acid and Rapeman, the Jesus Lizard continued those bands' relationship with the Touch and Go label, a seminal imprint that cut fifty-fifty handshake deals with its artists and helped establish the sounds of American hardcore and indie rock. On albums such as *Goat* and *Liar,* the Jesus Lizard reveled in odd time signatures, a cavernous and drone-y atmosphere, and shit-kicking punk rock. The powerful, revved-up groove of "Mouth Breather" heaves with crunchy guitar, jazzy fills, a huge bass, and singer David Yow's drunken, Nick Cave–like rage emerging from a muscular, guitar-driven blur.

The Jesus Lizard were also among the most compelling live bands of their time: The confrontational Yow stalked the stage, occasionally ending up stark naked, baiting the crowd, and making his asshole sing—all while managing to get his parts right. It was a fitting visual articulation of their swaggering cow-punk noise rock.
—BS

Slick Rick: *"Children's Story"* 1988

No chorus, no breaks, no lyrical hooks—just an intro, an outro, and one massive verse from Ricky Walters, coolly rattling off rhymed couplets about a teenage thug who robs the wrong guy and ends up getting plugged. When Slick Rick turned up in 1985 on Doug E. Fresh's "La Di Da Di," he had a sound like no other rapper—a nasal drawl with a thick British accent. His first album of his own, *The Great Adventures of Slick Rick,* went platinum on the strength of his cruel little narratives of power, sex, and party-rocking, and this tossed-off-sounding performance was its urban radio hit. "This ain't funny so don'tcha dare laugh," Walters mumbles, but his stance is pure sangfroid: Death is nothing to his rapper persona, and the

only time he lets on how pleased he is with his own mastery is when he pulls off especially tricky rhymes. Slick Rick's career got derailed shortly after *The Great Adventures* by attempted-murder charges, immigration troubles, a prison bid, and a string of undercooked records, but his flow and his attitude are still everywhere in hip-hop—the character voices and one-man call-and-response on this track alone set the template for Eminem's whole career.
—*DW*

Gang Starr: *"Just to Get a Rep"* 1990

The duo of Boston-born rapper Guru and Houston native DJ Premier did New York rap with fervent purism despite being out-of-town transplants. Gang Starr had a sort of Platonic ideal of rap in mind, a straightforward but nuanced union of sure-footed rhymes and clattering beats, and they spent a decade and a half working to get as close to that ideal as possible. They often hit their marks, and they always made it look easy: Guru's unhurried monotone had a way of bleeding deep into Premier's beats. And those thick, organic beats had a surgical precision that easily justified Premier's classicism. On "Just to Get a Rep," he chops up a burbling loop from experimental synth pioneer Jean-Jacques Perrey's "E.V.A." and a stray vocal snatch from N.W.A.'s Eazy-E, while Guru calmly rattles off a cautionary tale about a wannabe gangster. It could've been a well-meaning but toothless public service announcement—rap has certainly had plenty of those over the years. But Guru's dispassionate narration and Premier's virtuosic panache and perfect timing turn it into something else: a work of such intuitive grace that it transcends its subject matter.
—*TB*

Rob Base and DJ E-Z Rock: *"It Takes Two"* 1988

If you were drawing breath anywhere near a radio in the summer of 1988, you couldn't escape "It Takes Two." Built around a two-second loop of James Brown yelping in the background of Lyn Collins's 1972 single "Think (About It)"—as well as a sung hook from the same song that helped create the template for rapper/singer collaborations—it was a hip-hop hit and an unstoppable dance track that crossed over to mainstream audiences. It went platinum, a rare feat for a single, but stalled at number 36 on Billboard's

pop chart and number 17 on the R&B chart. Why? Well, that had to do with its label, the New York indie Profile Records. At the time, both radio and sales charts were based on what stations and stores reported was selling—which was largely based on a widely abused honor system, easily influenced by major-label money and clout. In the wake of NBC's 1986 report on "the new payola" (and Senator Al Gore's threat of a congressional investigation into radio promotion), it was still possible then for indie-label records to claw their way onto the American airwaves, but the historical documents of what people were listening to were another matter.
—*DW*

Salt-n-Pepa: *"Push It"* 1987

An Amazonian makeover of the same heavy-breathing-as-hook principle that propelled Kraftwerk's "Tour de France," Salt-n-Pepa's "Push It" works minimal components to serious party-rocking effect. Sprinkled with stutter-sampled announcements that "Salt-n-Pepa's here!" some wedding-DJ-worthy ad-libs ("this dance ain't for everybody, only the sexy people"), and gender-flipped lyrics, there's a loopy, whatever-works quality to Cameron Paul's production.

The song had a humble origin—a remixed B-side to the group's "Tramp," an afterthought olive branch to the dance floor. It was eventually slapped onto later pressings of their debut album after it began taking over pop radio. Growling like Etta James, Salt-n-Pepa's charismatic flow upstages the skeletal drum machines backing them, and it's their forthright kiss-me-you-fool assurance that make this a landmark moment in hip-hop. Other female MCs came first, but Salt-n-Pepa had heavier beats and a light-raunch pop flavor that prophesied the Lil' Kims and Foxy Browns who followed in their wake.
—*DD*

Beastie Boys: *"Hey Ladies"* 1989

After the novelty success of *Licensed to Ill,* the Beastie Boys didn't seem headed for a long-haul career, so their follow-up knocked naysayers sideways. With the aid of the L.A. production team the Dust Brothers, they whipped up *Paul's Boutique,* the cleverest montage of samples and snaps anybody had yet devised. Its first single, "Hey Ladies," dovetails snatches of more than a dozen

other songs more fluidly than any DJ could behind the trio's nonstop, delirious cascade of arcane pop-culture jokes ("I got more hits than Sadaharu Oh!"), trash talk, and old-school rap tropes. (You'd never guess from listening to their flow that hip-hop had evolved since 1982—which is why you'd also never guess that from most subsequent rap-rock, which picked up the Beasties' chalky yelping without their sense of humor.) The rest of the group's career has followed in the path of *Paul's Boutique* and its exhibition of their eclectic tastes, and they spent most of the 1990s as tastemakers and barometers of cool: Mike D parlayed their cachet into a label and a magazine (both called Grand Royal); and mullets, vintage sneakers, Spike Jonze, and Tibetan liberation all picked up cultural currency from being associated with the group.
—DW

De La Soul: *"Me Myself and I"* 1989

Once misread as a novelty, the Long Island rap trio De La Soul's best-known song and first hit is an altogether different sort of individualist anthem— unlike previous rap hits, it's not boastful, just self-assured. Annoyed by the floated notion that they were rap's "hippies," members Posdnuos and Trugoy (DJ Maseo rounded out the trio) don't shout or scream their indignation at being labeled "flower children." Instead, they blithely state facts: "Proud, I'm proud of what I am," raps Trugoy. It's a confident nobility that blends seamlessly with what was then an unconventional approach to rhyming: unselfish and fiercely intelligent.

Even alongside A Tribe Called Quest and the Jungle Brothers, De La Soul were the most challenging and witheringly hilarious group in the Native Tongues enclave. Their debut, the sprawling *3 Feet High and Rising,* sounds uninterested in traditional album structure; in fact, the group invented the now much-maligned rap "skit." But "Me Myself and I," an idiosyncratic, schizophrenically composed production, courtesy of unofficial fourth member Prince Paul, is pop-ready, buoyed by an irrepressible sample from Funkadelic's bouncing "(Not Just) Knee Deep." It became the group's biggest hit—plainly delivered, sharply drawn, and imbued with a righteousness devoid of preening.
—SF

Biz Markie: *"Just a Friend"* 1989

There's something incontrovertible about the dopey charm of Biz Markie, dubbed the Clown Prince of Hip-Hop by his peers, thanks to a gently oafish demeanor and a mouth that sounds like it dribbles saliva with each syllable spent. He earned his rep beatboxing for artists like Roxanne Shanté and Big Daddy Kane on producer Marley Marl's Cold Chillin' label, and later as a goofy wordsmith all his own. But his biggest hit, while silly in its own way, is also a sad song. It's a classic, uncomplicated story: Boy meets girl, boy likes girl, boy gets heart torn out. His paramour initially insists there's no one else, but at song's end Biz catches his lady *in flagrante* and is left scorned. What lifts it is the surprising sung chorus. Biz howls "You! You got what I need!…Oh baby, you!" in such a pained tone it's difficult to tell if he's lampooning heart-stricken troubadours (he donned a Mozart wig while banging on a piano in the song's video) or reappropriating their style for a hip-hop audience. It later became a sort of shorthand joke tune, but the sampling of Freddie Scott's similarly themed 1968 hit "You Got What I Need" is a knowing move: Biz may have been funny, but this clown was crying on the inside.
—SF

Public Enemy: *"Fight the Power"* 1989

Public Enemy had a long, hot summer in 1989. In May of that year, as the group was on the verge of its popular peak, anti-Semitic remarks attributed to "Minister of Information" Professor Griff appeared in the *Washington Times*. P.E. Leader Chuck D temporarily disbanded the outfit, yet soon unapologetically rehired Griff under a different job title, reigniting tensions and drawing the worst sort of attention to a group with otherwise positive convictions. At the same time, however, "Fight the Power" was in theaters as a signature anthem in Spike Lee's *Do the Right Thing* and on the radio as a single. A stunning combination of D's stadium-sized sermons, Flavor Flav's wiseass provocations, and Terminator X's atomic sonic montages, "Power" reestablished the group as the right kind of Public Enemy: The kind that affirms that doing "the right thing" can mean creating a new crop of villains, those who emerge when American social history is told by the losers; the kind who call Elvis a "straight-up

racist" and tell John Wayne to get fucked while crafting one of music's most forceful and controversial statements of African-American political identity.
—EH

Guns N' Roses:
"Welcome to the Jungle" 1987

The opening riff of "Welcome to the Jungle" is staggering in its simplicity—a single note, repeated, then run down over and over again as if someone's revving up a car for a long-awaited trip out of a personal hell. Axl Rose's opening "Oh, my God" only adds to the walls-closing-in feeling, those three syllables a sign that whatever was going on was worth a quick escape. What would follow—certainly in the next four minutes, as well as in the rest of the band's 1987 salvo *Appetite for Destruction*—was a portrait of Los Angeles as a bed of hedonistic delights that were available to all, or at least anyone who had the "money, honey."

Rose's lyrics hint that '80s Los Angeles fame wasn't all ingenue-sipped Schrafft's milk shakes and red-carpet glitz—there were debts to be paid, some with blood, some with sex, and all of them probably overdue. And dredging up this dark side of Los Angeles worked so well for the five G'N'R members because they seemed to be intimately acquainted with the sleaze—not tarted up in pentagrams like their Sunset Strip compatriots Mötley Crüe or menacing old Uncle Miltie like Ratt, but actually *grimy*, like they'd been dipped in whatever sludge was running through the sewers before crawling onstage at the Whisky. The transformation of Axl Rose in the video for "Jungle" from a wheat-chewing hayseed who boards a bus for L.A. to a hair-sprayed sex-and-violence hellion was no doubt an echo of his own post-Indiana transformation (though it's hard to think he was ever *that* naïve).

In the years that would follow, the band inevitably became a coopted caricature of the angry outsider—the rotating cast of rock lifers, the cameos with Elton John and Michael Jackson, the years of labor that puffed up and bloated *Chinese Democracy*. But on "Jungle," Rose's caterwauling, the blistering lead laid down by Slash, and the pummeling, snarling beat came together to create a picture of Los Angeles that was as terrifying as it was electrifying.
—MJ

Swans: *"Beautiful Child"* 1987

Emissaries of New York's fertile early-1980s downtown scene, Swans captured the stink of the decaying city and the cancerous underbelly of Reagan-era America. Unlike many of their peers, they did so without adopting theatrics or sanctimony; instead, singer Michael Gira addressed themes of power (filtered through sex, violence, faith, and the workplace) in a disconcerting first-person howl that seemed less a cry of protest than a helpless embrace of amorality.

Early records, with titles like *Fifth, Cop, Greed,* and *Holy Money,* were pure No Wave brutalism, all short, sharp shocks and reverberant clang. By 1989's *The Burning World,* Swans had begun to explore acoustic instrumentation and tangled baroque arrangements, along with increasingly humanist themes. "Beautiful Child," from 1987's *Children of God*—a turning point in their evolution—sounds like the last gasp of the Swans of yore. Opening with a series of gunshots over an oil slick of backmasked guitar, it quickly extends into a sheet of tribal drumming and hardscrabble detuned guitar, echoing the muscular blur of their peers Sonic Youth. Gira sings of his love for the titular tot, first caressing and then vowing to kill him, before concluding, "This is my only regret / That I was ever born." Hell isn't other people: Hell is inside each of us, and "Beautiful Child" is an elevator drop straight to its core.
—PS

John Zorn: *"The Sicilian Clan"* 1989

Some artists thrive in New York City by meeting the greats and rubbing shoulders with living legends; others stay for the archives and stores, where you can find any old record, crucial text, or Asian S&M film ever made. While composer, saxophonist, and born-and-bred New Yorker John Zorn shared stages with such late-1970s greats as DNA's Arto Lindsay and producer/bassist Bill Laswell, he spent as much time revisiting music history as making it. Starting in 1988, his supergroup Naked City—featuring such rising downtown improvisers as guitarist Bill Frisell, drummer Joey Baron, and art-rocker Fred Frith on bass—gave him the perfect vehicle.

Much of Naked City's repertoire included real or imagined movie soundtracks, from John Barry's James Bond themes to *Heretic,* a wholly improvised

erotic film score. "The Sicilian Clan"—from Ennio Morricone's work for the 1969 gangster movie of the same name—sets a scene through music, as Zorn's film noir sax smokes over Frisell's shifty guitar. While some elements, like the guitar tone, remain faithful to the original, the buzzing synths offer a different take on its wistful humor. Zorn's first high-profile release was his tribute to Morricone, *The Big Gundown*, which he almost titled *Once Upon a Time in the Lower East Side*. With "The Sicilian Clan," he once again modernizes the arrangement without knocking Morricone's spirit off its pedestal.
—*CD*

Prince and the Revolution:
"If I Was Your Girlfriend" 1987

In the 1980s, Prince was writing and recording songs far faster than he could release them. Among them was an album's worth of material intended to be issued under the name Camille—an oversexed, erotically ambiguous character Prince created by speeding up his voice. On the surface, "If I Was Your Girlfriend"— salvaged from the Camille sessions and issued on 1987's *Sign "O" the Times*—may be the most gender-fucked song a major artist has ever recorded, but it's more about relationship dynamics than drag fantasy: Prince wants to expand his role in his subject's life to being her bosom buddy, too. His arrangement mirrors the idea of sexual fluidity: Every instrument is treated and tweaked, bouncy and oozing, and Prince's stratospheric falsetto is underscored by hairy-chested harmonies. *Sign "O" the Times* was Prince's moment of being so securely on top of the world that he could get away with this kind of thrown-down gauntlet. He's still a provocateur, but his provocations don't often come from his records; instead, he's spent the '90s and '00s as a symbol, a self-imposed exile, a master without another masterpiece.
—*DW*

Madonna: "Like a Prayer" 1989

The climax of her incredible first decade as a performer, Madonna's "Like a Prayer" is pop culture at its most sublime. In the video, directed by Mary Lambert, Madonna went self-consciously controversial, changing her hair color, forming a pietà with a black Jesus (thus literalizing her name), and dancing nearly naked in front of burning crosses, her cleavage, like the Red Sea, barely parted. "I'm

down on my knees," Madonna sings, "I wanna take you there." This mashup of Catholicism, carnality, and civil rights lost Madonna a lucrative Pepsi sponsorship, but it inspired heated debate among parents and pastors and elevated the singer even further into the rarified realms of supercelebrity.

Of course, Madonna going gospel *sounds* like a terrible idea, right up there with her soundtrack to *Dick Tracy* or her beast-with-two-metal-hardbacks *Sex* book. But the music has outlived the controversy. Vacillating inventively between an angelic major key and a perverse minor key, Madonna gives one of her most exuberant performances, her vocals carried heavenward by percussionists Paulinho da Costa and Luis Conte as well as a joyful choir.
—*SD*

Deee-Lite: "Groove Is in the Heart" 1990

So this was one path the 1990s were going to take: A group with eclectic tastes and varying backgrounds (Kiev's Super DJ Dmitry Brill, Tokyo's Towa Tei, and New York's Lady Miss Kier) reaches back to disco, jazz, and funk and reassembles it into a limitlessly catchy house anthem, throwing in some hip-hop while they're at it. The disco originates from the relentless Latin percussion and Kier's classic diva vocals, which are slyly coquettish and, during the chorus, sleekly ecstatic. The jazz comes from *that* bass line, a nimble appropriation of the hopped-up groove from Herbie Hancock's *Blowup*-scoring number "Bring Down the Birds." The funk is covered by JBs/P-Funk alumni, with Bootsy Collins augmenting the bass line in his own inimitable way and Fred Wesley and Maceo Parker providing a terse but integral horn riff. And A Tribe Called Quest's Q-Tip brings the hip-hop, supplying a midsong rap breakdown that, while energetic and lyrically out there, is comparatively deadpan amidst the Technicolor revelry.
—*NP*

Pet Shop Boys: "Being Boring" 1990

They were two men in their thirties—a music journalist and an architecture student—who formed a pop group. At first they refused to play live, and in their rare TV appearances both were near motionless. One stood frowning over a keyboard; the other sang cynical lyrics in a dry, educated voice. Remarkably, they became stars, mixing synth-pop and club music, and scoring hit upon hit.

After four years of success, the duo wrote "Being Boring," singer Neil Tennant reflecting on how exactly his dreams came true. The PSBs warm and deepen their sound with padding drums, stardust keyboard flourishes, and gentle wah-wah figures, lending Tennant's singing an unexpected intimacy. He tells how he "bolted through a closing door" as a teenager, grabbed his opportunities, and reaped the rewards. His pride has a sad edge, though: "All the people I was kissing, some are here and some are missing in the 1990s." Tennant is gay, and several of his most moving songs can be heard as documents of how AIDS decimated a community. But the resonance of "Being Boring" goes beyond specifics and grows, the older you get. Every life story sees a change of cast; every boast worth making must also be a testament.
—TE

Sinéad O'Connor:
"Nothing Compares 2 U" 1990

In 1990, when Madonna's "Vogue" and Janet Jackson's *Rhythm Nation 1814* were ascendant, and before grunge had established a support system for alternative acts, Sinéad O'Connor's second album, *I Do Not Want What I Haven't Got,* couldn't help but stand out. Here was a beautiful, bald, angry Irish woman singing about motherly passions and police brutality over soft strums, hip-hop beats, and Celtic fiddle. Her voice could cut as easily as it could comfort, and its unpolished quality only heightened the anguish, especially on her cover of Prince's "Nothing Compares 2 U," which would be her only major hit.

Over a bed of strings and a stoically steady drumbeat, she compresses every stage of grief into five minutes: defiant when she sings "I can eat my dinner in a fancy restaurant"; accusatory on "Tell me, baby, where did I go wrong?"; and desperate whenever she repeats the title phrase. Yet her greatest gift is restraint: O'Connor lets her voice rise and fall tenderly and intuitively, a subtle progression that has more to do with old soul tracks than with anything else from 1990. Eventually, O'Connor became as unglued in real life as she was in the song—after her infamous *Saturday Night Live* stunt, tearing a picture of the pope on TV, she spiraled into a series of poor artistic and commercial choices—but "Nothing Compares

2 U" was her moment of clarity, and it was strong enough to fuel a long, uneven career.
—SD

The Orb: *"Little Fluffy Clouds"* 1990

Sometimes jokes give birth to genres. DJs Alex Patterson and Jimmy Cauty started "ambient house"—dance music with the beats taken out—as a conceptual gag in a London club. Then they realized it actually worked. "Loving You," a rambling early Orb single, was a twenty-minute sampler of their club set. For "Little Fluffy Clouds," they cut the length, tightened the focus, and discovered a new kind of playful beauty.

The track is built on an extended sample of a Rickie Lee Jones interview. It's hard to fathom quite what prompted interviewer LeVar Burton to ask "What were the skies like when you were young?" but pop owes that interchange a debt. The Orb cut and loop Jones's evocative answer, taking her charming hesitancy and turning it into dreamy babble. Synthesizer lines weave around her words like chains of flowers and then ground the track with a comfortable dub bass line that stops it from slipping too far into tweeness. Even so, the whole thing is dumbfoundingly pretty—though Jones apparently hated it and threatened legal action. The Orb went on to a brief and unlikely stardom, but they never made anything this coherent—or lovely—again.
—TE

The KLF: *"Wichita Lineman Was a Song I Once Heard"* 1990

Ambient music's 1970s pioneers made music that could pay off equally as background and foreground. What the KLF realized is that all pop music already works that way: The song you half-hear drifting from a store radio can grab you as easily as the one you reserve for severe headphone contemplation. So their ambient *Chill Out* album blends snatches of well-worn hits with road and rail noise, TV chatter, steel guitar, and electronic drift, all patched into a fictional nighttime road trip through the Southern United States.

These were places the British band had never been, but theirs was always a gestural art, ranging from the notorious (burning a million pounds on film) to the tiny (naming this track after a song that isn't referenced

within it). Instead of "Wichita Lineman" itself, the KLF replay their own hit, "Last Train to Trancentral," with its surging rave-music arpeggios turned into a beautiful four-a.m. ache. It's the one moment on *Chill Out* that can stand apart from its parent album, but let it sneak up on you as part of the whole and it's a sublime peak. The entire record is a dream that pop is having about itself, and this is the sunrise moment when it struggles awake.
—*TE*

808 State: *"Pacific State"* 1989

In the summer of 1990, the New Music Seminar, a music-business conclave in New York, hosted a contentious panel called "Wake Up, America—You're Dead!" The topic was how the new generation of dance music had totally failed to ignite in the U.S. the way it had in the UK and Europe. At the time, 808 State, a Manchester group named after the Roland TR-808 drum machine, briefly looked like it might break instrumental techno in a big way. They had an actual frontman (former rock musician Graham Massey); they had something like stage presence; and even better, they had a single with a big pop hook. "Pacific State"—aka "Pacific," aka "Pacific 202," etc.—was so clever that even people who weren't on ecstasy could dance to it: billowing synth chords, a triplet gallop that owed something to the New Jack Swing sounds coming out of the States, squelchy acid-house noises, and a four-note saxophone melody that pivoted like a picket-fence gate. 808 State have soldiered on ever since, but it's "Pacific State" that's now remembered as the anthem of a thousand raves—at least in Britain. It never quite caught on in America, which just kept sleeping.
—*DW*

Orbital: *"Chime"* 1989

Orbital's "Chime" straddled two decades in more than just the figurative sense. Originally created for fewer than £100 and released on the short-lived Oh'Zone label in December 1989, "Chime" was picked up by FFRR and rereleased in March 1990, where it hit the UK Top 20 and became one of rave's biggest crossover anthems.

Recording from his synths and his brother (and future collaborator) Phil's drum machine onto his father's tape deck, Paul Hartnoll took melodies

commonly associated with chiming clocks, staggered out the tones into staccato refractions, and laid it all over a warm analog sound bolstered by a tirelessly propulsive rhythm. The result was a euphoric techno masterpiece that drew on electronic dance music's recent past—you don't have to strain hard to hear the influences of early-'80s synth-pop, electro, or late-'80s acid house—and defined its future.
—*NP*

Depeche Mode: *"Enjoy the Silence"* 1990

It stands as a testament to both their prolific output and their willingness to remain on top of contemporary musical trends that British synth-pop pioneers Depeche Mode had their biggest transatlantic hit a decade into their career. It came at the ideal time: The concept of "modern rock" was just starting to take off, and the sounds and signifiers of industrial music and rave culture were bleeding over onto the pop charts. "Enjoy the Silence" could be synth-pop's finest moment, thanks in part to those influences; the gothic, minor-key synthesizer choir, burbling bass line, and sweeping orchestrations combine to form an epic arrangement that shows how far both the band and electronic pop in general had come since the canny simplicity of their 1981 hit "Just Can't Get Enough." Ironically, the composition is so intense and intricate that the lyrics are almost an afterthought—which is kind of funny, considering they're all about the tendency for words and communication to get in the way of affection. But even with the sentiments in the chorus ("Words are very unnecessary / They can only do harm"), it's hard to imagine this song being complete without Dave Gahan's vocals, brooding and anxious and lovestruck all at once.
—*NP*

My Bloody Valentine: *"Soon"* 1990

It was just after 1990 that rock music started being declared dead again. This didn't mean that rock was dead—it never does—but it was a pretty good sign that rockers needed to cope with the new sounds and subcultures, from hip-hop to electronic dance music, that were steadily demolishing the notion that rock was Just What Kids Listened To. My Bloody Valentine were only one of a parcel of British bands who were interested in reconciling guitar music with

Nanofads: From Grebo to Glitch

It would be easy to attribute the quick turnover of recent musical trends to the disposability of our accelerating digital culture, but most of these missteps predate the Internet and MySpace, and goddam emo has lasted longer than *Cheers*. No, these cul-de-sacs have more in common with the catwalk, as bungled microgenres splice subcultures into clashing hybrids like tube tops and tuxedo pants. Looking back, the two most common kisses of death when creating your new genre would be the suffixes -core and -billy. So, on paper, billycore will sell as well as…well, a Billy Corgan solo album.

Grebo: It sounds like a *Star Wars* prequel villain, but this genre pimpled in the early '90s from England's Midlands. Silly band names, such as Ned's Atomic Dustbin, Gaye Bykers on Acid, and Carter the Unstoppable Sex Machine, were a must. The look included dreadlocks, partially shaved heads, jackboots, and baggy military clothing. So, actually, it *was* just like a *Star Wars* prequel villain.

Digital hardcore: The entire genre centered around one band, Atari Teenage Riot, who earned critical hosannas with little more than a cool name. Their brand of computerized thrash heated up enough buzz to get a bunch of related acts signed to the Beastie Boys' Grand Royal Records. The label went out of business a few years later.

Happy hardcore: This accelerated techno raced with rodent-pulse drumbeats and fittingly lived about as long as a rodent in the care of meth addicts.

New Wave of the New Wave: Starting out the gate alongside Britpop with the Fierce Panda label's initial release, the *Shagging in the Streets* compilation 45, these leather-clad rockers simply got steamrolled by acts waving the Union Jack.

Cow punk: Honestly, it would be foolish to assert that the concept of country-tinged punk was merely a passing trend. Yet the moniker "cow punk" lasted months. The whole thing empirically crumbled, we're thinking, because contemporary Minneapolis punk band Cows were not cow punk. It was either that or the torn consciences of vegan guitarists.

Psychobilly: More a Halloween costume than a music genre, psychobilly acts dressed like zombie truck mechanics. Other failed "-billy" products include butterbilly, the breakfast spread that came in a faux pomade can, and Rubberbillies, the gabardine prophylactic.

Nu rave: On November 1, 1976, shortly before the release of the first single in this book, chemist Richard Van Zandt of the American Cyanamid Company filed U.S. patent number 4,064,428 for his "Chemical Light Device." The glowstick, as old as punk rock, has endured as a recurrent accessory for gaudy club trends. Of course, after they break, these genres tend to last as long as the plastic tube's luminescence.

Paisley underground: Illiterate Indian farmers put ink on the side of their fist and stamp it to walls to announce the time of harvest. The symbol became a textile motif, exported by Her Majesty's soldiers back to the Scottish weaving hub of Paisley. During the Summer of Love, maharishi-minded psychedelic bands applied those yins and yangs to guitars and blouses. Fashion is seasonal, and naming a musical movement after the paisley worked as well as OshKosh folk. Even the genre's biggest band, the Bangles, were named after jewelry.

Mathrock: The real tragedy of mathrock's brief lifespan is the absence of mainstream proliferation and spin-offs, which could have led to geometry funk, vector metal, and combinatorindie.

Glitch: Remember when Grandma first got e-mail and Photoshop and your inbox suddenly was filled with pictures of a schnoodle run through brush effects and garish color adjustments? Yeah, sometimes people get really excited about computers.
—*BD*

the giant leaps happening around it, and they had the good fortune to make their efforts before this stuff became a huge issue: For them and their peers, the samplers and electronics in the studio were just a fresh world of technology to leap into. But "Soon," one of the band's last singles, still stands as one of the most interesting and assured collisions to come out of the whole period.

"Soon" may not actually be dance music, but it certainly had its ear to the ground. These seven minutes roll along on the same type of sampled breakbeat that was driving electronic music's UK adolescence, and they bury the blocky chord changes you'd expect from a pop tune; instead, they lope by in a head-bobbing trance, thick with repeating, looping textures, as if they're playing to chill-out rooms at parties that won't be thrown for years. What's exciting is just how naturally MBV are able to fold those things into their usual blur—even after a terrific remix from dance maven Andrew Weatherall, this wasn't rock, or dance, or MBV-doing-dance, but just "Soon."

It finished off *Loveless* perfectly, with the promise that this band was ready to leap even further past its contemporaries than it already had. The years of unproductive silence that followed were surely better for their legacy: Listening to "Soon" is like watching a man jump seven feet in the air, then having the film cut off while his momentum is still carrying him up, up, up.
—*NA*

The Vaselines: *"Son of a Gun"* 1987

In the 1990s, the Vaselines got a boost thanks to their number one fan, Kurt Cobain: The short-lived Scottish outfit did a one-off opening stint for Nirvana, and Sub Pop reissued much of the band's material in 1992, with the shambolic sunshine of their first single, "Son of a Gun," sliding seamlessly into college-rock playlists. The nursery-rhyme melody, placed on big puffy clouds filled with just-out-of-tune guitar, was of a piece with the lovestruck indie pop of the time. But like much of that genre, its simple declarations of being head-over-heels in like were keenly deceptive. On the surface, "Gun" is a simple love song with declarative lyrics comparing the singer's always-shifting moods to the weather, with a female voice serving as a gender-balancing counterpoint to the

unfolding crush story. But not only do the repeated lyrics betray the monotony of infatuation, the frequent use of the word "gun" implies that this relationship may not be so healthy.
—*MJ*

Beat Happening: *"Indian Summer"* 1988

It's the song that's been described as "indie rock's 'Knockin' on Heaven's Door'"—the one everyone's covered. It probably doesn't hurt that it's very easy to play. Beat Happening, after all, were barely even a trio: Just two boys and a girl from Olympia, Washington, one bashing out rudimentary drum patterns, one plucking out three-note guitar parts, and another singing in the low, booming voice of a guy who was not quite a "singer." They were amateurish, sure, but there was also a mile-wide streak of dark energy and big emotion coursing through their primitivist pop. At its best, their music felt vital and defiant—more punk than any tough guy's screaming, and inspiring enough to justify all of the American "twee" bands for whom they would serve as godparents.

"Indian Summer" is one of the vital ones, as grand and rousing an elegy as can ever be milked out of so few notes: one guitar pattern chiming like church bells, one drum tapped like a funeral march. For three hushed minutes, they're gathering force, becoming more gripping with repetition. And so is Calvin Johnson's voice, which conjures up a love among orchards and abandoned farms, constantly circling back to the same vow—"We'll come back for Indian summer"—before accepting the aftermath: "then go our separate ways."
—*NA*

Daniel Johnston: *"Some Things Last a Long Time"* 1990

It's easiest to fall for Daniel Johnston's songs when you know his history—the lifelong struggle with mental illness, the time spent recording on tape recorders in his brother's garage, the girl he fell in love with in college and hasn't forgotten about for decades since. And so, while a lot of guys have written weepy songs about staring at old photographs, there's stuff in Johnston's biography, and in his voice, that lets you know exactly how much he means this one.

Truth is, no matter how much his mental illness, amateurish recordings, and lisping, yelping voice get him pegged as an "outsider" artist, Johnston is as much a student of pop music as anyone. He's soaked up songs from the Beatles and Bob Dylan to Elvis Costello and Hank Williams, and he writes earnestly—often cleverly—about the kinds of struggles common to everyone. You can hear this in the gentle chords of "Some Things Last a Long Time," and in the gathering sentiment behind them. You're listening to a man who's been robbed of the ability to function independently—a man who's never had much of a shot at finding love—and here he sits at a piano, calmly coming to grips with the passing of time and the incredible, awful weight of memory.
—NA

Mudhoney: *"Touch Me I'm Sick"* 1988

Smart-assed and scuzzy, Mudhoney formed in 1988 after the breakup of Green River, a Seattle rock band that included folks who also went on to play in Mother Love Bone and Pearl Jam. Mudhoney's sound—a repetitious, ultra-distorted blend of punk and metal with detached, howled vocals—was formative in the development of grunge; in fact, the band's guitar-toting vocalist Mark Arm is sometimes credited for coming up with the term.

"Touch Me I'm Sick" was the band's first single and has since been appended to an expanded edition of the group's debut EP *Superfuzz Bigmuff*—whose title offered a perfect description of the band's sound and the tools they used to get it. (The "Big Muff" in question is a distortion pedal for guitars.) *Superfuzz* was a big seller for the Seattle label Sub Pop, leading to the signing of similarly murky bands like Nirvana and Soundgarden. On "Touch Me I'm Sick," Arm's screeching and raw vocals, garage atmospherics, and distortion rock into a Stooges-style roar, dealing with sickness, alienation, and self-loathing: "I feel bad, and I've felt worse / I'm a creep, yeah, I'm a jerk," he moans, creating the template for the alt-rock 1990s in the process.
—BS

Pixies: *"Wave of Mutilation"* 1989

The first couplet of "Wave of Mutilation" is adapted from "Cease to Exist," a song Charles Manson wrote for the Beach Boys; the second is inspired by a 1989 news item about suicidal Japanese businessmen stepping on the gas and driving off into the deep blue sea. Amidst the roaring punk triumphalism of the Pixies' canonical *Doolittle* LP, this is a flat-out anthem. "Mutilation" is two minutes of violent, melodic glee.

A minor hit upon release, *Doolittle* would come to symbolize the transitional moment between the low-wattage moniker "college rock" and the focus group–tested, post-*Nevermind* commercial designation "alternative rock." In the process, the Pixies—along with Sonic Youth, Dinosaur Jr., and Fugazi—served as the culmination of '80s punk and hardcore. If bands can be measured by their disciples, the Pixies rank with the Velvet Underground, and the comparison extends from there. Over a short span of time, both groups fused high art with lurid, dark subject matter and novel musicianship in fascinating new ways; several years later, everyone else finally caught up.
—EH

Chapter Five:
1991–1993

The Lollapalooza festival that kicked off in 1991 strove to be its era's Woodstock. It toured the country annually, and claims that it was *the* festival of the early '90s bear up when you consider the itinerary: It brought the leaders of the newly coined and soon-to-be mainstream grunge movement onto the same bill as hip-hop acts like A Tribe Called Quest, industrial stars like Ministry, and Japanese noise artists like Boredoms. Side attractions included the Jim Rose Circus Side Show— featuring the Amazing Mister Lifto, who lifted weights from a genital piercing—and the Shaolin monks, who made their first trip to the U.S. just to kickbox for hipsters. The generation that had as many political beliefs as gas station shirts could all find something to dig at Perry Farrell's traveling festival.

The main stage boasted legends like George Clinton and Sonic Youth, and alt-rock upstarts like Rage Against the Machine. The second stage pushed underground acts such as the Flaming Lips closer to the mainstream, which was half the point of alternative rock: to make money. Nirvana's breakthrough validated the punk-bred and rebellious rock that was hidden on college radio in the late '80s. Rap also continued to prosper, with the rise of the positive Native Tongues collective and the decadent birth of West Coast gangsta rap. Underground bands could get a deal—but if they didn't take the bait, the grunge behemoth gave them something to react against, while college radio—(and Lolla's side stage) kept cheering them on.

In 1994, Nirvana was slated to headline Lollapalooza— and then Kurt Cobain committed suicide. To some, Cobain's death sounded a knell for alternative: After all, Nirvana's rise was supposed to save rock, and Cobain's suicide seemed to come at least two albums too early. Yet business went on as usual. Alternative stations kept spinning records in the space between Top 40 and those left-of-the-dial stations that had steered clear of the whole ruckus. And the kids who decided they liked industrial or hip-hop kept buying those records or moved on.

Garth Ennis's *Preacher* comic book series parodies the Nirvana phenomenon through a weak-willed young man who survives a self-inflicted shotgun blast to the face and is so disfigured, he's referred to as Arseface. His reason for the suicide attempt is childish: "Nobody cared." Lollapalooza taught Generation X the power of choice—the choice to enjoy any genre, to follow any movement that had a good pamphlet or a cute activist at the sign-up table, to pierce any part of your body, and to gawk at Shaolin monks. There was no movement—just a celebration of options that were exploding even before the World Wide Web gave everyone a virtual Lollapalooza that ran year-round. And if you still got bummed and blew your head off? Well, that was your choice, too.
—*CD*

Nirvana: *"Smells Like Teen Spirit"* 1991

It's the Song that Broke Punk, the incantation about self-despising entertainment that turned a dead-end Aberdeen kid into a supernova, the very last rock song everyone could rally around. (Check out the video of its first public performance on the *With the Lights Out* DVD; as soon as the drums kick in, the whole room learns how to levitate.) But the closer you listen, the more it sounds like straight pop. That four-power-chord sequence that never ever changes? It's got the rhythm from Boston's "More Than a Feeling," but it's not a riff anyone had heard before. If you'd asked one hundred Sex Pistols/Ramones wannabes how F-Bb-Ab resolved, one hundred of them would've told you it goes to C, duh. Kurt knocked the world on its ass by choosing Db instead. Turn up "Teen Spirit" even louder and the noise goes fractal, exposing the overdubs and high production values, and revealing the apotheosis of punk-rock authenticity as a magnificent simulation—better than the real thing could ever be.
—DW

Pavement: *"Summer Babe"* 1991

When it comes to 1990s mainstream rock and its quickly diminishing returns, all roads lead back to grunge. But when it comes to 1990s indie rock, all roads lead back to *Slanted and Enchanted.* Pavement's 1992 debut album has been cited as the origination of the "lo-fi" movement, the "slacker" aesthetic, and the widespread turn to irony in the underground music scene. But Pavement were never a band to take their sound too far in any one direction; paradoxically, their disinterest in the trappings of innovation made them a key touchstone. They didn't draw on a pool of influences all that different from those of their peers, but they were the first band to let so many different ideas and approaches stand in fractured and unresolved contrast. If Pavement can be credited with one seismic shift in alternative music, it's a move from the single-minded arty earnestness of college rock to the postmodern multiplicity of 1990s and 2000s indie.

Though they always made records on their own terms and at their own pace, Pavement never subscribed to the hard-line anti-industry stance of the do-it-yourself movement, instead forging an ethos that could best be described as "do it regardless." Malkmus and

Pavement cofounder Scott "Spiral Stairs" Kannberg released several seven-inches before they had a complete band, let alone a record label. When they needed a drummer, they enlisted Gary Young, the weird middle-aged stoner guy who ran the studio where they recorded. Had Pavement waited to record under ideal circumstances, they wouldn't have produced their charming, slapdash masterpiece.

Stephen Malkmus's singing is often described with words like "deadpan" and "laconic," but his performances are far from emotionless. Forgoing the myopic emotional intensity practiced by most rock singers, Malkmus cops a conversational style that allows for undercurrents of paradox, discomfort, limitation, self-sabotage, and redemption. To this effect, *Slanted* opener "Summer Babe" is a cage match between heart-on-sleeve romance and tongue-in-cheek irony—Malkmus begins the song with a clever lyrical nod to Vanilla Ice's "Ice Ice Baby." He even cracks up a little bit during the song's final verse—a slippage that might be distracting if it didn't perfectly complement the song's rupture and discontinuity.
—ML

Archers of Loaf: *"Web in Front"* 1993

The lead track on Archers of Loaf's debut album, *Icky Mettle,* is quintessential mid-1990s indie rock, with its gravelly vocals, tightly wound guitar interplay, and jittery, insistent drumming. But "Web in Front" is far from a rote genre exercise: It uses these elements to strike a balance between earnestness and intelligence, fulfilling indie rock's promise that music can be emotional without sinking into insufferable cliché. Eric Bachmann's lyrics are characteristically cryptic-romantic, impossible to parse literally yet tremendously resonant. When he sings, "There's a chance that things'll get weird / Yeah that's a possibility," his voice straining and cracking, the whiff of awkward romance is unmistakable. While some initially wrote them off as Pavement imitators, Archers of Loaf took little time to develop their own sound, defined largely by Eric Johnson's melodic and reverb-drenched guitar work. If anything, they were the workmanlike intellectuals to Pavement's inspired class clowns, turning out a solid and increasingly experimental catalog before disbanding with little fanfare in 1998.
—ML

Yo La Tengo: *"From a Motel 6"* 1993

It wasn't until their sixth album—a lifetime of work for bands on the get-in-the-van touring circuit—that Yo La Tengo cemented their position as one of indie rock's essential bands. While still indulging their well-documented Velvet Underground fixation, 1993's *Painful* finds guitarist Ira Kaplan and drummer Georgia Hubley discovering their own voice as songwriters and starting to cover a great deal of stylistic ground—everything from noisy guitar drones to 1960s pop pastiche.

The blaring un-riff of "From a Motel 6" is their shining moment. The tenderness of Kaplan's voice tempers the ferocity of his guitar playing, imbuing the song with subtle but palpable melancholy. Propelled by Hubley's insistent drumming and James McNew's fuzzed-out bass, "From a Motel 6" shows Yo La Tengo more metered than fellow dream-poppers Galaxie 500 and more upbeat than fellow noisemongers Sonic Youth. This combination of explosive sound and considered structure would serve the band well for years, but "From a Motel 6" remains their perfect storm in a teacup.
—*ML*

Sebadoh: *"The Freed Pig"* 1991

Lou Barlow might not have invented emo, but he deserves to have his name in the end credits. In one three-minute swoop called "The Freed Pig," Barlow eviscerates both his then-former bandmate (Dinosaur Jr. frontman J Mascis) and himself, inadvertently laying out the foundation for a million emo rock bands. There's no doubt that Mascis takes most of the damage, with the knockout punch coming in the couplet, "Your big head has that 'more room to grow' / A glory I will never know." But underneath all this withering sarcasm is the same guy who once screamed "Why don't you like me?" over and over like his inner child needed a binky and a new diaper. This song feeds off that fuck-you/love-me tension, and Barlow's sad-sack croon expertly exploits that tug of war. The final coup de grace, though, is its unavoidable catchiness. As Sebadoh ride this dirty pop gem into the sunset, it's clear that Lou Barlow has stumbled upon his own sort of glory.
—*DR*

A Tribe Called Quest: *"Check the Rhime"* 1991

A Tribe Called Quest are the avatars of hip-hop's posthumously garlanded "golden age" (gilded around 1986 and tarnished by 1993), which was principled, pacifistic, and preemptively nostalgic. Newly obsolete old-school masters were regarded as ancient gods, and fallen grace was often invoked. It was as if the genre's rapid evolution made recent history seem distant.

"Check the Rhime" came out in the autumn of the golden age, a couple of years before gangster rap usurped the mainstream. It's a classic distillation of an era when a diminutive MC with a squeaky voice could boast about not being a bully, and get respect for it. Its better-days reminiscence has come to seem more prophetic than stylistic, and it now scans as a time capsule. The horns are from "Love Your Life" by the Average White Band, one of the era's most frequently sampled sources. Q-Tip and Phife trade off genre-defining slang-laden punch lines, boastful disses, record-industry straight talk, and soapbox polemics, capped by this helpless, defensive edict: "Rap is not pop, if you call it that then stop." Of course, Tip would be proven wrong almost as soon as he said it, making his claim all the sadder.
—*BH*

De La Soul [ft. Q-Tip and Vinia Mojica]: *"A Roller Skating Jam Named 'Saturdays'"* 1991

What if hip-hop had remained more or less a subset of disco? It's too glib to assume an army of "Roller Skating Jam[s] Named 'Saturdays'" would be the end result: As MCs, De La Soul and A Tribe Called Quest's Q-Tip have styles too indebted to rap's post–Run-D.M.C. golden age for such a direct link to work. Besides, this song explicitly reminisces about a bygone era, which gives it some of its verbal lift and remarkable buoyancy.

Still, it's not hard to imagine "Saturdays" as part of a response to recent club-music trends. Only a year before, Q-Tip had lent a cameo to Deee-Lite's "Groove Is in the Heart," and while *De La Soul Is Dead* featured a house-music parody, that didn't necessarily stop Mase, Posdnuos, and Trugoy—

not to mention producer Prince Paul—from being curious about the then-revolutionary genre. Recycling early-1970s funk and rock was already de rigueur for rappers, but stepping into late-'70s disco was beginning to catch on elsewhere. Quoting Chic, Instant Funk, the Bee Gees, Frankie Valli's "Grease," and Chicago's "Saturday in the Park," De La and Q-Tip evoke their sunnier youth as adroitly as the samples.
—MiM

Black Sheep: *"The Choice Is Yours"* 1992

The Native Tongues movement that sprang up in the late 1980s was an early catalyst for "conscious" rap, with a focus on Afrocentrism and positive messages. But it also had the tendency to unleash its fair share of hook-heavy crowd-movers. And aside from A Tribe Called Quest's "Scenario," few could get a party amped like "The Choice Is Yours." Black Sheep, comprised of Bronx MCs Dres and Mista Lawnge, were relative latecomers to the Native Tongues movement, but their first and biggest hit solidified their membership. Having a monster of a beat helped: Between its heavy bop-jazz stand-up bass groove and its solid drum break, it sounded great through a subwoofer, and that naggingly catchy guitar twang in the chorus (a riff with origins in both Memphis funkateers the Bar-Kays and proto-metal psych rockers Iron Butterfly) was a nice bonus. But it's Dres's performance on the mic that really gets the track going, as he pulls off the impressive feat of sounding smooth and crazy at the same time.
—NP

Massive Attack: *"Unfinished Sympathy"* 1991

Within a few years of Massive Attack's debut, music journalists would refer to the output of the pioneering Bristol group and their followers as "trip-hop"— a sort of nebulous catchall that would eventually define almost anything moody, downtempo, or partially breakbeat-based. But until that term was coined, Massive Attack's *Blue Lines* was as category-defying an album as anything released in its day, and its centerpiece was a track that owed as much to 1980s house, 1970s disco, and 1960s Motown as it did to 1990s hip-hop.

The production was revolutionary enough; its combination of uptempo club-friendly hip-hop breaks and slow, dramatic strings merged dance grooves with luxurious melancholy in a way that hadn't been heard since the heyday of Philadelphia International Records's upwardly mobile disco-soul. But it might not have meant as much without guest Shara Nelson's powerful lead vocal. Evoking a line of classic R&B divas from Aretha Franklin to Chaka Khan, her voice is pained, angry, wary, pleading, and strong all at once, especially when she characterizes the damage done by an unattainable love which has rendered her "like a soul without a mind / In a body without a heart."
—NP

Tricky: *"Aftermath (Version 1)"* 1993

In 1992, ghoulish twenty-first-century bluesman Tricky—obsessed with hip-hop, reggae, his dead mother, and marijuana—started rapping like an old man who was two Lucky Strikes away from needing a breathing apparatus. He also hired a teenage singer from the neighborhood, Martina Topley-Bird, to leaven his croaking dread with winsome sexiness, and he made beats that creaked and clanged like the stairwell in a haunted housing project.

This demo version of his anti-anthem "Aftermath" is shorter and punchier than the almost eight minutes of paranoia that graced 1995's *Maxinquaye*. Opening with a snippet of dialogue from *Blade Runner* where a robot blows away a cop who dares to ask him about his parentage (robots being the ultimate metaphorical orphans for a guy mourning his mom), Tricky skulks around gray, possibly postapocalyptic British neighborhoods wet with rain. He is "feeling lonely, isolated," and haunted by the loss of his family as he's chased by a piano that sounds like a xylophone rented from hell's orchestra and an incongruous guitar lifted from 1950s rock and roll. His own gnarled mumbles lurk under Topley-Bird's crooning like they're two sides of the same untrustworthy conscience, and almost a decade after pre-millennium tension gave way to new-millennium ennui, "Aftermath" still sounds more like a personal breakdown than a song charting society's collapse.
—JH

Primal Scream:
"Higher Than the Sun" 1991

The rock remix usually amounts to little more than B-side filler or a quick paycheck for superstar DJs on the slum. There are certainly exceptions—remixes that improve upon and overshadow the original track (see the smash 2006 Justice/Simian mashup "We Are Your Friends"). More rare, however, is a remix that inspires its source artist to completely rethink its approach to its own music. When DJ Andrew Weatherall reassembled Primal Scream's 1989 Stonesy jam "I'm Losing More Than I'll Ever Have" into the indie/dance crossover hit "Loaded," he effectively showed this band of dyed-in-the-leather MC5 revivalists where the real revolution was happening, and set the stage for the Scream's Generation Ecstasy classic, *Screamadelica*.

On that record, the comedown is as entrancing as getting high: You don't so much listen to album centerpiece "Higher Than the Sun" as slip into it like a dream, with Bobby Gillespie's stoned, immaculate vocal guiding you through a shape-shifting panorama of dubtronic grooves, acid-washed synths, and thundering drum breaks (courtesy of producers the Orb). While *Screamadelica*'s string of club hits ("Loaded," "Come Together," "Movin' On Up") perfectly captured the acid house era's 1960s/1990s symbiosis, "Higher Than the Sun" offered a glimpse of the future—to trip-hop, post-rock, and, for better or worse, a million chill-out compilations.
—*SB*

Spiritualized: *"Step into the Breeze"* 1992

In 1990, after the demise of the British psychedelicists Spacemen 3, two of their three members went on to form Spiritualized. Since then, Jason Pierce—aka J. Spaceman, one of Spacemen 3's primary songwriters—has remained Spiritualized's only constant. Mixing dense atmospherics with fuzzy guitar and classical strings, *Lazer Guided Melodies* tightened and deepened Spacemen's sound, affixing it to a more rock and roll center. (Displaying their inflated ambition, some versions of the CD have its twelve songs cross-faded into four suites.)

On its own, in under three minutes, "Step into the Breeze" melds mournful violin bowing, echoing vocals, and the flanged swirl of elaborate strings with guitars, pulsing floor-tom drumming, and plaintive pop romanticism. It's a space-rocker's love song, a nugget wrapped in a symphony. Pierce's devotion to classic American popular music would eventually work gospel and blues into their mix (see the follow-up, *Ladies and Gentlemen We Are Floating in Space*), and here he starts his interest in U.S. rock with chord progressions from the Beach Boys, borrowed Velvet Underground melodies, pedal sustain, tremolo, and idyllic walls of sound.
—*BS*

Slowdive: *"Alison"* 1993

Some of the shoegazer acts of the early 1990s made noises that were furious, squalling, and cathartic, staring down at their feet and letting their guitars scream for them. Others, like Slowdive, painted their clouds in prettier, more delicate colors. This English five-piece made songs like the ocean: grand and serene, only sometimes whipping up into swells and storms. With crews like this sounding like they'd rather gaze into your eyes than at their own boots, critics even dug up a new word for it: dream pop.

Frontman Neil Halstead's sleepy strumming also held a secret kinship with folk and country music. "Alison" is the perfect collision of that sweet-sad-song aesthetic with the haze of shoegazing—a pop song to its very end, but one that calls for every lick of swooning guitar behind it. You could pile adjectives on its waves of sound—they're vast, blurry, and romantic, and Halstead sounds terrific in the middle of them, letting his languid singing draw up a crushing weight. But the gist of dream pop is a simpler trick: Have you ever had a strange beeping appear in the middle of a dream, only to gradually realize it was your alarm clock? Just imagine you'd had it set to AM radio instead.
—*NA*

Aphex Twin: *"Xtal"* 1992

The legend of Aphex Twin will always be steeped in mystery. Did he really play a DJ gig in London with nothing but sandpaper and a food mixer? Did he actually take to driving around city streets in a tank? Would we want to know if these stories were ever disproven? (The answers, insofar as they are verifiable:

yes, yes, and no.) The greatest mystery, to be certain, is how Aphex Twin managed to sound like no one else for so long. From its opening hiss and sigh, "Xtal" moves through a vast bank of sounds unique to the melodic and meandering mind of an electronic producer in his early prime. That's where Aphex Twin was upon the release of *Selected Ambient Works 85–92,* a collection that figured into the early '90s trend toward what the Sheffield label Warp dubbed "electronic listening music." As with much else on the album, the "ambient" appellation proves misleading: No less kinetic or stirring than a dance track fit for a club, "Xtal" skims over roiling rhythms and loops of womanly murmurs that oscillate between the sinister and the serene. They're not quite sounds structured for sleep; those would come later, on 1994's *Selected Ambient Works Volume II.*
—*AB*

Talk Talk: *"Ascension Day"* 1991

Mark Hollis's spiritual awakening on *Spirit of Eden* and *Laughing Stock* is remarkable, not for its honesty—plenty of rockers have loudly gone to the pews—but for the immediacy and grace with which he chronicles it. While both of Talk Talk's final LPs follow an arc from doubt to faith, *Laughing Stock* is the lonelier and more challenging of the two, and "Ascension Day" marks its darkest hour. Tim Friese-Greene's organ and Lee Harris's steady drums lay a vibrant bed under Hollis's restless, thrashing guitar. The struggle yields to noise and is not resolved until later in the album, when Hollis concludes that "Christendom may come Westward" and starts to find peace.

Many hours of edits and experiments fed *Laughing Stock*'s success: The jazz influences, dissonant chamber instruments, and pop melodicism make a unique vessel for its message. But the despair in Hollis's guitar and the desire in his voice form the core, capturing a seeker whose lyrics are so personal they're practically mumbled. Some have pegged *Laughing Stock* as one of the seeds of post-rock—and many bands have borrowed its delicate chamber instruments and its patient sighs and silences—but few of them reached such a lasting resolution.
—*CD*

Slint: *"Good Morning, Captain"* 1991

Both sides of *Spiderland*—the second and final album from Louisville's Slint—end with solitary protagonists bludgeoned by despair. Side one's Don and side two's Captain are both left trying to atone for something looming from the past: Don needs chemicals and friendship but finds only the contempt of being an outsider, and Captain needs shelter and safety but finds only tragedy. Captain was probably proud, but here—after a storm takes his crew and his boat—he struggles up the shore to a house. Reduced to bleeding, begging, shivers, and tears, he waits by the door. Finding only a flush-faced boy, he remembers he's got nothing left. As he screams "I miss you" and mumbles "I'll make it up to you," he's speaking to possibilities he once knew through the conduit of an innocent child. In eight taut minutes, "Good Morning, Captain" makes a strong man weaker than a scared boy. Likewise, this cut's qualities—a near-funk rhythm juxtaposed with chilly narration, scathing guitars, and a nerve-torching crescendo—make younger bands wince in envy.
—*GC*

Disco Inferno: *"The Last Dance"* 1993

Disco Inferno were part of the "lost generation" of British independent bands—uncompromising modernists whose experiments were just getting under way when Britpop arrived and hoovered up what little attention they'd won. DI's big idea was to use their guitars to trigger MIDI samples of snowfalls, glass shattering, or found sounds. This made for a fascinating cacophony, but their album title—*DI Go Pop*—was more hope than promise. At their best, Disco Inferno sounded instead like they were beating pop up, leaving fine songs punch-drunk and reeling, hopelessly breached by the noise of everyday life.

Paring down the din, as they did on "The Last Dance," revealed sparse, pained songwriting and delicately clipped guitar work. Ian Crause, half-speaking the lyrics, is a voice of mournful reason, begging for space in a culture increasingly dominated by repackaged memories and cozy ghosts. The only sample is the strict, double-time

ticking of a stopwatch. "In the end it's not the future, it's the past that'll get us," Crause sings, as an abundance of cyclical, repetitive pop and "centuries-old feuds updated with high-tech weapons" prepare to prove him sadly right.
—TE

Stereolab: *"French Disko"* 1993

It's a rare disco in which a monotone call for solidarity could qualify as rousing, but Stereolab know how to draw drama out of flatness. "French Disko" established itself as a Stereolab anthem on the strength of a few hypnotic parts pushed into overdrive. Chugging guitar and swinging bass situate the sound somewhere between shiny-booted 1960s go-go and trancey 1970s krautrock, but the main power source of Stereolab has always been their futuristic discharge of vintage organs and synthesizers. Blasts and baubles stream from a spaced-out mix of tools including vocals, Farfisa, and Moog, and it would be hard to overstate the aural heat generated by analog equipment pressed to drone on for minutes at a time. The repetitive charge and gritty sound of "French Disko" showcase Stereolab as a formidable rock band—a distinction later obscured in a discography that hews toward the space-age bachelor pad. But there's little that counts as decorous lounge music in a song that marries angstful swirls of noise to lyrics like "Though this world's essentially an absurd place to be living in / It doesn't call for total withdrawal."
—AB

Acen: *"Trip II the Moon Pts. 1 and 2"* 1992

After the UK's second Summer of Love, acid house and rave culture made inroads around the world. The music morphed into increasingly harder and then darker sounds, and the harsher realities of life in places like London, Berlin, and Rotterdam were replaced by a sort of utopia on the dance floor, with the uniformity of that familiar 4/4 beat serving as a great leveler and the shared foundation of what became a worldwide community.

"I get hype when I hear a drum roll," Rakim said in 1987 on "I Know You Got Soul"; five years later, when the English rave producer Acen Razvi sampled the line for "Trip II the Moon," he not only claimed the

words but made their sentiment his tune's entire MO. Of course, "hyper" was the prevailing idea behind early-1990s hardcore rave music, especially the breakbeat-driven stuff that would lead to jungle and drum 'n' bass, and "Trip II the Moon" shared—along with countless other records from the time—a basic template of squealing vocals, heavy bass, palsied snares, and two-fingered keyboard riffs. But Acen never merely juggles his patterns; he structures them as intricately as a maze, full of unexpected stops and starts that heighten the dramatic tension: "I can't believe this feeling!" a helium-voiced diva shouts, and the upward-spiraling synth surrounding her makes those feelings flesh. Justly, this crazed mélange made the British Top 40; today, "Trip II the Moon" holds up not just as a magnificent time capsule but a classic of avant-garde pop and bubblegum alike.
—MiM

The Future Sound of London: *"Papua New Guinea"* 1991

Techno has always had a love of beauty, whether you're talking about the melodic twinkles of Kraftwerk's neon lights or Derrick May's heart-tugging strings of life. But since most techno producers were beat-heads who'd rather mess with a drum machine, the Future Sound of London didn't bother foregrounding the winsome melodies and pretty sound effects that they had painstakingly played on fussy keyboards. At least, that is, until a generation of ravers had decided they were done with the nightlife, burnt out on the weekly ritual of clubbing until dawn. The first thing that strikes you about the proto-chill-out groove of British techno duo the Future Sound of London's "Papua New Guinea" is what you often remember first about dance music: the melodic hook. In this case it's a wordless vocal ululation sampled from Lisa Gerrard, the pallid siren of goth faves Dead Can Dance, which snakes around a funereal piano figure. (Various spaceship noises zip around the mix, too. This *is* techno, after all.) The combination is enough to give you goosebumps all on its own, but FSOL's trump card is that "Papua New Guinea" is also exceptionally rhythmic, with an insistent bass line lifted from Meat Beat Manifesto and a rough breakbeat drum pattern that's ultimately as hypnotic as Gerrard's vocal.
—JH

Human Resource:
"Dominator (Joey Beltram Mix)" 1991

The vacuum cleaner was patented in 1908 by inventor James Murray Spangler, whose cousin-in-law William H. Hoover improved the design and formed a company to distribute the device. Eighty-three years later, Brooklyn producers Joey Beltram and Mundo Muzique, working under the moniker Second Phase, created a rave track called "Mentasm," whose primary figure was played on a synth that sounded, appropriately, like a microphone being dragged across a shag carpet. The "Hoover riff" was born.

Beltram's steel-nerved remix of "Dominator," by Belgian dance quintet Human Resource, is the ultimate utilization of the Hoover riff, not to mention the logical endpoint of hip-hop's noisier end. Its air-raid sirens and "Funky Drummer" cut-ups are straight from the Public Enemy playbook, and there's plenty of James Brown in here as well—particularly the refrain, stolen from "Super Bad": "Wanna kiss myself!" Eventually, they do: "Mwah! Mwah!" As much as any record of the hardcore-rave era, "Dominator" is the spiritual godparent of the noisy, messy, fun-first late-2000s blog house derided by sourpusses all too ready to tell you that this stuff is really Serious Art. Students of history should be amused to learn that they missed the point back then, too.
—*MiM*

Metalheadz: *"Terminator"* 1992

With the relentlessly mesmerizing squelches of acid house and the rapid-fire, high-BPM hyperactivity of hardcore standing as the most predominant forms of techno in the early 1990s, it was just a matter of time before something came along to place a few sticks of dynamite under it all and set the pieces flying. Goldie's work under his early alias of Metalheadz was labeled upon arrival as "darkcore," after its tendencies to subvert hardcore techno's upbeat mood with sinister atmospherics; but it's easily recognizable as a catalyst for the jungle sound that was poised to take over dance music. By shifting the pitch and time of the drum breaks so they piled upon each other and grew more frantic even as they maintained their tempo, Goldie built up a rhythm that threatened to fly off the rails. And by throwing in a few mutations of familiar sounds (including a brief swipe of Second Phase's "Mentasm") and letting them ricochet off an increasingly frantic backdrop, he wound up with a pivotal example of what technology could do to a break—and wound up becoming jungle's first star.
—*NP*

Omni Trio: *"Renegade Snares (Foul Play VIP Mix)"* 1993

By 1993, the second wave of UK rave had hit critical mass, while the parties were just becoming a reality in the U.S., and the many mutants of earlier house and techno styles were breeding feverishly. At this point, the frenetic breakbeats of hardcore started being fine-tooth-combed, and one of the artists leading the charge was Rob Haigh, aka Omni Trio. "Renegade Snares," the title cut of his third EP, took his already steely sound down to nothing: tremulous diva vocal, rough-cracking snares, cannonball bass, and New Age piano. That's it, and even in its original form that was all Haigh needed. Only it took a few more hands—the drum 'n' bass trio Foul Play—two tries to work those ingredients to perfection.

The "Foul Play VIP Mix" (to distinguish it from the earlier "Foul Play Remix") intensified the original track's depth and contrast so as to conjure a pitch-black sonic space flecked with flickering light from the piano and snares, with occasional curves suggested by the voice, a thrill-ride between the barest of elements doing dazzling things. "Renegade Snares" isn't the precise spot where drum 'n' bass turned minimal and foreboding, but as a marker, it stands in beautifully. Even more important, it's one of the great pieces of pop minimalism, a record that focuses your wonder on the many ways rhythm communicates.
—*MiM*

Red House Painters:
"New Jersey" (second version) 1993

Everyone always mentions the same story—the one that says Mark Kozelek, this band's singer, battled drug addiction at an early age. Once you've read that, it's hard not to imagine hearing a hard-luck kid in his voice, which is warm, expansive, and dense with longing: Like Nick Drake before him, he reached his midtwenties already sounding tired. If other singers seem like actors on the stages of their songs, Kozelek inhabits music more like a voice-over—calm, declamatory, and thoughtful.

The band made music to fit: funereally slow, always caught between an achy prettiness and the dark, weird clouds behind it. They recorded "New Jersey" twice, the first time with just voice and guitar, and the second time—this time—with the full band, an ominous marching snare, and an undertow of guitar noise. In most people's mouths, you'd think the lyrics were a little rough on their subject, a burnt-out twenty-nine-year-old mother who needs reminding that "New Jersey ain't the whole world." But when this song hits its peaks, something happens: "Don't you leave me out here too long," Kozelek sings. The safe bet is that he's switching to her point of view, letting her call out for rescue. But with that voice, it's just as easy to imagine it's still him, calling out for her—dying dreams, "bum childhood," and all.
—NA

Teenage Fanclub: *"The Concept"* 1991

With its blend of barely controlled fuzz guitar and sweet, gentle vocals, "The Concept" perfectly straddles Teenage Fanclub's early, proto-grunge years and their later guise as modern standard-bearers for power pop. Norman Blake's portrait of a scenester girl makes wry observations about her lifestyle ("Says she don't do drugs / But she does the pill") but it's offset by a poignant chorus where the group, in harmony, offers her comfort and solace. The long, well-played guitar solo was an oddity for its time, and it emphasized the band's underlying classicism.

Halfway through, the song transforms from a midtempo pop tune into a slow-motion guitar meltdown. Wordless vocals and clean-toned guitars—one strummed, one bowed—set the stage for a second, arcing solo that's as anthemic as anything on classic-rock radio, and the coda lasts three minutes, nearly half the length of the song. The *Bandwagonesque* LP solidified the place of Blake and his fellow songwriters, Raymond McGinley and Gerard Love, in Scotland's long history of outstanding guitar-pop bands, and there's no greater distillation of the album's aesthetic than its powerful opener.
—JT

Heavenly: *"C Is the Heavenly Option"* 1992

Formed from the ashes of shambling pop outfit Talulah Gosh, Heavenly—led by the biting vocals of Amelia Fletcher—quickly became a fanzine favorite after they came together in 1990, thanks to their whip-smart lyrics and falling-and-laughing guitars. Indie-pop haven K Records released the band's second album, *Le Jardin de Heavenly,* in the U.S., and K founder (and Beat Happening singer) Calvin Johnson was so besotted with the group he decided to chime in on a track. The result was "C Is the Heavenly Option," a playful duet based on those personality quizzes in teen rags; like those tests, most of the options (personality makeovers, fashion critiques) were plainly stupid to anyone with a sense of romance. Johnson and Fletcher's tag-team advice urged the cardigan-clad girls and boys out there just to let love bowl them over, with the track's singsong cadence doing at least 50 percent of the job. It probably wasn't much of a coincidence that the kool things who ran *Sassy* launched their "Dear Boy" advice-from-the-guys column the year after "C" was committed to tape.
—MJ

Tindersticks: *"City Sickness"* 1993

In the early 1990s, Tindersticks was a band apart from any current trend or movement, and the Nottingham, England, sextet crafted a world of sound that was at once elegant, refined, debauched, and crumbling. The group's sense of tragic romance is embodied by the dramatic baritone vocals of Stuart Staples, who telegraphs world-weariness in every syllable he sings. "City Sickness" is a masterpiece in miniature: The playing from each member is a model of economy and lack of ego, and Dickon Hinchliffe's beautiful string arrangement lends Staples's down-trodden musings an effortless grace and beauty.

Staples sings from the perspective of a man who knows the pleasure he feels is too intense for this world. "I'm hurting, babe / In the city there's no place for love." Most people have felt that alienation, and the band captures the light and shadow of urban life—the train, the nightlife, the traffic, and the loneliness of being surrounded by people you don't know are all somehow palpable in the simple beat, sparse vibraphone, and shivering violin.
—JT

Unrest: *"Make Out Club"* 1993

Within an indie-rock scene marked by scuzzy sounds suggestive of 1990s slacker lassitude, Unrest distinguished themselves as a pop band partial to clarity and subtle refinements of tone. It all revolved around a guitar sound as singular as any in rock: Through his beloved brand of Sears Silvertone amps, Unrest mastermind Mark Robinson played unduly fast, scattering crystalline chords in patterns that ricochet before they have a chance to register. In "Make Out Club," the result is a peppy rhythm guitar that whips up layers while strings struggle to transmit signals as fast as they're being strummed. Robinson's hand was paced to outrun by design, but the band behind him keeps up: Drummer Phil Krauth and bassist Bridget Cross play a frantic, propulsive groove that proves both loose and locked-in, with splashy cymbals and melodic bass runs that evoke New Order in a sunny mood. The spirit carries over into the vocals, which address "the very first one / making out all over me" with a cryptic cuteness and staccato temper typical of Robinson as a writer and as a singer.
—AB

Tenor Saw/Buju Banton: *"Ring the Alarm Quick"* 1991

Mown down by a speeding car on the streets of Houston in 1988, Tenor Saw's death was a huge blow to reggae music. Just twenty-two, he had already secured his place in dancehall history with a run of popular tunes, including "Golden Hen," "Pumpkin Belly," and, most of all, "Ring the Alarm," his definitive interpretation of Winston Riley's "Stalag" riddim.

Born Clive Bright, Saw's appeal as a singer is almost entirely peculiar to Jamaican music; he couldn't carry a tune in a bucket, but his technical deficiencies were far outweighed by the spontaneity and genuineness of his songs. Saw's unpolished crooning style and Riley's unctuous, bass-heavy instrumental could have made "Ring the Alarm" sacrosanct, beyond any kind of improvement. Luckily enough, reggae has never had much time for such proscriptions, and 1991 saw Tenor Saw's original verses juxtaposed with the gruff precision of a new set of vocals by Buju Banton. It's an audacious and electrifying combination, both

artists' styles clashing and complementing in equal measure—with the stark digital beat that backs Banton's rhymes adding a rasping, contemporary touch to the already-classic sonic template.
—DS

Dr. Dre [ft. Snoop Doggy Dogg]: *"Nuthin' but a 'G' Thang"* 1992

While N.W.A. at last shifted rap's focus to the West Coast in the late 1980s, the group's producer, Dr. Dre, made the interest stick with his sonically startling solo debut *The Chronic*. Released on the notorious Death Row Records, the album's lead single, the strolling "Nuthin' but a 'G' Thang," hardly screams "seismic shift" with its subtle bass line and astute funk interpolation of Leon Haywood's "I Want a Do Something Freaky to You." But the voice of a smooth operator named Snoop Doggy Dogg took those restrained notes to an altogether new place— smart and playful, but harder than anything before it.

"'G' Thang" wasn't the first time Dre and Snoop had worked together. After being introduced by Dre's stepbrother Warren G, the producer recruited the then-teenage Long Beach rapper for a soundtrack cut called "Deep Cover." That song, where Dre warns he'll be "Killin' motherfuckers if I have to," didn't quite fit Snoop's languorous tone. "'G' Thang" was softer and yet still more menacing. And although it's a solo coming-out party for the long-celebrated Dre, Snoop opens the song—marking one of the first times Dre acknowledged his key talents lie in discovery and production.

The song became a smash, ushering in the gangsta rap movement, with its glorification of drug use (especially pot) and explicit depictions of violence and misogyny. But the story of gangsta rap's rise, like most media-created movements, was essentially apocryphal. "Nuthin' but a 'G' Thang" didn't become iconic because it lionized decadent behaviors. *The Chronic* was, instead, an enormously accomplished piece because it's steeped in funk history, unrivaled in thump, and viciously evocative with its imagery. Parts of that imagery will be forever emblazoned in a generation's mind thanks to this song's video, a morning-to-night take on a day in inner-city Los Angeles, from BBQ to basement blowout. For the first and possibly last time, the West Coast was the center of the rap universe.
—SF

Ice Cube: *"It Was a Good Day"* 1992

"Anything you wanted to know about the riots was in the records before the riots," said Ice Cube on *The Predator*'s "Fuck 'Em," responding to a reporter's question about the 1992 battle for Los Angeles. Fair enough. Cube's N.W.A. pedigree, his repeated clashes with the media and the police, and his status as one of the lone voices that spoke for the South Central section of the city made him something like a prophet in the days after Rodney King's beating at the hands of four L.A. cops. Cube's extensive experience with the more wretched aspects of African-American poverty culture at that time also qualified him as a sort of metaphysical weatherman; if Cube said it's been a good day, odds were it had.

In retrospect, "It Was a Good Day" was beloved as much for the Isley Brothers' languid soul sample as its creeping social message. Still, look at how many things had to go right for this day to turn out OK— no carjackers, crooked cops, or dead friends. Like its spiritual cousin, Lou Reed's "Perfect Day," "Good Day" felt so triumphant because it represented a momentary, ecstatic break from all the many things that were so badly wrong at the time.
—*ZB*

2Pac: *"I Get Around"* 1993

Tupac Shakur lives on in the popular consciousness as a sensitive thug, a raw force of gangsta charisma, and, above all, a tragic figure—but under all that, he was simply a dude who could just flat-out rap his ass off. While "I Get Around" was originally meant for Digital Underground's album *The Body-Hat Syndrome,* 2Pac's former crewmates turned the track over to him (keeping MCs Money-B and Shock-G along for the ride, for a couple of bars) and sat back and watched as it became Pac's first Top 20 hit. As player anthems go, its love-'em-and-leave-'em attitude is less control-freak pimp than restless rambler. And there's rarely been a breakdown and defense of the one-night stand as tightly constructed as this; the way Pac rattles off internal rhymes ("Conversations on the phone 'til the break of dawn / Now we all alone, why the lights on?") bumps just as much as the classic g-funk beat beneath.
—*NP*

Souls of Mischief: *"93 'Til Infinity"* 1993

Around the same time that the wide-screen nihilism of Dr. Dre's *The Chronic* was making its seismic impact on West Coast rap, a few California crews were finding alternate routes to national prominence, taking cues from the warm, jazzy beat collages and starry-eyed idealism of New York's Native Tongues crew. Los Angeles's Pharcyde and Freestyle Fellowship and the Bay Area's Hieroglyphics wound joyous and virtuosic fast-rap cadences around slow, organic samples and, more often than not, came off sounding like kids goofing off in the back of their AP English class.

Souls of Mischief, a young Bay Area group and part of the Hieroglyphics crew, perfected that approach on the title track of their debut album. The content isn't particularly original; the four members rap about girls and weed and rapping. But their sense of fun is infectious; on the first verse, Opio rhymes "digits" with "Bridget," "midget," "dig it," "swig it," and "frigid." The beat, from group member A-Plus, layers an echoing trumpet blast over a glimmering guitar and drum shuffle while the rappers interweave hyperactive syllable-sprays all over the track, interrupting and finishing each other's thoughts. The track runs just five minutes, but sounds like it could go on for hours.
—*TB*

Suede: *"The Drowners"* 1992

The cover of the April 25, 1992, issue of *Melody Maker* showed four young men in button-down blouses and bangs, like glam rockers from an Evelyn Waugh novel, and declared them "The Best New Band in Britain." To that point, Suede had appeared in only a handful of concert reviews, where the band was billed below such nobody acts as Midway Still and Mega City Four. It was still three weeks before the group released its debut single, "The Drowners." This well-intentioned enthusiasm spawned tabloid indie fervor and accelerated the UK papers' cycle of hype, ushering in the nationalistic, classicist Britpop movement in the process.

"The Drowners"—with its monster glam-rock stomp and Brett Anderson's charmingly androgynous vocals and lyrics ("We kiss in his room to a popular tune")—

supported premature media buzz, yet allowed Suede to transcend it. They had changed their name from Suave and Elegant but kept that as an ideology. Here, glittering chords sashay down the runway, allowing four foppish rakes to carry the burden of expectations to a number 1 UK album.
—BD

Blur: *"For Tomorrow"* 1993

Before they became the archetypal British indie band of the 1990s, Blur fumbled from idea to idea, first as baggy chancers and, on part of their underrated second album *Modern Life Is Rubbish,* dabblers in the kind of art rock favored by guitarist Graham Coxon. Success came courtesy of singer Damon Albarn, who filled out *Modern Life* with a trio of singles that highlighted a new appreciation for '60s mod. Unlike the original mods, who reacted against stuffy, gray-skied Britain by adopting the fashions of the continent and the sounds of America, now Albarn and co. were reacting against dreary, stultifying Americanism, hoping to rid the UK of dour, grunge-era U.S. rock. Albarn's first successful offensive was "For Tomorrow," which he promoted with self-described "British images" of bulldogs and World War II bombers. Melodic and jaunty, the song's London-set lyrics about Primrose Hill and being lost on the Westway tapped into a history of British pop that blended universal moods and communal sensibilities with detail-specific settings. At home it made them superstars, much to Coxon's dismay. The indie hero never did find the humor in quips like "What's fifty feet long and has no pubes?" "The front row of a Blur audience."
—SP

Elastica: *"Stutter"* 1993

Justine Frischmann, having recently quit the nascent Suede, placed an ad in *Melody Maker* reading: "Guitarist wanted, influences the Fall, the Stranglers, Wire." Donna Matthews, a Welsh dropout, answered, and Elastica was not "born" so much as pieced together from their influences. "Stutter," their two-minute-sprint debut, infamously concerns erectile dysfunction. Often misconstrued as a kiss-off of belittling girl power, "Stutter" romantically promises monogamous patience.

Beyond the subject matter, it remains the seminal Elastica song for not blatantly recycling a Wire riff or Blondie refrain, the way many of their other peaks did. At the height of their popularity, Elastica sent Christmas cards depicting the band as macrocephalic anime characters. Across the top, in hiragana text, ran the word "RECYCLING." With "Stutter," Frischmann remembered it's best to reconstitute rather than simply reuse.
—BD

Ween: *"Doctor Rock"* 1991

Ween may have been an honest joke at first—two teenage friends singing about weasels and making stoned backroom pastiches of Prince, prog, hair metal, Springsteen, pop, and everything else under the sun. Thing is, they were good at it. Scarily good. It's as if the mushrooms they were surely taking were tapping them into some new dimension of rock genius. And so as the years went by, and their budget went up, and they stopped cracking up in the middle of their songs, they got so great that it became kind of confusing: This stuff was too good to be a joke, but too ridiculous—and too often about food and/or infectious diseases—to be serious.

"Doctor Rock" comes from their early, low-rent days—just two kids in a moldy shack studio called "the Pod," complete with a bunch of aerosol bongs, a load of janky equipment, and the apparent belief that nobody would be listening anyway. Dean Ween lays down a raunchy guitar strut like a drunk old man at a Guitar Center, plus a solo that gets confused midway through; Gene Ween sings like a demented Sabbath fan at a role-playing convention and only laughs once; the whole thing sounds a little like Ozzy Osbourne fronting the Cars. And Gene's ridiculous metal high notes—you can practically see him extending his scarf hand toward the sky—are like the abridged version of the whole band: awesome, hilarious, and then just plain awesome again.
—NA

Wu-Tang Clan: *"Protect Ya Neck"* 1992

When they arrived on the scene in 1993, the Wu-Tang Clan were rawer, hungrier, and more revolutionary than any other crew. In fact, they changed the whole concept of what a crew could be, gathering numerous MCs and letting them all develop to the point where each could carry his own solo record. They incorporated a philosophical outlook that built on the realities of black life in project housing, expanded it to a multitheistic view of how to live that drew from Islam, Christianity, Taoism, and Confucianism, and let martial arts films and comic books fill out the pop-culture background. You could find fragmented precedents for this formula in the works of borderline-underground East Coast peers like Brand Nubian and Organized Konfusion, but the Wu-Tang's first single, "Protect Ya Neck," is the track that seamlessly put it all together.

Going over the details of all eight MCs' contributions (the ninth member, Masta Killa, was incarcerated at the time this track was recorded) reveals a group that was on the precipice of a world-conquering future. While some of them had yet to develop the more distinct personae that would show up in their solo albums, and U-God is limited to a rugged-sounding but brief ten-second cameo, all the signs are there. RZA lays down the prototypical Wu beat, all fragmented pianos, distorted strings, and hazy bass, and turns religion and poverty into competitive boasting. Meanwhile, Inspectah Deck and Method Man bring the rawness, Ol' Dirty Bastard plays the unhinged maniac, Raekwon and Ghostface Killah run through tight prototypes of their intelligent-hustler styles, and the GZA closes things out with an all-time classic label-killing tirade ("First of all, who's your A&R / A mountain climber who plays an electric guitar?"). The version of the song that would show up later, on debut album *Enter the Wu-Tang (36 Chambers),* opens with a call-in segment from a City College radio station where a DJ replies to what, from his tone, sounds like the fiftieth request for the Clan. "Wu-Tang *again*?" he asks incredulously. "Ahh yeah," replies the caller. "Again and again!"
—NP

Geto Boys:
"Mind Playing Tricks on Me" 1991

On the cover of the Geto Boys' twelve-inch single "Mind Playing Tricks on Me," Bushwick Bill—one third of the Houston rap group—sits with a hospital gown draped over him, a black Raiders cap hiding his face, and an enormous white bandage covering half his

head while Scarface and Willie D, the other two thirds, loom over him. The picture was taken in the hospital after Bill tried to force a girlfriend to shoot him in the face. The suicide attempt, which cost Bill his eye, gives context to the dread and desperation all over the track, the Geto Boys' biggest national hit.

There's humor in Bill's verse, a hallucinatory, demonic narrative, but that humor comes laced with the sort of paranoia that leads an up-and-coming rapper to try to end his life, and the other two rappers mirror it. Scarface, already sounding like a wizened old gunslinger at twenty-one, sits staring at his walls while someone, he's sure, is about to kill him. Willie D imagines a car following him. The track swipes an eerie minor-key guitar-line from an Isaac Hayes record, building it into the sort of lush, organic beat that Texas rap would come to be known for. Before "Mind Playing Tricks," a thriving national rap scene was barely aware that anything was happening outside the twin poles of New York and Los Angeles.
—TB

Pete Rock and C.L. Smooth:
"They Reminisce Over You (T.R.O.Y.)" 1992

Troy Dixon wasn't conventionally famous during his lifetime. He was known primarily as a member of Heavy D and the Boyz—a dancer, back in that odd period of the late 1980s/early 1990s when hip-hop crews actually had dancers—who died in 1990 at age twenty-two when he fell off a balcony after a concert. But he had two close friends in Pete Rock and C.L. Smooth, a couple of young artists coming up in the rap world, who put together an emotionally resonant eulogy, a moment of familial love. C.L. Smooth spends most of the track recollecting his own single-mother upbringing and the uncle who helped raise him, but the third verse's tribute—"Only you saw what took many time to see / I dedicate this to you for believing in me"—ties it all together. Only Pete Rock could've built a backing track like this, turning Tom Scott's lite-jazz cover of Jefferson Airplane's "Today" into a hard-kicking, sax-heavy beat that both adds to the sentiment and balances it out with a good dose of head-nodding force.
—NP

On My Block: Regional Rap

As rap expanded outward from the twin poles of New York and Los Angeles, it soaked up the flavors of its practitioners' locales. By the mid-'90s, two of the world's greatest rap groups hailed from the unsung burgs of Port Arthur, Texas, and Orange Mound, Tennessee. Many of these local heroes went on to form enormously popular musical empires; plenty didn't. But all of them left behind deliriously weird artifacts like these.

"Life Is…Too $hort," **Too $hort:** Oakland's Too $hort could be as profane as 2 Live Crew, but his delivery was all controlled insinuation where theirs was amped-up roar. Over long, melodic bass grooves like this one, he calmly, coldly, and cruelly spun tales of sex and exploitation, leaving an indelible impression on several generations of Western and Southern rappers.

"Scarface," **Geto Boys:** These deranged Houstonians went national with "Mind Playin' Tricks on Me," a freaked-out paranoiacs' lament. More often, though, they'd leave introspection out of it, preferring instead to tell stories of killing and fucking over warm, organic beats like this one. Scarface, one third of the group's classic lineup, taught today's rappers how to imply regret and self-hatred without skimping on the threatening swagger.

"Dirty South," **Goodie Mob:** These days, Atlanta's Dungeon Family crew are best-known for nurturing OutKast. But back when Big Boi and Andre were still stealing speed-rap tricks from Das EFX, Goodie Mob were injecting healthy doses of harsh economic perspective into melodically thick blues-rap and giving their region its name.

"Pimp in My Own Rhyme," **8Ball and MJG:** Like Too $hort, these gold-grilled Tennesseans built their body of work talking about the world's second-oldest profession. But unlike $hort, Ball and G never let us forget about the moral quandaries and psychological exhaustion of a pimp's life. On this chilly slow-churn beat, they both sound like they're about to crack.

"South Side," **DJ Screw:** Sometime in the mid-'90s, Houston's DJ Screw hit upon a life-altering epiphany: Under the influence of codeine-laced cough syrup, rap music sounds a lot better at half speed. Unfortunately, his drug of choice may have contributed to his premature death in 2000. Before dying, though, Screw invented a uniquely homespun psychedelic music, forming many of his city's most promising rappers into the Screwed Up Click and letting them rap over his woozy, funereal tracks.

"One Day," **UGK:** The Port Arthur duo of Bun B and the late Pimp C always snarled with the hardest of them, but they were at their best laying out images of poverty and tragedy with heartbreaking clarity. "One Day" is a slow acoustic-guitar lament with some of the saddest lines you'll ever hear, "My brother been in the pen for damn near ten / But now it look like when he come out, man, I'm going in."

"Adrenaline Rush," **Twista:** While Southerners were slowing down, Midwesterners like Do or Die and Bone Thugs-N-Harmony were speeding up, twisting rapid-fire syllables around lush, hammering tracks. On "Adrenaline Rush," Chicago's Twista, once the Guinness Book record-holder for fastest rapper, sounds like a rap version of the fast-talking guy from the old Micro Machines commercials, his threats blurring into a half-comprehensible hail of syllables.

"Bout It, Bout It II," **Master P:** Largely on the strength of a hyperviolent, mesmerizingly awful self-released straight-to-video movie called *I'm Bout It,* Master P built his New Orleans label No Limit into a pop powerhouse. P's delivery was always clumsy, but here his demonic sneer does more than enough to compensate, and the track, from No Limit house producers Beats by the Pound, sounds like a Dr. Dre beat played on blown-out speakers.

"Ha," **Juvenile:** By 2000, No Limit's crosstown rival Cash Money Records had come to equal and maybe even eclipse its ground-up crossover success. That's an unlikely coup considering the all-out bizarreness of tracks like "Ha," which featured Juvenile slurring impenetrable local slang while producer Mannie Fresh kept handclaps and cheap synthesizer burps flying in all directions. New York still hasn't caught up.

"Southern Hospitality," **Ludacris:** Ludacris was never a thug, and he's not really a Southerner, either; he's a Midwesterner who moved from Illinois to Atlanta as a teen, and he raps without the slurry drawl of most Southern rappers. On "Southern Hospitality," he adapts Atlanta drug-dealer slang with the zeal of a recent convert over the Neptunes' heavy, mathematical beat, summoning the fired-up intensity and sly humor that would make him a star.

—*TB*

Bikini Kill: *"Rebel Girl"* 1993

Bikini Kill's enduring anthem "Rebel Girl" is inextricably linked to the early-'90s riot grrrl movement, which began through fanzines (like *Girl Germs* or the band's own *Bikini Kill,* put together by members Kathleen Hanna, Kathi Wilcox, and Tobi Vail) and spoken-word events in Olympia, Washington. Promoting DIY community, punk-inflected culture, and female empowerment, riot-grrrl bands wanted women up front at their shows; sometimes Bikini Kill handed out lyric sheets so the audience could sing along. Despite eschewing mainstream outlets and often ignoring the press, which they thought was commodifying the movement, Hanna showed up in Sonic Youth's "Bull in the Heather" video and her graffiti inspired the title of "Smells Like Teen Spirit."

"Rebel Girl" mixes chugging distorted guitars, simple garage-punk drums, Hanna's X-Ray Spex–esque snarl, and a message of female empowerment with a performative *Sassy* edge: "That girl she holds her head up so high / I think I wanna be her best friend." Like much of Bikini Kill's work, the song is political but also fun, a trait that ran through the group's work and which Hanna continued in the late 1990s and early '00s with punk-electronic female trio Le Tigre.
—*BS*

Melvins: *"Hooch"* 1993

In the nine years between Melvins' inception and Nirvana's ascension to alt-rock ubiquity, Kurt Cobain tried out for the elder band. He would eventually have to settle: When Atlantic snatched up Melvins after Nirvana's commercial breakthrough, they tapped Cobain to produce his heroes' major-label debut, 1993's *Houdini.* On arrival, the album owed more of a debt to metal than it did to punk. Album opener "Hooch" kicks off with Dale Crover slapping his drum kit like John Bonham kicking off *Licensed to Ill,* and the band's ringleader and vocalist, Buzz Osbourne, unabashedly channeling Dio's fantasy-metal vibrato. Later, Melvins would be remembered as one of grunge's many also-rans, as a stylish influence to check (the Japanese trio Boris named themselves after a song on *Bullhead*), and for pioneering a genre—stoner rock—that was basically the metal they loved, with an emphasis on bass and psychedelics.
—*ZB*

Dinosaur Jr.: *"Start Choppin'"* 1992

Recorded after J Mascis's band's major-label debut, *Green Mind,* and before MTV-candy "Feel the Pain," "Start Choppin'" was Dinosaur Jr. at their most commercially loopy. *Nevermind* had jacked their soft-loud-soft-loud-solo routine and printed money with it; on *Where You Been,* Dinosaur leader Mascis cribbed back, but with more falsetto and better guitar parts. After many presumably difficult years as a graying slacker and in-band pariah, Mascis took grunge's success as an opportunity to make a cool-guy aesthetic out of his mumbling social incompetence and ragged clothes.

Where You Been, with its "November Rain"–caliber ballads ("I Ain't Sayin") and its Skid Row flourishes ("Not the Same"), was a bizarre synthesis of the hair metal Dinosaur Jr. had helped dethrone, the alt-rock they'd helped create, and the radio-ready major-label fare they were just then trying to get a piece of. On "Start Choppin'," this meant less feedback, a couple of fewer riffs, and a chorus you could actually spot—not least because Mascis improbably wrestled the end of his hook into an unabashed shrieking falsetto. This guy was never more weird than when he was trying to be normal.
—*ZB*

Pixies: *"U-Mass"* 1991

Trompe le Monde turned out to be the Pixies' final statement, and it's both their most accessible album, full of space-age power ballads and hard rock, and their most esoteric, with lyrics concerning stuff like the biggest damn volcano in the universe (which just happens to be on Mars). "U-Mass" falls somewhere in the middle, a knowingly dumb glam-rock stomp about the band's original stomping ground. That was where Black Francis, as a baby-faced anthropology student, first synthesized the bug-eyed mix of pagan culture and UFO worship that he's usually roaring about in the band's lyrics. But here he's paying tribute to the pieties of a liberal-arts education over Joey Santiago's robo-caveman riffs, which scythe out a grinding space between Devo and ZZ Top.

Even when he's writing about college, Black Francis still sounds more like a displaced alien trying to make sense of humanity through inscrutable grunts

Revolution Grrrl Style Now: Riot Grrrl

"Did you tell them how punk-fuckin'-rock my pussy is, man?" screamed Kathleen Hanna in the Bikini Kill single "Anti-Pleasure Dissertation." The ingenue and motivator of early-'90s riot grrrl was airing out a player, but it could have been a mission statement for the third-wave-feminist masses. The riot grrrls (and boys, too) were mostly left-coast lady revolutionaries: making zines, shredding guitars, screaming much-needed manifestos, and, more importantly, indicting the white male hegemony of both the punk underground and the broader patriarchy. It was a short blip of a scene-sized earthquake, but these groups' influence shook up the underground and still inform feminist bands, literature, and culture.

"Double Dare Ya," **Bikini Kill:** The first growling song on BK's first album set up the movement and gave an easy headline for the thousand riot-grrrl articles (and sidebars) that came after it: "REVOLUTION. GIRL! STYLE! NOWWWWWWW!"

"Cherry Bomb," **Bratmobile:** These minimalist masters cover the Runaways' bad-girl anthem in their signature lo-fi aesthetic.

"Call the Doctor," **Sleater-Kinney:** An early example of the trio's tumultuous interplay—yearning voices, rumbling guitars, and drums—and how they put feminine heart into their feminist rebellion.

"Her Jazz," **Huggy Bear:** Unbridled and punk as fuck, Huggy Bear got deep into the gender coalition—the coed group called themselves "boy/girl revolutionaries"—and proceeded to scissor up the scenery with screeches and distortion.

"I Had Mark Arm," **Skinned Teen:** A group of teen Britons who got together after seeing a Huggy Bear/Bikini Kill show; this song was a bit more bare-bones than any of their other unraveled DIY guitar joints, but the sentiment—reverse objectification on a Mudhoney man-hunk—effectively put the spotlight on the sausage party.

"Horse Girl," **Tourettes:** The most accurate band name ever. "Horse Girl" is jerk-and-twitch femmecore wherein lyric-deciphering is impossible, but this burst of nonsensical bomb-droppage (from ladies who'd later join Out Hud) is short but gratifying, like exhaling.

"What Kind of Monster Are You?" **Slant 6:** Maybe not officially riot grrrls, they still repped the Washington, D.C., leg of power chicas with dude problems—killing the seven-inch scene in the process.

"Strawberry Julius," **Bikini Kill:** Not their most popular, but Kathleen Hanna's emotional urgency matched the power-punch of its guitars. And her impressionistic lyrics about abuse and healing showed how she was a master of subtext when she wasn't sloganeering.

"Make You Come," **Kicking Giant:** Rachel Carns, who would later join epic/operatic metallurgists the Need, and graphic designer Tae Won Yu, who made now-dead teen-girl mag *Elle Girl* look fresh, go in like gangbusters on their guitar and stand-up drums, working out sex politics via DIY punk.

"Water's Edge," **Tsunami:** Yes, the melodic Simple Machines band, but don't front: Jenny Toomey's Tsunami not only embodied the spirit of riot grrrl via feminist lyrics and an activist mindset, she organized some of the first-ever D.C.-area riot grrrl meetings at the legendary Positive Force House.
—JS

and groans than the boy who grew up as Charles Thompson in a devout household. The drooling way he leers through the final howl—affirming that his experience at U-Mass was all very "edd-uuu-kay-shuun-aall"—is one of the best gags in the band's catalog, and not something they teach you in school. —*JH*

Liz Phair: *"Divorce Song"* 1993

When Oberlin grad and dorm-room-taping legend Liz Phair released her debut album *Exile in Guyville* in 1993, rock critics seized on her penchant for singing about fucking—and sounding completely deadpan while doing so, thanks to her low, raw voice. But on *Guyville*'s chiming, shuffling "Divorce Song," Phair also proved herself to be adept at chronicling the small cruelties that men and women inflict on each other in the name of love.

The song follows a meta-argument between two spouses in the midst of a long, bad road trip. Each of the vacation's hiccups (a lost map, a request for separate rooms at a motel) seems to amplify the notion that the relationship on which we're eavesdropping has ended: "And the license said you had to stick around until I was dead / But if you're tired of looking at my face I guess I already am." Phair's plainspoken, conversational tone gives the argument at the song's crux a depressingly realist tone, and the music—complete with harmonica outro—never really resolves. Which seems appropriate, since it's arguments like these, which cyclically mask big issues behind small quibbles and semantic disputes, that precipitate the biggest gulfs between friends and lovers. —*MJ*

PJ Harvey: *"Rid of Me"* 1993

It simply isn't possible to hate another human being more than Polly Jean Harvey hates whomever she's singing to on "Rid of Me." It also isn't possible to desire someone more. Harvey has spent her career exploring that sweet spot where extreme love and lust meets violent anger—there isn't a song in her catalog that's only *kind of* pissed off or just enjoying a playful little crush. Everything is either the best thing ever or the worst—and often both at once.

The tension between the two extremes is ably reflected in Steve Albini's seasick production, which leapfrogs from quiet to loud with sledgehammer force. Truly, the best position to be in while listening to this song is with one hand on the volume knob and the other between the legs. Both eardrums and loins deserve protection when Harvey shrieks "Lick my legs, I'm on fire!" at the track's end. This petite woman who grew up on a rural English sheep farm is way more terrifying than even the most menacing gang of marauding thugs—at least they won't make you lick their wounds. —*APh*

The Afghan Whigs: *"Debonair"* 1993

To treat the effects of a steady diet of sexless indie rock, doctors recommend heavy doses of Greg Dulli. As frontman for the Afghan Whigs, this Cincinnati lothario probed every dark aspect of lust and the gritty intricacies of attraction. And nowhere did he dig deeper or hurt harder than on the Whigs' 1993 album *Gentlemen*.

The Afghan Whigs were signed to Sub Pop during the height of grunge hysteria; while their labelmates whined about how life sucked or whatever, Dulli was covering Al Green and posing with a topless woman straddling his torso in a music video. The band made the major-label leap to Elektra for *Gentlemen* and became modern-rock radio stars with "Debonair" and the title track. "Debonair" distills Dulli's lubricious persona down to its base, with the singer spitting venom while the band shudders behind him. When he snarls, "This time the anger's better than the kiss," it sums up everything that's exciting about the group. To borrow a phrase from a certain television program, this is what happens when people stop being polite and start getting real. —*APh*

Rage Against the Machine: *"Killing in the Name"* 1993

At first, nobody knew it by its actual title: It was "Fuck You I Won't Do What You Tell Me," the indelible cry that's repeated for the song's final minute. There was a bitter irony to stadiums full of fans chanting that line, as there were bitter ironies at every stage of Rage Against the Machine's career. The loudest

voice of political radicalism in 1990s rock, they were inextricably part of the machine their rap-metal anthems protested (being on a major label will do that) and broke up at the end of the Clinton era, splintered by the same kinds of ideological conflicts that bedevil the American left. The centerpiece of their self-titled debut album seems unlikely on paper—it's basically just five lines, each shouted over and over, and three top-heavy riffs. But Zack de la Rocha paces his delivery like a furious master orator pointing his troops into battle, and guitarist Tom Morello underscores those shouts with crisp flutters of noise before breaking out into a pitch-shifter solo that sounds like a transistor radio morphing into a ballistic missile. By the end of the song, you're ready to tear apart the enemy with your bare teeth.
—DW

The Lemonheads:
"It's a Shame About Ray" 1992

Evan Dando's offstage legacy—between 1992 and 2002, he descended from dopey, alt-rock pinup to washed-up crackhead—eventually eclipsed his reputation as a songwriter, which is tragic, because It's a Shame About Ray is packed with charmingly gloomy pop songs about doing drugs and eating cereal. The record's title track (cowritten with Tom Morgan, and, like much of the album, featuring Juliana Hatfield on backing vocals and bass) somehow feels both epic and nonexistent. Dando's vocals are dim and nonthreatening, and he delivers tiny observations over gentle electric guitar and light percussion. The whole thing is so innocuous it should be boring, but it's arresting instead—three unlikely minutes of perfect, gooey pop warbled by a blond, stringy-haired kid in a stained T-shirt.
—AP

Beck: "Loser" 1993

Beck Hansen could have been a one-hit wonder. When alternative-rock DJs furiously spun "Loser" on the radio, Gen Xers were immediately struck by its doofy beats and slide-guitar hook, but best of all, its catchphrase chorus: "I'm a loser baby / So why don't you kill me." And to cap it off, Beck's low, throaty vocals suggested a man older than his twentysomething years.

The sheer number of throwaway lines should've tipped us off that Beck was playing it for laughs and, in fact, was just some goofball on a label called Bong Load. It took a few more years for Beck to rebuild himself into a star of a more serious kind, but "Loser" remains a Gen X memento: Contemporaneous with self-serious, self-effacing dreck like the film Reality Bites, it nailed the uselessness of a generation that never escaped the shadow of the baby boom. And unlike other artists who took slacker ennui a little too seriously, at least Beck was in on the joke.
—CD

The Breeders: "Cannonball" 1993

Sure, the Pixies are legendary, influential, mighty, unfuckwithable. But more people on this planet have the bass line from "Cannonball" engraved in their brains than have ever even heard a Pixies song. The Breeders began in 1988 as a way for Pixies bassist Kim Deal and pal Tanya Donnelly of Throwing Muses to blow off steam; by the time the group's second album, Last Splash, landed in 1993, the Pixies had broken up and Donnelly had been replaced by Deal's sister Kelley.

A fractured surf-rock fun-fest centered on a swinging bass line and Kim's repeated "Ah-oooh"s, the song has more in common with good-time frat-rock tunes like "Surfin' Bird" than the moody bluster of its alt-rock peers. And just as the goofiness of "Cannonball" offered an alternative to grunge's dour outlook, the Breeders' refusal to glam up their femininity offered welcome respite from rock and roll's tradition of exploiting female sexuality.
—APh

Nirvana: "Scentless Apprentice" 1993

After the enormous, industry-shifting success of Nevermind, Nirvana sought the assistance of audio engineer Steve Albini, long known for his cynical pronouncements, purity regarding sound (few effects, huge guitar), punk-rock ethics, and work with both underground bands like Scratch Acid and crossovers such as the Pixies. Ostensibly, Nirvana were going to record a heavier, angrier album. Ironically, the band was unhappy with some of Albini's work—and brought in R.E.M. producer Scott Litt to flesh out singles "Heart-Shaped Box" and "All Apologies."

Still, much of *In Utero* was more combative and self-conscious than its predecessor, offering tracks like the feedback-drenched "Radio Friendly Unit Shifter" and "Serve the Servants," both explicitly documenting the band's uneasy relationship with their success.

The noisiest and rawest song from the album, "Scentless Apprentice" narrates and personalizes Patrick Süskind's 1985 novel *Perfume,* much loved by Kurt Cobain. Süskind's book spins a tale about a man born without body odor but with a keen sense of smell, who apprentices himself to a *perfumier,* killing women for their scents in order to find one that can mask his own nothingness. The song is punctuated by Cobain's pained screams—as if he was exorcising his demons, his own fear of nothingness.

By the next year, Cobain's addiction to heroin had resurfaced, he attempted suicide, and he grew more outwardly conflicted and confrontational about Nirvana's success. A week after being checked into a drug rehabilitation center, Cobain escaped over a wall, flew back to Seattle, and on April 8, 1994, was found dead at age twenty-seven of a self-inflicted gunshot wound. Nirvana, though, had opened the major-label doors for alternative and uncompromising artists, creating a legacy that continued well after Cobain prematurely closed the chapter on his (and his band's) life.
—*BS*

Chapter Six:
1994–1996

By the mid-'90s, the flush of excitement around alternative gave way to the realization that rock radio had surrendered to something with the fervor-tamping name "grunge." The middle of the decade gave alternative's new stars a chance to mature. In some cases, that meant slowing down and experimenting: While Hole's Courtney Love gave the most gut-wrenching performances of her career, Smashing Pumpkins' Billy Corgan grew curious about drum machines, and Björk walked an ever-more-intriguing tightrope between electronics and pop. Green Day became another in a chain of brash young bands to revisit punk—but soon after, they scored a smash hit with one of the sappiest acoustic power ballads of the '90s, "Good Riddance (Time of Your Life)." Everyone was growing up.

Under the wide umbrella of alternative music, new cross-genre artists had a chance to flourish. DJ Shadow used to prowl record stores, moving his stoner/sampler classic *Endtroducing...* from the "electronica" section to the "hip-hop" bins where he felt it belonged. Beck followed the Beastie Boys into an embrace of samples and beats, while Dr. Octagon (aka Kool Keith) scored a cult classic with his scatalogical *Dr. Octagonecologyst LP*. And while the catchall genre of post-rock brought new textures and longer instrumentals to guitar-based bands, alluring female vocals helped ballads like Portishead's "Sour Times (Nobody Loves Me)" and Mazzy Star's "Fade Into You" into incessant rotation, laying the seeds for some of the smoother indie rock that would follow an aging Generation X into the '00s.

Crossover hits also brought rave, house, techno, and other forms of dance music to the popular consciousness under the name "electronica." The term—derided by fans as a crass but convenient shorthand for marketing a massive range of music—is still in wide use, and for precisely that reason.

Yet while acts like Orbital and the Prodigy could score hits under this new rubric, the impact of electronic music touches almost every artist from this point on. While rock and synth-pop acted like mortal enemies in the '80s, drum machines and personal computers insinuated themselves into almost every genre during the 1990s, bringing nearly limitless arrangements of sounds to the basic guitar/bass/drums setup that had dominated rock since its inception.

But the biggest change lay on the business side. Where alternative rock was first fueled by the tension of underground bands attaining widespread recognition and success, by the mid-'90s the major-label fishing expeditions that signed acts as far afield as Butthole Surfers started to wind down. Being small meant just that—you were small—and the concept of "selling out" changed to "making good." Hip-hop especially had a hand in this transformation: Artists like the Notorious B.I.G. were blunt about their ambition and turned their personal finances into engaging singles. College rock, meanwhile, burrowed back underground, relearning to think small: Strains of humble and charming rock led to artistic successes such as Belle and Sebastian and soft-spoken singer-songwriters such as Elliott Smith. They made a virtue of whispering while hip-hop loudly seized the charts.
—*CD*

Hole: *"Violet"* 1994

The structure of "Violet" is textbook pop-grunge: three chords, soft-loud verse-chorus, ringing guitars followed by distorted ones. Slow it down and let your stereotypical pale dude in flannel mope over it, and you've got Silverchair. Speed it up with Patty Schemel's rapid-fire drumming and Courtney Love at the peak of her powers, and you've got a testament to feminine rage—the similarity of the word "violet" to "violent" is no accident.

Love's gale-force howls could be directed at a former flame, but more likely at the cruelest lover of all: fame itself. "When they get what they want, they never want it again," she sneers. "Go on take everything, take everything, I want you to." And indeed, everything was taken: Love's husband Kurt Cobain committed suicide just days before the release of Hole's *Live Through This*, and Hole bassist Kristen Pfaff died of a heroin overdose two months later.

Looking at Courtney Love through the tabloid haze of her later legal troubles, bad plastic surgery, grotesque scene-making, and dubious handling of Cobain's estate, some might find it hard to remember when she was a vital artist. But *Live Through This* and "Violet" are reminders of a time when a woman as beautifully messed up as Courtney Love was not only a source of worldwide fascination but beloved by critics and record-buyers alike.
—APh

Smashing Pumpkins: *"1979"* 1995

Smashing Pumpkins' third album, *Mellon Collie and the Infinite Sadness,* was comprised mainly of the Black Sabbath stompers and psychedelic epics they had built their reputation on, but its biggest hit was the surprise change-up of "1979," a delicate, minimal piece of synth-pop nostalgia. Weirdly, to kids who came of age on a diet of Seattle grunge and Los Angeles pop metal, "1979" sounded like the most futuristic thing ever.

Of course, Billy Corgan was simply indulging his long-suppressed New Order fanboy impulses, with a spot-on forgery of a Peter Hook bass line and canned string flourishes. Coupled with the video and the time stamp of the title, it was practically a faded snapshot of the singer's suburban youth. Corgan couldn't leave well enough alone, and he reinvented the Pumpkins

around the formula of "1979," following *Mellon Collie* with the momentum-derailing *Adore* in 1998.
—RM

Green Day: *"Longview"* 1994

By 1994, radio rock had become very serious and very sludgy. Any punk in "alternative" had become swamped by stale hard rock, trading thrust and hooks for a smug sense of book-learnin' self-importance. Many premature fogies didn't consider Berkeley's Green Day very punk either once they started squatting on the pop charts, but the trio—barely out of their teens, and having already cut two raggedy skate-park classics for Bay Area indie label Lookout! Records—had plenty of what punk needed to remind us what we'd lost: speed and snot and singer Billie Joe Armstrong's atrociously affected (and totally endearing) Cockney sneer.

Green Day were also just accomplished enough as songwriters to catch the ear of major label Reprise, and once their for-all-intents debut single "Longview" hit MTV, a new generation of Converse-wearing chronic masturbators finally had pop stars to call their own. Over a classic walking bass line that ambled with the bowlegged gait of Shaggy from *Scooby-Doo* and double-time thrash that made grunge feel as quicksand-slow as it too often was, "Longview" brought back the urge to pogo at a precise moment, reaffirming the value of being young and full of dumb bubblepunk riffs—at least until Green Day, too, turned into stale hard rock, trading thrust and hooks for a smug sense of book-learnin' self-importance.
—JH

Weezer: *"Say It Ain't So"* 1994

Just as the Cars' 1978 debut streamlined New Wave into a fully digestible form of pop music, Weezer's self-titled 1994 debut—commonly referred to as "the Blue Album"—breathed new life into the post-grunge "alternative" of the '90s with its irresistible melodic sensibility and slick production (courtesy of the Cars' own Ric Ocasek). Album standout "Say It Ain't So" boasts a softly plucked verse and explosive, power-chord-laden chorus taken straight out of the Pixies/Nirvana playbook. But unlike the majority of their contemporaries, Weezer displayed no interest in self-serious macho posturing. At a time when it was fashionable to be dark, mysterious, and brooding, Weezer sang about sweaters, surfing, and D&D.

Even the wrenching familial angst of "Say It Ain't So"—the song tackles the potential consequences of an alcoholic parent—is channeled into syrupy-sweet harmonies and alternately chiming and chugging guitars. Rivers Cuomo sings with just a whiff of self-effacing nerddom, tempering the song's emotional intensity without pushing it toward the geek kitsch of the Blue Album's first two singles "Undone–The Sweater Song" and "Buddy Holly." Indeed, "Say It Ain't So" established Weezer as more than just a bespectacled novelty act and marked a crucial shift toward unapologetic catchiness and self-aware humor in alternative music.
—ML

Blur: *"Girls & Boys"* 1994

In his memoir, Blur bassist Alex James recalls advice from his producer, Stephen Street: "A hit record is nearly all about the drums and a bit about the vocal." Hit records often bloom from nightclubs, dens of din where numb eardrums filter only rhythms and sing-alongs, and "Girls & Boys" both satirized and embraced this hedonism. For the video, the band played before a cheap blue screen displaying dance floors and water slides. A toy disco beat throbs synthetically at 120 bpm. Damon Albarn leads a chorus chant of gender bending as addictive as a tongue-twister.

By Street's principle, everyone else in the band could do whatever he liked. The more punk-inclined Graham Coxon takes the first forty-seven seconds off before stabbing bursts of guitar into the song's sashaying spine. As for his role, James gleefully confessed, "I had total freedom to groove my pants off." He mimics Chic.

The whole thing is too steeped in the bacchanalia to be mere ridicule—and in the end the formula worked: "Girls & Boys" became Blur's first U.S. top 5 single.
—BD

Oasis: *"Live Forever"* 1994

Like every Oasis song, it's complete nonsense: She's into botany ("your garden grows"), he's into aviation ("I just wanna fly")—what's that got to do with the pursuit of eternal life? Nothing, obviously, but then Oasis's greatest talent was making the mundane seem majestic. For three years at least, they managed to convince all of England (and a few

million Americans) that a singer who barely moved onstage and a guitarist who shamelessly cribbed classic-rock riffs like they were restaurant after-dinner mints could be the core of the world's most exciting rock band.

"Live Forever" likewise works magic out of misdirection: The drumbeat is sluggish, Liam Gallagher stretches the limits of his Lennon/Lydon vocal parameters, the second verse is the same as the first (so's the third), and the rhyme schemes are grade-school remedial (fly/die, pain/rain, be/be). And yet the fucking thing just soars, thanks to Noel Gallagher's comfortably numbing David Gilmour-esque solo and a heaven-bound chorus that marks the only time lad's-lad Liam has shown off his sensitive-guy falsetto. Living forever is folly, of course, but as the song gears up for its third and most rousing verse/chorus cycle, Oasis sound self-possessed enough to believe in it—and to this day, the song's brazen bravado is enough to make you forget that each subsequent Oasis album proved just how mortal they really were.
—SB

Pulp: *"Common People"* 1995

The angriest Britpop record starts with boy meets girl. She's from a wealthy home and curious about common people—how they live, how they love. Pulp singer Jarvis Cocker, her intended lover and tutor, replies simply: Forget it. The experience of everyday poverty is unknowable unless you live it—and live it with no hope of escape. Cocker had built a reputation as a master of lyrics about sexual disappointment, and "Common People" is less of a shift than it seems. It's full of a fury and spite that being objectified—culturally or sexually—fuels.

"Everybody hates a tourist," he sings, with precise venom. You don't need to know Britain's class politics to understand. Cocker is ring-fencing the authentic, marking out something that can't be packaged but must be lived from start to end. This is an impulse as old as mass culture—there have to be things the market can't reach, even if they're things, like poverty or despair, that nobody should want.

But as soon as something is beyond reach it becomes more glamorous, and popular music has always tried to break down the very fences Cocker is building. "Common People" became an anthem in

Britain, and a very large number of the people who bought it weren't common at all. Pulp never attracted the broad demographics that Britpop rivals Blur and Oasis did; instead, they became indie gods, student superheroes. When Cocker sings of the common people ("they burn so bright whilst you can only wonder why") and his newfound audience nods along, he's fueling the very thing he hates, which makes him angrier still.

Its lyric made this song an event; its performance lets it endure. Pulp had waited fifteen years for an audience to arrive, and this is the sound of them seizing a chance. They'd worked fanlessly through everything from folk pop to disco revivalism and kept the most effective bits, reaching a pulsing keyboard-led sound with sudden surges exactly suiting Cocker's neurotic physicality. "Common People" barely has a melody, but the way music and vocals roll and peak together is utterly gripping. It builds carefully and conversationally, and when its rage breaks through, it's a laser of certainty and moral force.
—TE

The Notorious B.I.G.: *"Juicy"* 1994

Rags-to-riches stories are inherently predictable and therefore often boring. The key to elevating any such tale is in the details—the grit, the dirt under the fingernail. Brooklyn's pudgy proletarian Christopher Wallace was a king when it came to the details. His Horatio Alger moment, the intricate, accessible smash "Juicy," is riddled with clever minutiae that complement the song's big, bold hook and its reflective backstory. He reminisces throughout the first verse, wistfully recalling the early days of rap radio in a way that made those old enough to remember feel good and those too young feel in on the story.

The clarion call of the third verse—"Super Nintendo, Sega Genesis / When I was dead broke, man, I couldn't picture this"—became a rallying cry for aspirational kids everywhere. But unlike the larger-than-life rap superstars that would follow, we were always with Biggie, never watching him from afar. He was still a chubby kid with insecurities at heart. "Juicy" is the most profoundly pop song in his catalog, thanks to a sticky, smoothed-out sample from Mtume's "Juicy Fruit," but it's also the evocative prologue for hip-hop's best, brightest storyteller.
—SF

Nas: *"It Ain't Hard to Tell"* 1994

When a twenty-year-old Queensbridge kid named Nasir Jones rocked over a loop from Michael Jackson's hit "Human Nature," the entire landscape of rap writing changed. The Large Professor's subtly entrancing sampling, mixed with stiff, lean drums, became the bedrock for something exquisitely visual, officiously cocky, and wondrously memorable.

"It Ain't Hard to Tell" was the lead single from Nas's monumental *Illmatic,* an album that stunned upon its release and remains a revered hip-hop document. Weaving together his forebears' skills—Rakim's stone-cold aura, Big Daddy Kane's effortless cool, and Kool G Rap's menacing street lore—the youthful Nas could turn seemingly simple couplets into brain-busting exercises in efficiency ("'Cause in my physical, I can express through song / Delete stress like Motrin, then extend strong"). "Hard to Tell" isn't about anything per se, but in that way it is about everything: power, perseverance, and purpose.
—SF

Mobb Deep: *"Shook Ones, Pt. 2"* 1995

Mobb Deep—two smallish, virulent kids barely out of their teens—recorded their second album with little fanfare after the flop of their debut, *Juvenile Hell,* two years earlier. But the Queensbridge residents that comprised the group, sullen MC Prodigy and sneering producer Havoc, discovered generation-spanning relevance with "Shook Ones, Pt. 2," their best and most chillingly violent document of mid-1990s New York street life. Prodigy raps like a man torn between rage and devastation ("When the things get for real my warm heart turns cold"), while Havoc is a coil of existential doubt ("Sometimes I wonder: Do I deserve to live?"). The soundtrack is a simmering executioner's song: crackling drums underneath a skeletal piano line and a shrieking orchestral loop that sounds like ghosts screaming in the night. The perfect track for two young men dodging death each day, the song became emblematic of a bigger concept: fearlessness in the hearts of the young.
—SF

GZA: *"4th Chamber"* 1996

GZA's first post–Wu-Tang Clan LP, *Liquid Swords*— a haze of gutter-crunch drums, Asian film samples,

Runaway Trainwrecks: The Post-Grunge Nadir

By the time *The New York Times* unwittingly published a list of fake grunge slang terms in November 1992, there were plenty of people in the know who were already sick of the stuff. However, it took the general public a few more years to experience the same fatigue, and after the first wave of groups stepped away from the spotlight, there were plenty of second-stringers—new, old, home-grown, or imported—ready to take the stage. Sadly, these are only *some* of the worst offenders.

"Far Behind," **Candlebox:** The fact that Candlebox were from Seattle gave their inadvertent trend-humping a certain special schadenfreude when their tiny bubble quickly burst. As with the hair-metal that grunge nominally replaced, it's the power ballad that gets Candlebox the gold, and as with most power ballads, it's a turgid sack of crap.

"Glycerine," **Bush:** Gavin Rossdale and co. came up with the brilliant idea of melding heartfelt (possibly wrong headed) sincerity with a bathetic orchestral backing, which made his pretty nonsense easier to sell to folks not fond of his group's usual plug-and-chug routine.

"Misery," **Soul Asylum:** A group that was in the race long before a bevy of young upstarts began lapping them, Soul Asylum languished in critical-darling limbo for years before finally hitting the big time with 1992's *Grave Dancer's Union.* Three years later, they gave the world, and a bevy of their soon-to-be ex-fans, "Misery."

"Molly (Sixteen Candles)," **Sponge:** The plight of Detroit's Sponge was the same as that of many groups who were discovered and discarded in the record industry race to milk millions from the grunge groundswell: peak fast, fade faster, and become a footnote on some nostalgia-baiting clip show.

"Lakini's Juice," **Live:** Once a little band from Pennsylvania under the watchful eye of former Talking Head Jerry Harrison, Live sold eight million copies of *Throwing Copper* and found just as many TV shows willing to abuse "Lightning Crashes." In 1997, they returned with *Secret Samadhi* and whatever humility singer Ed Kowalczyk possessed prior to superstardom tumbled like a placenta to the floor. If you're one of the few that stuck with the group after witnessing his awkward "spiritual" pantomime in the "Lakini's Juice" video, then you're possibly deaf and blind.

"Tomorrow," **Silverchair:** We'd like to think there were a bunch of teenagers around this time writing music that puts Silverchair's shameless grunge homage to shame. Then again, I doubt very many of them had a frontman who was a dead ringer to one Mr. Kurt Cobain. But for that one indisputable selling point, I doubt so many would know that the water in Daniel Johns's world is, indeed, very hard to drink.

"My Own Prison," **Creed:** While it's stupid to blame a subgenre for anything it might have influenced, someone needs to answer for Creed.

"Shine," **Collective Soul:** Like Creed, this Atlanta-based group's first single also dabbles in a little *Christianity for Dummies,* but with less bombast. A little less.

"Push," **Matchbox 20:** Back before dreamboat Rob Thomas became a VH1 mainstay, he was slumming in the alt-rock arena, sporting black nail polish and trapped in a video with a director who couldn't keep a shot in focus. Folks slowly growing out of their flannel could easily get down with Thomas's pseudo-intense groveling and the group's radio-rock sheen, so it's not a surprise that this song launched their career. It's also not a surprise that many of nu-metal's less spiritual proponents keep taking the push-you-around ethos to the bank.

"Superman's Dead," **Our Lady Peace:** In case you're lucky enough not to remember "Superman's Dead," this is the song about the world being a subway, done by the group with the lead singer that sounds like Perry Farrell's gamey third cousin. Thankfully, this was their one and only moment in the U.S. sun—the rest of the time, they were Canada's problem.
—*DR*

and virtuoso wordplay—helped this most self-disciplined of rappers become the truest embodiment of the Wu's quiet power. "4th Chamber" opens with dialogue from 1980 kung-fu cult favorite *Shogun Assassin:* "Come boy, choose life or death," a father matter-of-factly asks his young son. While the child chooses to live, producer RZA's loping mix of heavy-metal guitar, krautrock bleeps, and dub scrunch could pass for hell's national anthem. ("Unprecedented, opium-scented, dark-tinted," says GZA, describing the track with characteristic succinctness.) The levelheaded rapper doesn't just casually obliterate opponents willy-nilly ("unnecessary beef is more cows to breed") but he's no pushover, either. Sometimes, a steel will can be the fiercest, most intimidating weapon of all.

—RD

Pavement: *"Gold Soundz"* 1994

Pavement, formed by childhood friends Stephen Malkmus and Scott Kannberg in Stockton, California, were arty indie-rock wisenheimers too smart for their own good. Irony, a word heard pretty much every five minutes throughout the Gen X 1990s, was something they did very well, but Pavement never allowed themselves to be easily pigeonholed. "Gold Soundz," a single from their second full-length, *Crooked Rain, Crooked Rain,* shows their warmer, softer side: They come over as optimistic, generous, nostalgic, melodically gifted, and ready to take on the world. Sure, the lyrics are a little fuzzy. "You're the kind of girl I like," says one verse, seemingly a paean to reckless youth—but then they follow with "Because you're empty, and I'm empty." But nothing was ever simple with these guys; to them, songs with only one meaning were boring. The deeper truth is in the effortless tune, the relaxed jangle of the guitar, and how they combine to evoke the timeless glow suggested by the title.

—MR

Built to Spill: *"Car"* 1994

Though they titled their 1997 major-label debut *Perfect from Now On,* Built to Spill's key moment came a few years earlier, with "Car," from 1994's *There's Nothing Wrong with Love.* The song is almost embarrassingly spare and sweet, but its wide-eyed innocence is earned, not forced. Like much of Built to Spill's early output, "Car" is elegant in its awkwardness, accenting

impeccably arranged guitars with a lone, uncomfortable cello. It's a song that yearns for understanding and connection, a laundry list of desired experiences punctuated with declarations of "I wanna see it now." Though a far cry from the excellent prog-pop opuses the band would later record, "Car" betrays an astounding degree of structural sophistication, winding its way through asymmetrical bridges and verses before arriving at an anthemic coda: "I wanna see movies of my dreams."

—ML

Modest Mouse: *"Broke"* 1996

In early 1996, the members of Modest Mouse were still living in rural Issaquah, Washington, and they had yet to release their full-length debut, *This Is a Long Drive for Someone with Nothing to Think About.* They were also pretty much boys: Lead singer and songwriter Isaac Brock was twenty, but on "Broke," the A-side of Modest Mouse's second seven-inch, he sounds even younger. The song begins with the prettiest and most delicate guitar part of the band's early career, with chiming arpeggios that announce: "You are about to hear a heartrending indie-rock single; please find a special place for this single on your next mixtape." But the lyrics are anything but typical, expertly mixing pathos with self-deprecating humor in a way that became a band trademark. "Broken hearts want broken necks," Brock offers early on, clever and succinct, but a couple of lines later he follows with, "Sometimes I'm so full of shit that it should be a crime." It's a disarming admission—but once you reach the ecstatically noisy climax and corresponding "Huh-oh-ah-ho" vocalizations, you're ready to follow this dude anywhere.

—MR

Frank Black: *"Headache"* 1994

When Black Francis folded the Pixies in 1993, he flipped his name around and began to bring into his music all the parts of his record collection that his previous band hadn't covered. By his second solo album, *Teenager of the Year,* he was moving out from the Pixies' shadow and creating a sound that looked forward and backward at the same time. "Headache" scored him his biggest solo hit, and in retrospect it's the closest thing to a bridge between the Pixies and his later, more straight-ahead work with the Catholics.

The song is mostly chorus, and Black flirts with country music in a way only someone with his oddball sensibility could, by stringing C&W strumming and bluegrass-inspired backing vocals over a pounding rock beat and filling it with vivid, surreal imagery like "My heart is crammed in my cranium / And it still knows how to pound." The song's two strange, hissing verses revisit the minor-key drama of the Pixies' *Bossanova,* but with less reverb. Kurt Cobain had anointed Black an elder statesman of indie rock a few years earlier, and "Headache" gives the impression that Black had begun to relish the role.
—*JT*

The Jon Spencer Blues Explosion:
"Bellbottoms" 1994

In the authenticity-obsessed 1990s, neo-blues-rock bands such as the Make-Up and the Jon Spencer Blues Explosion drew as many detractors as devotees. The JSBX, and the energetic showman who led them, also orbited the irony-obsessed Beastie Boys and Beck, furthering claims that Spencer himself was a mere charlatan.

But where those crossover artists made music from collage, Spencer and his band did almost the opposite: The fiery, urgent "Bellbottoms," from 1994's *Orange,* is practically a *décollage* of a live rock album, stripping away the fat until you're left with only the manic highlights. Never working itself into a proper song structure or any sort of discernible pattern, Spencer's Elvis/revivalist preacher impersonations and the song's pileups of riffs and breakbeats instead give the song an almost fluid, improvisatory feel. After *Orange,* the group further embraced the cut-and-paste methods of their peers, bridging the space between guitar music and hip-hop culture by working with remixers such as Mike D, Beck, GZA, UNKLE, Moby, and Calvin Johnson's Dub Narcotic Sound System.
—*SP*

Guided by Voices: *"I Am a Scientist"* 1994

Of the thousand or so songs that Robert Pollard has written, none makes for a better mission statement than "I Am a Scientist." One of the last compositions penned for *Bee Thousand,* "Scientist" marks a turning point for the band. While Guided by Voices' earlier output found them struggling to fit arena-sized anthems onto a basement four-track, by 1994 they had fully

embraced the unique sonic potential of lo-fi rock. This combination of childlike curiosity and obsessive musical craftsmanship is the cornerstone of Pollard's output; as a result, *Bee Thousand* is both GbV's most fully realized and their most magnificently scattershot album. "I Am a Scientist" speaks to this spirit of exploration, as Pollard declares "I am a scientist, I seek to understand me," and "I am a lost soul, I shoot myself with rock and roll" with equal conviction.
—*ML*

Nine Inch Nails: *"Closer"* 1994

Trent Reznor has never had trouble singing about sex. Yet to say that "Closer" is blunt is an understatement, and it's also beside the point. Reznor's lyrics are meant to be coldly expressive objects, cogs in a meticulous system that incorporates ideas from industrial, metal, and electronic music to accost the listener on all fronts. The Mark Romanek-directed video portrays Reznor's subconscious as a musty gallery of horrifying psychosexual curios, and for anyone who came near MTV in 1994, the hissing, throbbing drum machine is inseparable from the video's opening image of an artificially pulsating human heart. "Closer," like much of Reznor's work, blurs the typological distinctions between eroticism and dread, and between man and beast. The song's most frightening quality, however, is also perhaps the most obvious: It's incredibly seductive. Why waste time digging for hidden meanings, it suggests, when you could be fucking like animals?
—*EH*

Björk: *"Hypor Ballad"* 1995

In 2002, Björk's official website conducted a poll to organize the tracklist for the singer's greatest hits collection, and "Hyper-Ballad" earned the most votes. One of the eccentric artist's most straightforward songs, "Hyper-Ballad" swells and accelerates to a thumping house beat as she belts a devotional refrain of "to be safe up here with you" that melts down to a mantra of "safe up here safe up here safe up here." Eumir Deodato, a Brazilian 1970s funk-fusion composer, conducts strings that trigger knee-weakening. As the title suggests, it sounds exceedingly romantic.

The song's protagonist, alone atop a mountain with her lover, surreptitiously rises each dawn to stand at

a cliff and toss housewares while contemplating her own splattering suicide. Through purging these black thoughts in solitude, she spares her partner her dark side. Compared to quixotic love songs, is this cynical humanism? No: Björk delivered a clinical song of romantic realism.
—BD

Beck: *"Devil's Haircut"* 1996

Some of the skittering drums on Beck's blaring ode to demonic 'dos are lifted from a cover of a James Brown song by Van Morrison's early group Them. The sample's lineage is a perfectly convoluted mix of white and black, funk and rock, appropriation and inspiration. Along with cut-and-paste maestros the Dust Brothers, Beck genre-skipped his way out of one-hit-loser-dom with *Odelay,* a stylistic smorgasbord that redefined alternative rock by smashing it into bits and piecing it back together again, drum break by drum break.

"Devil's Haircut" is the album's wig-blowing opening gambit. Flashing a four-note Godzilla riff taken from yet another Them track ("I Can Only Give You Everything"), the song sounds like the untold, paranoid aftermath of Robert Johnson's infamous deal with the devil. "Heads are hanging from the garbage man trees," deadpans the shape-shifter, conjuring an abstract underworld where *Naked Lunch* is required reading. Toting an ungodly collision of metal, rap, blues, and hip-hop, Beck was a living mashup descended from "Walk This Way" and the Beastie Boys. But, even more than his progressive forebears, the singer completely obliterated the thick lines commonly used to pigeonhole artists. "Rock and roll, know what I'm saying," he proclaimed, encapsulating the genre's rebelliousness with the bust-it-up attitude of an original punk.
—RD

Portishead: *"Sour Times (Nobody Loves Me)"* 1994

The ten-minute art-house espionage film *To Kill a Dead Man* wasn't notable as cinema, but it served as a demo reel of sorts for the film's composers, Geoff Barrow and Beth Gibbons of Portishead. *Dummy,* the album that emerged as a result, proved the duo could create evocative, cinematic music without any need for visual accompaniment. Barrow's previous

job as a recording studio tape operator allowed him to witness the recording of Massive Attack's *Blue Lines,* and during the studio's off-hours he first laid to tape his and Gibbons's defining moment, "Sour Times (Nobody Loves Me)." The song samples the haunting Middle-Eastern jangle of "Danube Incident," from Lalo Schifrin's *Mission: Impossible* score, pairs it with Adrian Utley's slithering, echo-drenched guitar, and adds a murky hip-hop pulse, creating an exquisitely foreboding backdrop for Gibbons's seductive femme fatale. Her despairing refrain, "Nobody loves me…Not like you do," is probably just bait, but like the song itself, it's impossible to resist.
—EH

Saint Etienne: *"Like a Motorway"* 1994

Saint Etienne were born from a fusion of 1960s pop and 1990s dance music, delighting in how both genres reveled in the promise of the endless Now. By the time of 1994's *Tiger Bay,* the English group's songs had evolved into something grander, reaching for a timeless classicism while still steeped in techno modernism. Anchoring it all is Sarah Cracknell, whose marvelously understated vocals imbue each phrase with delicate nuances. From joy to regret, she holds herself in check even when the music around her explodes with feeling.

On the impeccably titled "Like a Motorway," the group resurrects the pulsating synthetic grooves of disco producer Giorgio Moroder to soundtrack a tale of suburban tragedy, as Cracknell tells of a friend whose lover has mysteriously disappeared. At once epic and precise, the song moves effortlessly from the panoramic sweep of a life of disappointments to the minutiae of small details: jeans torn at the waistband and skin that smells like petals. The lover claims the motorway is like life itself, at once expansive and oppressive, and the group evokes those traits with its majestic synth arpeggios and looping breakbeats. The song has no chorus and no release: "Like a Motorway" might be a melodrama, but Cracknell avoids playing along, instead using the sighed refrain "he's gone…" to express the depth of her empathy.
—TF

Basic Channel: *"Octagon"* 1994

Berlin's Basic Channel didn't invent minimalism, but they did more than any other artist to repurpose reductionism for the dance floor. Interview-shy and antifame, the duo of dub enthusiasts and former post-punks Mark Ernestus and Moritz von Oswald reduced everything to aesthetics, beginning with their generic-sounding moniker and extending to their austere yet oddly hypnotic record designs. Basic Channel's sleeves blurred the line between individual and collective, creator and title, preferring to smear relevant information across the center sticker in an indistinct blur. Vertically integrated, the collective was as DIY as it gets, opening its own record store—Hardwax, a mecca for techno tourists visiting Berlin—and even a vinyl pressing plant.

Of the nine vinyl twelve-inches that appeared on the label between 1993 and 1994, the thirteen-minute-long "Octagon" is one variation among many: a 4/4 kick running slightly upwards of 130 bpm, a blurry suggestion of high-hats smuggled in from disco, and a steady shoomp of reggae chords pumping piston-steady. All the action is in the effects. Elements normally foregrounded, like beats and notes, lie beneath the surface, while filters and delays give shape to the underlying topography, carving resonance into subtly humanizing machine-made rhythms. In essence, it's the old studio-as-musical-instrument model of Phil Spector and Lee "Scratch" Perry; Basic Channel's innovation was to translate the sinewy possibilities of the mixing desk into a kind of musical mind-control in which thirteen minutes could be stretched to infinity when folded into the DJ's hall of mirrors.
—PS

Paperclip People: *"Throw"* 1994

"Throw" is a classic example of Detroit techno in which drama derives from a sneaky collusion of momentum and repetition. The parts are basic: a brooding bass kick, an insistent high-hat that flexes and bends, a minor-key synthesizer played with a mind for Motor City seriousness. The way those parts rise, however, owes to the complexity of their creator, Carl Craig. A protégé of techno figurehead Derrick May, Craig released "Throw" under his Paperclip People guise in the midst of Detroit techno's enduring second wave. His stoic sense of rhythm remained faithful to the mechanistic bent of his forebears, but Craig differentiated himself with a feel for the more human aspects of what convention has long-since celebrated as "soul." A fleshy electric-bass

line positions "Throw" between techno and disco—you can practically see a funky session player's neck pop as the strings at his fingers quiver—and recurring visitations of vocals help prime the ecstasy seeded in a track that builds without straining for change. The message comes clear as an alien voice sermonizes at a helium pitch: "I want to see you throw your hands… up." Craig engineered the response to be inevitable.
—AB

DJ Shadow:
"Midnight in a Perfect World" 1996

About twenty years after the birth of hip-hop, Josh Davis (aka DJ Shadow) marked one of the genre's more subtle evolutionary milestones with his 1996 debut LP, *Endtroducing…* Davis is a crate-digging and sampling freak, but his use of worn-in grooves isn't simple nostalgia. Unlike fellow second-hand masters Eric B and Dr. Dre, Davis didn't make funk-fueled highlight reels for a fragmented, postmodern era. Instead of party-starting with the beloved spirits of James Brown and George Clinton, Shadow created his own personal history through pure excavation and craftsmanship.

But even with all the record-nerd samples (Meredith Monk! David Axelrod!) found on *Endtroducing…*, the album is never bogged down by its creator's push-pad virtuosity. Along with hooks and favorite phrases, Davis delves deeper into his sources, extracting their unfiltered essence and lovingly recontextualizing them. "Midnight in a Perfect World" isn't just cinematic—it's cinema. Like classic noir by way of Miles Davis's *In a Silent Way,* the sharp snares skulk in high-contrast black-and-white as the cooing vocals and warm organ evoke haze under a lone streetlight. Characteristically Shadow isn't quite visible in this scene, but his presence is felt.
—RD

Dr. Octagon: *"Blue Flowers"* 1996

Kool Keith had always been one of hip-hop's most visceral surrealists, dating back to his days with the NYC underground legends Ultramagnetic MCs. But by the time he moved to California in the mid-1990s, his capacity for disturbing imagery and bizarre metaphors had increased to the point that, under the alias Dr. Octagon, he developed into one of the then-nascent independent rap scene's

earliest critical darlings. Delivered with a diabolical and calculated calmness over 1970s splatter-flick Moogs and a queasy loop from Bela Bartók's "Violin Concerto No. 2" (production touches courtesy of future underground hip-hop fixture Dan "the Automator" Nakamura), "Blue Flowers" is the most memorable track from *Dr. Octagonecologyst,* a psychedelic dirge that doesn't bump so much as it scrapes. The lyrics are simultaneously graphic and abstract—"Drawing by the pond, look, it's raining yellow"; "Supersonic waves combine and burn as brainwaves"—to the point where Keith comes off like a hybrid of Timothy Leary and Dr. Nick Riviera.
—NP

Common: *"I Used to Love H.E.R."* 1994

In the early 1990s, mainstream hip-hop became a mirror image of itself. The then-prevalent Afrocentric style exemplified by the Native Tongues posse was verbally spry, jazzy, pacifistic, and rooted in New York City. It celebrated spiritual power. Its usurper, g-funk (blueprinted in Dr. Dre's *The Chronic*), was laconic, funky, violent, and Californian. It celebrated physical and financial power.

Chicago-based hip-hop purist Common issued the seminal statement of this sea change in 1994's "I Used to Love H.E.R.," when he was still called Common Sense. Over a jazzy beat by future Kanye West associate No ID, who found apt source material in George Benson's "The Changing World," Common weaves an extended personification of hip-hop as a woman on the skids. After moving to L.A. (a dig that initiated Common's feud with West Coast rapper Ice Cube), she decides that "pro-black is out of style" and starts "popping glocks, serving rocks, and hitting switches." Since the song's objectification of women is a definitive trait of the music it rails against, it's notable both as a segue and as a timely crystallization of a dying hip-hop worldview, right at the moment it expires.
—BH

Jeff Buckley: *"Grace"* 1994

Jeff Buckley's voice flies all through this song, smearing across tidal washes of cymbals, guitars, strings, and the singer's own sense of withering drama. It's heady, romantic stuff, if hardly cerebral:

Buckley's various strains of siren song were made for exploding into euphoria, but not necessarily for examining under a microscope. The song's lyrics are impressionistic, vague, and poetic ("There's the moon asking to stay / Long enough for the clouds to fly me away"), but the real magic is in hearing the melody dash and flutter through layers of lush, pristine rock noise. Guitarist Gary Lucas (who cowrote the tune) provides an easy launching pad for Buckley with a song structure almost perfectly sculpted for dramatic tension and release, but it's still that voice that lingers longest.
—DL

Mazzy Star: *"Fade Into You"* 1994

Mazzy Star were neither the first nor the last band to write a tune this sleepy-slow and languorous; it's a style that runs back to old country and there are always new bands giving it their best shine. It's no accident, though, that "Fade Into You" turned into a hit. The video probably helped—singer Hope Sandoval, with her arresting beauty and flimsy tank top, stuck out like a dream amid the din and clatter of MTV. But it wasn't just that: There's a seductive, once-in-a-career magic to this recording, a sound that decades of rainy-day folkies have spent whole discographies trying to perfect.

Part of it is the music, which swoons in the background: the steady strum of acoustic guitar, subtle embellishments on piano, slide guitar lilting between the lines. Mostly, though, it's Sandoval's bewitching voice, as she glides lazily around the notes. She slurs her words or even leaves them unsaid: "I think it's strange, you never…" She might sound sedated, if only her lines weren't so clear-eyed or controlled; this is less like a stoned muddle than the tired-out clarity that descends after a long jag of crying. She sings about wanting to help you—wanting to "hold the hand inside you"—but she sings it like someone who's just realized it's never going to happen.
—NA

Arthur Russell: *"This Is How We Walk on the Moon"* 1994

Though his greatest commercial success came with a string of disco tracks that confounded urban

Running to Stand Still: Slowcore

Extending the less-is-more principle of hardcore punk to tempo and dynamics, slowcore bands made austere, hypnotic music based on minimal chord changes and trudging drums.

"Snowstorm," **Galaxie 500:** Galaxie 500's languid guitar, warbling falsetto, and behind-the-beat drumming shine through a fog of reverb to evoke the late-night contemplation of the open road. Dream pop starts to become slowcore on this Boston trio's 1989 album *On Fire.*

"Dinosaur Act," **Low:** Duluth, Minnesota–based trio Low came to define slowcore in the 1990s with spacious dirges that built up tension until they attained an unadorned majesty. On "Dinosaur Act," from 2001's Steve Albini-recorded *Things We Lost in the Fire,* husband-and-wife team Alan Sparhawk and Mimi Parker could be describing their own lumbering sound, their harmonies bolstered by trumpet but still skeletal.

"Sick of Food," **American Music Club:** The depressive laments of San Francisco's American Music Club show why the terms "slowcore" and "sadcore" were usually interchangeable. From 1991's *Everclear,* "Sick of Food" examines the spiritual hunger of an AIDS patient whose medication has drained his appetite. The sculpted guitar noise lends dignity to singer Mark Eitzel's anguished vocals.

"Katy Song," **Red House Painters:** One of the few songwriters arguably sadder than Mark Eitzel is Mark Kozelek of fellow San Francisco band Red House Painters (and later Sun Kil Moon). From the first of two self-titled 1993 albums, "Katy Song" wallows in lonesome despair for more than eight minutes, drawing on the introspective folk of Nick Drake.

"Bedside Table," **Bedhead:** Led by brothers Matt and Bubba Kadane, Texas's Bedhead buried half-spoken (and seemingly half-awake) vocals in delicately interlocking electric guitar lines. Debut single "Bedside Table," released in 1992 and available on 1994 album *WhatFunLifeWas,* is a template for the band's sound, rising gradually from reflective beginnings to a violently distorted climax.

"Pickup Song," **Codeine:** The title of New York trio Codeine's 1990 debut, *Frigid Stars,* sums up the slowcore movement's aesthetic better than anything except maybe the name of the band itself. Cold and distant but still glowing, album highlight "Pickup Song" veers from druggy melancholy to grand, celestial guitar glides.

"Topical Solution," **Duster:** The San Jose, California–based duo of Ewing Clay Parton and Canaan Dove Amber brought the scraggly lo-fi charm of early Pavement to Galaxie 500's strummy ruminations. Recorded at home on four-track, "Topical Solution," from 1998 debut *Stratosphere,* finds Duster cooing, "Rock out, rock out." They suspended their chiming guitar riffs in tape hiss instead.

"The Magnificent Seventies," **the American Analog Set:** Texas-based quartet the American Analog Set formed from the remnants of avant-garde electronic outfit Electric Company, but the futuristic touch they brought to slowcore was the Farfisa organ— an instrument most commonly associated with '60s garage rock. The first track from 1997's *From Our Living Room to Yours* inserts Andrew Kenny's lightly sung pop hooks into slowcore's unwavering drones.

"Burn Girl Prom Queen," **Mogwai:** Mogwai are routinely tagged as post-rock, not slowcore, but in more serene moments the Scottish band demonstrate how close the two nebulously defined genres can be. On "Burn Girl Prom Queen," dolorous horns play a melody not far from "Silent Night" as guitars drift back and forth over the same couple of chords for eight minutes.

"Maybelle," **Ida:** Like Low, Brooklyn-based Ida were led by a married couple—in their case, Daniel Littleton and Elizabeth Mitchell. With their plaintive harmonies, Ida owe more to American folk music than most of their slowcore peers; after the piano- and acoustic guitar–based "Maybelle," from 2000's *Will You Find Me,* it's no surprise to learn that they also appeared on Lisa Loeb's 1994 folk-pop hit "Stay."
—MH

dance floors in the late 1970s and early '80s, corn-fed composer Arthur Russell also spent much of his career as an idiosyncratic singer-songwriter and one of the under-recognized pioneers of the deeply personal art of home recording, piling up dozens of quiet, fragile tapes over two decades. The records that made it out of Russell's bedroom while he was still alive, like 1986's *World of Echo,* mingled his gauzy, folkie falsetto with an amplified cello that buzzed with feedback; unreleased songs added pop-funk beats and New Wave synthesizers to the mix. These were private tone poems written in Russell's apartment with reverb and delay pedals, too unmoored and eerie to pin to any one genre.

Released on 1994's *Another Thought* two years after Russell died from AIDS-related complications, "This Is How We Walk on the Moon" has more shape than the dust motes that drift through *World of Echo,* but only just. Like much of Russell's best work, it makes incompatible sounds harmonize in strange ways. There's an irregular hand-drum pulse to guide it, with Russell bowing long angelic sighs from a cello that often sounds like a hoarse extension of his own soft breathing. It's as weightless as its title implies, at least until an unexpected horn section pokes out at the end, suddenly turning this downcast, murmuring avant-garde sketch into something like a bright, brassy pop song.
—JH

Low: *"Words"* 1994

Formed in the extreme northern climate of the lakeside industrial town of Duluth, Minnesota, Mimi Parker and Alan Sparhawk have spent most of their career as Low exploring a sonic space somewhere between nightmare and blissful sleep. Along with somnambulant mid-1990s contemporaries Red House Painters and Codeine, Low were a leading light of the slowcore scene, a short-lived reaction against alternative rock's chain-rattling.

"Words," the opening track to the group's 1994 debut *I Could Live in Hope,* established their sound right out of the gate: a bass line providing the song's melody, Parker's light percussion (tapped out on a two-piece drum kit), Sparhawk's simple, shimmering guitar, and stunning harmonies.
—APh

The Auteurs:
"Unsolved Child Murder" 1994

Luke Haines is the cynic's cynic, and he matches the acid in his words with menacing vocals delivered just above a whisper. Recorded with Steve Albini at Abbey Road after the band had already established itself as a thorn in the side of John Major's England, "Unsolved Child Murder" demolishes tabloid culture and a modern lack of community with swift efficiency.

Haines captures the full range of emotion implicit in the premise—thoughts of his own mortality, disgust at shrieking headlines, hate, and false hope. "When they find him / We can cure him," goes the heart-breaking optimism of the final verse, but Haines's weary tone gives the darker truth away. The way Albini captures James Banbury's cello adds a sawing quality that harks improbably to the Beatles' "Piggies," though there's nothing baroque about this song. No word or note is wasted, and its musical starkness is a great illustration of the band's ability to make very little into something hauntingly memorable.
—JT

Jawbox: *"Savory"* 1994

A masterful play at contrasts, "Savory" is at times angelic, at times traumatic, and usually both at once. Though the unmistakable opening chord is riddled with dissonance, J. Robbins makes it both shimmer and jangle. Robbins and Bill Barbot's guitars snarl and menace during the song's verses and wag submissively during its chorus. Drummer Zach Barocas, a fan who joined the band just prior to the recording of *For Your Own Special Sweetheart,* adds both muscle and jazz-tinged nuance. The result is a balance of beauty and explosive aggression, the perfect backdrop for a song about the impossible and contradictory expectations placed on women in our culture.

With the release of *Sweetheart,* Jawbox found themselves subject to a different set of impossible expectations, incurring the wrath of indie purists by jumping from archetypal indie label Dischord to major Atlantic. And yet "Savory" turned out to be not only one of the most provocative and uncom-promising songs to emerge from the Washington,

D.C., post-punk scene, but one of its biggest crossover singles as well—a fitting achievement for a band that always thrived on contradiction.
—ML

Drive Like Jehu: *"Luau"* 1994

Belatedly tangled up in early waves of emo and post-hardcore, Drive Like Jehu were often overshadowed by the better-known Fugazi—as well as guitarist John Reis's more straightforward group, Rocket from the Crypt. But whatever you call DLJ's sound, their music encouraged punk bands to embrace odd time signatures, complex riffs, and pop structures without sacrificing either tempo or bile. We get plenty of the latter in the heaving rhythms of "Luau." With its sustained tension and fellow San Diegoan Rob Crow (of Pinback) adding a nice contrast to Rick Froberg's desperate vocals, "Luau" was as pop as the band got. It was also nearly ten minutes long, a stitched-together mix of jagged, circular guitar riffs that stands like a monolith in the midst of the band's otherwise economical *Yank Crime.*
—JC

Brainiac: *"Pussyfootin'"* 1996

Plenty of bands find their way to a unique sound, but Brainiac seemed to run on a paradoxical and volatile energy source all their own. "Pussyfootin'" is a hot-wired robot dance party, all jerky movements and big blue sparks. It's fun and sinister at the same time, sexy yet ridiculous, metered yet completely unhinged. The flashes of Moog-filtered vocals on their 1993 debut *Smack Bunny Baby* only hinted at the bizarre combination of *Flintstones*-style primitivism and *Jetsons*-style futurism that Brainiac would touch on in their all-too-short career. By the release of their final full-length *Hissing Prigs in Static Couture* in 1996, the band was gleefully probing the seedy underbelly of electronic slickness, layering seasick synthesizers and razor-sharp guitars under frontman Timmy Taylor's warped croon. On "Pussyfootin'," Taylor sings with an air of unstable menace, like someone punching himself in the face before a fight just to freak out the other guy. When Taylor died in a one-car crash in 1998, indie rock lost some of its uninhibited weirdness.
—ML

Napalm Death: *"Twist the Knife (Slowly)"* 1994

Napalm Death are credited with inventing the metal subgenre grindcore (founding drummer Mick Harris coined the term), making thrashing, guttural music with crust-punk riffs and death metal vocals in songs that usually lasted less than two minutes. On its fifth album, *Fear, Emptiness, Despair,* the British band turned a corner, incorporating more experimental tendencies into its expanded attack, including a bigger (and slower) groove, buzzing black-metal riffs, and an industrial cast.

"Twist The Knife (Slowly)" opens with fuzzed guitars joined by math-y, rolling drums and Barney Greenway's growl: "Feeling like a knife's being twisted in the hole of how it is / False hope, an inch of pride that died when I left to hide from nonstop battering of conditioned opinion." (Not that you can actually understand what he's saying.) The song title is appropriate considering, in grind terms, how slow the song is: Its call-and-response toward the end, the return to the opening guitar part, the final flourish, and drum 'n' scowl dynamics show a band ambitiously rewriting the genre it created.
—BS

Darkthrone: *"En Ås I Dype Skogen"* 1994

Norwegian black metal—an extreme sound characterized by high-pitched vocals, a deemphasis on heavy bass, and epic song structures—gained dubious international prominence in the early 1990s after folks associated with the scene burned down a number of historic churches. The notoriety was upped when Dead, the first vocalist of the band Mayhem, shot himself; then, in 1993, Varg Vikernes, known mostly for his solo work as Burzum, fatally stabbed his Mayhem bandmate and friend Øystein Aarseth.

Darkthrone had already released two albums before issuing their first black-metal record in 1993, around the time of the Mayhem murder and church burnings. They started their aesthetic climb with 1994's *Transilvanian Hunger,* a record steeped in the scene's notoriety: the album title refers to Dead, who was wearing an "I heart Transylvania" shirt at the time of his suicide. Vikernes wrote lyrics for half of the album's tracks, including the excellent finale "En Ås

I Dype Skogen" ("A Hill in the Deep Forest"), which typifies Darkthrone's raw, primitive black metal—strangulated, up-front vocals; escalating hyper-fast guitar scissoring; blistering energy; and distant cardboard drums.
—BS

Ol' Dirty Bastard: *"Brooklyn Zoo"* 1995

The sprawling Staten Island collective known as the Wu-Tang Clan never hurt for eccentrics. So it's a testament to his unconquerable personality that Ol' Dirty Bastard was the group's most unhinged member. His hair an unkempt twirl of braids, his teeth full of scratched gold, and his eyes nearly bleeding from psychosis—they were all telltale signs of an unmatched intensity that blazed new territory for hip-hop. "Brooklyn Zoo," ODB's debut solo single, bubbles over with bile: "I don't even like your motherfucking profile!" he snarls.

That he could bring an innate musicality and singsong cadence to such crazed musings ("I drop science like Cosby droppin' babies!") made it all the more devastating. One of the few non-RZA-produced tracks from his debut, this bluesy True Master–helmed turn is nothing more than a short piano loop and muffled snare pattern—utterly appropriate for the ranting and raving it accompanies.
—SF

Snoop Doggy Dogg: *"Gin and Juice"* 1994

While Snoop Doggy Dogg was brought up on murder charges during the making of his debut album, *Doggystyle,* it's hard to imagine the laid-back dopesmoker even mustering up the effort to bust bubble wrap. In a culture where keeping it real often meant keeping it locked and loaded, Snoop sounded his most real when he was just having a good time. And even if Dr. Dre's Minimoog sound makes it seem like the cops are just a few blocks away and closing in fast, the only real drama in the world of "Gin and Juice" involves freeloaders mooching booze and weed. As the block- and house-party music video indicated, this was a slice of downtime gangster life brought to you by two of hip-hop's finest at the height of their powers. Despite the number of hits to his credit, Snoop's 'round-the-way charm wasn't as

irresistible after leaving Dre's care. Likewise, the dangerous laid-back cool of Dre's g-funk never sounded so sweet as when a young Snoop was first dropping his izzles into the pop lexicon.
—DR

Luniz: *"I Got 5 on It"* 1995

Five dollars could once make a perfect day. In 1995, just as the glossy decadence of rap-as-pop began to take off, a humble duo from Oakland dropped one of the most hypnotic rap singles in a decade full of them—with almost no aspiration. While self-proclaimed drug kingpins such as Jay-Z or Biggie Smalls spent the decade riding yacht decks, Luniz (rappers Yukmouth and Knumskull) took the ache of being broke and sober and turned it into a soaring smash.

The "5" is five dollars, as in enough money for half of a dime bag of marijuana—a small, relatable number for anyone who's ever split anything with a friend. In the case of Yuk and Knum, it became a calling card, thanks largely to the song's mystifying keyboard line, dashing horn bursts, and the burnished croon of Timex Social Club singer Michael Marshall. Marshall's indelible hook, which ended with the memorable "Potna, let's go half on a saaack," and the enchanting production, which hinted at trance, was always more celebrated than Luniz's excited, unambitious lyrics. But that gleeful selfishness and youthful understanding of value made "I Got 5 on It" an unforgettable West Coast curio.
—SF

Cutty Ranks: *"Limb by Limb"* 1995

It's only fitting that, before becoming one of the most recognizable voices in dancehall, Cutty Ranks made his living as a butcher. Thanks to his charismatic presence and gutsy control of the microphone, his take on the stripped-down "Fever Pitch" riddim is a powerful and visceral experience. This was, and still remains, a song in which all the lyrical and instrumental fat is trimmed away; nothing left behind but sinew, muscle, and bone. Hugging and kissing his gun and even sleeping with it at night, on "Limb by Limb" Ranks rejects roots reggae's central theme of redemptive spirituality and also subverts the loverman archetype, defiantly glorifying gangsterism and violent machismo. It's also intensely playful,

In its formative years, alt-country suffered a crisis of identity; even the movement's flagship publication, *No Depression,* advertised itself as "The Alternative Country (Whatever That Is) Bi-Monthly Magazine." In the decade since its heyday, the field has welcomed Nashville refugees, country punks, torch-song chanteuses, rockabilly revivalists, backwoods weirdos, and Starbucks folkies—all of whom defined the genre according to their own particular formulas.

"Side of the Road," **Lucinda Williams:** Everything that characterized Lucinda Williams in the 1990s and '00s is present in this painfully conflicted love song: Her wounded vocals, poetically plainspoken lyrics, strong sense of place, and—most crucial of all— her profound distrust of contentment.

"Gun," **Uncle Tupelo:** The band that more or less created the genre shows how flexible alt-country can be: Jay Farrar's churning guitar switches between sped-up classic rock and slowed-down hardcore, and Jeff Tweedy's Midwestern twang and wounded pride fuel one of the genre's highest-caliber choruses.

"Goodbye," **Steve Earle:** From Steve Earle's first album following his incarceration and rehab, "Goodbye" derives its considerable force from its simple acoustic arrangement and Earle's hard-hearted regrets.

"Gone to Stay," **Freakwater:** Few vocalists, alt-country or otherwise, are better matched than Freakwater's Janet Beveridge Bean and Catherine Ann Irwin, whose bone-chilling harmonies haunt this God-challenging dead-baby ballad.

"More Brother Rides," **Palace Music:** From Will Oldham, the most abstruse of all alt-country singers, comes a song that sounds like a 45 melting on your turntable.

"Big Brown Eyes," **Old 97's:** Rhett Miller was alt-country's greatest wit, Ken Bethea its unsung guitar hero, and "Big Brown Eyes" the best showcase for both.

"Weightless Again," **The Handsome Family:** A California gothic: A stop for coffee in the Redwoods inspires Brett and Rennie Sparks to muse on marriage as one long Western Passage, compelled by a death-rattle two-step beat and mordant thoughts on suicide, sanity, and touring.

"Come Pick Me Up," **Ryan Adams:** With its lovely banjo and elegant chorus melody, "Come Pick Me Up" was such a beautifully pessimistic love song that it made us optimistic for Adams's solo career. What a heartbreaker.

"Twist the Knife," **Neko Case and Her Boyfriends:** Owner of alt-country's biggest voice and reddest hair, Neko Case typically sings the hell out of every song, but this one features her most wrenching and wounded performance.

"Up with People," **Lambchop:** The umpteen-piece Nashville orchestra Lambchop lean toward the countrypolitan end of the spectrum, lionizing Owen Bradley the same way others do Gram Parsons. Mixing in a dollop of gospel, "Up with People" more than lives up to its title.
—*SD*

though, and even given the grittiness of its subject matter there's something avuncular about Ranks, to the point where it's easier to picture him dressed in a white coat, tipping his hat to the local ladies on market day than shooting out anyone's eyesight. —DS

The Prodigy:
"No Good (Start the Dance)" 1994

It may be hard for Americans to imagine, but there was a time when England thought the Prodigy were too cute. The rave trio and their well-known fauxhawks may be forever date-stamped to the late '90s, when they broke internationally on the back of grimacing industrial-techno bangers like "Firestarter" and were saddled with the unfortunate term "electronica." But when mastermind Liam Howlett first started knocking together speedy techno tracks out of purloined hip-hop beats and squeaky cartoon samples in 1990, this Essex lad shamelessly wore as big a smiley face as anyone, so much so that dance magazine *Mixmag* infamously castigated him as the man who made underground dance music appealing to grade schoolers and unfit for everyone else. So Howlett went woodshedding with his computers, and the time away from the dance floor left him downright grim.

1994's "No Good (Start the Dance)" is the finest moment of this second, oh-so-serious Prodigy phase, sonically not all that far from the candy rave Howlett claimed to be ditching. But whereas before his tunes seemed to yelp for joy, here the pitched-up diva repeating "You're no good for me / I don't need nobody" sounds like the ecstasy has turned frighteningly frigid, the hair-raising Morse-code synth riff warns dancers to flee the club like a fire alarm, and Howlett's frantic rhythm track adds a sinister undertow to his spastic, sugary music. —JH

Underworld: *"Born Slippy (NUXX)"* 1995

In the wake of grunge's early-1990s ascendance, savvy marketers desperately searched for an equally lucrative trend to satisfy the freshly minted alternative audience. They hoped to find it in electronica—electronic dance music, basically, but performed by album artists rather than faceless DJs. Nonetheless, electronica became a sort of shorthand for any music featuring drum machines, sequencers, and synthesizers, so when Underworld's "Born Slippy (NUXX)" started getting airplay in 1996, it was posited as an electronica anthem.

The instrumental "Born Slippy" was originally released a year before, to limited notice, with the "Born Slippy (NUXX)" remix as its B-side, but prominent placement on the popular *Trainspotting* soundtrack forced folks who wouldn't know drum machines from washing machines to take notice. The remix featured vocalist Karl Hyde's stream-of-consciousness lyrics—normally elegantly gliding over the band's hypnotic progressive house—now shouted on top of a relentless booming beat. As with fellow breakthrough singles like the Prodigy's "Firestarter" and the Chemical Brothers' "Setting Sun," it was this sideways connection to rock as much as Rick Smith's and Darren Emerson's impressive studio alchemy that made the song a U.S. hit. Indeed, "Born Slippy (NUXX)" was capable of rousing dance fans and rock fans alike, bobbing in sync as the track worked its kinetic magic. —JK

The Chemical Brothers
[ft. Noel Gallagher]: *"Setting Sun"* 1996

Just as Run-D.M.C.'s "Walk This Way" dusted off classic rock and roll to break hip-hop into the mainstream, "Setting Sun" was supposed to be dance music's mainstream breakthrough. Featuring a sneering Noel Gallagher at the height of Oasis's fame and a massive beat lifted from the Beatles' "Tomorrow Never Knows," the song was poised to usher in a euphoric new rave epoch where synthetic pink pills revived the dead, glow sticks gave the blind sight, and bass shifted the heavens. And, for a brief moment, it did exactly that, hitting number 1 in the UK and even breaking onto the U.S. charts. But "Setting Sun" didn't lead to a long-term revolution; if anything, the song might have set the bar too high. The drums are the star, bursting forth like an exaggerated, syncopated cartoon heartbeat, while ferocious air-raid sirens pan left to right. This simply sounded like the future—an engulfing blend of hip-hop, psych, rock, noise, and techno that transcended 1990s pastiche culture and predicted twenty-first-century eclecticism. —RD

Daft Punk: *"Da Funk"* 1996

After a brief foray into indie rock that resulted in a *Melody Maker* review tagging their music as "a bunch of daft punk," Guy-Manuel de Homem-Christo and Thomas Bangalter abandoned guitar pop for a stake in the early-1990s house scene—and promptly blew up with their second single. With city-street ambiance and tape-deck acoustics muffling its electro-clap beat, the first forty seconds or so of the French house duo's breakthrough hit "Da Funk" feel like a surreptitiously recorded b-boy throwdown circa 1983. And even though it explodes into a robotic, arena-filling, acid-house banger—complete with a severe, insistent, wall-shaking 4/4 bass throb, and a hyperventilating Roland 303 in the track's second half that still stands as one of the sickest riffs ever to come out of the synthesizer—it earns its title with that persistent, bouncy wah-wah hook and a slick, midtempo strut of a rhythm that makes it sound like a sinister version of Roger Troutman and Zapp. It's hard not to like a house track that works equally well at warehouse raves and roller rinks.
—*NP*

Belle and Sebastian: *"The State I Am In"* 1996

Songwriter/singer/guitarist Stuart Murdoch's entire aesthetic is, as he later put it, wrapped up in books, and in bookish young people nervously reaching out for one another. Murdoch met bassist Stuart David in the mid-1990s in Glasgow, and the singer's music business course at Stow College arranged for them to make a limited-run vinyl-only LP, so they assembled a band to play a bunch of Murdoch's songs. The release party was their fifth-ever gig. And there the story might have ended—except that the product, *Tigermilk*, was so good that cassettes of it started passing from hand to hand across the international pop underground.

Why was *Tigermilk* so hot? You can start with the opener, "The State I Am In"—Murdoch's statement of purpose. It seems to be autobiographical or confessional, but instead he's just creating the first of his many characters who've grappled with faith and the idea of sin; he's specific about emotions and dates, and deliberately vague about certain tantalizing details. A lot of Belle and Sebastian's early records were about valorizing shyness, so the group's performance is beautifully understated at a moment when most of their contemporaries were turning it up as loud as possible. And Murdoch already had a magnificent sense of how to let melody carry the emotional arc of a song—his long, sinuous lines distill everything he'd learned from his favorite records, including the Sarah Records roster, the Smiths, and especially Love's *Forever Changes*.

Also, for a track about wallowing in misery and loneliness, "The State" is incredibly funny. The song is jammed with witty, often dark little details, beginning with the title: "The state I am in" sounds like a sober self-assessment, but turns out to refer to a vicar's tell-all collection of confessionals. The lyric is one long critique of self-pitying, tormented youth: He's not just charting the territory, he's planning his escape.
—*DW*

Elliott Smith: *"Needle in the Hay"* 1995

Just before the dissolution of his first band, Heatmiser, Portland, Oregon–based singer-songwriter Elliott Smith began recording spare, acoustic laments on borrowed four-tracks, murmuring grim-but-gripping folk songs about broken hearts, feeling hopeless, and consuming piles of drugs. In 1994, Smith released his debut solo LP on local label Cavity Search; the following year, he signed to Kill Rock Stars and issued a self-titled follow-up. "Needle in the Hay," that record's opening cut, skewers Smith's three primary demons: thwarted love, heroin addiction, and mental illness. Although Smith purportedly plotted a full-band version, he ultimately opted for just acoustic guitar and voice, and all those gentle coos and apologetic strums provide a devastating counterpart to the song's dark lyrics.

In 2001, the track was featured in Wes Anderson's *The Royal Tenenbaums,* spinning while Luke Wilson's character stared blankly into a bathroom mirror, clipped his hair and beard, and dug into his wrists with a straight razor. Two years later, when Smith died from two stabs to the chest, the song—and the scene—would take on added, unwanted weight.
—*AP*

The Magnetic Fields: *"Take Ecstasy with Me"* 1994

Stephin Merritt is an arch, ultra-mannered gay man who apprenticed himself to the hard-won tradition of

classic pop songwriting and sings in a cadaverous, monochromatic baritone croon that keeps his camp, ornate wordplay at a remove. These facts supposedly mean that he was out of step with his contemporaries at the height of the earnest, emotive indie rock of the mid-1990s. But even though his voice felt purposefully affectless, and even though he embraced a slick combination of Tin Pan Alley craftsmanship and creaky synthesizers, Merritt's songs were pure college rock, full of knowing irony and steeped in kitsch. On "Take Ecstasy with Me," backed by a tinker shop's worth of wind-up toys and a grinning keyboard melody, Merritt implores a lover to turn on to the love drug in a voice that sounds one step from suicidal ennui. It's the most delicious of all of Merritt's emotional/lyrical juxtapositions, and exactly what you'd expect him to sound like on MDMA: a guarded stiff loosening up just enough to crack a wan smile, without ever dropping his sense of sarcasm. It's also beautiful, proving that even postmodernists can fall prey to good ol' fashioned sensualism every now and again.
—JH

Palace Music: *"New Partner"* 1995

From 1993 to 1997, shape-shifting, Kentucky-born eccentric Will Oldham performed and recorded—along with brothers Ned and Paul—under several variations of the name Palace Music (for example, Palace, Palace Brothers). 1995's *Viva Last Blues* is arguably the collective's finest LP, a collection of rowdy, folk-rock stompers and eerie ballads.

In 2004, Oldham rerecorded *Viva Last Blues'* "New Partner," whipping it into a smarmy, honky-tonk sing-along, but Palace Music's original rendition is impossibly poignant—an earnest, scrappy love song full of vocal cracks, tinny percussion, and a chorus ("You are always on my mind") reminiscent of Willie Nelson. "New Partner," like almost all of Oldham's studio work, benefits from his penchant for under-rehearsing; the song feels transitory, serendipitous, and ghostly, anchored only by Oldham's awkward Appalachian twitters. Still, that fragility is an integral part of what makes him such a compelling performer: "New Partner" feels so temporary and fated that it's hard not to imagine the song dissipating into the atmosphere upon completion.
—AP

Arab Strap: *"The First Big Weekend"* 1996

Summer 1996 was the peak of Cool Britannia, and amidst nationalistic back-patting and necrophiliac consensus-building, Arab Strap—along with fellow Scottish or Welsh bands Super Furry Animals, Belle and Sebastian, Mogwai, and Gorky's Zygotic Mynci—were tonics to the '60s nostalgia of Britpop. Those groups also highlighted just how far the goalposts had moved within UK indie: The bigger English indie-rooted bands were now desperately chasing mainstream success, leaving indie's creative energy in the capable hands of these assorted freaks and geeks.

"So that was the first big weekend of the summer": Drinking, striking out with girls, passing out in the middle of the day, discovering powerful cider ("8.2 percent…mmm"), running into your ex-girlfriend, having disturbing nightmares from booze and possibly cheese. And yet somehow these mopes, with their impenetrable spoken-word Scottish brogues, slowcore guitars, and primitive drum machine make it sound like the greatest time in the world.
—SP

Tortoise: *"Gamera"* 1995

Maybe it was the sudden mainstream popularity of loud-and-dirty alternative rock, but the 1990s saw a lot of independent bands start pulling their inspiration from places further afield than punk. In Chicago, a whole new confluence bubbled up. Guys with indie-rock backgrounds met guys with jazz ones, and the records in their collections they deemed most important weren't pop albums: They were dub reggae, Ennio Morricone film scores, avant-garde electronic works, heady funk. Tortoise were the flag-bearers of this new "post-rock" wave, and you might assume the music they made wants to be difficult. But that would mean missing the friendly, bubbly feel of their compositions, which groove along with a generous spirit. This wasn't music for highbrow mind-blowing: It was music for stoned kids to lie back and imagine the different landscapes—jungles and deserts and underwater paradises—the music seemed to be kicking through.

The twelve-minute "Gamera," one of the band's early successes, is just that kind of trip—across landscapes and, just as much, through the record collections of its makers. It starts with acoustic guitar,

Her Hair Is Everywhere: Post-Fugazi Emo

Emo was born in 1985 when Washington, D.C., hardcore bands Rites of Spring and Embrace started wearing their hearts on their coat sleeves. But it didn't develop into a nationwide movement until after Fugazi, whose members spawned those pioneering groups, had hit their stride. The term "emo" was short for emotive punk, and it would grow whinier, more collegiate, and eventually more adolescent. It was rarely cool, but it did have its moments. Here's to teenage nostalgia:

"In Circles," **Sunny Day Real Estate:** Seattle's Sunny Day Real Estate infused Ian MacKaye–led Fugazi's jagged punk with dramatic bombast and melodic focus, but the biggest development came with singer Jeremy Enigk's aching lyrics. "I dream to heal your wounds," he howls on this song from the band's genre-defining 1994 debut *Diary,* "but I bleed myself."

"I'm Afraid of Everything," **Braid:** Confessionalism and sensitivity grew even more intense in the hands of Braid, an Illinois four-piece whose members went on to form Hey Mercedes. "Why is it I lost my courage and passed your exit?" Bob Nanna shouts, like a teenager, on this spiky 1995 single. Let's hear it for the suburbs.

"Tired of Sex," **Weezer:** After the breakthrough success of their self-titled debut album, Weezer's 1996 follow-up *Pinkerton* turned introverted and bitter. While nowhere near as popular as their previous album, it gave many mainstream suburban kids an entry into emo, and never ran more contrary to prevailing high-school opinion than on this feedback-chafed opener.

"Nothing Feels Good," **the Promise Ring:** Milwaukee's the Promise Ring offered an undergraduate middle ground between Braid's frustrated cries and the slacker sophistication of indie rockers like Pavement. On "Nothing Feels Good," 1977's big punk "no" becomes 1997's "I don't," as erstwhile Cap'n Jazz guitarist/vocalist Davey von Bohlen complains: "I don't know anything / I don't go to college anymore."

"Sweet Avenue," **Jets to Brazil:** Blake Schwarzenbach's first band, the bleakly literary San Francisco pop-punks Jawbreaker, had amassed a fervent fan base by the time it disbanded in 1996. Two years later, Blake was in Brooklyn, working with Jeremy Chatelain and ex–Texas Is the Reason drummer Chris Daly in the dreamier Jets to Brazil. This closing track from their debut, *Orange Rhyming Dictionary,* is a classic emo heartbreaker.

"Cold Enough to Break," **Knapsack:** The California band Knapsack floated frontman Blair Shehan's whispery intimacy over slower, softer electric guitars, bass, and drums. "Cold Enough to Break," from 1998's *This Conversation Is Ending Starting Right Now,* adds strings and bells as well, as Shehan pleads: "Keep me safe tonight."

"Mass Pike," **the Get Up Kids:** Once Weezer's *Pinkerton* began to attract hooky, plainspoken followers, many of them added some of the jolt of late-1990s pop-punk. Kansas City's the Get Up Kids also covered New Order, and this track from 1999's *Red Letter Day* EP uses keyboards and drum programming that anticipate sentimental lap-poppers the Postal Service.

"San Dimas High School Football Rules," **the Ataris:** Though formed in Indiana, the Ataris made their name with catchy, caffeinated pop-punk for the beaches and highways of California. "San Dimas High School Football Rules" took its title from a line in *Bill & Ted's Excellent Adventure,* and the song turns unrequited romance into a dare over crackling power chords: "Just dump your boyfriend and go out with me / I swear I'd treat you like a queen."

"Lucky Denver Mint," **Jimmy Eat World:** Before 2001's *Bleed American* and its hit "The Middle" made Jimmy Eat World arguably the first emo band to break through to the mainstream, their music was more introspective and atmospheric. "Lucky Denver Mint" is atypically aggressive, the song's ringing guitars and insistent chorus evoking U2 as much as Sunny Day Real Estate.

"A Movie Script Ending," **Death Cab for Cutie:** By the time Death Cab for Cutie signed to a major, emo meant Fall Out Boy, Thursday, and My Chemical Romance. But on songs like "A Movie Script Ending," the first single from 2001's *The Photo Album,* plaintive singer/guitarist Ben Gibbard sounds like the bedheaded heir to Jets to Brazil. In fact, one of DCFC guitarist and eventual producer Chris Walla's first production credits was for an EP by Camden—a Milwaukee band who signed to Braid's Grand Theft Autumn Label and toured with the Promise Ring.
—MH

plucked with the back-porch Americana feel of folkie legend John Fahey. Two minutes in, though, the six-string bass emerges, as well as the kind of aquarium-tour groove that became this band's signature. The tricky, weaving rhythms of John McEntire's drums are always entertainment enough, but the other elements that fold in and out of this ride are all a joy: a sunny analog synth line introducing melodies, guitars that slide in and quaver from foreground to background, a bass that pulses nimbly and even tickles its way into the song's center. Just relax and let it fill up your free time.
—NA

The Sea and Cake: *"Parasol"* 1995

They shared drummer John McEntire with Tortoise, and other members came from jazzy and sophisticated Midwestern guitar-pop outfits the Coctails and Shrimp Boat, so it seems entirely reasonable to lump the Sea and Cake in with Chicago's post-rock scene. But they're really not a "post" kind of band; their music doesn't come after anything. Instead, it seems to ooze up from the cracks at the edges of genres, the jagged lines where the instrumental proficiency and tricky chords of jazz exist alongside the bubbly guitar figures of Afro pop and breathy singing of 1970s AM pop.

The Sea and Cake's fondness for in-between spaces extends to their lyrics, which virtually never have clear meaning. In "Parasol," a crystalline slow-burn ballad that has emerged as this band's peak moment, impressionistic lines by vocalist Sam Prekop ("Real on time lay rest the sugar / Lay rest the holiday") exist as sounds alongside other sounds, his smooth diction and airy phrasing riding a hypnotic circular guitar pattern that feels equally weightless. Words like "ghost" and "floating" pop out, not as rock lyrics but rather subliminal commentary on what we're hearing as the song unfolds. The whole thing sounds dramatic and mysterious, like a noir version of 10cc's "I'm Not in Love," but it's also a wonder of structural beauty, the satisfying snap of each piece fitting snugly in place.
—MR

Pavement: *"Rattled by the Rush"* 1995

After "Cut Your Hair" grazed the pop charts, the music business was hoping Pavement could do something that would endear them to modern rock radio. So, naturally, they made the huge, unwieldy, awesome *Wowee Zowee*. "Rattled by the Rush," its first single, comes on like a classic-rock song, thanks to the big, simple riff that dominates the whole thing in various guises. The more you pay attention to it, the more confusing it gets. Very few lines of its lyric connect even to the next, even though Stephen Malkmus aims to wring any emotional depth he can out of them. Then, in the instrumental break that takes up half the song, the band interferes with whatever shreds of straightforwardness are left, piling on harmonica honks, haunted-house synthesizers, a heroic guitar duel that wanders in and out of sync with the rest of the band, and Malkmus yowling another offbeat mantra: "No soap in the john, no soap in the john." It's an invitation to bang and scratch your head at the same time.
—DW

Guided by Voices: *"Game of Pricks"* 1995

Guided by Voices' earliest records, recorded at home on beery evenings by guys with regular jobs, sound like transistor radios playing from inside the trunk of a car. But the cheap, tinny production values didn't prevent "Game of Pricks"—from 1995's *Alien Lanes,* the band's last album created on lo-fi four-track recorders—from sounding anthemic. Singer Robert Pollard cuts through the hiss with a clear, assured vocal and an indelible tune and cuts to the chase with a sharp lyric about betrayal and paranoia: "I never asked for the truth, but you owe that to me," goes the chorus.

At a minute and a half, it's a mercilessly concise distillation of Pollard's guitar-pop aesthetic. He crafts hooks worthy of his British Invasion heroes, not a given considering the perennially scattershot nature of his songwriting. It's possible that Guided by Voices' tenuous position during this period—in the fuzzy zone between band-as-hobby and band-as-life—helped bring out the best in them. During this time of uncertainty, when he'd just begun to tour away from wife and kids and his band flirted with interest from major labels before signing with big-time indie Matador, Pollard wrote a song with the energy, brevity, and universal applicability to stand near the peak of his massive catalog.
—JC

Weezer: *"El Scorcho"* 1996

Rivers Cuomo learned a harsh lesson when his band followed its triple-platinum, self-titled debut with *Pinkerton*: Music by popular artists isn't supposed to be quite so raw and confessional. "El Scorcho" gets just a little bit too intimate with the inner workings of Cuomo's mind, as the singer confesses his half-Japanese fetish, stalks some poor Harvard undergrad with no apparent remorse, and builds a chorus out of third-grade note-passing sentiments.

Brilliantly, the song is also like a skewed, low-self-esteem, crush-drunk version of Weezer's breakthrough: The riff is basically "Undone–The Sweater Song," with Muppet noises replacing dude-brah dialogue and no silly clothing metaphors. Revving up to punk gear and remembering that he's supposed to be a rock star, Cuomo hits upon a meta-statement that could be a motto for all the good and (mostly) bad emo *Pinkerton* inspired: "How stupid is it? I can't talk about it / I gotta sing about it, and make a record of… my heart." Weezer would never be so creepy—or so good—again, but *Pinkerton* will always be out there like the stalker's stolen diary.
—*RM*

Chapter Seven:
1997–1999

Money. There was a lot of it around at the end of the 1990s. In the United States, the economy was good, unemployment and inflation were low, and whatever was going on in the rest of the world, well, that was probably nothing to get too worked up about. A general sense of financial well-being led, naturally enough, to conspicuous consumption. In popular music, this trend found some expression in tunes and videos by the rapper the Notorious B.I.G. His larger-than-life style, helped along by his friend and label boss Sean "Puffy" Combs, found him celebrating his escape from childhood poverty at every turn, as millions of fans celebrated along with him. To this movement in rap there came the inevitable backlash, as hip-hop groups like the Roots and Black Star sought to steer the music toward a headier plane.

In the steadily unraveling world of alternative, escape—either through consumerism, dilettantism, or plain old withdrawal—was the order of the day. By 1997, the "cocktail nation" phenomenon was in vogue. It was a kitsch culture celebrating the swinging sounds of the early 1960s—another time of affluence and rapid technological change. Easy listening bled into swing bled into ska; reissues of records by the campy orchestral bandleader Juan Esquivel had been trickling out and were being scrutinized critically; Sub Pop, the label that had launched Nirvana and put latter-day rock abrasion on the map, was releasing music by fussy retro lounge outfit Combustible Edison. The present moment, such as it was, became a little hard to define.

A lot of deservedly forgotten groups came out of this era, but the reassessment of genres led to some fascinating places. Bands like Stereolab, Air, and Broadcast were recombining old styles and forms—spacey Moog explorations, French pop, krautrock—and making them fresh, vital, and even truly futuristic. The rise of the Internet and telecommunications meant more cultural exchange and a smaller world; both artists and listeners were making the most of being able to draw from anywhere.

Others either set aside the trappings of the day or tried to steer their music to a more exalted place rooted in a different past. Troubadours Elliott Smith, Cat Power, Bonnie "Prince" Billy (aka Will Oldham), and Smog embraced austerity, affirming that great songs delivered with voice and guitar would always have currency. Psych-pop bands Olivia Tremor Control, Neutral Milk Hotel, Flaming Lips, and Mercury Rev went the other direction and began to think in the terms of that relic from the 1960s and '70s—the concept album. All of these bands were marked by a deliberate search for weightiness during a time of easy pleasure.

The rising prosperity of the late 1990s was due in part to the rapid growth of the information sector, which in turn had its own effect on music. The encroachment of technology in the smallest aspects of our lives led to anxiety. No one knew what was going to happen with this "Y2K" business. The increasing power of computers meant that previously unimaginable textures were now possible. And one band in particular, Radiohead, stood poised for this moment.
—MR

Radiohead: *"Paranoid Android"* 1997

"Creep," Radiohead's 1992 paean to self-loathing, cast the band as a post-grunge one-hit wonder, but their critically acclaimed 1995 follow-up, *The Bends*—with singles "Fake Plastic Trees" and "High and Dry" essentially launching the post-Britpop of Coldplay, among others—proved the band were much more than a flash in the pan. Yet 1997's *OK Computer* was something else entirely: a gorgeous and frighteningly timely album that encapsulated the era's pre-millennial tension. *OK Computer* went platinum in both the U.S. and the UK after less than a year, and it marked Radiohead's entry into the vaunted realm of the world's most respected and popular rock bands.

As the centerpiece of *OK Computer*, "Paranoid Android" starkly indexes the record's strongest theme: a desire to escape the rapid pace of technological progress and its strangulating effects on the human spirit. Thom Yorke was inspired to write the song after visiting a trendy L.A. bar, casting its networking yuppies and "kicking, squealing Gucci little piggies" as technoculture's zombies, the result of commercial culture's fusion with the human psyche. Yorke's vocals, which fluctuate between a plangent wail, a disfigured scream, and an ethereal moan, personify this schizophrenia—reinforced by the richly layered soundscape, which morphs from gossamer to grotesque and back again.

Thematically, "Paranoid Android" merges *Night of the Living Dead*–style psychological terror with an Old Testament form of cosmic retribution, creating a masterwork of musical science fiction in which the narrator's most pressing fear is his own defenselessness in the face of the omnipresent white noise. The conclusion of "Android" is a gorgeously macabre happy ending, in which the wicked are eliminated in a slow-motion torrent of furious punishment.

As the first single from a highly anticipated album, "Paranoid Android" showed that Radiohead were determined to meet the public on the band's terms. The song, recalling the bombastic '70s prog rock of Queen, King Crimson, and Pink Floyd, was a huge leap from the group's previous work, and Magnus Carlsson's unsettling animated video threatened to alienate MTV along with the band's fan base. Of course, the gamble paid off: Radiohead's greatest success came from ignoring the perceived wisdom about how high-profile rock bands should operate

and trusting their fans to follow them down a difficult path at the most crucial point in their career. They followed, all right, and Radiohead rightfully earned their reputation as one of the most widely admired rock bands of the '90s and beyond.
—*EH*

Björk: *"Joga"* 1997

Following her stress-induced on-camera thrashing of a television reporter in a Bangkok airport and a letter bomb and videotaped suicide from a psychotic fan, Björk began 1997 by abandoning her public life in London for the remote comforts of her native Reykjavik, in turn rekindling a love affair with Iceland that manifested as *Homogenic*. Where her previous solo albums, *Debut* and *Post,* were exuberant outings, *Homogenic* came across as sober and stoic. There was even an underlying methodology at play; Björk originally wanted each of the album's tracks to consist of only "beats and strings," the former to represent Iceland's mountains and glaciers, the latter to represent its more dynamic, shifting elements, such as lava, geysers, and bubbling mudpots. Described by Björk as a sort of Icelandic national anthem, the sweeping "Joga" is a concoction of stirring strings and craggy rhythms that stays true to her original blueprint. It also signposted her move away from dance music and toward the modern-classical, avant-garde, and minimal electronic experiments that defined her career over the next decade.
—*MP*

The Verve: *"Bitter Sweet Symphony"* 1997

When the Verve incorporated a string sample from an orchestral cover of the Rolling Stones' "The Last Time" for "Bitter Sweet Symphony," Stones rights-holder ABKCO Records sued. Eventually, they allowed the Lancashire five-piece to continue publishing and performing the song, as long as all royalties went to ABKCO and songwriting credits went to Mick and Keef. The ironic thing is that of all the Britpop hits that ruled the earth in the 1990s, the sound of "Bitter Sweet Symphony" is among the least indebted to the Stones, the Beatles, or any other British Invasion staple. Frontman Richard Ashcroft made a colossal work out of that contentious sample by building heavily on it—piling on monolithic drums, deeply chiming guitars, and his own orchestration—until he

transformed a syrupy cooptation of rock music into a towering pop anthem. Reminiscent of Phil Spector's wall of sound, Ennio Morricone's film scores, and a lineage of soul that stretched from the Drifters' "There Goes My Baby" to Isaac Hayes's "Walk on By," the song is remarkably majestic, even as Ashcroft's voice just about gives up hope: "'Cause it's a bitter sweet symphony, this life / Trying to make ends meet, you're a slave to money, then you die."
—NP

Elliott Smith: *"Between the Bars"* 1997

Though "Miss Misery" made him an indie star, the elegant "Between the Bars" remains Elliott Smith's most enduring statement, as well as his most incisive and dysfunctional love song. "Between the Bars" is about power, shame, and keeping somebody close to you by keeping them trapped in their own past. As is often the case with his best work, the simple fluidity of Smith's lyrics masks their unsparing wit. His sharp, fatalistic tone is present from the song's first verse, as he calls out "the potential you'll be that you'll never see" and "the promises you'll only make." Smith would go on to explore similar themes the following year on the more grandiose *XO,* but he never again wrote a song as darkly romantic as "Between the Bars."
—ML

Cat Power: *"Cross Bones Style"* 1998

Before she came out of her shell, Chan Marshall was a legendary mess. She broke down during shows, played with her back to the audience, abandoned songs mid-verse, left the stage without explanation. The Cat Power moniker probably never would have made it past a few small releases and a forgiving cult audience had her withering nature not made songs like "Cross Bones Style" sound even more haunted. A Southerner who had relocated to Brooklyn, Marshall took herself out of her element for her fourth album, *Moon Pix*; she traveled to Australia to record with guitarist Mick Turner and drummer Jim White of Melbourne instrumental act the Dirty Three.

On "Cross Bones Style," that rhythm section hammers out a sinewy and seductive groove as Marshall, an underrated guitar player, traces her own curvy lines throughout the song. Even as she sings the cryptic invitation "Come, child, in a cross bones style," she distances herself from the listener, splitting into

two Chans: one singing low and intimate, like she would on her 2006 Memphis soul stew *The Greatest,* the other higher and a little desperate in her afflictions. That makes the song's other central line—"'Cause you have seen some unbelievable things"—doubly ambiguous and further masks the song's meaning, as if this introspective singer sought to guard her mysteries.
—SD

The Clientele: *"Reflections After Jane"* 1999

With a sound this classically English, you'd think the Clientele would have found favor at home. But at a time when the UK media was primed to jump on promise at a track's notice the band quietly sneaked out a half-dozen singles. Among them was 1999's "Reflections After Jane" (and its equally exquisite B-side "An Hour Before the Light"), an instant antique from a group who seemed caught out of time.

Like all the Clientele's early songs, "Reflections After Jane" is soaked in reverb, so at first it seems like one big gauzy cloud. Listen closer and details emerge: Snatches of resonant lyrics, a wistful chorus hook, and the careful intelligence of the band's rhythm section as it delicately picks a way through the reverie.

The Clientele's initial fans relished the band's classically gorgeous melodies and the subtle shifts in feeling that underpinned apparently similar tracks. And once the band started recording albums, they gradually let more space and joy into their sound. But the Clientele are still the same group that made precious miniatures like this—even now, the mood's the thing.
—TE

Bonnie "Prince" Billy: *"I See a Darkness"* 1999

Will Oldham's music has always been haunted, but only on *I See a Darkness*—his first record under the Bonnie "Prince" Billy moniker—does Oldham stare down his own ghost. *I See a Darkness* is an album obsessed with morality and mortality, with the way we live our lives and with their inevitable end. The album's title track is both a hymnal and a drinking song, a celebration of friendship and a fearful acknowledgement of our capacity to do evil. As the song's whisper-quiet verse builds to

IDM: Artificial Intelligence

"Intelligent dance music": With a name like that, the genre was in trouble from the start. Still, there was a need to classify this music for the sake of discussion. It grew out of rave in the early 1990s, was electronic-based, and paid attention to rhythm, but ultimately had no dance-floor aspirations. "IDM" was easy shorthand to show that you weren't talking about techno and you weren't talking about ambient. You were talking about…IDM, a possible revolution that often sounded like a garbled and alien whisper.

"Polynomial-C," Aphex Twin: It all starts (and many would say, ends) with the boundless imagination of Aphex Twin. This early track shows what he could do with inventive drum programming and a retro-futuristic melody that sounds beamed in from another planet.

"Object Orient," Black Dog: This is as close as the early-'90s "classic" era of IDM gets to dance; it's kept from the floor only by the trio's playful production trickery, which keeps knocking things off course.

"In a Beautiful Place Out in the Country," Boards of Canada: After the retreat of Aphex Twin, Boards of Canada found themselves the (rather shy and obscured) face of IDM. They created an airy, pastoral brand of electronic music and liked to tell stories; try to guess where this one is set.

"Frosch," Mouse on Mars: Mouse on Mars are German and have worked with a former member of Kraftwerk, but they're never sleek; this characteristic early track, which does a gentle butt bump with ambient house, reveals the Cologne-based duo as masters of the fuzzily textured, whimsical, and sensual.

"Do Dekor" Jan Jolinek: This music is all in the details. Here we have nanotechnology applied to the cause of sonic reconfiguration; it's a track created by sampling jazz where the fuzz in the vinyl grooves is more important than the vibraphone solo.

"Smile Around the Face," Four Tet: His programming and timbres are as sophisticated as the '90s artists he came up on, but Four Tet's Kieran Hebden has a more conventionally musical ear, demonstrating here how a cluster of woozy, synthetic sound can come together to sound like a cheery pop tune.

"Come on My Selector," Squarepusher: Tom Jenkinson, virtuoso bassist and friend of Aphex Twin, regularly explored the rarely traveled six-corner intersection of fusion jazz, drum 'n' bass, and abstract electronics. "Come on My Selector" leans in the d 'n' b direction, showing how zany, high-speed snare rips could get when you didn't have to worry about club play.

"4," Aphex Twin: Combining surging drum 'n' bass beats with a tense, bittersweet melody that could be scored for a chamber orchestra, "4" saw Richard James's musical ambitions expanding to where no genre could contain them, something the best IDM always strove for.

"Dael," Autechre: IDM producers sometimes like to present their tracks as virgin births, but Autechre gave props to old-school electro producers like Kurtis Mantronik. You can hear his icy, ridged funkiness at work in this eerie tune, which slithers around its bass melody like a mechanical snake.

"Endless Summer," Fennesz: With its simple acoustic guitar strum, computer treatments that crackle and gurgle, and surprisingly tuneful melody, this track by Austrian producer Fennesz made it seem like every kind of music could benefit from deconstruction—even sentimental themes from old surf movies.

"Do While," Oval: Markus Popp of Oval once said that what he does is not music or art but rather "file management." His deeply serious immersion in dense poststructuralist theory somehow led to the creation of one of the most hypnotically beautiful pieces of '90s electronic minimalism, an epic track wherein the "glitch" (in this case, from skipping CDs) reveals a machine's warm soul.

"Straight Outta Compton (Kid-606 Remix)," N.W.A.: Nutty processing (made possible only by very powerful computers) meets a rap classic. By time-stretching the vocals, amplifying the already hard beats, and cutting the original samples to ribbons, Kid-606 made the original sound alternately meaner and more vulnerable.
—MR

a chilling chorus, Oldham intones, "Did you know how much I love you?" like it's actually a question, all tenderness and heartbreaking vulnerability. This disarming openness bleeds from "I See a Darkness"; while Oldham's earlier work as Palace was chock-full of Appalachian folk anachronisms, this song forges a starkly grand sound that's far more candid and immediate. That Johnny Cash covered it (with Oldham singing backup) was apt; like the best of Cash's work, "I See a Darkness" unflinchingly approaches broad, timeless issues with awe and humility.
—*ML*

Smog: *"Teenage Spaceship"* 1999

As Smog, Bill Callahan combines simplicity and mystery. If he writes a song called "River Guard," it's going to be about working as a guard down by the river; something called "Rain on Lens" is going to be about how condensation can mess up a camera shot. But his voice is typically flat, low, and deadpan, urging the listener to wonder what he "really means." This lovely ballad, from Smog's 1999 album *Knock Knock,* is the pinnacle of his aesthetic. "Teenage Spaceship" is about an anthropomorphic craft going through its awkward stage with an inspiring sense of confidence and dignity. "I was beautiful with all my lights," Callahan sings, evoking the Disneyfied fantasia of a kid with an active imagination. The austere musical accompaniment—just a few notes on piano and a lightly scraped guitar—is enough to move the song along, not needing a note more. Then Callahan finishes by pausing an extra second during the line "I was a teenage…Smog." By suddenly mentioning his band name, and later, the title of his first album, he causes the song to fold in on itself. It's a strange reveal to end a gem of economy and understatement—in other words, Callahan doing what he does best.
—*MR*

Silver Jews: *"Random Rules"* 1998

An associate of and precursor to Pavement, a recovering drug addict, and a respected literary figure, David Berman knows the difference between what makes good poetry and what makes good song lyrics. Witness the opening line to "Random Rules": "In 1984, I was hospitalized for approaching perfection." Comparably clever words and sharp images follow, but, more than that, every syllable is a careful fit to the music—which, with help here from

Pavement frontman and one-time Berman roommate Stephen Malkmus, is more vivid than the sour and Spartan sounds on previous Silver Jews albums.

Berman's flat vocals and out-of-tune strumming were now augmented by languid lead guitar and well-placed horns, all evoking the half-empty country-and-western bars and backwater burgs that his characters inhabit. It comes together in a subtle build that underlines the song's linchpin image, a final parting shot after a cold, broken tryst, and one that further demonstrates Berman's eye for detail: "Before I go I gotta ask you, dear, about the tan line on your ring finger."
—*JC*

Autechre: *"Arch Carrier"* 1998

As IDM—"intelligent dance music"—unraveled into abstract electronic music in the late 1990s and early 2000s, Autechre's last great gasp of beats came on 1998's evocatively titled *LP5.* "Arch Carrier" was tucked away near the end of the album, and it featured all of the group's previous hallmarks: razor-sharp updates on electro and industrial dance; obscured but interesting, almost mystical "melodies" (which were more the product of rhythmic manipulation than chord sequences); and massively programmed variations on the basic midtempo groove. In one sense, it was a culmination of Autechre's early sound, just before the UK duo of Sean Booth and Rob Brown abandoned any obligations to obvious forward momentum in favor of ultra-complexity.

The song's insistent statement and restatement of its chord pattern over the constantly mutating and painstakingly tweaked rhythm track is reminiscent of Ravel's "Boléro," wherein a simple melodic figure is transformed into mantra through repetition. There is a story in which a confused audience member accused Ravel of madness after hearing the piece, to which the composer replied that she had understood it well. Three years after "Arch Carrier," Autechre released *Confield* to similar accusations.
—*DL*

Boards of Canada: *"Happy Cycling"* 1998

With their warm, woozy, nostalgic take on IDM, Michael Sandison and Marcus Eoin have had an immense influence on the rest of electronic music. The duo established its basic sound with a variety of mixtapes and EPs in the early to mid-'90s and hit big with its 1998 debut *Music Has the Right to Children.* An inspired blend of ghostly atmospherics, decaying synths, nature sounds, and hip-hop rhythms, that landmark LP alternated between friendly and sinister tones with disarming ease. By way of its artwork and time-distorted samples of children talking, it also established BOC as uncanny articulators of the gauzy fragments of childhood memory. Although only issued as a bonus track on that album's U.S. release, "Happy Cycling" is now held as one of the band's signature moments due in part to the way it memorably folds a sample of seagulls into its syncopated rhythms.

Outside of their music, Boards of Canada rarely grant interviews or play live shows and prefer not to talk in depth about their personal beliefs. On record, though, they're the kind of band that Wikis were invented for. Their music is suffused with hidden references to the occult, numerology, and David Koresh's Branch Davidians. "Happy Cycling" is no different: Playing the outro backward reveals snippets from an interview with ELO's Jeff Lynne on the subject of backmasking.
—*MP*

Herbert: *"So Now..."* 1998

Although a gifted producer with a talent for inter-locking nimble rhythms with fragile sounds, Matthew Herbert has always put nearly as much emphasis on his process as on the music itself. In the same way that Danish filmmaker Lars von Trier tried to restore a certain level of transparency to his films with the Dogme 95 manifesto, so has Herbert with his own self-penned "Personal Contract for the Composition of Music." In addition to hard-and-fast rules prohibiting the use of third-party samples, drum machines, or factory presets, Herbert's PCCOM also stipulates that songs should only use "sounds directly related to [a] topic." Correspondingly, whether it's 2001's *Bodily Functions* (the human body) or 2005's *Plat du Jour* (food preparation), many of Herbert's albums are concept albums, built around the sounds of their chosen subjects.

With its shuffling house rhythms, gloopy synths, and cool, jazz-inflected vocals (supplied by Herbert's wife and longtime creative partner Dani Siciliano), 1998's dreamy "So Now..." represents an early coming-together not only of Herbert's signature elements,

but also of his sampling practices. That's because it's taken from *Around the House,* the first of Herbert's albums to work within a predefined set of sampling parameters—in this case, it was items found within the home. Listen to "So Now..." enough and you're likely to start hallucinating everything from cookie cutters to ironing boards into the mix; this is music that demands as much imagination from the listener as it does from its creator.
—*MP*

Aphex Twin: *"Windowlicker"* 1999

Richard D. James's career has been dictated primarily by his own stubborn whimsy rather than by public interest. For many fans, James's slippery legacy of pseudonyms, left turns, purported white-label releases, question-mark-leaving, and all-around antagonism represents something to be admired. For some, though, it's a point of frustration, and the magnificent "Windowlicker" has a lot to do with that. Originally released as a one-off single in 1999, it's a slithery, twisted six minutes of wet funk and a near anomaly in the Aphex Twin catalog. But despite overflowing with some of his most grotesque sounds, it's also a strangely accessible, even hummable record—one that gives glimpses of what James' imaginary pop album might sound like.
—*MP*

Uilab: *"St. Elmo's Fire"* 1998

Fusion was a great thread through music in the 1990s, as bands, perhaps sensing that from-nowhere innovation was becoming more difficult, looked for new ways to combine the sounds of the past. Stereolab were masters of this sort of thing, but their influences were much broader than those of their peers. They also made the most of collaboration, building bridges across genres and scenes by working with members of Tortoise, Nurse with Wound, and Mouse on Mars, among others. More than any single group in the '90s, Stereolab showed how music from earlier generations could be reconfigured to inspire new music that seemed oddly futuristic.

Stereolab combined with American post-rock outfit Ui for a one-off EP built around a cover of "St. Elmo's Fire" by Brian Eno, another polymath whose open-ended approach to sound was a touchstone for all involved. True to the original in terms of structure,

Uilab updated the song considerably in terms of sonics. Beginning with the steady pulse of a tinny drum machine, Laetitia Sadier's voice fades up, holding a single-note drone, and then the shuffling, lazily funky beat kicks in, calling to mind the trip-hop that was then in vogue. Sadier's silken tone contrasts sharply with Eno's functional nasality in the original, and the richness of the production—Beach Boys coos at the end of every line, deeply resonant bass, a gurgling Moog—results in a mysterious and transporting track that serves as a nexus for about five different strands of art-rock/pop.
—MR

Air: *"Le Soleil est Près du Moi"* 1997

In 1997, the Prodigy and the Chemical Brothers scaled the international charts with pummeling rhythms and intestine-rattling pulses, but Frenchmen Jean-Benoît Dunckel and Nicolas Godin couldn't be bothered with such barbarism. The perfectly coiffed pair was more interested in chilling out in style, a popular pursuit in the middle of a 1990s mini–lounge revival also fueled by Stereolab, the High Llamas, Cornelius, and Pizzicato Five.

Modernizing the cognac-sipping smoothness of Serge Gainsbourg, Air introduced themselves to the world with singles that seamlessly mixed analog warmth and digital panache. "Le Soleil est Près du Moi" (translation: "The Sun Is Close to Me") starts elegantly, with strings, bass, and keys slipping into a classy groove. But this duo isn't interested in mere pastiche. The song's processed, robotic vocals seem novel at first—a bit of smirking, self-aware kitsch— but as the animatronic cocktail lizard casually repeats the track's cryptic titular phrase, its hazy voice grows more human, and more tragic. Instead of simply making a gimmicky tribute to lady-killers of the past, Air break down bachelor-pad suaveness and arrive at something surprisingly honest and affecting: the hidden tears of a letch.
—RD

Massive Attack: *"Teardrop"* 1998

Massive Attack defined trip-hop with cool, dark vocals and cinematic beats. While 1994's *Protection* showed a sense of hope and humor, most tracks on the 1997 follow-up *Mezzanine* hung with menace: The bass is a tremor, vocals drift like smoke, and everyone seems seconds away from growing fangs. But compare "Teardrop," featuring the sighing vocals of Cocteau Twins' Elizabeth Fraser, to anything else on the album—or really, to almost anything in Massive Attack's catalog—and the difference is stark. While crackling vinyl shadows the ringing harpsichord, the song is uplifting, precise, and porcelain. From the first note to the ragged close, Fraser's voice is fragile and strained. Years later, she'd fight in concert to hit the same firm whisper. But the strain is the hook. For Massive Attack, it's the exception that proves the rule: They had their biggest hit with their most precious cut.
—CD

Black Star [ft. Common]: *"Respiration"* 1998

Mos Def and Talib Kweli, two bookish Brooklyn rappers, named their 1998 project after Marcus Garvey's return-to-Africa steamship line. Their focus for Black Star, however, was directed toward their own borough's unique brand of violent cosmopolitanism. "Respiration," the standout track from their self-titled record, opens with two successive voices. First comes a young black graffiti artist describing one of his tags; second, as the track starts taking shape, a Latina woman's voice whispers, "Escuchela…la ciudad respirando," or "Listen to it…the city breathing."

Mos and Talib's subsequent rendering of city life is accordingly anthropomorphic. Their stated goal is to "describe the inscrutable," and they succeed, conveying a striking image of a Brooklyn supported by a metal and fiber-optic skeleton, breathing "against the flesh of the evening," yet choked by conflict and contradiction. In a broader context, Black Star reintroduced Native Tongues–style rap consciousness to the nation at large, in the process jumpstarting rap's turn-of-the-century independent renaissance via New York's own Rawkus Records.
—EH

The Notorious B.I.G.: *"Hypnotize"* 1997

"Hypnotize" became Biggie's first number 1 pop hit on May 3, 1997. It remained on the Hot 100 for four months. As the song finally exited the chart in September, Biggie's "Mo Money Mo Problems" became his second number 1 pop hit. Coming after the rapper's March 9 murder, these successes

Bootybass

Ghettotech: The Detroit term "ghettotech" was coined by then-teen producer/DJ Disco D, a talented prodigy of many genres who, sadly, took his own life in 2007. As a sub-subgenre of Detroit electro, ghettotech takes the dance-floor-rocking mission of booty bass and Chicago house and cranks it through its own D-Town slant, most explicitly seen through the eyes of its aptly named papi, DJ Godfather. As one Databass Records compilation put it, "Don't stop til you jit enough"— "jit" being the Detroit-based battle dance that fits hand-in-glove with the ghettotech m.o. These sped-up synths and trebly tweeters twerk it 'til the morning light.

"Ass-N-Titties," **DJ Assault:** Dance-floor classic extolling the virtues of the well-endowed while admonishing those broke-and-stanky chicas, wherein Assault repeats porn keywords as a chorus over jacked-up electro. So wrong, it's right, basically.

"Whut U Like," **Mr. Dé:** A paired-down man-woman flirtation electro number in which former DJ Assault partner Mr. Dé and Dé's wife compare assets—cheddar, hair, nether parts. Ghettotech gold from a production genius who deserves more due outside the D.

"Tittles and Ass," **DJ Deeon:** Brilliantly flipping Assault's classic chorus, longtime ghettotech producer Deeon makes a nastily minimal polar opposite, replacing the original's sugar-bass with tinny drums and an echo chamber.

"Bang Dat Butt," **Bitch Ass Darius:** He's from the kindred city of East St. Louis, but Bitch Ass Darius is signed to Godfather's Databass Records and his small catalog has some of the best tracks in ghettotech; this one switches from 808 spark plugs to outer-space melodies with barely enough warning to switch up your booty stance.

"I'm a Ho," **DJ Slugo:** A sort of unlikely community-building song: Slugo, his voice screwed down to a crawl, beseeches all men, women, and children to join the ho massif—and over sweaty 909 beeps and a Jell-O-vibrating low end, even the squarest wallflower could be convinced.

Miami Bass: Miami bass came out of late-'80s electro and turned into booty and car bass, that shit that blows out your ears and moves your ass at once— and gave birth to new genres like crunk, favela funk, and Baltimore club music. Now bow down to the Roland TR-808 synthesizer, without which we would have none of these tinny cowbell tinks or echo-chamber bass kicks.

"Return to the Planet of Bass," **Maggotron:** Maggotron went all-out on this early hit, nestling a kitchen sink of samples in extra-melodic yet menacing synths and guitar solos: Bugs Bunny, Salt-n-Pepa, Darth Vader, Madonna, and Chic all make cameos in this epic classic. The rapped verse comes in like a narrator and is curiously distorted so dude totally sounds like the wizard behind the curtain—but really maybe he was just the wizard beneath the carburetor. You know, of *your jeep.*

"Just Give the DJ a Break," **Dynamix II [ft. Two Tough Tee]:** The vocodered chorus—"Just give the DJ a break," of course—is answered by vinyl scratches and a hefty 808 bass-cowbell tag-team, spliced in with soul-chorus samples and…is that a dog barking?

"Wiggle Wiggle," **Disco Rick and the Wolf Pack:** As the '80s played out, 2 Live Crew got Congress-famous, and their magic Roland electro drum-machine joint got more refined. Bass music branched off deeper into booty pep rallies, complete with choruses sung by ladies who would make terrific cheerleaders. This super-fast jam gets a bobbysox sample and instructs las chicas to wiggle it—just a little bit— in pretty tame terms. This is maybe the only Miami bass song you could play for a three-year-old.

"Throw the D," **2 Live Crew** / **"Throw the P,"** **Anquette:** Long before Luke and them were throwing the First Amendment back in the face of the porn-busting religious right, they were making nice instructional dance tracks that merely amplified the good clean fun and sexual undertones of dudes like, you know, Little Richard or whoever. "Throw the D[ick]" put a little porn in with its wind-and-grind and used cowbell to jump-start the jams—and interestingly, it inspired an answer track (on Luke's label!) in the form of Anquette's "Throw the P[ussy]." The ladies, having our say from jump!

"Shake That Ass Bitch," **Splack Pack:** This track illustrates exactly why bootybass is actually a secret form of rhythmic magic: Many women would probably smack any strange dude who rolled up on them on Broadway and commanded, "Shake that ass, bitch, and let me see what you got." Add a posse-barked chorus, a helping of bass, a suave disco melody, and a couple of dance move instructionals, and voilà! The ladies are shaking it, the daring are scrubbin' the ground, and the whole club is sweating.
—JS

were both undeniable triumphs and frightening confirmations of the "you're nobody 'til somebody kills you" mentality Biggie espoused during his twenty-four-year lifespan. But "Hypnotize" isn't a eulogy. It's a pinnacle of the entire Bad Boy aesthetic—part street-rat mercilessness, part gaudy Clinton-era flamboyance, part foolproof funk.

Highlighting these qualities is the track's action-movie-inspired video, which doubles as a feel-good, escapist balm in the face of brutal reality. In the generously funded mini-thriller, Biggie, sidekick Puffy, and a few bikinied associates are chilling on a yacht—using cash as coasters—when black choppers encroach from above. What are a couple of silk-pajama-wearing playboys to do? Cue up a carefree club bomb and tweak peril into euphoric drama—more or less the same formula that took Biggie from Brooklyn street corners to big-budget videos in the first place.
—RD

OutKast: *"Spottieottiedopaliscious"* 1998

Already innately gifted students when they debuted in 1994—as two teenagers draping their adolescent drawls over a silky Atlanta take on California's low-riding pimp rap—OutKast fast-tracked themselves into mainstream futurists, mixing old-school, back-woods funk with Southern hip-hop's bass-heavy machine rhythms and a streak of spacey mysticism that's equal parts sci-fi comic book and church gospel. By the time of 1998's *Aquemini,* and the eight-minute "Spottieottiedopaliscious," rappers Big Boi and Andre 3000 were nearly on their own as radio-bound boundary-pushers in a playalistic world that their early work had both nurtured and undercut.

Over a loose, live bass groove that sounds like it was recorded during a three-a.m. basement jam with more pot smoke in the air than oxygen, producers Organized Noize whip up voodoo—with shakers, wah-wah guitar, and percolating drum-machine counter-rhythms—and hit like Parliament at their most sensual. Andre and Big Boi spit almost-rhymes in a cryptic self-help spoken-word style—but, reversing the hip-hop norm, their lyrics make up only a fraction of the track's length, with the slow-motion rhythm and the grimy horns trading a call-and-response that works the stoned vamp for every second. It was the first time critics and fans raised the question of whether or not OutKast could be tagged as hip-hop, and the

fact that they were still questioning ten years later is a testament to the duo's restlessness and potency.
—JH

The Roots: *"The Next Movement"* 1999

"Inevitably, hip-hop albums are treated as though they are disposable. They're not maximized as product, even, you know, not to mention as art." The Roots chose this sample to begin not one but two of their first four albums, summing up demons they couldn't quite shed: On the one hand, commerce and all its attendant demands for hooks, charisma, and formula; on the other, art. In the 1990s, the Roots mainlined this dilemma: As traditionalists without traditional skills and as hip-hop culture loyalists who traded beats for real instruments, the Philly collective had to reinvent the basics.

If they lost sleep over their contradictory aspirations, the struggle also backed them into great corners. 1999's *Things Fall Apart* saw their most concerted effort to go pop, and yet the hook in "The Next Movement" is a glorified stutter from MC Black Thought, and the track's most quotable line might well be "At your music conference I'm the panelist." But "Movement"—authored by bandleader ?uestlove, augmented by guest turntablist DJ Jazzy Jeff, and fielding a cadre of instrumentalists about ten guys deep—boasts one of the most densely concentrated and detailed stretches of Roots music in the group's career.
—ZB

The Flaming Lips: *"Waitin' for a Superman"* 1999

Throughout the late 1980s and '90s, when Oklahoma psych-rockers the Flaming Lips tackled subjects like mortality and faith, they left themselves an escape route in the form of obscure references and dark, surreal humor—so a lyric like "If God hears all my questions / How come there's never an answer?" would be found in a song called "Placebo Headwound." But the band's 1999 album *The Soft Bulletin* was different, as evinced by "Waitin' for a Superman."

Here, a community that's used to having a hero swoop in to solve its problems has to deal with an issue whose weight is beyond Superman's ability. While the track references comic-book fantasy, the delivery is so straight, and the song so achingly melodic, that humor and irony are laid aside entirely. The musical shift is just as dramatic, with piano chords Elton John might have fit into a ballad, strings and horns providing additional sweetening, and absurdly loud drums accenting the refrains. When heard next to the Flaming Lips' fantastical and acid-damaged early material, its earnestness is especially striking. With "Waitin' for a Superman," the Flaming Lips reimagined the modern rock song as a gentle, affirming prayer.

—MR

The Beta Band: *"Dry the Rain"* 1997

The Beta Band blossomed from fever dreams. A year before their first demo, an influenza virus clogged singer Steve Mason's sinuses. For two weeks, Mason shivered in bed, and when the mucus waned he spontaneously wrote "Dry the Rain," a dusty ballad forged of junkyard loops and Mason's wistful, choirboy voice. Fittingly, then, the song begins in a haze, before drums rush in like white blood cells and horns blow away the clouds.

The lilting, shuffling, acoustic-driven song made the band the toast of discerning music fans almost as soon as it was released, but it also hamstrung the rest of its career. The Betas' sound continued to be exploratory, encompassing house, ramshackle blues, and spacious dub. Each of their releases contained a smattering of ideas and genres—not only over the course of a record, but often within each song. Those willing to follow the group ranked them as one of the most promising of the new decade, but many listeners wanted more of those traditional dusty ballads, and in 2004, dejected and too often overlooked, the Beta Band bowed out with the sadly appropriately titled *Heroes to Zeros*.

—BD

The Olivia Tremor Control: *"Hideaway"* 1998

The Olivia Tremor Control, from indie hotbed Athens, Georgia, were best known for their membership in a loose federation of bands—along with Neutral Milk Hotel, Apples in Stereo, Elf Power, and others—known as the Elephant 6 collective. OTC's trippy guitar pop can be seen as an experiment designed to answer one question: What would happen if a band recorded at home on their own banged-up equipment but pretended they were the Beatles at Abbey Road? Most lo-fi groups of the 1990s either incorporated sonic scuzziness into their music (Sebadoh, Smog) or wrote such catchy songs you forgot about the bad sound (Guided by Voices). The Olivia Tremor Control wanted everything—all the control and unfettered imagination of bedroom self-production and the rich, multilayered sonics of careful studio work.

"Hideaway" came closest to realizing that dream. The song works as both sing-along rock and a collage of sounds arranged in a comely mass. Liner notes make mention of "10 acoustic guitars... added two at a time as the mix progresses," but the hook holds out more in the way of spacey backing vocals and brassy horns primed for a surrealist parade. It's a monument to the simple pleasures of pop—as well as an artifact from an era when sounds of the psychedelic '60s started coalescing into something newly homey and modern. That it's ultimately a celebration of creativity ("don't hide away from your imagery" is the refrain) makes "Hideaway" inspirational in a very direct way: You hear it and you want to get together with friends and make something great.

—AB

Neutral Milk Hotel: *"Holland, 1945"* 1998

"Holland, 1945" is the key track on a very key indie rock album. *In the Aeroplane Over the Sea* extended the horizons of the genre in terms of sound and subject matter. But even those who don't care for the band or album—and there are many—often find a place in their hearts for this song. It reaches beyond the group's sizable cult because it tempers some of Neutral Milk Hotel's divisive quirks—leader Jeff Mangum's yelping vocals are held under the warm Alka-Seltzer fizz of Robert Schneider's production, for example—and sweeps them along with a relentlessly buoyant melody.

Still, while it's the most accessible song on *Aeroplane*, "Holland, 1945" pulls no punches lyrically. Since it was the last song written for the album, it's hard not to see it as a kind of summary. The title and lyrics refer to World War II and specifically the story of Anne Frank, a recurring motif on the record. Frank's persona—the tender, poetic innocent in love with the simple beauty of the everyday, destroyed by the ultimate expression of human evil—turned out to be an ideal archetype for the kind of worlds Jeff Mangum wanted to build. "Holland, 1945" celebrates humanity's instinctive sense of wonder while registering disgust at its propensity for destruction.

The song is filled with dark pictures and striking details ("Indentions in the sheets / Where their bodies once moved but don't move anymore"), and as the images pile up, held aloft by fuzzy chords and fanfare-style horns, "Holland, 1945" begins to feel hurried and breathless, like Mangum has so much to say that he's not sure he'll have time to get it all out. The song conveys the feeling of a manic state, when the rush of thoughts, ideas, and feelings becomes almost too much to bear, and by the time it ends with a cluster of horns holding a chord, Mangum's obsessions have become ours.
—*MR*

Super Furry Animals:
"Ice Hockey Hair" 1998

Few bands reward a modest international cult of obsessives with more or merrier pranks than Super Furry Animals. Since forming in 1993, this Welsh group has created a vast and largely self-contained world that spans psych pop, progressive rock, punk, and techno. Whether crafting multilingual puns, tooling into festival gigs in a blue "peace" tank, or dropping the f-bomb more than fifty times in a Steely Dan–sampling single, SFA established themselves as musical anarchists with the tunes, ideas, and charisma to back up their wacky stunts. It's only fitting that the band's crowning achievement would be, um, the title track to an EP named after a Scandinavian variant of the mullet hairstyle.

In the surging, fuzzbombing chorus to 1998's "Ice Hockey Hair," SFA frontman Gruff Rhys goes so far as to ask for advice from a woman who sports the shaggiest 'do. Released during the interim between career LP high points *Radiator* and *Guerrilla,* the song would garner SFA their loftiest UK singles-chart placement yet. More importantly, it encapsulates a career's worth of good-natured guitar-pop mindfucks. "Ice Hockey Hair" is the band at its most decadently irreverent, a full seven minutes of candy-coated distortion and vocoder-like vocals all eventually giving way to outer-space electronics.
—*MH*

Stardust:
"Music Sounds Better with You" 1998

A one-off release from Daft Punk's Thomas Bangalter, French house heavy-hitter-in-waiting Alan Braxe, and singer Benjamin Diamond, 1998's "Music Sounds Better with You" followed up on the Eurohouse goodwill amassed by Daft Punk's 1997 breakthrough *Homework.* Considering Stardust were an ad hoc band (they would never put their name on anything again), the single's impact was tremendous: It shot to the top of the U.S. dance chart and scored a number 2 on the UK singles charts. But compared to the output of other crossover dance acts such as Chemical Brothers, Faithless, and Prodigy—who were all charting with tracks that made concessions to traditional song structure—"Music Sounds Better with You" sounded like it was piped directly from the booth in Paris's Rex Club. Even for a house track, there's staggeringly little going on here; there's no intro, no bridge, no buildup—just an infectious, spangly, rolling groove (lifted from the beginning of Chaka Khan's "Fate"), expertly filtered into peak-time perfection.
—*MP*

Basement Jaxx: *"Jump n' Shout"* 1999

They rarely repeat themselves, but Basement Jaxx's perverse approach to house music remains instantly recognizable, exploding with ideas no other producer would dare to use. Starting life in the mid-'90s as perfectionist curators of traditional house, the UK duo quickly became obsessed with writing their own scripts: On 1999's "Jump n' Shout" they arrive at their desired destination by running in the opposite direction, creating an effortless crossover house-pop anthem through an uncommonly brutish reiteration of house music's core principles.

Simultaneously stripped-back and overblown, the song's wall of sound is constructed from little more than a galloping beat, sludgy bass riffs, and a cavalcade of sirens and whistles. The final ingredient is MC Slarta John, whose tongue-twisting ragga sermon is delivered with such breathless enthusiasm that the track seems to accelerate exponentially, threatening to spiral out of control at any moment. It's an illusion: Throughout, the arrangement's exacting precision reveals Basement Jaxx to be ruthless disciplinarians, demanding total submission to their

nonstop beat. Their sonic blueprint only expanded after this: On 2001's unofficial sequel "Where's Your Head At," the duo toyed with full-blown guitar-churn carnage. A nice addition, but arguably redundant: With "Jump n' Shout," they'd already concocted a sound as heavy as metal.
—*TF*

Wilco: *"Via Chicago"* 1999

"I dreamed about killing you again last night, and it felt alright to me," shrugs Wilco leader Jeff Tweedy at the outset of this disjointed murder ballad. While the words read as bloody and intense, the Midwestern troubadour delivers his opening line with all the passion of an office drone. Is it a deadpan joke? An unsettling harbinger of things to come? The song's shady internal logic and unscrupulous motivations distinguish it from Tweedy's previous work—clearly, this isn't the kind of straightforward yarn about a well-meaning screwup Tweedy had perfected with Uncle Tupelo and early Wilco albums *A.M.* and *Being There.*

Indeed, if 1999's slyly poisonous *Summerteeth* marked a transition from the Chicago band's folksy, classic-rocking roots to the more abstract, free-associative style they would later pursue with *Yankee Hotel Foxtrot,* "Via Chicago" was the tipping point. More Lou Reed or Henry Miller than Woody Guthrie, the song's theme is matched by its uncertain instrumentation. A squealing guitar offers constant threats beneath the track's traditional acoustic guitar veneer, and "Via Chicago" eventually breaks into a cacophony of stammering drums and Sonic Youth–style distortion. It's the sound of a band burying its past and foreshadowing its own stunning resurrection.
—*RD*

Pulp: *"This Is Hardcore"* 1998

If 1995's commercial breakthrough *Different Class* constituted a velvet-rope-toppling coup for this long-suffering art-pop band, with 1998's *This Is Hardcore*—and its foreboding title single— Pulp realized that the scene inside the VIP room was just as insufferable as life on the fringes. In retrospect, "This Is Hardcore" signaled the end— not just of Britpop's halcyon days, but of the alt-rock-dominated 1990s, the capper to an era when major-label-sponsored acts could make a funereal six-minute dirge about low-budget pornography and call it the single.

Released just as Pamela Anderson and Tommy Lee's sex tape was becoming the web's first viral-video phenomenon, "This Is Hardcore" renders the unsavory intimations of a would-be amateur-porn auteur in an Ingmar Bergman–eqsue pallor, and the song's ominous allure is intensified by drowsy brass fanfares and seismic orchestra swells that seem to emanate from beneath the earth. But the song turns more dramatic as Jarvis Cocker's pervy protagonist grows ever more desperate to get his shot: "This is hardcore / There is no way back for you," he insists, speaking both to his starlet's forever-lost innocence and his own band's future as an international chart proposition. But if this was commercial suicide, it was executed with a Kevorkian-like sense of precision and pride in the work.
—*SB*

Belle and Sebastian: *"Lazy Line Painter Jane"* 1997

At the start of 1997, Belle and Sebastian seemed poised on the verge of a breakthrough. Their second album, *If You're Feeling Sinister,* had confirmed them as standard-bearers for lyrical, jangling, old-school indie, while their elusive debut, *Tigermilk,* grew ever more mythical. Would they finally conjure a hit single, cross over, and, as many predicted, become the Smiths of the 1990s? Or were they happy to cultivate their indie-pop cottage industry away from the mainstream?

In typically eccentric fashion, they somehow managed both, releasing a series of four-track EPs, the second of which was *Lazy Line Painter Jane.* While its name seemed to allude to the hushed influence of Nick Drake, the title song was actually the most ebullient example yet of their church-hall Phil Spector aesthetic, thanks largely to guest vocalist Monica Queen, on loan from Glasgow perennials Thrum. Appearing more than a minute into the song, she transforms Stuart Murdoch's teenage frustration and seedy longing into a grand yelp of defiance: "You will have a boy tonight / Or maybe you will have a girl tonight!" she howls, spurring the band into a gear they never knew they had, dizzy with reverb, and whirling with fairground exuberance.

For a moment it seemed as though B&S could achieve pop success without sacrificing their homespun independence—but the EP stalled one place short of the UK Top 40.
—ST

Yo La Tengo: *"Autumn Sweater"* 1997

Georgia Hubley and Ira Kaplan, for better or for worse, for richer or for poorer, are indie rock's eternal homecoming king and queen. By the time they released *I Can Hear the Heart Beating as One* in 1997, they had spent nearly twelve years together, rewriting (or reinterpolating) the music they loved in their own voices, a living fakebook for over forty years of popular music. In a lot of ways, Yo La Tengo's catalog is itself an autumn sweater—comforting, warm, lived-in without feeling overworn, the one thing you always reach for when you want to unwind. In this light, it's only fitting that the elder statesmen (and woman) of indie rock would pen the subculture's "Unchained Melody." If there were ever an instrument that could embody the awkward exuberance and fear of young love in the 1990s, it's Ira Kaplan's humble, introspective croon. But even the most ham-fisted Ethel Merman understudy couldn't undercut the sublime simplicity of those oft-quoted nothing-to-say lyrics, which perfectly encapsulate the exhilaration and fear felt before opening the door to someone you may fall in love with. Four warm organ chords wind through the song like leaves skittering across the ground as Hubley stands by her man, her understated syncopation moving this beautiful mess to its only natural conclusion—the boy asking the girl one last time to get away from it all, and the question remaining unanswered.
—DR

Sleater-Kinney: *"One More Hour"* 1997

In the early-1990s Pacific Northwest, riot grrrl was mostly a youthful thing, as fervid and passionate and life-changing as youthful things usually are. But Sleater-Kinney, birthed in the indie incubator of Olympia, Washington, was the band that took the fury and energy of that initial explosion and carried it with them into adulthood. Over an immensely rewarding seven-album career, the trio kicked enraged agitprop with the best of them, but it also brought that same urgency to its songs about love, music, motherhood, politics, and breakups.

"One More Hour" is a monster of a breakup song. Corin Tucker's world-devouring yowl unleashes torrents of anger and disappointment while the girl-group harmonies of Carrie Brownstein ("Don't say another word / About the other girl") and Janet Weiss cut the desperation with sweet fondness. Tucker and Brownstein's guitars weave together, combining conversational ease with jangling force and nudging each other in different directions, while Weiss's huge drum cracks keep everything anchored. In the band's early years, Tucker and Brownstein briefly dated, and it's fun to speculate that they were singing to each other. But ultimately it doesn't much matter: What sticks is the song's instinctively turbulent grace, the sort of grace that only happens when someone internalizes a moment of subcultural excitement and turns it into something eternal.
—TB

Refused: *"New Noise"* 1998

Refused broke up the same year they released *The Shape of Punk to Come,* and at the time it seemed sadly inevitable. Having learned sarcasm and suffocating self-awareness from their hardcore forebears in Born Against, and how to stylize an otherwise radical political program from D.C. agitators Nation of Ulysses, the Swedish quartet came into 1998 backed into a corner. Refused were aware of the irony: Self-defined as violently and vocally anticapitalist, the band made, as their last act before self-destructing, what might still be their genre's most viable commercial product— a song destined for video-game soundtracks, skate tapes, and *24.*

Though they sometimes cloaked their songwriting in free jazz and spoken-word interludes (two more goofy talismans of radicalism they copped from NoU), "New Noise" couldn't be obscured. Here, pinprick guitar riffs build, subside into silence, and come back ocean-sized. Halfway through, the song dissolves into a feedback echo before the guitars punch back in, Dennis Lyxzén's voice ramps back up, and Refused pipe in crowd noise—a canny predictor of the track's future as a punk-rock gateway drug.
—ZB

Sitting back and playing armchair astrologer for a band is easy from a distance; once their careers wind down, the overall trajectory is easily drawn. But in a few special cases, an artist releases a song that's less a warning sign than an air-raid siren. Even idle observers can see there'll be no graceful decline into old age for these groups. From here, it's a screeching halt.

"What's Your Fantasy?" **Travis Morrison:** This horrific Ludacris cover seemed, at worst, to be a misfired joke when the ex–Dismemberment Plan singer posted it to his website. Instead, it was a harbinger of *Travistan,* a masterpiece of bad humor.

"Why Can't I?" **Liz Phair:** Phair's cred may have been built on a thin foundation of swears and lo-fi production, but "Why Can't I?" was a headfirst dive into generic pop schlock, built for Clearasil ads and sitcom montages.

"Dope Nose," **Weezer:** Rivers Cuomo's fascination with the power of riffs was a cute dalliance of post-hiatus Weezer for a song or two off The Green Album. But when he remade "Hash Pipe" less than a year later as "Dope Nose" (so different!), people started wondering when the band would take another break.

"All Around the World," **Oasis:** The Gallagher brothers' musical mission may well have been to find the point where rock excess switches from triumphant to bloated. They finally succeeded with the interminable "All Around the World," with its horrible world-word rhymes and eight-thousand-piece orchestra.

"Look at Your Game Girl," **Guns N' Roses:** The covers record is generally the point where vultures start to circle, but Guns N' Roses raised the bar by recording maybe the most distasteful remake ever, of a song by one Charles Manson. The resulting bad karma kept them comatose for years.

"Ava Adore," **Smashing Pumpkins:** Billy Corgan went all-in on the guess that electro-goth was the future… or at least the best way to compensate when you've fired your addict drummer. Now he's cursed to a lifetime of "Return to Rock!" comeback gimmicks.

"Ch-Check It Out," **Beastie Boys:** Rap has yet to find a way to age gracefully, and returning to your old-school roots after your hair's turned gray is never the solution. So bad they were shamed into making an instrumental record.

"Crazy Beat," **Blur:** Let's take Graham Coxon's side on this one; when you're playing with the Disco Duck effects, it's time to let the band splinter into side projects.

"This Is What She's Like," **Dexys Midnight Runners:** Kevin Rowland's anxiety over following up "Come On Eileen" manifested itself in a fascinating record of spoken word and leitmotifs that was nonetheless single-proof and forever enshrined the band's picture under "one-hit wonder" in U.S. dictionaries.

"War" (live on *Saturday Night Live*), **Sinéad O'Connor:** Usually, stars benefit from a good old-fashioned album-burning crusade, but Sinéad found out the hard way that nobody got out of a diss war with Pope John Paul II alive. The man took lead!

"Stinkin Thinkin," **Happy Mondays:** Credit *24 Hour Party People* for re-creating the exact moment the Factory Records staff realized the Happy Mondays had suicide-bombed themselves (and their label) with this lead single from their Barbados recording session/drug excursion.
—RM

The Dismemberment Plan:
"The City" 1999

The Dismemberment Plan's breakout sophomore album *The Dismemberment Plan Is Terrified,* was a plea for passion and sincerity in a been-there-done-that scene, a playful and well-crafted taunt at "modern, uh, postmodern" hipsters and kids who don't dance at shows. The band answered its own battle cry with 1999's *Emergency & I,* abandoning the wink-and-nod self-awareness of *...Is Terrified* while maintaining its undeniable urgency.

"The City" is *Emergency & I*'s beating heart, a dark and gorgeous meditation on how a city changes in the absence of a loved one. It hits like a ballad and sounds like a rave-up, an incredible testament to the band's ability to cover a huge emotional range without compromising its electrifying energy. *Emergency & I* finds singer Travis Morrison at his most clever and charismatic, but on "The City" he allows himself to sound genuinely hurt and vulnerable. Eric Axelson's squiggly synth bass echoes the melancholy in the "streetlamps' hum" and the "iridescent grid." The Dismemberment Plan will be best remembered for their high-energy live shows, but "The City" remains a vivid and immaculate document.
—*ML*

Boredoms: *"Super Shine"* 1998

Japan's Boredoms are about as far from a singles band as you can get. Their records—and there are lots of them—tend to be built from a handful of zany ideas, with each track offering variations on a theme. "OK, for this one we'll record the drums on the beach, partially submerged in water" or "Let's cover a short punk song and extend it to twenty minutes." "Super Shine," then, may be the greatest single Boredoms song, because it has a little of everything that made them interesting.

Coming in 1998, in the middle of the band's creative peak, it opens with a few seconds of wonky, random-sounding tape experimentation. Then there's a blast of grating noise, which settles into a relatively laid-back psychedelic groove. On albums past, they might have let this section go on for a dozen minutes then allowed it to fade into nothing, but "Super Shine" has bigger ideas. A martial drum beat kicks in, then

some chanting, then some guitars, then more drums, more voices, more guitars, and then…more, more, more. Before you know it, the song sounds like fifty people dancing around a bonfire sending a message of love to the heavens, with the shouted "Shine! Shine! Shine!" being the most ecstatic use of the word since John Lennon's "Instant Karma." Boredoms used noise, distortion, and chaos to express not anger or aggression but overwhelming joy, which gives "Super Shine"—a challenging, abrasive acid-rock song of epic length—a surprisingly spiritual quality.
—*MR*

Mogwai: *"Like Herod"* 1997

Mogwai never confined themselves to the quiet/loud post-rock structures for which they're best known. Over a decade, the Glasgow titans have tinkered with stretching pop melodies through cool atmospheres or roaring through grinding, nervy anthems. They've done soundtracks and made music that itself sounded like a projection screen. But "Like Herod," the twelve-minute, two-crescendo monster that drifts into the second spot on 1997's *Young Team,* duly cemented that early, overarching reputation. Originally titled "Slint," "Like Herod" mirrors the Kentucky band's "Good Morning, Captain"—brooding and quiet until it suddenly flashes out, heavy, piercing, and, above all, *loud.*

The original "Like Herod" take is a righteous template, lurching forward with sinister, two-guitar-and-bass crosstalk that incinerates after three minutes. But it's the eighteen-minute version recorded in 1999 for the BBC and included on *Government Commissions: BBC Sessions 1996–2003* that stops playing nice. The rhythm is tight and crisp, and its first catapult into loudness—painfully teased by muted guitar strings that turn seconds into minutes—is like walking into a backdraft.
—*GC*

Jim O'Rourke:
"Halfway to a Threeway" 1999

Perhaps best known for his time as mixer and producer for Wilco and a temporary member of Sonic Youth, Jim O'Rourke strengthened both bands' songs by refining the elements that clashed against them: beds of noise and wide-open space with Wilco and shrieking guitar vamps with Sonic Youth.

But O'Rourke's whirlwind twenty-plus-year career is much bigger than parentheticals: He played in Gastr del Sol with David Grubbs, enabled the renaissance of undercanonized minimalists like Tony Conrad and Arnold Dreyblatt, and collaborated with artists from Fennesz and John Fahey to Merzbow and Joanna Newsom.

As "Halfway to a Threeway" proves, he's got an ear for hooks, too. Like a short film tucked neatly into a finger-picked, whispered-harmonies framework, "Halfway" delivers the promise of a fantasy ménage à trois with a lover who "ain't getting any sleep tonight." To end the first of its four verses, he hopes his anonymous lover won't run away. In verse two, she's confined to a wheelchair, and he knows she can't roll away. In verse three, she's a balding epileptic in leg braces, and he knows she can't run away. And in verse four, the fantasy reaches its corroded fulfillment: He'll pull the plug on his lover's life support and make it quick, singing, "I know that you'll just fade away." Such noxious images stem from the desire for companionship, pushed here to absurdist, appalling extremes. The beauty beneath just makes that sick sting stronger.
—*GC*

Sigur Rós: *"Svefn-g-Englar"* 1999

"Svefn-g-Englar" is a mission statement— a helium-sucking surprise hit with the hope of a fresh millennium riding on its winged back. It's tempting to mythologize the otherworldliness of this Icelandic band's epic breakout, as if it bubbled up from Atlantis. (The track's sonar-blip introduction would not refute this theory.) But Sigur Rós's nowhere sounds manage to shatter language barriers and elicit sobs from the most ardent hard-asses because they tap into a universal past. In slightly more modern terms, Sigur Rós are My Bloody Valentine chopped and screwed.

This single wraps everything from prevocal tics to ancient hymns to EBow into a shoegaze track that peers past the laces into a deep blue yonder. Jónsi Birgisson's unmistakable eunuch cry steers the song's wary New Age birthing tale. It's sung mostly in Icelandic, but the central meaning—filled with images of "liquid hibernation" and "new light"— is innately lucid.
—*RD*

Chapter Eight:
2000–2002

The new millennium didn't mark a clean break from the past, but the seeds planted in the first years of the twenty-first century have altered the music industry in ways greater and more profound than at any time in the past thirty years. The suits blame their woes and their declining sales on the dereliction of their audience, but the major labels arguably committed suicide when, faced with the widespread sharing of music across the Internet, they chose to fight this technology rather than adapt to it. The result: A generation of kids who don't think twice about stealing rather than paying for music, and the psychological damage of believing that music itself therefore has no specific value.

For listeners, however, the Internet has opened countless doors. Rather than have to hunt for months (if not years) to locate a record, much of the history of pop music is now at our fingertips. And at the beginning, as Napster first exploded, this was undoubtedly a positive thing. Music fans from around the globe, and with different sensibilities and biases, gathered online to seek out music, acquire it, and discuss it. New conversations began, conventional wisdom was challenged, and a younger and more varied set of voices evangelized about everything from the usual sacred cows to Southern hip-hop, metal, noise, microhouse, dance-punk, and chart pop.

Fortunately, too, there were a lot of conversations worth having. From the scatological and racial-line-blurring rhymes of Eminem to the New Rock Revolution of the Strokes and the White Stripes to Radiohead's electronic frontiersmanship to Timbaland and the Neptunes' merging of the avant-garde and pop, it was a good time to have access to a multitude of sounds. The eclecticism paid off: Chart music was as creatively rich as it had been since the New Pop era two decades earlier; Daft Punk and Jay-Z released defining albums, easing staunch rock fans into the worlds of contemporary dance and hip-hop; and artists such as the Avalanches toyed with the lines between genres while mashup culture obliterated them altogether.

For us at Pitchfork, this was a great time to be a music fan, but these are also the first years in which every author in this book was now also a critic. And we celebrated the freedom of being an online magazine unencumbered by industry influence by talking about anything from mixtapes to mp3-only releases and by placing virtual unknowns on our site alongside established stars. Where the traditional mainstream press is forced to save its pages for celebrity culture and cover artists who will sell on the newsstand, online editors and bloggers could reach hundreds of thousands of readers and still choose their subjects on simpler, even purer criteria: Is this artist's music worth discussing, even celebrating?

As the readers caught on—and thanks to blogs, became critics themselves—much of the online press would eventually confuse criticism with enthusiasm, raving about bands but considering the discussion of ideas or context to be self-indulgent. In 2000–02, however, listeners and readers were hungry for both, as well as for any new sound they could get their right-clicking hands around. "I found a world so new," the Avalanches gushed, but in many ways these years were a hyperspeed update on the earlier progression-obsessed, genre-busting late 1970s—right down to post-punk and underground disco revivalism.
—SP

Daft Punk: *"One More Time"* 2000

By the time Daft Punk dropped their second album, *Discovery,* the French dance scene was dominated by the filter-disco sound—woozy disco and funk samples looped over chewy house beats. At its best, it was the sound of almost tangible yearning, the release of disco heartbreakingly deferred. At worst, it was joyless and lazy. *Discovery's* melting pot of cybernetic balladry, soft rock, electro, and house was a way out of the filter-disco impasse, but lead single "One More Time," built on a clipped and phased horn sample, is also a supreme example of the style.

The message of "One More Time"—to defy exhaustion and just keep dancing—is mirrored by its form: pulling out the old filter-disco tricks for the last time. It's also reflected in the way guest singer Romanthony's voice is bent and auto-tuned until he sounds out of breath, fiercely pushing himself on. Then the beat stops.

The breakdown in "One More Time" runs a full two minutes over soft keyboard washes. Romanthony pleads in a series of shattered gasps: "Celebrate… don't wait too late…mmm…no…you can't stop." He sounds like he's praying. It's a starkly intimate moment—written by two guys in robot masks.
—*TE*

Radiohead: *"Idioteque"* 2000

Although much was made of the influence of IDM musicians like Aphex Twin and Autechre on 2000's *Kid A,* Radiohead immersed themselves just as deeply in electronic music's marginalized early avant-garde. It's no surprise, then, that *Kid A* owes as much to those radical, lab-coated attempts to evoke "the ghost in the machine" as it does to the more stylized, streamlined sounds of Warp Records. Nowhere is that influence more evident than on "Idioteque."

The rising chord pattern that powers the song is sampled from a work by electronic music pioneer Paul Lansky. Created in 1973, the eighteen-minute long "Mild und Leise" was composed on a mainframe workstation roughly the size of a refrigerator. One of the first original pieces of music to be composed on a computer, it sounds nothing like what we've since come to regard as electronic music. Its evolving tones and strange, twisting mutations are both eerie and primordial. In the context of "Idioteque," though,

the sample does a different kind of work, in essence providing the same kind of melodic coloring as an acoustic guitar. The deployment of unconventional sounds working in conventional ways is something Radiohead have always done well, but nowhere better than on *Kid A.*
—*MP*

Godspeed You! Black Emperor: *"Storm"* 2000

Like every track on Godspeed You! Black Emperor's stunning 2000 double album *Lift Yr Skinny Fists Like Antennas to Heaven,* "Storm" is several pieces bundled into an informal suite, each movement carrying a character and subtitle of its own. With their sweeping strings and built-in grandeur, Godspeed can evoke Aaron Copland, the score to a John Ford film, or the guitar orchestrations of Glenn Branca. And true to the sprawling Montreal collective's leftist political ideals, "Storm" surges with a communal spirit, each instrument deployed expressly to serve the overall momentum. When the full ensemble bears down, it crafts epic music for an unheroic age.

The first movement (subtitled "Levez Vos Skinny Fists Comme Antennas to Heaven") opens with several rapturous minutes of pure ascension, as cello and violin are soon joined by French horn, guitar, and percussion to form a triumphal chorus. From there, the track transforms into the agitated drone-rock of "Gathering Storm" before winding through the downcast "Welcome to Barco AM/PM," which features the alienating, disembodied voice of an automated PA system. Though Godspeed's predominantly instrumental work leaves its thematic designs to the listener's imagination, there is no mistaking the music's defiance and power.
—*MMu*

The Avalanches: *"Since I Left You"* 2000

"Welcome to paradise," an unknown man says glibly at the beginning of "Since I Left You." The first track on the Avalanches' 2000 album of the same name is as pure an expression of loveliness as you'll find, with its layers of sighing strings, gauzy backing vocals, and aching woodwind solos treading dangerously close to irony but passing by unscathed through sheer self-belief.

The Avalanches have a celebrated modus operandi—every sound on *Since I Left You* is sampled from another record—but their music rarely draws attention to the process of its creation. The group traipses through shimmering disco, clattering hip-hop, and glistening ambient pop with equally impressive results, but the orchestrated easy-listening glide of "Since I Left You" is the perfect introduction to its aesthetic: "Since I left you, I've found a world so new," a pop diva exclaims, and it's less a declaration of independence than a snapshot from the most amazing travel diary ever.
—*TF*

Broadcast: *"Come On Let's Go"* 2000

Broadcast formed through a mutual admiration of obscure 1960s psychedelic group the United States of America, so it's no surprise that their music reflects that decade's free-loving, rose-colored view of the world, filtered through England's fascination with a more sinister future, characterized by the droogs of Stanley Kubrick's film *A Clockwork Orange* and Dr. Who's robotic nemeses, the Daleks.

"Come On Let's Go" might be just another space-age nostalgia trip were it not for the earthy, matronly warmth of Trish Keenan's voice. As the music echoes and modulates, Keenan calmly navigates the analog mist, hand-holding the song's subject through their shared experience while asking questions that don't need answering. Her performance seems as effortless as the haunting melody she sings and lends Broadcast's technological flights of fancy a much-needed tether.
—*DR*

Aaliyah: *"Try Again"* 2000

For all that's been written about the rise of Napster and mp3 culture, and what it's done to the business side of the music industry, comparatively little has been written about how it's changed people's listening habits. Yes, the removal of a financial barrier to entry meant that listeners could stretch their tastes, but the privacy of earbuds also meant they could sneak time with music they didn't want to broadcast. Not coincidentally, the mainstream underwent a creative renaissance during that period; if pop, electronic, hip-hop, and avant-garde could sit comfortably side-by-side in a laptop playlist, why couldn't they commingle in the real world as well?

Along with singles from Britney Spears, OutKast, and Missy Elliott, Aaliyah's bittersweet "Try Again" counted for a huge part of that movement. "Try" was one of Timbaland's most seminal productions; from its syncopated accents to the squelching 303 synth lead, "Try Again" introduced elements that would become pop cornerstones for the next ten years. It also rescued mainstream R&B from a melisma-induced slump by dramatically updating its sound palette. But while "Try Again" has aged remarkably well, it's also tinted by tragedy; about a year after releasing this, the twenty-two-year-old Aaliyah died in a plane crash off the coast of Abaco Island, Bahamas.
—*MP*

Justin Timberlake: *"Cry Me a River"* 2002

It says a lot about Justin Timberlake's decision-making abilities that he's gone from being the Brillo-haired runt in a boy band to one of the 2000s' most forward-thinking pop singers. From his Neptunes-produced solo debut single "Like I Love You," which brought minimalism to the mainstream, to the Timbaland-aided, rave-inspired "My Love," Timberlake's always had a canny instinct for boundary-pushing pop. Even stood next to other pop singles with similarly bizarre palettes, "Cry Me a River" (again, courtesy of Timbaland) still sounded like it was beamed down from another planet. A sonically audacious production, "Cry Me a River" managed to make Gregorian chant, second-rate beatboxing, and a gospel choir play nicely together, while Timberlake's typically intuitive vocal performance (it takes a special kind of courage to lean so hard on a falsetto) acted as grounding. Oh, and this one apparently had to do with Timberlake's former girlfriend: Britney somebody.
—*MP*

Luomo: *"Tessio"* 2000

Sasu Ripatti, sometimes known as Vladislav Delay, already enjoyed a reputation as a master craftsman of dub-inflected ambient music when, in 2000, he released three singles (compiled to create the album *Vocalcity*) under the name Luomo. A former jazz drummer, Ripatti might have seemed an unlikely candidate to devise "The Next Episode in House," as a sticker on the cover of *Vocalcity* proclaimed.

Threat Level: This Was Our 9/11

Musicians confronting the attacks of September 11, 2001, had to tackle their fears: fear of backlash or radio censorship if they didn't sound sufficiently patriotic; fear of sounding trite or safe if they retreated to elegies and cheerleading; and the more insidious fear that in making art from the most traumatic, widely covered event of their generation, they might totally blow it.

"The National Anthem," **Radiohead:** Before there was post-9/11 anxiety, we had pre-millennial tension, and in the mainstream, nobody captured it better than Radiohead. With just a few grim lyrics and a killer bass line, this cut from 2000's *Kid A* sums up the alienation between man and state, and the practice of rule by fear.

"This Mess We're In," **PJ Harvey [ft. Thom Yorke]:** In 2000, Harvey's *Stories from the City, Stories from the Sea* paid tribute to New York City with equal parts thrill, hope, and dread—as if the city's excitement had to come with whispers of disaster. On "This Mess We're In," Harvey evokes a Bonnie fantasy with an unlikely Clyde (Radiohead's Thom Yorke) while ominous helicopters whir overhead.

"O Superman (for Massenet)," **Laurie Anderson:** Anderson famously taped "O Superman" in concert right after 9/11, with the 1981 hit's lyric "Here come the planes" taking on an all-too-vivid reality. As with so many apocalyptic fantasies, it sounded a lot cooler before it actually happened.

"Far Away," **Sleater-Kinney:** Sleater-Kinney pay tribute to the working men who ran to the danger while the president spent the day in hiding, but the song is less about score-settling than about family and feeling suddenly helpless to protect your own, no matter how far you lived from Ground Zero.

"The Bombing," **Elephant Man:** On one of the first songs to respond to 9/11, Jamaica's Elephant Man sounds sincere and unpretentious, from praising the firemen who lost their lives to complaining about the stepped-up airport security: "No weed cyaan smuggle again, through the bombing."

"Fly Me to New York," **Cassetteboy:** Not everyone lit candles for America. This British satirical duo's mashup narrated the attack on the World Trade Center and cast Frank "New York, New York" Sinatra as one of the jihadists. A Morrissey sample sums up their message: "There's no one but yourself to blame."

"My Two Front Teeth, Parts 2 and 3," **Travis Morrison:** "The second I saw, but the first was suckerpunch-city," recalls ex–Dismemberment Plan singer Travis Morrison, who uses a story about getting beaten down in front of a Gap as a metaphor for 9/11. Sometimes the anecdote pulls him away from the point, but by the end, when he wails, "All I want for Christmas is my two front teeth," the meaning is clear: He misses his teeth (i.e., the Twin Towers). He wants them back. For Christmas.

"Road to Joy," **Bright Eyes:** Less awkward is New York City newcomer Conor Oberst's impressionistic "Road to Joy," which runs a gamut of stumbling, contradictory reactions—from retreating into booze to shrugging his way into gung-ho militancy: "When you're asked to fight a war that's over nothing / It's best to join the side that's gonna win."

"John Walker's Blues," **Steve Earle:** America embraces rebels, upstarts, and even mass killers like Charles Manson. But trying to grasp why an American boy like John Walker Lindh would sign up with the Taliban was too much for the critics of this song and way too much for the Nashville establishment. (Earle's explanation didn't help: "The culture here didn't impress [Walker Lindh], so he went looking for something to believe in.") In 2006, Slayer courted similar controversy with their song "Jihad," which quoted head suicide terrorist Mohammad Atta.

"The Rising," **Bruce Springsteen:** Ultimately, while young artists wrestled (and, often, ran away from) the post-9/11 world, America sought heroes with the maturity and gravity to bring order to the world in the wake of a tragedy, and with *The Rising*, the Boss rose to that challenge.
—*CD*

But "Tessio" lived up to the hype, confirming that a pale European dude with one foot in the avant-garde was capable of making warm-blooded, soulful dance-floor fillers.

"Tessio" takes its time to get going, waiting over two minutes to drop its 4/4 kick drum. The introduction is a beatless swirl of pulsing keyboards and billowing delay over which male and female voices sing an ambiguous tale of heartbreak; the melody resurfaces over the course of the song's twelve minutes, always without warning, finally building to an R&B-infused emotional climax. Ripatti's luxurious production leans heavily on rubbery bass lines that split the difference between dub reggae and the Human League— no easy feat. But even better is the song's curiously pneumatic feel, as the percussion's crispy high end dissolves into a murky middle range suffused with grit and pockets of air, where every element seems to move in two directions at once.
—PS

Vitalic: "La Rock 01" 2001

Vitalic's ice-cold, maximalist dance-floor stompers were christened "champagne techno" by pundits quick to note their European catwalk-to-club ubiquity, but a better substance for comparison would have been Everclear. Constructed as a ruthlessly efficient arc toward climax, "La Rock 01" is classic French techno, in which each discrete element serves a single purpose. Over a galloping flanged intro, three kick drums punch through the mix, each successively "bigger" than the last, all in anticipation of the blowout to come.

The first two minutes are a tease of delayed gratification as a bass line slinks onto the stage and then goes berserk. The song's programmatic title might as well be "Filter 101," because the main event is a simple but devastatingly accurate transformation of the bass line from a moody trickle into a raging torrent of synthetic lava, subtly knocked off-kilter by portamento glides and squeals that lend a woozy, amyl-nitrate perfume to the revolving-door structure. After a subaquatic goth breakdown, the bass line returns—presto!—even louder than before, now armored with claps and ride cymbals that glint like studs on an haute couture biker jacket.

The song was so transformative that Internet seekers scrambled to hunt down other mixes and tracks by

the elusive producer, making him one of the first puzzles (and first solutions) of twenty-first-century dance music.
—DD

Kylie Minogue: "Love at First Sight" 2001

Arriving at the tail end of commercial dance-pop's absorption of French house, "Love at First Sight" is the genre's apotheosis. Producers Richard Stannard and Julian Gallagher understood how manipulative French house could be, and they ruthlessly exploited their sonic arsenal for maximum emotional impact: The song's waxing and waning intensity commands anticipation and release with all the subtlety of a drill sergeant, while the ridiculously fizzy, string-swept chorus is as chemically charged as that of any rave hit.

Kylie, of course, has had many big dance-pop anthems, but what lifts this above her previous efforts is how thoroughly she ignores her status as a tongue-in-cheek camp icon. Instead, she serves up blissful abandon and the first flush of new love with a touching devotion and intensity. Ultimately, her performance feels bittersweet because her joy is unattainable: Even her story of falling in love with the DJ sounds like pure fantasy.
—TF

Jay-Z [ft. UGK]: "Big Pimpin'" 2000

After blaxploitation movies turned the pimp into a questionable antihero, hip-hop ensconced his amoral flash and random violence as an archetype beloved by city and suburb dwellers alike. Pick it apart and it's plain gross, pandering to consumerism and misogyny at their most unredeemable. Append it to a beat and a swaggering vocal and it becomes harder to dismiss, even if it's only because you're seduced by the drama.

In hip-hop at the turn of the millennium, no one swaggered harder or milked more drama out of retrograde gangsta rap materials than Jay-Z. He rose from the untested hustler on his 1996 debut, *Reasonable Doubt,* to self-proclaimed emperor of all things hip-hop in only a few years: By 2000's "Big Pimpin'"—technically first released on December 28, 1999—no one argued Jay's claims as he flowed imperiously over the subcontinental flutes and computer hydraulics of one of producer Timbaland's

most memorable beats. Southern hip-hop vets UGK make guest appearances and work harder than their host, who barely deigns to blot his brow. At his best, Jay sounded like he was really enjoying it—casually shaming the skills and rote, moneyed boasts of his peers—and when he felt there was no one left to shame, he began a long, lazy slide into his own brand of complacency. But "Big Pimpin'" was Jay at his peak, no longer hungry but still enjoying the lifestyle enough to make us commoners want to stow away on his yacht.
—JH

OutKast: *"B.O.B."* 2000

The music video for "B.O.B." begins with a psychedelic revision of the training scene from *Rocky III*, as a delirious horde of hyper fourth-graders chases Andre 3000 across an expanse of purple grass. It's a pretty good visual analogy for the song itself—an ecstatic headlong leap into the unknown.

OutKast had been titans in their field before *Stankonia's* "B.O.B." The Atlanta duo released three of the greatest, most complete albums in Southern rap history, every one of them expansive, articulate, and adventurous. But nothing anticipated the turbocharged insanity of "B.O.B."; the song represents the moment that OutKast left worldly concerns behind, reaching instead for a dizzy twilight zone of disconnected imagery and kinetic fury. In the first five seconds, an ominous music box plays while Andre, whispering, counts to four. And then we're off, with a blindingly fast Miami-bass drum pattern.

It's almost physically jarring, so much so that it takes a while to even notice all the other shards of music that find their way into the attack. A gothy, miasmic organ gurgles throughout. Isaac Hayes chicken-scratch guitars bust in, rushing to keep up with the jackhammer tempo. Electro synth blips oscillate. The Morris Brown College Gospel Choir wails "Bombs over Baghdad" again and again, like a mantra or prayer. Screaming hair-metal guitars duel with frantic turntable scratches. And Andre and Big Boi's voices twist, duck, and dodge the carnage, neither pausing for breath. When we can make out the words, they seem to address actual real-world concerns, but in a vividly impressionistic way.

In the years leading up to "B.O.B.," Andre and Big Boi increasingly became an ever-more-odd couple,

Andre kicking free-associative rhapsodies and pairing grass skirts with football shoulder pads while Big Boi remained accessibly slick and regal. After *Stankonia*, Andre and Big Boi would diverge completely: Big Boi stuck to his literate thug-rap roots while Andre soared ever outward into impenetrable prog-soul pastiche. Neither has been quite as great ever again, but the sense of woozy possibility on "B.O.B." still devastates.
—TB

Eminem: *"The Real Slim Shady"* 2000

The first huge pop star of the twenty-first century, Eminem had it all, including an(other) alter ego that allowed him to vent any half-formed homophobia or misogyny he had rolling around in his ever-so-troubled head. But however the whole Slim Shady enterprise may have spun Eminem's career trajectory into relentless self-parody, it also gave him the opportunity to make tracks like "The Real Slim Shady," a magnificent bit of myth-making and one of the most hilarious songs in a catalog full of them.

The notion of a legion of Eminem imitators was hardly far-fetched when this song—and its "will the real Slim Shady please stand up?" refrain—was released in 2000, and though lines that reference Carson Daly, Tom Green, and Fred Durst may eventually need footnotes, they're still pretty hilarious. Slim, hinting at his future withdrawal from the music industry, imagines his prankster making the most of his inevitable retirement to a nursing home. He then brags about keeping it realer than "90 percent of you rappers out there" (which in this context, actually comes off as modest), before finally dropping the most indisputable line of all: That no matter the mass of followers, no one else will ever be quite like him. Very funny, Slim Shady, very funny.
—DL

Ghostface Killah: *"Nutmeg"* 2000

On "Nutmeg," the opening track on *Supreme Clientele*, Ghostface references storytelling hip-hop classic *The Great Adventures of Slick Rick*, and if that album represents rap's linear, romantic period, then this song finds the Wu-Tang Clan's most gifted MC channeling the experimental modernist ethos. Part James Joyce, part Al Capone, the rapper threatens and preens while rattling off the kind of dense prose that requires several readings, exhaustive footnotes, and a Wu decoder ring.

"Nutmeg"—ostensibly named for the alarmingly hallucinatory high one can get from ground nutmeg—initially seems like a showboating cascade of inventive non sequiturs: Nods to tennis hothead John McEnroe, fairy-tale starlet Rapunzel, and ancient Egyptian-style headwear abound. But like the world's most graphic Magic Eye poster, the track's gun-toting quasi-narrative slowly congeals as the apparent randomness dissipates. RZA's circular, sample-based beat—not to mention his sublimely spazzed-out closing verse—only heightens the song's outlandish pull. "Yeah, you see what I mean?" taunts Ghost midsong, after two and a half minutes of some of the most brilliantly weird rhymes hip-hop's ever heard.
—RD

Missy Elliott: *"Get Ur Freak On"* 2001

Saying that Missy Elliott is the baddest lady to ever spit sticky-icky rhymes over beats sells her short, as gender-based distinctions always will. She's one of pop *and* hip-hop's all-time greats, regardless of sex. But in a hypermasculine, often blatantly sexist genre, singer, songwriter, rapper, vocal arranger, and producer Elliott has never been anyone's bitch, and her long-standing sexual and sonic autonomy, flaunting a zaftig body and a sense of the absurd that finds her dressing that body in robot suits, is a beacon. And yet many of her most astounding moments are the product of an intense partnership with a man—producer and childhood friend Timbaland.

The pair spent the early '90s stewing in Virginia Beach, cutting demos and blowing through a series of go-nowhere groups and collaborations. These pre-celebrity experiments were their first cloudy combinations of the smoothness of R&B, the clunky rhythms of Jamaican dancehall, the trunk-rattling bass of Southern hip-hop, and the electronic gleam of techno. But from 1996 until 2005, when Elliott released her first album that wasn't entirely produced by Timbaland, critics and fans argued about just how big a role Tim played in Missy's music.

What should have been apparent from Timbaland's collaborations with hip-hop losers like the Lox, however, is that crazy beats could only get you so far. Tim may have been the one to bust hip-hop's sense of timekeeping permanently, but it was Missy who

filled in the gaping spaces with a forty-foot personality. Ravenously sexual and coyly romantic, Elliott shaped Tim's rhythms into cross-platform smashes.

And nowhere did Tim's mixing board wild style and Missy's everything else come together crazier than on 2001's "Get Ur Freak On," a dance-floor burner that argued, why shouldn't Indian bhangra suddenly be blaring from stores in middle-American shopping malls? Tim surrounds a deep kick-drum thud with splattered Indian tablas and horror-film drones, a mix so unexpected it deflects all criticisms of exoticism. As with most of Missy's music, "Get Ur Freak On" is about partying or sex or the collision thereof, which doesn't make it "deep," at least by the standards of the "serious" hip-hop fans who mete out such judgments. But there's no one's party, or after-party, you'd more like to find yourself at. Just don't forget your robot suit.
—JH

The White Stripes: *"Dead Leaves and the Dirty Ground"* 2001

It's amazing that a sound like the White Stripes' ever needed reviving, yet the idea of a blues-based hard-rock band living outside of the classic-rock dial in 2001 was about as unfathomable as another swing-dance craze. But with "Dead Leaves and the Dirty Ground"—the opening track of their third album, *White Blood Cells*—two-tone ex-lovers/fake siblings Jack and Meg White took the primal throwback rock they'd gestated in Detroit basements to the world, announcing themselves with a guitar squeal so loud and nasty one expected Marty McFly to come bursting through the wall.

As that guitar crunches its way through a chord progression that triggers Pavlovian head-banging, and as Jack spews his iconic bravado, it's hard to blame critics for succumbing to hollow "Rock is back!!!" platitudes or heralding the Stripes as the grand marshals of a new garage-rock era. The truth is that garage rock didn't grow any more versatile in the forty years since it was invented, just that the Whites executed its limited recipe to perfection, with Meg's brutish drumming providing the spare, primal backbone that crucially balances out Jack's guitar-god prowess.
—RM

The Strokes:
"The Modern Age" (single version) **2001**

There are so many things about the Strokes that are infuriating: Their slackness, their upper-class pedigrees, their passive-aggressive chauvinism. So it's no surprise that a Strokes backlash occurred practically simultaneously with their arrival, the battle lines quickly drawn between supporters and enemies in the newfangled salon of the Internet. But with some much-needed temporal distance, the whole skirmish seems ridiculous. Compared to the slower, slicker version on *Is This It?* the original single version of "The Modern Age" is about as pretentious as any school-age band's demo—just forget for a moment that the institution in question was a Swiss boarding school.

Jangly and grungy, hyper and hungover—and with a vocal from Julian Casablancas that redefines phoned-in to include throwing a phone-booth temper tantrum—the Strokes packed a whole lot of contradictions into a three-minute song. The ultimate deception was that the Strokes were a band concerned with style over substance, too cool to try too hard, while their songs belied the kind of New Wave catchiness that alt-rock had forgotten—until their UK success launched a transatlantic wave of followers (Franz Ferdinand, Arctic Monkeys, Futureheads, and dozens more not worth mentioning) cashing in on the same.
—*RM*

...And You Will Know Us by the Trail of Dead: *"Another Morning Stoner"* **2002**

...And You Will Know Us by the Trail of Dead's major-label debut, *Source Tags and Codes,* is the sound of a band's ambition outpacing its talent. Could the Austin five-piece make the world's greatest rock and roll album? Probably not, but that wasn't going to stop them from trying. "Another Morning Stoner" strikes a perfect balance between the Trail of Dead's well-honed aggression and their newfound aspirations, bringing a previously unheard elegance to their Sonic Youth–inspired guitar racket. Gradually building momentum through its string-swept verses and serpentine bridge, the song culminates with a call-and-response coda that would sound horrifically cheesy if not for Conrad Keely's unrestrained,

spittle-flecked conviction. For all its overblown grandiosity, *Source Tags and Codes* remains an explosive record, overflowing with big ideas and the desperate need to communicate them.
—*ML*

Interpol: *"Obstacle 1"* **2002**

While the rest of New York's post-punk class of 2002 was making dates with the night, Interpol were setting their alarm clocks for the next morning, projecting an air of steely professionalism—office attire, clean haircuts, monochromatic album art—and paying Manhattan rents while the party was raging in Williamsburg. "Obstacle 1," from their debut *Turn on the Bright Lights,* provided an instant snapshot of Interpol's stern-faced intent—and effectively unleashed the deluge of Ian Curtis comparisons that will haunt singer Paul Banks for life.

But if anyone should be filing a copyright suit here, it's Television: The song is essentially "Marquee Moon" played at 45 rpm, with guitarist Daniel Kessler echoing its staccato riff, Sam Fogarino laying down a fierce drumbeat that's almost bar-band brawny, bassist Carlos Dengler buffing the jagged edges with high-note melodies, and Banks having a panic attack before the first verse is over. When he starts crying, "She can read!" he makes literacy sound like a national-security issue. If "Obstacle 1" is oblique in its allusions to lost romance, it still announces Banks as one the most guileless voices in indie rock: Even when he tosses in one of the most egregious throwaway lines ever ("her stories are boring and stuff"), it's understood that his unsettled state has simply left him at a loss for words.
—*SB*

Electric Six: *"Danger! High Voltage"* **2002**

Originally known as the Wildbunch, before a lawsuit from the Tricky/Massive Attack–associated DJ crew of the same name, Electric Six had been kicking around the Detroit garage rock scene for a good half-decade before "Danger! High Voltage" The song was first released on seven-inch in 2002, a full year before hitting its stride as a single. But when it popped up on 2 Many DJs' mashup opus *As Heard on Radio Soulwax, Pt. 2,* the band was quickly signed to XL, which rereleased the song in early 2003. It debuted at number 2 on the UK singles chart.

"Danger" consists of a four-on-the-floor disco beat, guitars that alternate between garage fuzz and sexploitation noodling, a pair of sax solos, and exactly seven lines of lyrics, two of which are "Fire in the disco! / Fire in the Taco Bell!" Frontman Dick Valentine's oily delivery is more than enough to sell the song, but what catapults it to silliness heaven is his duet partner, a deranged, love-struck shrieker who sounds an awful lot like the White Stripes' Jack White. Even half a decade later, White had still not copped to the performance.
—APh

Golden Boy with Miss Kittin:
"Rippin Kittin" 2001

Around the turn of the millennium, big-city clubs saw an unexpected revival of 1980s electro music— brash, intentionally sleazy, complete with robotic drum machines, two-note bass lines, and chilly, monotone vocals. Fashion-averse rock guys across America spent years writing the whole thing off as the most bankrupt fad in history, all without realizing they'd be deprived of the last laugh: Not only did the brief flash of electro and "electroclash" produce loads of great music (especially in Europe), but its vibe anticipated the tone of the decade better than anyone could have guessed. By 2005, the echoes of electro were all over pop charts, the trashy basement-party style of the stuff was showing up in countless rock bands, and we'd moved from a 1990s of Salvation Army flannels to a new decade slathered in skinny jeans, makeup, Vans, and hipster-trash chic.

Among the most memorable songs of the original new-electro wave, "Rippin Kittin" is sleek, glowing, and elegant—jewelry dipped in honey. Guest vocalist Miss Kittin may be better known for dead-eyed sneering, but she's singing here, and her iciness is all about poise: "I feel like taking a life," she sings, in a voice calm and self-amused enough to approach frightening. The whole thing—produced by Switzerland's Golden Boy—struts along with remarkable grace, then ends with a synth solo that sounds like it's walking in circles through a gold-plated revolving door.
—NA

Jürgen Paape:
"So Weit Wie Noch Nie" 2001

Jürgen Paape is, along with Michael Mayer and Wolfgang Voigt, the co-owner of Kompakt, one of the world's preeminent techno imprints. Among Paape's main tasks for the label is to run the Kompakt record store in Cologne, and it's a pity that this business obligation seemingly prevents him from cutting more tracks—his "So Weit Wie Noch Nie" stands out as one of the label's loveliest out-and-out pop songs. Kaleidoscopic and transporting, the track lifts off into an ecstatic hyperworld of bouncy minimal beats, swoony melodies, and unforgettable female vocals. It's one of Kompakt's most successful crossover tracks, a favorite of everyone from indie pop fans— many of whom were introduced to it by Erlend Øye's eye-opening *DJ-Kicks*—to hardcore technoids.

"So Weit Wie Noch Nie," along with a handful of Kompakt tracks that followed, almost single-handedly helped to rejuvenate German techno's fan base. By appealing to the hearts of rockers, popists, and disco heads, the label amassed a loyal worldwide following of newly converted techno fans seemingly overnight, and built itself into a go-to brand and seal of quality, the sort of reputation enjoyed by classic independent rock labels such as Rough Trade, 4AD, and SST.
—GD

Osymyso: "Intro-Inspection" 2001

They've never gone away, but mashup bootlegs— where vocals from Record A were laid atop music from Record B—peaked in popularity between 2001 and 2003. It wasn't a coincidence: This was when the Internet's explosion of the pop marketplace began in earnest and helped expand musical awareness even beyond that of the CD generation. If disparate styles and genres were meeting on the hard drive, why not hybridize them further?

"Intro-Inspection"—a twelve-minute collage of 101 song beginnings—is that moment's most mammoth placeholder. The track may not go as far as Strictly Kev's forty-minute "Raiding the 20th Century" (2004) or Girl Talk's *Night Ripper* (2006), but it's still jaw-droppingly ambitious. Its kitchen-sink approach— owing slightly to John Oswald's classic 1989 Proto-Mashup LP, *Plunderphonics*—magnifies its triumph:

Unclassics 2000: The New Electro

Ten gems from the early 2000s revival of electro music—full of fuzzy synths, sleazy vibes, campy glamour, and cold, mechanical beats. It helps to have an urge to dance, and it helps even more to have a sense of humor.

"Space Invaders Are Smoking Grass," **I-F:** It was this I-F track—not to mention his *Mixed Up in the Hague* compilation of classic Italo disco— that was credited with sparking the electro revival in Europe. "Space Invaders" is early, raw, and unslick: mostly just a grainy synth bass line pushing endlessly forward.

"Fitzcarraldo," **Legowelt:** From the same Dutch electro underground as I-F, there's Legowelt, who dressed like a metalhead and made tracks full of gritty, lo-fi, no-nonsense stomping. The fluttering analog synths on "Fitzcarraldo" sound haunted, devilish, and…classical?

"Frank Sinatra 2001," **Miss Kittin and the Hacker:** "Frank Sinatra 2001" is one of the most lovable tracks to come from the European home of the era's best electro: the International Deejay Gigolo label. Sneered over an arch disco groove, Miss Kittin's lyrics sum up all the ironic glamour of the scene: "To be famous is so nice! Suck my dick." Note that Miss Kittin was not that famous.

"Emerge," **Fischerspooner:** It's one of the biggest pop hits of the new electro wave, by an act who summed up all the arty pretension of the New York scene. Many a hater, distracted by this band's hilarious self-importance, missed the fact that the song— and most of its many remixes—was actually terrific.

"Nausea (Restructured)," **Adult.:** Detroit's Adult. made electro that raced instead of grooved, and with pinpoint precision "Nausea" is a high-speed car chase to which you'll find yourself shrieking "Nausea!" in the same vampire-schoolmarm voice as singer Nicola Kuperus.

"Missy Queen Is Gonna Die," **Tok Tok vs. Soffy O:** Two masters of tweaked-out German techno team up with a commanding cool-girl singer and turn out one of electro's most fun singles. The music here is dead simple high-energy pop, and Soffy O rides happily over it like a Madonna song from 1983.

"14 Zero Zero," **Console:** A catchy, high-octane electro-pop song—as sung (literally) by a poor, outmoded, unloved computer. That doesn't keep it from being strangely heartbreaking when the computer sings "I love you" and follows it up with gushing, emotional synthesizer stabs, before finally suffering some sort of drive failure.

"Discotraxx," **Ladytron:** Ladytron's singles are all elegance, drawing more on chart-topping early '80s synth-pop than any dance-floor pounders. The airy voices cooing quietly through "Discotraxx" have style down to a science and hooks to spare.

"Silver Screen Shower Scene," **Felix da Housecat:** A glitzy electro touchstone from this veteran Chicago house producer, with grainy synthesizers belching left and right. Note that Miss Kittin, as on "Frank Sinatra 2001," can be found whispering about her favorite topic: having sex in limousines.

"Keine Melodien" (single version), **Jeans Team [ft. MJ Lan]:** Sounds like a robotic Prussian dictator marching his mutant army over a hill. And then it gets funky.
—*NA*

There are loads of great little moments here, as when the leadoff riffs of "Smells Like Teen Spirit" and "Stayin' Alive" begin to march in tandem, or the way it closes off with Frank Sinatra's "My Way" sinking into Fleetwood Mac's "Albatross" on its way to the Doors' (what else?) "The End." It soon produced a glut of nondescript admixtures, but the best parts of "Intro-Inspection" suggest that some things sound even better played all at once.
—MiM

The Knife: *"Heartbeats"* 2002

A "99 Luftballons" for the hipster set, this springy bit of electro-pop represented a breakthrough for the Swedish brother/sister duo of Olof and Karin Dreijer. An already unconventional mix of cement-heavy synths, chirpy organs, and deeply unfashionable percussion sounds, this otherwise conventional pop song turned into a funhouse curiosity with the added presence of Karin's witchy singing style. "Heartbeats" was a minor hit in select circles, but it wasn't until fellow Swede José González's pensive acoustic version was featured in a high-profile Sony Bravia ad that it really took off. While the ripple effect of being in one of the year's most talked-about television commercials had an instant impact on González's fortune, the Knife didn't feel the effect as dramatically. Nonetheless, the spot's lucrative payout gave them the comfort they needed to work on their follow-up record at their own pace. The result was 2006's masterful *Silent Shout,* which saw them evolve from a colorful—if eccentric—electro-pop act into something more twisted, sinister, and macabre.
—MP

LCD Soundsystem: *"Losing My Edge"* 2002

One major flaw of music criticism is that it operates in an entirely different arena from its subject matter; as much as it attempts to describe and discuss the world of music, it can only approximate its character with the handicapped one-dimensionality of the written word. Yet musical forms of music criticism are rare, typically consisting of either brute sloganeering ("I Love Rock and Roll") or bone-dry sermonizing (a shitload of backpacker hip-hop). James Murphy proved an exception to the rule with his first single, debuting his LCD Soundsystem project with "Losing My Edge," as acidic, hilarious, and necessary a piece of musical criticism as has been released in the Internet age—and a great song to boot.

The message of "Losing My Edge" is hardly direct; it's both love letter and hate mail to The Scene, and it employs classic music-reviewer creative stunts to avoid being merely a list of complaints. Murphy is in the first person for half of the song, sketching out the universal indie fan midlife crisis: the horrible realization that one is now older than both the people onstage and the people in the crowd. Faced with this shock, Murphy falls back on the favorite scenester crutch of detailing his credibility résumé, portraying himself as the underground's Forrest Gump. Eventually this self-inflation bursts into a hailstorm of record collection name-dropping, a knife-stab to a culture where recitation of band names too often suffices for conversation. The final word is a voice singing, "You don't know what you really want," over and over again; it's directed at Murphy himself, but also at the entirety of independent music.

Written out as prose, "Losing My Edge" would still be a brilliant parody. But as a piece of music, Murphy's rant is even more effective, castigating the tired tropes of turn-of-the-millennium indie rock while pointing the way forward. The song starts with a noisy guitar-and-drums mess, the kind of self-conscious squall produced by that most tired rock-star maneuver, the end-of-set stage demolition. But within seconds, the mess is replaced by an icy-clean drum machine, which sets up shop for the song's entire eight minutes. From there, it's a slow, patient build of percussion and synthesizers, about as far as you could get in 2002 from the nth revival of garage rock and Pavement clones that ruled the indie scene. Flip side "Beat Connection" may have made a more convincing musical case for tearing down the arbitrary borders between the indie rock and electronic genres, but the combination of editorial firepower and electro-punk horizons in "Losing My Edge" makes it ideal for dancing to dancing about architecture.
—RM

The Rapture: *"House of Jealous Lovers"* 2002

"House of Jealous Lovers" was an anthem that shifted underground rock almost immediately upon release, and with its scintillating mix of convulsive beats and

livid screams, it remains the defining gesture of what would come to be known as dance-punk. It was very much a gesture: When the Rapture teamed with New York production duo the DFA (Tim Goldsworthy and LCD Soundsystem's James Murphy), they consciously set out to craft a manifesto that could play both as a rock song and as a dance track. Hints were suggested by the song's release format—twelve-inch vinyl, the medium favored by club DJs—but the message proves most distinctive in its sound, which mingles the excoriating guitars and yelping vocals of post-punk with a big throbbing bass line and high-hats that sashay like the drums in disco. The cross-platform experiment worked: Hear it on a proper dance floor, as scores of underground rock fans did when dance-punk started teaching them to be less suspicious of their bodies, and the Rapture's functional masterpiece makes good on its shrieking vocal command to "Shake dooowwn!" But more epochal than that, is how well "House of Jealous Lovers" reimagines raucous punk as a mode fit for rhythm.
—AB

The Streets: *"Weak Become Heroes"* 2002

Most of the Streets' early work deployed a rudimentary and fitful take on syncopated UK garage beats to create shifty hip-hop that ingeniously combined hardness and weakness. On "Weak Become Heroes," pasty British rapper Mike Skinner wants to evoke house music, but the frailty of the MC's own jumbled memories of rave hedonism—an undifferentiated rush of disconnected details—are a world away from the shimmering perfection of the early-1990s club music he eulogizes. Perhaps they're saying more about the life his younger self grasped for than the life he actually led ("never seen so many fit girls," he observes, a bit tragically)—and maybe that's the point: Moments of peace, love, and understanding are fleeting even when the drugs are good. Impossible simply to repeat, they live on in the afterlife of memory, the intense flashback, and the sudden, foolish grin.
—TF

Aesop Rock: *"Daylight"* 2001

"Daylight" is anchored by a memorable and discernible hook: "All I ever wanted was to pick apart the day / Put the pieces back together

my way." That's a pretty good summation of what Aesop Rock likes to do: stitch together impenetrable metaphors and fragmented images and deliver them double-time with his distinctive quack-rap.

The horns and flutes of "Daylight" are not only sad but terse; its woodblock-like percussion sounds like the music itself is following the bouncing ball over the unusually dense lyrics. There are too many quotables to begin to list but needless to say, Aesop affirmed his vision here: cynical, exhausted, and overwhelmed. Cramming more syllables and images into his rhymes than most other rappers doesn't necessarily make him better, but it does make him a more apt reflection of modern urbanity—or at least a more appealing tour guide.
—JC

Rjd2: *"Good Times Roll Pt. 2"* 2002

"Fingertips, Pt. 2," "Shout, Pts. 1–2," "Hot Pants, Pts. 1–2"—the archives of R&B and soul are strewn with examples of classic songs that their creators, for one reason or another, thought would be best appreciated in multiple parts. This habit clearly didn't escape the notice of veteran cratedigger Rjd2, aka DJ/producer R. J. Krohn. On his stellar debut, *Deadringer,* an album that still stands as a high-water mark for instrumental hip-hop, Rjd2 broke his source material down at an almost genetic level to build startling new originals. Mixed and edited with a keen eye for period detail, "Good Times Roll Pt. 2" has surely led more than one inattentive listener to mistake it for the work of some long-lost 1960s R&B combo.

Of course, Rjd2's scrupulous historical accuracy wouldn't matter much if "Good Times Roll Pt. 2" wasn't so satisfying in its own right. Buoyed by vibrant brass and vocal samples, and overlaid with the warm crackle of old vinyl, "Pt. 2" joins the party when it's already in peak swing. (This despite the confusion in the call-and-response chorus when half the crowd scream "Yeah!" while the rest holler back "No!") Without stopping to sort things out, Rjd2 plows ahead with his endlessly inventive breaks, secure in the knowledge passed down from that earlier generation of soul men: When the sound is right you can't help but go back for seconds.
—MMu

Bright Eyes:
"The Calendar Hung Itself" 2000

There are two incarnations of Conor Oberst, the Omaha-bred musician known as Bright Eyes. Each reflects the other in reverse, as befits someone for whom mirrors (along with fevers, calendars, and clocks) are perennial motifs. Modern Oberst— a politically engaged, emo-country ministar—is an antidote to teenage Oberst, who recorded poisonous folk and primitive electronics on a reel-to-reel in his basement, his dread-laden self-obsession spanning the tonal spectrum between maudlin fragility and furious brutality. To be young and suburban on the cusp of the twenty-first century was to recognize the impotent guilt, bottomless longing, unfocused urgency, and belligerent introspection Oberst so faithfully replicated in song.

"The Calendar Hung Itself" is the younger Oberst's creative apex, a final adolescent salvo before his raw-boned music and desperate alienation pivoted toward polish and populism. The bathroom floors, telephone booths, and "red-rouge, sun-bruised fields" that represent his jealousy and self-immolation spin like a zoetrope. He yelps the lyrics like a boy on the run, while telegraphic guitars and creepshow synths amplify the sense of panicked flight. Of course, the ex whom Oberst addresses is a spectral presence at best, and this marks one of the last times he would mistake hating himself for loving someone else.
—*BH*

Wilco: *"Poor Places"* 2002

The early word on Wilco's *Yankee Hotel Foxtrot* was that it was such a weird and challenging album that it would make you simultaneously bleed out your eye sockets and question whether you've ever truly heard music before. Okay, so that wasn't true, but a couple of moments were unorthodox enough to make Warner Brothers wonder, famously, what happened to their humble little Midwestern country-rock band, causing them to put the record on the proverbial shelf. "Poor Places" is one of those songs, Jeff Tweedy's deconstructivist experiment taken to its most haunting extreme. It's not hard to hear the undercarriage of a typical Tweedy folk-rock tune here, but every move is calculated to dissect the arrangement without letting the song completely

disintegrate. Crowding out the brief respites of Beatlesesque comfort rock, there are ominous drones and white noise; out-of-phase, ghostly keyboards drifting in and out of range; and a climax of screeching power-drill feedback and ham-radio transmissions. The disorienting environment mirrors the agoraphobia of the lyrics, where the protagonist himself is falling apart piece by piece as the comforts of home morph into a prison cell. *YHF* may not have been anywhere near experimental enough to justify its suspiciously beneficial release controversy, but "Poor Places" shows that it was still distinctly disquieting American rock, from a band unafraid to sabotage itself.
—*RM*

Queens of the Stone Age:
"No One Knows" 2002

Some of the strongest Queens of the Stone Age tracks first saw the hungover light of day during the musical key parties that guitarist and singer Josh Homme hosted under the Desert Sessions moniker. It's no wonder: Though Homme is the grand poobah of all things Queens, he hits his highest highs when paired with bandmates who both complement and challenge him, as this song proves. Not only does this track come from the last Queens album featuring former bassist Nick Oliveri it also features a former drummer from a popular flannel-clad rock trio that knew a thing or Foo about bringing melodic grunge to the great unwashed. Here, as on the rest of the band's *Songs for the Deaf* LP, Dave Grohl locks into the Queens' pop-motorik assembly line flawlessly, tightening the screws on an already well-oiled machine. Homme's cocky swagger has never been so ably abetted as it was with Oliveri and Grohl spurring him on—it's a shame this meeting of like minds was so short-lived.
—*DR*

My Morning Jacket:
"The Way That He Sings" 2001

At the tail end of the '90s, Louisville-based My Morning Jacket stumbled onto a Southern crossroads where rootsy Neil Young jams could open into the spacey psychedelic euphoria of the Flaming Lips. They probably got into the whiskey cabinet, too. Songwriter/guitarist Jim James's reverb-laden vocals

A History of Bastard Pop: Mashups

From Negativland's politicized sampling of U2 to Girl Talk's hyperspeed pop combustions, mashups take appropriation and recontexualization to new levels of postmodern absurdity by mixing together two (or more) songs to create one mutant hybrid. Transgressive by nature, they jump past all boundaries of legality, culture, language, and taste.

"Doctorin' the Tardis," **the Timelords:** The godfathers of prank pop, the KLF had a combative career featuring numerous challenges to fair use and copyright laws—and they didn't shy from challenging pop's aristocracy, using portions of songs by the Beatles and ABBA in their earliest records. Under the name the Timelords, the duo also scored a UK number 1 in 1988 with this dynamite (and legal) blend of Gary Glitter's stadium anthem "Rock and Roll (Pts. 1 and 2)" and the theme from cult TV show *Doctor Who.* Hey!

"U2," **Negativland:** As Negativland's Mark Hosler puts it, "We never had a hit record. Negativland had a hit lawsuit." The band's kazoo-laden "U2" became famous thanks to the drawn-out legal battle U2's label initiated over its unauthorized samples and misleading cover art. Today, the rebellious mess remains a better lesson in fair use and satire than in songwriting.

"I Wanna Dance With Numbers," **Girls on Top /** *"A Stroke of Genius,"* **Freelance Hellraiser:** The Romulus and Remus of modern mashups, these releases lit the fire that sparked across web pages throughout 2001 and 2002 and helped establish the most common template for bastard pop: chart-pop female vocals over more cred-worthy, usually '80s-tinged music. On the former, Richard X imagines a mechanical showdown between dance-pop robot Whitney Houston and krautrock robots Kraftwerk. On the latter, an anonymous UK producer perfectly grafts Christina Aguilera's debut single onto the Strokes' Lower East Side guitar chug.

"Gold Teeth Thief," **DJ/rupture:** Though web freebies would become commonplace over the next few years, this full-length mix was an illicit thrill when it first appeared. The sixty-eight-minute set finds explosive collisions and common causes in five or six continents' worth of beats, making a statement on both the power of the global Internet and the reach of the booty diaspora in the '00s.

"Lisa's Got Hives," **Conway:** Proving that rap-rock doesn't have to be a dated pursuit, TLC's Lisa "Left Eye" Lopes is added to the Hives' rehashed punk, accomplishing the neat trick of taking two good songs and turning them into one great one.

"Can't Get Blue Monday Out of My Head," **2 Many DJs:** Making the most of an immense silver LP stage prop, Australian pop star Kylie Minogue helped to legitimize the burgeoning mashup trend when she performed this alternate, New Order–enhanced version of her single "Can't Get You Out of My Head" at the Brit Awards.

"Freak Like Me," **Sugababes:** Bringing the concept of mashups even further into the mainstream, producer Richard X reworked his original Gary Numan–sampling underground bootleg with British pop tarts Sugababes and ended up with a number 1 hit in the UK.

"Poor Leno (Silikon Soul Remix)"/"There Is a Light That Never Goes Out," **Erlend Øye:** The Norwegian singer-songwriter hits upon a mashed gold mine by making Morrissey sound downright funky while singing Smiths karaoke over a disco-dance throb courtesy of fellow Scandinavians Röyksopp.

"Bingo," **Diplo/M.I.A.:** Featured on M.I.A.'s hype-igniting *Piracy Funds Terrorism* mixtape—one of the first to bring this hip hop promotion staple to indie kids—the cosmopolitan MC displays her own brand of no-nonsense hustle over Timbaland's untouchable "Big Pimpin'" beat.

"99 Problems," **Danger Mouse:** Generational icons clash as Jay talks bitches and hos over the Fab Four's blister-bursting "Helter Skelter." By mashing up Jay-Z's new *Black Album* with the Beatles' "White Album," Danger Mouse tampered with some of the most verboten samples in the licensing world—and by giving away his *The Grey Album* online, the producer got away scot free, earning nothing but stardom for his efforts.

"Smash Your Head," **Girl Talk:** When Biggie Smalls's "Juicy" meets Elton John's "Tiny Dancer" in the middle of this ADD smashup clinic, Girl Talk elevates novelty into heart-wrenching art—and a centerpiece of his rabble-rousing live sets.
—*RD*

are the band's centerpiece, howling like Confederate ghosts down lonesome country roads intersected by twangy guitars. In contrast with the often-tortured Southern Gothic of fellow Kentuckian Will Oldham, MMJ are a bunch of romantics, as their 1999 debut, *The Tennessee Fire*, established with songs like "I Will Be There When You Die." While 2001's follow-up, *At Dawn*, added a keyboardist and lengthier instrumental sections, the mix of plaid-shirted country-rock and uncomplicated emotional yearning remained.

At Dawn's swaying, sunburned "The Way That He Sings" epitomizes both the sound and the sentiment of early MMJ. Opening with wordless harmonies before settling into a moseying Sunday-afternoon gait, the song asks questions about love and music and the appeal of each. The answers, James concludes, must be something intangible: "It's just the way that he sings, not the words that he says, or the band." The lyrics would seem to render rock critics moot, and here they describe James's appeal better than we could, anyway.
—*MH*

Modest Mouse: *"3rd Planet"* 2000

On "3rd Planet," Modest Mouse singer Isaac Brock shouts, "The universe is shaped exactly like the earth / If you go straight long enough, you'll end up where you were." The song came just as Modest Mouse were leaving behind their beginnings, looking unlikely to double back. In 2000, the longtime Pacific Northwest indie rockers released their major-label debut, *The Moon and Antarctica*. Over the next seven years, this would catapult them to platinum status, a number 1 album, and the addition of the Smiths' Johnny Marr as an extra guitarist. "3rd Planet" is the lead track from that landmark record, and it's where singing guitarist Brock sets out his vision of a cosmos infinitely swallowing itself.

With Red Red Meat's Brian Deck producing, clean guitar plucks and pinging harmonics jut into crashing drums, lap steel, and those ADD-addled vocals. Despite the songs's lofty musings and self-loathing, the single would help Modest Mouse grab ears on alternative radio, making way for modern rock chart-topper "Float On" to propel the band, four years later, into a new, bigger universe.
—*MH*

Clinic: *"Distortions"* 2000

Liverpool four-piece Clinic perform in surgical masks, and their alien alloy of surf rock and garage psych is similarly furtive, wobbling with anxiety and paranoia. Their low-key hymn "Distortions" is a millennial slow dance for people who aren't sure they believe in love. With its prom-ready refrain, "I love it when you blink your eyes," this could've been an anthem, were if not for its humble nature: A long-toned sheen of analog organ sloshes and glows. Spindly mechanical percussion ratchets up the intensity. Ade Blackburn's vocals are small but searchlight-intense, laced with gentle vibrato and spectral harmonies. The lone melodica after the chorus is impenetrably strange, as is the elliptical narrative: Blackburn wonders what people say about him behind his back, imagines his beloved dead, lusts after her sister, and concludes with a corporal manifesto of sorts: "I want to know my body." It's as if the singer, as mystified by his oracular decrees as we are, takes us on a flying, desperate leap toward the solid ground of self-knowledge. If we don't exactly find our feet, a few moments caught in the climax's phantom updrafts are the next best thing.
—*BH*

Shellac: *"Prayer to God"* 2000

When it comes to making music and voicing opinions, famed indie audio engineer and Big Black leader Steve Albini has never been one to mince words. So it's no surprise that this song of love-gone-wrong—from a man better known for screaming about slaughterhouses, self-immolation, and televised suicides—goes for the throat rather than mooning and weeping. Atop one of the band's signature minimal, metallic backdrops, Albini's narrator asks God to kill his former lover and her current man. The brute simplicity of the request ("fucking kill him") lends it a resonant honesty that any number of sad-sack troubadours would fucking kill to emulate. And while the musical backing punctuates each "kill" with a primal thud that's perfect for Shellac's usual audience of cross-armed head-bangers, there's a ballad inside this storm that could just as easily find a home within the repertoire of a world-weary blues or country singer.
—*DR*

Mclusky:
"To Hell with Good Intentions" 2002

Cowed and confused by trendy late-1990s artists who were often influenced by dance, some journalists rushed to laud anybody who picked up a guitar or fingered a blues scale in the early aughts, naming them the saviors of rock. But none of these over-praised artists embraced anything as unpredictable or ugly as the underground rock of the Pixies, the Jesus Lizard, or even Nirvana. It took three men from Wales to give us a swift reminder with their second and most potent album, 2002's *Mclusky Do Dallas*.

With just a few mechanical stabs of bass and a guitar riff like a buzzsaw inching toward some dashing spy's pelvis, "To Hell with Good Intentions" is one of many examples of the band's off-kilter humor, which ranges from absurd boasting about drug-taking and their fathers' wealth to turning emotion into a dick-measuring contest ("My love is bigger than your love")—all of which sounded perfectly logical to the rabid pocket of fans they abandoned when they broke up three years later. When the song slides into the goosebump-raising cacophony that teases a chorus that never comes, everything they shout sounds desperate and righteous, not to mention: "When we gonna get excited??" Uh, right fucking now.
—*JC*

Lightning Bolt: *"Ride the Sky"* 2001

Noise rock poked its head above ground a little in the 1980s and '90s, but the turn of the century saw many more such groups rise from basements into the alt-mainstream consciousness. This happened all around America, but a particular concentration gelled in the unlikely nook of Providence, Rhode Island. The leaders of this demi-movement, hyperactive duo Lightning Bolt, injected prog riffs and speedy chops into the kind of noise-rock pioneered by Japanese juggernauts Boredoms and Ruins, as well as the muscular groups on Minnesota's Amphetamine Reptile label.

Live, bassist and singer Brian Gibson (usually with a mic in his mouth) and drummer Brian Chippendale (usually in a colorful mask) don't play on stages; instead, they performed in the audience, fans crowding around their athletic workouts. "Ride the Sky," from their second LP *Ride the Skies,* captures

this chaos, as Gibson churns out a stupefyingly simple riff and Chippendale responds with a rhyming pound. Soon the pair dissolve into a noisy cloud that seems to speed up even without actually varying its beat. Despite their ability to overload into blissful mess, Lightning Bolt could also be an awe-inspiring machine, and "Ride the Sky" has the frantic efficiency of an assembly line in overdrive.
—*MM*

The Microphones: *"The Moon"* 2001

Indie rock's lo-fi movement grew out of the hissy four-track recordings of guitar/bass/drums acts like Sebadoh, Pavement, and K Records founder Calvin Johnson's Beat Happening. By the late '90s, however, Athens, Georgia's Elephant 6 collective had shown that the lo-fi approach could also be applied to lushly orchestrated psych-pop. Naturalistic recording techniques met an ideal theme—the beauty of nature—on the 2001 masterpiece *The Glow Pt. 2,* by K Records mainstay Phil Elvrum.

As the Microphones, the Washington-based singer-songwriter created dynamically explosive headphone music. Album standout "The Moon" begins with a minute of faltering, stereo-panned acoustic guitars before bursting into a steady thrum of distorted cymbals, blissful trumpet, and delicate fuzz. Elvrum's soft murmur is submerged into the mix like just another instrument. An acoustic version from the rarities collection *Song Islands* better showcases Elvrum's poignant lyrics, about romantic evenings spent under "the blue light of the moon" and the narrator's effort to forget them. "There is nothing left except certain death," Elvrum sighs—but, as on Nick Drake's lo-fi precursor "Pink Moon," there's plenty of time for wistful contemplation first.
—*MH*

The New Pornographers:
"Letter from an Occupant" 2000

Sorting the good power-pop from the bad is like being a dog-show judge; the basics are so codified by this point, it's all in the subtleties. But "Letter from an Occupant" is an easy best-of-show call, with all the early Who and Beach Boys cues juiced up with a triple espresso and one hell of a show-stopping lead vocal. It was clear all the way back in the mid-'90's, when he fronted the Zombies-esque Sub Pop group

Zumpano, Carl Newman had the uncanny ability to plant melodies deep in one's memory. But drafting Neko Case as his occasional mouthpiece—not to mention Destroyer's Dan Bejar to push him off kilter—bumped Newman up a tier from the cheerily pedestrian likes of Fountains of Wayne. "Occupant" is the CMJ all-star team nailing it on the first pitch, mostly thanks to Case's Nashville-worthy pipes blasting like a foghorn through the song's random-word-generator lyrics, stretching every syllable like she's smuggling a vocoder in her throat. It's a jaw-dropping diva performance in an arena dominated by fey male vocals; shocked, as speechless as the listener, Newman can only *oo-woo* in response.
—*RM*

The Shins: *"New Slang"* 2001

The Shins came out of nowhere—Albuquerque, to be exact—with *Oh, Inverted World,* playing up Brian Wilson harmonies and early-R.E.M. impenetrability (sans mumbling), inadvertently sculpting the shape of mid-'00s crossover indie in the process. Hummable and instantly familiar, album highlight "New Slang" boasts an immediacy and a surefooted folk melody that disguises singer James Mercer's dark thoughts as he looks for a new way to bemoan a mistimed romance.

The song's cracked heart comes from Mercer's certainty that this missed opportunity will color the rest of his days: "I'm looking in on the good life I might be doomed never to find," he sings near song's end, just before that tambourine taps out into eternity. Slowly giving up its secrets, "New Slang" sounds like a personal lament drawn from a particularly foul mood.
—*SD*

The Decemberists:
"Here I Dreamt I Was an Architect" 2002

Decemberists frontman Colin Meloy has two modes: flamboyant high school drama geek, spinning yarns of war and forbidden love in his best from-the-diaphragm voice; and wistful indie geek, much like a thousand others but a little more graceful and literate. "Here I Dreamt I Was an Architect," from the Decemberists' debut *Castaways and Cutouts,* catches him in the latter phase, and while it's not unlike so many other soft, unassuming ballads of its time, the

beauty of the verse and the yearning in the chorus are striking. In three vignettes, he role-plays a soldier, a Spaniard, and an overambitious builder, and each one tells a different tragedy. On their next records, the band started showing off its chops and Meloy grew more ostentatious—but it was hard-pressed to make anything this affecting. When he reaches the song's end "We are vagabonds…we live this close to death," he doesn't declaim it from the safety of the stage; instead, the drama overwhelms him.
—*CD*

Radiohead: *"Life in a Glasshouse"* 2001

Around the turn of the millennium, many critics hoped Radiohead would become the biggest band in the world; instead, they threatened to become the best—a group that could match the emotional resonance and grandeur of rock with the limitless sonic possibilities of electronic music.

After the success of 2000's *Kid A,* it seemed like Thom Yorke's band would accomplish both goals—creating twenty-first-century art rock and dragging the more mundane elements of the guitar-centric world with it. Instead, Radiohead temporarily lost some of its cultural cachet with the release of 2001's *Amnesiac,* an adventurous, rewarding album that pushed too far away from the supposedly authentic and organic for many of those who had exalted the group over the past half-decade. It remains a spectacular record, however, closing with "Life in a Glasshouse," a New Orleans funeral jazz lament about political apathy in the relatively comfortable years immediately preceding 9/11. "I'd like to sit around and chat, but someone's listening in," a paranoid Yorke wryly warns, before presciently observing that "once again, we are hungry for a lynching." With the twenty-first-century emergence of city-wide surveillance, wiretapping, and preemptive war, Yorke's tale of a toothless citizenry being seen (but not heard) at all times is even more powerful.
—*SP*

Broken Social Scene:
"Cause = Time" 2002

Broken Social Scene had been nominated for a Juno award in Canada by the time their 2002 sophomore release, *You Forgot It in People,* also broke in the States. The band's core members had also been in the

They Don't Know: Grime

This post-millennial sound grew out of the dance-music movement known as two-step garage and later evolved into the ghostly form of dubstep. The connecting agent between them was the active rhythmic urge behind old drum 'n' bass, which grew up, slowed down, got poppy, and started searching for meaning in words.

"Destiny," **Dem 2:** An incandescent gem from the early days of two-step, "Destiny" catalogs all the traits that gave the style its initial shine: diagonally aligned drums and splashy high-hats, processed diva vocals that fall in line with futuristic R&B, and a dapper bass line haunted more by house music than by anything dark and hard.

"Shut the Door," **Todd Edwards:** A rare U.S. player in a scene mostly situated in the UK, Todd Edwards helped seed the two-step sound with a singular production method that paired fleet beats with an atomizing vocal technique that cut samples into what sounds like hundreds of pieces. "Shut the Door" plays like an angel's song crafted from stutters, swoons, and sighs.

"Neighbourhood," **Zed Bias:** The ruff-neck tendencies of two-step played out in heavy tracks like "Neighbourhood," which twitches and snaps over a monstrous bass line designed to make speakers nervous. This more manic and volatile "sound of the pirates" was often accompanied by a melodic MC who toasts like a barker at an old Jamaican soundclash.

"Battle," **Wookie:** With "Battle," Wookie introduced a strain of eerily moody soul into a scene that had grown comfortable in clubs with luxurious lights and flutes of champagne. Electric piano and svelte harmonies still signal an affinity for aural lushness, but the vocals sound sparse and spectral.

"Has It Come to This?" **the Streets:** Mike Skinner, the rapper known as the Streets, was a storyteller from the start. In the stirring voice of a contemplative everyman, he intones a windy poem about weed and dashed dreams.

"21 Seconds," **So Solid Crew:** Toggling between the postures of American hip-hop and a mode of rapping that was more homegrown, So Solid Crew brought cocksure vocalizing to the forefront of UK garage and helped birth grime as we know it. The premise here is simple—an army of MCs take over the mic for twenty-one seconds each—but the result is otherworldly in its density and range.

"Booo!" **Sticky [ft. Ms. Dynamite]:** The star here is Ms. Dynamite, an MC whose singsongy island cadence boasts all the potential energy of a fuse burned just short of its charge. Her only competition is a bass line big enough to shake concrete walls, but she outweighs it with a staccato delivery that sticks as much as its sprays.

"Cha Ching (Cheque 1, 2 Remix)," **Lady Sovereign:** Before she became a favorite of Jay-Z, Lady Sovereign was the teenage darling of grime on the strength of upstart tracks like "Cha Ching." She sounds like four or five different rappers in the same song, but they're all bratty, bossy, brash—and more commanding than their origins in a cheeky teenage mind would seem to make possible.

"Eskimo," **Wiley:** Wiley fashioned himself as the grime producer of choice with a chancy, chintzy sound that focused on thin synthesizers and brittle beats. Both figure highly in "Eskimo," with its epochal grime backdrop that sounds licked by a sinister mix of fire and ice.

"Destruction VIP," **Jammer:** Grime in its prime trafficked in MCs trading verses like chaotic characters on a pirate-radio broadcast. "Destruction VIP" features four of them—Wiley, D Double E, Kano, and Durrty Goodz—and the result is fluent lunacy of the highest order.

"Gorgon Sound," **Horsepower Productions:** An early foray into the largely voiceless sound that would come to be known as dubstep, "Gorgon Sound" skulks through a thwacking garage rhythm in thrall to the atmosphere of old dub reggae. Snatches of vocals echo through the mix, but the message speaks more through the grain of a red-lined bass sound gone to gray.

"Distant Lights," **Burial:** Burial embodied the disembodied sound of dubstep with "Distant Lights," a scene-making single that sounds like drum 'n' bass with the life scared out of it.
—AB

scene for years: Primary songwriter Kevin Drew had made two albums with Do Make Say Think's Charles Spearin as K.C. Accidental, and singer/bassist Brendan Canning had cut his teeth with Canadian alt-rock bands hHead and By Divine Right. The band's combined experience comes through loud and clear on "Cause = Time," a slow-release anthem that masterfully builds to Andrew Whiteman's guitar fireworks and a blistering hook—one that, almost overnight, helped catapult the Toronto collective into indie rock's top tier.
—ML

Deerhoof:
"This Magnificent Bird Will Rise" 2002

This Bay Area band doesn't merge genres so much as use them to neutralize one another. While singer Satomi Matsuzaki's high, cute, and heavily accented vocals evoke Japanese pop, the band dives into blank-faced, start-and-stop No Wave, pushing the music into an absurd formlessness checked only by the prog-rock grandeur and power drumming that make up its engine. Thematically, 2002's *Reveille* rests on that knife's edge: Premonitions of a religious awakening and final judgment are tempered by the suggestion that adorable animals are behind the whole thing. (Yes, nature's angry—but as its voice, Matsuzaki is more meerkat than lion.) Leading off with a spoken-word intro that heralds Judgment Day, "This Magnificent Bird Will Rise" is the overture to a highly unpredictable album. A wooden flute tone and dippy wordless vocal offset the huge, tear-into-the-sky riff and Greg Saunier's sprints of drumming: One moment it's building to grandeur, the next it stops and changes gears as if something could actually pause the end of the world.
—CD

Spoon: "The Way We Get By" 2002

This is a song about losers who don't actually seem like they're losing. They get up, they get high, they steal stuff, they get high some more, they listen to the Stooges, and naturally, they get by. However, where Iggy would scream, "I feel all right," as if he felt anything but, Spoon singer Britt Daniel's perspective on these slackers is more nuanced: "We believe in the sum of ourselves," he rasps near the end of the track, cutting the rough-and-tumble talk with some Up With People self-actualization. Fittingly, the music also

avoids the road more traveled, riding the rails atop piano work and percussion that has more in common with "Mr. Big Shot" than "I Wanna Be Your Dog." The tight spaces within the song's precise arrangement, however, are pure post-punk: Just because this was the moment Spoon started to find a larger audience doesn't mean they abandoned their roots.
—DR

Dizzee Rascal: "I Luv U" 2002

Up to 2002, Dizzee Rascal's career highlight was providing the hook and a brief, thirteen-second verse on London-based grime crew Roll Deep's underground hit "Bounce," which combined UK garage, dancehall, and hip-hop into the genre that would shortly be known as grime. But by the end of the year, a test pressing of a new solo Dizzee track had leaked to the Internet. Commercially released in spring 2003, when Dizzee was still seventeen, "I Luv U" defined the persona of grime's first international breakthrough star—and, in turn, the personality of the genre itself. The production is grime writ large, opening with a stuttering, robotic female voice that turns the phrase "I love you" into a throat-clenching threat, then dropping into a quick-jog rhythm that scatters coughing, hyperventilating synths over face-slapping beats and window-rattling bass. At the core of the track is Dizzee's delivery: harried to the point of paranoia ("She just keep ringin' me at home / These days I don't answer my phone"), he combines anger and fear into an uncontrollable anxiety, making his phrasing a raw expression of teenage frustration.
—NP

M.O.P.: "Ante Up" 2000

There was never anything smooth about M.O.P., and yet the Brooklyn duo still managed to score their biggest hit just when rap's ostentatious materialism was reaching untold heights. They were unreformed knuckleheads; when everyone else on Hot 97 was talking about *owning* diamonds, Billy Danzenie and Lil' Fame were rapping about *stealing* them. As rappers, both delivered their threats in full-bore throat-shredding, vein-popping bellows, sacrificing finesse and technique for straight-up adrenaline. "Ante Up" is their finest moment, four straight minutes of violence and desperation, a chain-snatcher's manifesto.

Producer DR Period turns a chopped-up horn stab from Sam & Dave's "Soul Sister, Brown Sugar" into a riotous clarion call while Danze and Fame unleash hell. (Practical advice from Fame to the poor: "Kidnap that fool!" Soul-searching introspection from Danze: "I'm nine-hundred and ninety-nine thou short of a mil!") During the summer of 2000, "Ante Up" felt like a visceral reawakening of rap's repressed dark side, and the drawn-out horn blast on the intro would start mosh pits in clubs before the drums even kicked in. That reawakening wouldn't last: After "Ante Up," M.O.P. bounced from record label to record label, constantly being told their material wasn't commercial enough to see record-store shelves. They're men out of time, lost relics of a scarier era.
—TB

Clipse: *"Grindin'"* 2002

There's spare, there's stark, and then there's Spartan—and in the summer of 2002, the Spartan sounds of production team the Neptunes ruled the day. Working with their rap protégés, Virginia duo Clipse, Pharrell Williams and Chad Hugo launched the trunk-popping "Grindin'" and helped revitalize an obsession with the drug trade in hip-hop. Clipse (brothers Malice and Pusha T) attacked the track's stuttering snares and vocal pops with insidious verve and an insider's playbook, rapping in unfiltered slang about the drug-dealing corner trade. In the third verse Malice spits, "My grind's 'bout family, never been about fame / From days I wasn't able, there was always 'caine," alluding to the Bible, brotherhood, and his trade in one quick run. Lyrically, this isn't the best of what would come from the Thornton brothers—Pusha in particular hadn't quite found his voice yet, or perfected his serpentine flow—but it's easily the Neptunes' most sonically arresting song. It seems ostentatious to leave such complicated musings so open to the beat's wide, negative space. But these are the risks great producers take.
—SF

Talib Kweli: *"Get By"* 2002

Highly skilled and well regarded by his peers (Jay-Z is an admirer, among others), Talib Kweli has nevertheless spent much of his career serving a niche audience. It hasn't been for a lack of effort, though: Starting with 2002's *Quality,* Kweli ventured outside his fertile relationship with Rawkus Records

house producer Hi-Tek to work with a wide range of more commercially minded producers.

Lucky for Kweli, he counted then-ascending producer Kanye West among his *Quality* collaborators. Even in West's exhaustive library of tracks, "Get By" stands tall, a tough yet graceful interpolation of "Sinnerman" by Nina Simone, to whom Kweli and Hi-Tek had paid exhaustive tribute on 2000's "For Women." "Get By"'s lyrics are conscious without lapsing into sanctimony: Kweli is sympathetic to hustlers and strugglers while still pining for change. After years of earning respect, Kweli not only proved he could measure up when given an obvious hit track, but reminded us that a great beat should serve the MC, not vice versa.
—JC

Jay-Z: *"Takeover"* 2001

By century's end, rap beef was often broiled, rarely served raw. But after Queensbridge's favorite son, Nas, began taking shots at Jay-Z in 2000, the Marcy Projects native reinvigorated—even elevated—a swollen art form: the dis track. Responding not just to Nas, but also Mobb Deep and a handful of others, "Takeover" is the fiercest rebuttal ever. Here, Jay at last unleashed a rapid-fire series of bullets at his targets. See the staggering, career-altering verse three—it's the stuff of legend. (Nas eventually hit back with the bitter, simplistically punishing "Ether" and relaunched a flagging career.)

"Takeover"'s might is void without one of Kanye West's production high-water marks. Sampling the Wurlitzer gallop, stutter-thump bass line, and Jim Morrison's yowling "Come on!" from the Doors' "Five to One," it's the thickest, grimiest thing he's ever constructed. But even at his most brutal, Jay was elegantly dexterous. Near the song's end he ambiguously raps, "You know who did you know what with you know / Let's keep that between me and you." Even in the midst of outspoken grandeur, he still leaves something to the imagination, thumbing his nose at his enemy in the process.
—SF

Chapter Nine:
2003–2006

It's the middle of the first decade of the twenty-first century, and one of the more acclaimed albums in indie rock comes from Beirut (aka Zach Condon), a nineteen-year-old American kid who sings with a heavy vibrato that sounds like it belongs on a lost 78. His lyrics are brashly sentimental but evocative creations about lost love, while his band—horns, ukulele, accordion—sounds like it bumped into him on some street corner during an Eastern European festival.

Meanwhile, on the German indie label Tomlab, electro-acoustic duo the Books, whose concrete aesthetic is built around spare guitar, cello, and a vast library of vocal samples, are reaching high school students and thirty-something NPR listeners—no prior knowledge of experimental music required. In Brighton, England, the Go! Team, an exuberant five-piece, draw inspiration from orchestral '60s pop, early hip-hop, and cheerleader routines, and make their peculiar genre mish-mash seem perfectly natural, if not inevitable. And then there's Animal Collective and Liars, two bands that like to reinvent themselves with every album, blending searing, abrasive sound work with communal pop chants. And in 2006, these bands found ways to flourish; the age of the niche was in full swing.

How did artists like these reach so many people? One factor, surely, was that the Internet's ability to connect bands with their audience had finally begun to mature. The matrix of connections established on social networking sites had reached critical mass, and the flier stapled to a telephone pole became the blog post read by thousands. With young music fans keeping up with more music so easily, tastes broadened, and specialization followed. A band no longer needed to be everything to any one fan; it was enough for them to do one or two things very well—and another band, with another few mp3s, was always on tap for when the next mood struck.

There was also the new ways music was being used on television as MTV shifted its focus away from videos. It would have been strange in the '80s for a prime-time TV drama to feature a musical interlude set to, say, a song by the Smiths, or a company like McDonald's to use a song in an ad by a guitar pop band on an indie label, like the Shins. But in the twenty-first century, such use of independent music became commonplace, providing another intersection where artists and fans might meet.

These changes meant that artists could get weird— a frontman talking and joking throughout his songs like Eddie Argos in England's Art Brut, Japan's Boris taking noise guitar to the outer limits of psychedelia, Sufjan Stevens writing concept albums about states—and still achieve an impressive level of recognition. Bands could also stand out by putting a new twist on moves that once seemed banal to the indie audience, like playing stirring, unabashedly passionate arena-ready anthems (Arcade Fire) or bar-band rock with good riffs and better stories (the Hold Steady). To be clear, we're not talking about platinum-sellers; these bands aren't stars in the traditional sense. But they are able to find fans around the country and around the world, make a decent living, and enjoy a high level of cultural penetration, often on the strength of one good record.

As technology helped odd little bands to become modestly successful, it also made room for more cultural variety. In this environment, Sweden can become the new center of indie pop. A vocalist originally from Sri Lanka can introduce people to political conflicts they never knew existed. A classically trained harpist exploring baroque, medieval balladry can put a new twist on American folk. France can become a locus for grinding dance music and epic shoegazer rock. And teenagers, like Beirut, singing in an antiquated style about the old country, can connect with other teenagers. No doubt the globalization of the music landscape, where elements from every place and time are up for grabs, has only just begun. Here's what it looked like as it was just beginning to hit its stride.
—MR

OutKast: *"Hey Ya"* 2003

In 2003, Atlanta's OutKast decided to resolve their creative differences by releasing a double album—one disc for Big Boi to make lush, solid hip-hop, and another for Andre 3000 to follow his muse into scattershot, genre-mixing pop experiments. Big Boi may have steered clearer of potential embarrassment, but it was Andre's "Hey Ya" that sold both halves. Pop fans, rock fans, rap fans, children, Mennonites, high-school principals, the elderly, terrorists—everybody loved this song. Animals loved it. Silverware loved it. You could play it in a forest with nobody to hear it and have complete faith that the very *trees* would throw up their branches.

It's not hard to hear why. "Hey Ya" sounds entirely like a product of the twenty-first century, but its spirit shoots straight back to the last '60s moment when rock and soul still snuggled up to a common ancestor. It's got joyous hooks, participatory handclaps, and a tricky half-measure to keep you on your toes. And best of all, for a song this ecstatic, it's filled with a kind of righteous, frustrated passion, and packs one of the broadest, weightiest lines to hit pop radio in a long time—the one where Andre thanks dear old mom and dad for staying together, something younger generations haven't managed as well. If everyone loves it, maybe it's because Andre is asking a question on behalf of everyone, ever: Why is it so damned hard to make it *work*? The song might be painful if it didn't seem to promise that reassuring thing that all the best pop songs promise: that we're all in it together, and we'll probably manage somehow.
—*NA*

Kanye West: *"Through the Wire"* 2003

A rap producer with label troubles, little mainstream name recognition, and a jaw literally wired shut after a car wreck releases his first single, an autobiographical track built around the heavy slur incurred by the constraint of a medical device. Such was Kanye West's formal entrance to stardom, rapping in a voice that sounded little like his own but with a determination unheard in years. Speeding the tempo of Chaka Khan's "Through the Fire" for his trademark "chipmunk soul" effect, "Wire" is one of West's most elementary and affecting concoctions. Its style made hip-hop's sampling tradition obvious and bold, leaving little to the imagination and courting larger audiences in the process.

The sound of his voice—on verse one recounting the accident's aftermath and on verse two delivering a statement of purpose ("He wasn't talking 'bout coke and birds, it was more like spoken word")—is garbled, yearning to break loose. It's that clenched tone that renders West's sometimes goofy double entendres disarmingly honest and translates his oft-flaunted middle-class pomp to all audiences. West would go on to tempt bombast and controversy and take his sound to greater heights, but no moment ever felt as earned as "Through the Wire."
—*SF*

R. Kelly: *"Ignition (Remix)"* 2003

The album version of "Ignition" was a slow-jam redo of Prince's "Little Red Corvette" that kept itself narrowly hemmed in by its framing conceit that driving a car is like having sex: funky, yes, but not the shameless sing-along party anthem it was to become post-remix. The big change from the wallflower original to its drunker, sexier offspring is a matter of poetics let off the chain. Similes are a particular weakness of Kelly's, and the barrage of romantic comparisons unleashed in the remix's new rhymes are so relentlessly off-topic and ridiculous that they successfully skew his reputation for "sick flow" away from watersports and back to polymorphously perverse free association.

No sooner is his intended described as a car than she's like "a football coach," and by the time you've figured that out, Kelly's already moved on to catering. The point here is to celebrate the ladies and the fellas having a good time together, conceptual tightness be damned. Alternately crooning and toasting with a faintly reggae lilt, R. Kelly's genius decision to bedazzle his song with an intensely catchy, brand-new chorus featuring a sung/slurred "I'm like so what I'm drunk" drops the cherry on the cake.
—*DD*

Beyoncé [ft. Jay-Z]: *"Crazy in Love"* 2003

When this song exploded, Beyoncé Knowles was already an established superstar, having deservedly scored major hits in Gen Y's very own Supremes, Destiny's Child, and teamed with Jay-Z on "'03 Bonnie & Clyde." "Crazy in Love"—her second Jay-Z collaboration—was the first single from Beyoncé's debut solo LP *Dangerously in Love,*

and its Chi-Lites-derived hook and Meters-powered beat made explicitly clear what seemed all but obvious before: Her voice, look, and mass appeal were fashioned from a different era, where concepts like the Entertainer—or even Pop—were built to apply to every single person in the world. This song makes people dance, sing in their cars, and suddenly develop blue-chip soprano vocals. And yes, we've seen *Dreamgirls*: There may well be singers with more natural talent or better show-stopping runs, but no twenty-first-century R&B star yet commands more attention with each passing single, each sports mag swimsuit cover, each run through the chorus of this tune than Beyoncé does.
—DL

Gnarls Barkley: *"Crazy"* 2005

It may have seemed like it, but "Crazy" wasn't the product of musical neophytes: producer Danger Mouse parlayed the notoriety of his Beatles/Jay-Z mashup, *The Grey Album,* into high-profile production gigs for underground rap icon MF Doom and Damon Albarn's cartoon rock band Gorillaz, while vocalist Cee-Lo was well-known as Goodie Mob's multitalented MC/singer, a man who could spit tommy-gun raps one moment and ease into gospel-inflected Al Greenisms the next. But when "Crazy" first aired on the band's website, it sounded weird and surprising enough to catch a lot of people off guard; a few months later, it became the first song to hit number 1 on the UK charts based solely on download sales, and in summer 2006 it spent seven weeks at number 2 in the U.S.

Danger Mouse's beat is deceptively simple, a segment of Gianfranco and Gian Piero Reverberi's 1968 spaghetti western score for *Preparati la bara!* tweaked and rearranged until it's turned into a mournful yet slinky break. Cee-Lo's voice pushes it over the edge; it's a moody wail that transitions between ghostly and full throated, splitting time between rapid-fire spitting and tranquil crooning to capture the lyrics' tone of enviable lunacy. And all those great highlights of his performance— the half-demented, half-cordial reading of "ha ha ha—bless your soul," the tossed-off "word" before the second chorus, the wounded delivery when he sings, "but it wasn't because I didn't know enough / I just knew too much"—were captured in the first take.
—NP

!!!: *"Me and Giuliani Down by the School Yard (A True Story)"* 2003

New York mayor Rudolph Giuliani was the poster boy for post-9/11 resolve, as he put aside his characteristic grandstanding and authoritarian fervor and calmly encouraged his battered citizenry to get on with the healing process. But for punk-funk octet !!! (pronounced "chk-chk-chk"), a big part of that healing process was to remind everyone that their humble hero was also responsible for draconian laws that regulated dancing in the city that birthed disco and hip-hop. Their response arrived in the form of a tremendous twelve-inch that, along with the Rapture's "House of Jealous Lovers" and LCD Soundsystem's "Losing My Edge," completes the trinity of post-millennial NYC post-punk.

"Me and Giuliani Down by the School Yard" takes a nine-minute late-night subway ride from the Knitting Factory to the Paradise Garage, soundtracked by a fluid, peak-hour disco (not disco) mix of Liquid Liquid, Pigbag, Arthur Russell, Can, New Order, and— with its climactic "Everybody cut loose!" breakdown— Kenny Loggins' *Footloose* theme. But there's great significance to that kitschy source material: Like the movie, "Me and Giuliani" reinstitutes dancing as an act of defiance—and in the song's foot-stomped/ hand-clapped finale, you hear !!!'s staunch refusal to leave the floor even after the music stops.
—SB

TV on the Radio: *"Staring at the Sun"* 2003

At first, TV on the Radio dabbled in four-track experiments—barbershop quartets, raunchy rhymes, and entrancing loops and collages. Those early experiments were relegated to a CD-R, *OK Calculator,* which they dropped in cafés and hid in couches of furniture showrooms. But their free-for-all phase paid off. By the time they recorded their first proper release, the *Young Liars* EP, they had honed a style: Vocalist Tunde Adebimpe and producer/guitarist Dave Sitek combined elements of soul, electronics, post-punk, and gospel in a manner never quite heard before. Beating at the album's melodic heart is the gorgeous "Staring at the Sun," a hypnotic meditation that's reluctant to give up its mysteries despite its addictive playability.

In the late 1990s, the creative impulses—and eventually the scale—of dance music collapsed. After roughly fifteen years of relentless innovation, electronic music stalled, both with the close of European superclubs and the inability of the U.S. music industry to make electronica a lasting success. Instead, the rhythms and texture of dance scattered in multiple directions—in New York City, a fascination with late '70s and early '80s underground disco and post-punk; in Paris, the filter disco of Daft Punk and their progenitors; in Germany, the dubby, minimalist, and bookish microhouse. But dance continued to impact the charts, where producers cannibalized the best ideas in "faceless" DJ music without sacrificing time-tested qualities like star power and songcraft.

"Around the World," **Daft Punk:** Daft Punk's *Homework*—boosted by eye-catching videos from Spike Jonze and Michel Gondry—went gold in the U.S. despite making no attempt to meet rock audiences halfway with guest vocalists or verse-chorus-verse structures. "Around the World" became not just mantra but prophecy, as electronic music went from an outlier to becoming almost synonymous with pop.

"Are You That Somebody?" **Aaliyah:** Dance's influence was eventually felt throughout hip-hop and R&B—and much of the credit goes to producer Timbaland. Infusing his songs with everything from woozy bleeps and bloops to Bollywood, Timbo found his perfect foil in Aaliyah, whose soulful, egoless coos made "Are You That Somebody?" the first of a string of classic singles until her untimely 2001 death.

"Bug-a-Boo," **Destiny's Child:** Producers such as She'kspere copped Timbaland's moves on hits for R&B groups TLC and Destiny's Child, who on "Bug-a-Boo" helped finally smuggle elements of rave music into the *Billboard* charts.

"Girls Like Us," **B15 Project:** UK dance music—long the domain of dark, masculine sounds like jungle and hardcore—had already begun to feminize by the time U.S. R&B incorporated elements of off-kilter rhythm and texture. 2-step returned the favor with upbeat, chaotically whipsmart singles such as this 2000 hit.

"Groovejet (If This Ain't Love)," **Spiller:** In the short time between the rise of Daft Punk and Madonna's *Music*, the French house technique of filter disco produced a string of European hits (including Modjo's "Lady [Hear Me Tonight]" and Armand van Helden's "U Don't Know Me"), but none better than this Sophie Ellis-Bextor-sung gem.

"Snoopy Track," **Jay-Z:** As hip-hop began to get E'd up, scenes of opulent club culture became common in not only music videos but on record as well, here soundtracked by a lurching, almost alien Timbaland sound comparable to neck-snapping IDM.

"Romeo," **Basement Jaxx:** In the late '90s, Basement Jaxx revived the classic house template by infusing it with ragga, rock, and other rougher sounds. The Jaxx consolidated those strengths on 2001's *Rooty*—in particular the overstuffed, charmingly complex single "Romeo."

"Work It," **Missy Elliott:** Songs like Brandy's "What About Us," Nelly's "Hot in Herre," and any number of crunk and hyphy hitz took the kitchen-sink approach as a dare. No one did that better than Missy Elliott, whose playful, hilarious, sonically exploratory singles like "Work It" became events.

"Like I Love You," **Justin Timberlake [ft. Clipse]:** In the early 2000s, electronic hip-hop so dominated the U.S. pop market that it seemed to swallow whole the stars of late-90s teen-pop—artists like Britney Spears, Christina Aguilera, and Beyoncé switched almost overnight from shiny, adolescent Disney cuts to dirtier, sexier sounds. Nobody made the move more completely or effectively, however, than Justin Timberlake, who here employed the Neptunes and Clipse to smooth the transition.

"Milkshake," **Kelis:** While minimalism dominated German techno in the '00s, the Neptunes almost single-handedly brought the approach into the charts. Their longtime, long-suffering house chanteuse Kelis finally had a deserved smash with "Milkshake," built only from a diner bell, a bare-bones drumbeat, a few synth sounds, and her own outsized sexuality.

"Biology," **Girls Aloud:** Throughout the 2000s, new wave and '80s revivalism characterized indie-dance cultures from electroclash to underground disco revivalism to mashup culture. UK production team Xenomania buffed and shined these trends, funneling the best of their high-octane modern electro-pop through Girls Aloud, the most consistently wonderful girl group of the new decade.
—*SP*

Drawing inspiration from the thirteenth-century Sufi poet Rumi, the lyrics of "Staring at the Sun" reflect upon the nature and fate of the soul, using its ecstatic language ("Pour out like light, like answering the sun") to artfully blur the boundaries between death and romantic passion. Layering drones and luminous vocal harmonies, Sitek's detailed arrangements expertly complement the lyrics' offhanded sophistication, while Adebimpe's graceful falsetto—an instrument almost wholly foreign to indie rock—levitates above the mix like a spirit ascending. Self-assured and revelatory, "Staring at the Sun" signaled the arrival of TV on the Radio as a major new creative force, with the further peaks of 2006's *Return to Cookie Mountain* and beyond already visible on the horizon.
—MMu

Yeah Yeah Yeahs: *"Maps"* 2003

Onstage and on record, the Yeah Yeah Yeahs' Karen O is a gleeful hellion dressed like a haute couture Cyndi Lauper and leering like a truck driver—simultaneously the coolest, weirdest, sexiest, and yes, scariest girl in the room. As she'd sing on 2006's "Cheated Hearts," sometimes she thinks that she's bigger than the sound. "Maps"—the breakout hit from the New York City trio's debut full-length, *Fever to Tell*—is not one of those times.

Here, Karen O doesn't shout or squeal or flirt. There's power in the way her voice breaks as she delivers the song's key lamentation: "Wait! They don't love you like I love you." But when guitarist Nick Zinner zooms in at the end of the chorus, it's a riptide drowning everything that came before it.

A classic power ballad, "Maps" was written for Karen's then-boyfriend, Angus Andrew of Liars. As the song gained popularity in the summer of 2004, critics and fans crowed about how the lovelorn singer of "Maps" was the "real" Karen O, and the video, featuring Karen crying real tears, certainly helped. But when she's let loose onstage, screaming about how she's got a man who makes her want to kill while pouring beer down her dress—and having the time of her life doing it—that's real, too. The vulnerability of "Maps" just makes Karen O's persona even stronger and the woman herself an even more thrilling rock star.
—APh

The Walkmen: *"The Rat"* 2004

New York City's the Walkmen have an ear for grandeur. Their glacially jutting arrangements and the scenery chewing of singer Hamilton Leithauser make them sound like an uptown version of U2, with prep-school smarm subbing for ecopolitical earnestness and Brooks Brothers peacoats for wraparound shades. In reality, they're emotionally deeper, burying heartfelt meditations on loneliness beneath their cocksure swagger. They usually build delicate ambiance from detuned scraps of upright piano and wintry analog synths, but this is a rat of a different color: Without warning, it howls like a locomotive barreling out of a tunnel into the blasted expanse of Leithauser's disaffection, where rhythm guitars glitter and drums explode. Leithauser is indignant one moment, but plaintive the next. No matter who he's addressing, a terse bridge—"When I used to go out I would know everyone that I saw / Now I go out alone, if I go out at all"—clues us in to whom he's really at war with: himself.
—BH

Devendra Banhart: *"A Sight to Behold"* 2004

For all his road-hippie imagery, strange celebrity connections, and the freehand surrealism of his lyrics, Devendra Banhart manages to endear himself to almost anyone who doesn't already have a life-grudge against Haight-Ashbury revivalism. This song is from his second record, 2004's *Rejoicing in the Hands,* and it's the finest primer for all things freak-folk: simple, elegant finger-picked guitar; similarly graceful melody, carried by ever-so-slight warble; poetic lyrics ("It's like finding home in an old folk song that you've never ever heard / Still you know every word"). The song also features string accompaniment and warm, uncluttered production courtesy of original Banhart-booster and former Swans leader Michael Gira, thereby cutting off haters before they can cry foul of flowery, precious excess.
—DL

Joanna Newsom: *"Peach, Plum, Pear"* 2004

California harpist Joanna Newsom boasts one of the most divisive sets of pipes around. High, warbly, and vaguely spastic, her vocals are peerless:

Squeeze your eyes shut and conjure a tottering little kid in a fairy costume, huffing helium out of a yellow balloon, careening around the backyard, yodeling nonsensical poems about fruit and gathering floozies.

Whether or not she likes it, Newsom—along with pals Devendra Banhart and Vetiver—is considered a key member of the contemporary freak-folk movement, a noncommunity of artists heavily influenced by American psychedelia and late-1960s British folk (Pentangle, Vashti Bunyan, the Incredible String Band). One of the highlights of her full-length debut, 2004's *The Milk-Eyed Mender,* "Peach, Plum, Pear" is a charming account of meeting a cute boy in a store, expertly layered over a tinny, chirping harpsichord line. Newsom's vocals might be the most striking component of her sound, but they're also remarkably well-suited to her whimsical, anachronistic lyrics: "We were galloping manic / To the mouth of the source," she twitters, voice somersaulting. All that affect can sometimes make Newsom seem emotionally distant, but on "Peach, Plum, Pear," it's hard not to love her, squeaks and all.
—AP

Sufjan Stevens:
"*Casimir Pulaski Day*" 2005

Sufjan Stevens gets much of his press out of being charmingly ambitious, be it with his fifty-state project, dress-up stage shows, or improbably ornate arrangements. But Stevens's proficiency as a folk singer is his musical foundation, skills that are on full display during "Casimir Pulaski Day," a story-song with a sentimental land mine of a premise. Few songwriters could spin a tune out of a teenager's first-person account of his girlfriend's cancer death without it turning into a Lifetime original movie, but Stevens handles it with characteristic delicacy. There are no choruses, just three-line stanzas that pack in the plot and the emotion through only the sparest of details, while soft guitar and banjo give way to trumpet solos that are as wounded as the words themselves.

Poignantly, "Casimir Pulaski Day" reveals Stevens's spiritual depth amidst an indie scene that bristles at unironic mentions of the Bible or the Lord. Though it appears to be a particularly cynical form of Christian rock, with its imagery of ineffective prayer and a selfish God, "Casimir Pulaski Day" rings true as being authored by someone who has deeply considered his faith, rather than knee-jerk rejected it.
—RM

Antony and the Johnsons:
"*Hope There's Someone*" 2005

Music is seldom more spellbinding than "Hope There's Someone," the haunting torch song that opens Antony and the Johnsons' breakthrough 2005 album *I Am a Bird Now.* Essentially a solo piece for voice and piano, "Hope There's Someone" draws much of its dramatic power from the subtle tension between its straightforward lyrics and the pull of Antony Hegarty's androgynous voice. And though it's a performance that unmistakably reveals Antony's spiritual links to the AIDS-stricken history of the downtown New York scene, the song's themes of loneliness, the fear of mortality, and the need for love make the song as universal and affecting as any traditional hymn.

"Hope there's someone who'll take care of me when I die," Antony sings, articulating the lyric's central fears with unshakable clarity. His vocal is mirrored throughout by his soft piano chords, and toward the song's end the music takes a sudden turn upward. This final section closes "Hope There's Someone" with a cathartic trace of optimism, allowing the song to serve at once as a graceful elegy and as a fervent prayer whispered to fend off the encroaching darkness.
—MMu

Animal Collective: "*Leaf House*" 2004

"Leaf House" seems more like a psychedelic dream than a song. Musically, it's a mixture of cloudburst melody; harmonies akin to the wildest moments on the post–*Pet Sounds* Beach Boys records; beats born from stomps, claps, and kicks; and a droning acoustic guitar figure that shows the influence of an earlier outsider from another land, Brazil's Tom Zé.

Though their lineup often varies, all voices and instruments on "Leaf House" are by David "Avey Tare" Portner and Noah "Panda Bear" Lennox, Animal Collective's chief songwriters. The group had been making records for four years at this point, and though its sound had varied considerably, it had generally come across as a dark, noisy, and strange outfit—accomplished within its sphere, but ultimately a specialty item. "Leaf House" was the first track from what proved to be their breakthrough album, *Sung Tongs,* and it found AC pushing their experimental tendencies in a brighter, more tuneful direction; they sound fearless (perhaps naïve) as they lurch into whatever lies ahead. The closing lyric—"Kitties / Meeeeeeow"—leaves the listener not so much baffled as hanging on in suspense, wondering where these guys might go next.

—DL

The Books: *"Take Time"* 2003

It's become a common trick to drop an evocative vocal snippet—a hellfire-breathing preacher, for instance, or a scratchy Victrola recording—into a song. But for electro-acoustic duo the Books, these bits of cultural detritus are the foundations of their music. American multiinstrumentalist Nick Zammuto and Dutch cellist Paul de Jong build their sonic collages from the samples outward. Their music has often been misconstrued as being left partly to chance—a designation at odds with their carefully selected samples, the daring intuitive leaps between them, and their meticulous instrumental arrangements.

This fastidious pruning is apparent in "Take Time," which leaves no room for the random amid its syncopated glitches. Tangled loops of pitched percussion, flurries of alternately blocky and fluid banjo runs, and a titular nursery-rhyme chant comprise its sparse framework. Within this structure, they arrange foreign-language samples, laughter that blurs into screams, and plainspoken metaphysical paradoxes ("Something is happening that is not happening") that fit snugly together. The combined effect is music as a hedge maze, a track you happily wander and puzzle through that provides a new perspective around every corner.

—BH

M83: *"Don't Save Us from the Flames"* 2005

Now that indie rock and electronic dance music enjoy a symbiotic relationship, it's easy to forget they used to be a binary. The former emphasized manual dexterity and human slippage; the latter, conceptual dexterity and mechanical precision. But as consumer electronics became cheaper and more user-friendly, they started to dovetail with indie's DIY aesthetic, and in the 1990s, labels like Germany's Morr Music cultivated the idea that electronic music could be wedded to indie rock (particularly shoegaze) to produce new emotive possibilities.

France's M83—at first a duo, then the solo work of Anthony Gonzalez—forewent the cerebral aspects of IDM, blending shoegaze's broad, glowing melodies with screaming synthesizers to make Technicolor panoramas. "Don't Save Us from the Flames" nabs grunge's abrupt loud/soft dynamics and fills them out with fey vocals, ghostly harmonies, hard-charging guitars, and celestial synth swirls. But the ghost of techno lingers in its stormy mechanical drum rolls and simmering, house-music-styled verses. It's an overawing example of the analog and the digital lowering their weapons to join in an embrace.

—BH

The Postal Service: *"Such Great Heights"* 2003

With breakout first single "Such Great Heights," the Postal Service—a collaboration between Death Cab for Cutie frontman Ben Gibbard and Dntel/Figurine knob-twiddler Jimmy Tamborello—hoisted the nascent indie-yuppie movement upon its fluttery wings and took off for the mountain of gold glittering in the distance. But as hard as it is to separate the song from the sundry screen love scenes and technology-product commercials it's accompanied, "Such Great Heights" is still a thing of beauty. Tamborello's pointillist bleeps and tender synth swells lift Gibbard's heavenly melody to, um, such great heights, despite the almost unbearable emo-ness of the lyrics. ("I am thinking it's a sign that the freckles in our eyes are mirror images / And when we kiss they're perfectly aligned.")

After "Such Great Heights," the Postal Service became a phenomenon, with their album *Give Up* selling more copies than any Sub Pop record since Nirvana's *Bleach.* The song was covered by Iron and Wine for the 2004 film *Garden State,* and the original version was featured in *The O.C.* and *Grey's Anatomy,* cementing its reputation as the high-water mark for twenty-first-century indie-rock lifestyle branding.

—APh

Annie: *"Heartbeat"* 2004

Annie's "Heartbeat" served as the chief ambassador of the '00s Internet pop underground—the increasing ubiquity of mp3 trading via blogs, file-sharing networks, and message boards boosted DJ/diva Anne Lilia Berge-Strand, of Bergen, Norway, to small-scale international stardom before she had even released any music or played any shows outside of Scandinavia. Simultaneously, discovering the pleasures of someone like Annie helped erode the barrier many conservative indie fans had placed between themselves and mainstream dance pop.

DSL lines worldwide were lit up by "Heartbeat"'s classic narrative of falling for a stranger on the dance floor, sung by Annie with such giddy, glassy breathlessness that she seems on the verge of fainting. Producers Torbjørn Brundtland and Svein Berge (of Röyksopp) counterbalance the melody's brittle antigravitational pull with four-on-the-floor bass and live drums that pulse, of course, like a heartbeat.
—*APh*

M.I.A.: *"Galang"* 2003

At its core, M.I.A.'s "Galang" is a great school-yard nonsense song, a bubbly ditty with a shuddering jump-rope beat and bratty chant-along chorus, perfect for braiding hair and talking about boys. Yes, its lyrics reference shotguns, the Feds, and blow jobs, and it's sung by a woman whose father is a leader of the Sri Lankan extremist group the Tamil Tigers. Its video features cartoon tanks and explosions. But if "Galang," like all of Maya Arulpragasam's music, wasn't so much fun, so infectious and full of verve, would anybody care?

It can get messy digging into the nitty gritty of M.I.A.'s politics. She's no saint, and she's the first person to admit it. But it's telling that in the few years since "Galang" first ignited the blogosphere, M.I.A.'s primary cultural influence hasn't been a grand dialogue about terrorism or immigration or sexism: It's the way her rhythmic, pan-global sound has infiltrated the Top 40. Her polyglot textures would be heard all over hit pop albums throughout much of the rest of the decade.
—*APh*

The White Stripes: *"Seven Nation Army"* 2003

Following the unpredicted success of the White Stripes' *White Blood Cells,* Jack White opened follow-up *Elephant* with seven notes that sound like a bass line but are actually played on guitar. It's an inside joke and a defining Stripes moment, a clever rebuke to all those baseless accusations that his drums-and-guitar band was too skeletal, that he and bandmate/ex-wife Meg needed a low end.

The rest of "Seven Nation Army" works even harder to prove their bravado. Reverting to recognizably guitar-generated sounds, Jack elaborates on that central riff like he's working the soil, while Meg follows close behind, forcefully chucking beats into the ground. Poor Meg gets no end of hassle from the band's detractors for not being a "good" drummer, as if "good" means playing lots of fills. But here her rudimentary rhythms keep Jack's sophisticated guitar work in check, so that the song strikes with a blunt, primitive force. The Stripes never reveal the full extent of their arsenal—a strategic restraint—and never morph into the kind of proficient rawk that many listeners wanted (and got, with diminished results, from Jack White's other band, the Raconteurs). "Seven Nation Army" not only serves as the best argument for the duo's self-imposed limitations, but lets them poke fun at expectations of excess.
—*SD*

Franz Ferdinand: *"Take Me Out"* 2004

At a moment when the UK's music weeklies were still obsessed with the Strokes, this Scottish band's breakthrough single spent its entire first minute playing the kind of choppy, eighth-note pop most Strokes imitators would have been thrilled to cook up for themselves. But then they stopped, stomped, changed tempo, and broke out into something else entirely—a loose-limbed dance-rock tune that's as much Duran Duran as anything else, complete with a suave, arched-eyebrow bridge that reeks of total, casual confidence. Cheeky, right? They dangled what you might enjoy and expect right in front of your nose, then whipped back the curtain: Just kidding!

After the end of the 1990s' Britpop explosion, those British rock magazines struggled to figure out where to go next: They got curious about chart pop, flirted with covering the emo and nu metal younger kids

were getting into, and found themselves settling for putting American bands on their covers a lot more often. This single was, for better or worse, one of a wave that reinvigorated the kind of British post-punk guitar pop those magazines had been devoted to for years—and soon enough Franz Ferdinand and bands like the Futureheads, Bloc Party, and Arctic Monkeys returned homegrown pop rock to its central place in the UK music media.
—NA

The Fiery Furnaces:
"Here Comes the Summer" 2005

The fact that "Here Comes the Summer" is actually the middle section of a three-song suite pretty much explains straight away why the Fiery Furnaces are as love-it-or-hate-it as bands come. Zealots fall for their giddy compulsion to add multiple layers to their songs and their soft spot for British Invasion concept records; haters find their arrangements overcooked and their juvenilia cloying. "Summer," however, is truce territory, a moment where the band's unabashed garage-pop powers peek out like the sun amidst the concept-heavy clouds.

There's still a lot to chew on, including a chatty wah guitar and a good half-dozen keyboards, but it's not so busy as to overwhelm the song's melodic heart, a reminiscence that takes on the catchy nursery-rhyme meter of so many Furnaces tunes. In it, the Chicago-bred Friedbergers romanticize the warm-weather months as only people born in frigid cities can. Meanwhile, all that synthesizer mayhem proves itself necessary to the plot, as it overwhelms the melancholy piano of the verses to simulate a street-fair arcade on the choruses, a seasonal contrast clever and subtle enough to satisfy Furnace lovers and haters alike.
—RM

The Mountain Goats: "No Children" 2003

John Darnielle has performed as one-man band the Mountain Goats since the early '90s, but on 2003's *Tallahassee,* he finally ditched his straight-to-boombox recording technique and brought a full band to bear on his Alpha Couple, a pair of recurring characters whose relationship he's explored throughout his discography. The thread binding the pair doesn't snap during "No Children,"

but our narrator—a hard-drinking firebrand with a fleeting soft spot—wishes it would. He stuffs eighteen fantasies into a song less than three minutes long, summed up by the brutal clincher "I hope you die / I hope we both die." Despite the acoustic guitar and the piano that winks beneath it, this is an anthem for total annihilation, branding the black destruction of heavy metal into a northern Florida disaster of desire and despair.
—GC

The Wrens: "She Sends Kisses" 2003

The accordion doesn't get much play in indie rock, and hearing its earnest whine in the first few seconds sets the tone for this swooning, unapologetic ballad. Live, The Wrens ended it in a meltdown of distortion, but here they're content to let it simmer and make its point more eloquently; the lurch of its first wordless chorus is that much heavier without an underline.

"She Sends Kisses" is one of many examples of the Wrens recycling their own lyrics and weaving layers and mythologies out of them; the same exchange of letters described here would cause some friction in "Ex-Girl Collection" later on the same record, and as far as confessional lyrics go, "she worked lost and found / I put your face on her all year" is some cold shit. For other artists, going back to the well would be a red flag, but the Wrens just find more and more inspiration. These navels run deep.
—JC

Les Savy Fav: "The Sweat Descends" 2004

It might not be completely true, but it's as close to the truth as lead singer Tim Harrington's likely to get: "My tight young skin covers up a sick palimpsest." The skin is attached to a frontman best described as a cuddly whirling dervish. Part Iggy Pop, part Uncle Buck, Harrington's a performer as calculated as he is spontaneous. During a live show, he's just as likely to jump into the crowd to scream into your face and smother you in his chest hair as he is to unfurl a Slip 'n Slide, strip down to his tighty-whities, and give it a go.

As for this palimpsest, it's covered with alluring and lurid phrases about sweat and skin and mouth and tongue, tied together by consonance, repetition, and Harrington's indomitable delivery. Meanwhile, the rest of the group succeeds in matching Harrington's lyrical and physical twists and turns—guitarist Seth

Jabour embarks upon another of his glorious Andy-Gill-at-Red-Rocks heroic moments, while the rhythm section puts four to the floor and sets the death disco's roof on fire. The end result of this hodgepodge is a rocking post-punk bomb blast where the phrase "meet me where the sweat descends" is all at once an invitation, a rallying cry, and a threat.

—DR

Ted Leo and the Pharmacists:
"Where Have All the Rude Boys Gone?" 2003

From fronting Chisel, a marginally successful power-pop group in the '90s, to bigger success leading the Pharmacists, Ted Leo has endeared himself to his fans in part by acting like one himself. Cramming his lyrics with literary and musical references, Leo has stepped onstage to Dexys Midnight Runners, worn Thin Lizzy jackets in his liner photos, and made studious nods to his heroes throughout his songs. Nowhere is that clearer than *Hearts of Oak*'s "Where Have All the Rude Boys Gone?", Leo's valentine to the Specials. Second-wave ska it's not—the rapid rockabilly guitars and softer keyboards evoke someplace where pompadoured punks can swing with the New Wave kids with caked eyeliner—but almost every lyric is a nod to the 2 Tone band.

Leo's guitar chops—try following every note of that skipping sleight-of-hand riff at the beginning—are not unwelcome in the material he pays tribute to, or even in indie rock in general. Yet despite Leo's dexterity on the guitar, his inimitable, elastic voice, his high-minded lyrics, and his relentless tour ethic, he still somehow comes off as a music-loving everyman. Sometimes the smartest man in the room is also the most likable.

—JC

The Exploding Hearts:
"Modern Kicks" 2003

Portland, Oregon's Exploding Hearts could have been a page straight out of the Big Book of Rock and Roll Clichés: four dudes decked out in leather pants and denim jackets, sneering and cursing and banging out two-minute, three-chord songs. But more than thirty years after the Ramones, the Clash, and Cheap Trick debuted, they somehow made well-studied reimaginings of all things punk and power-pop—buzz-saw guitars and teenage romanticism—sound new. Their 2003 debut, *Guitar Romantic,* opens with "Modern Kicks," which finds the Hearts at their most anthemic and exuberant, drawing equally from the jangly pop of Raspberries and the propulsive punk of Buzzcocks. When three of the band's four members died in a car crash in July 2003, it marked the tragic and untimely end of a band willing to make exactly the music they wanted without fear of being misunderstood or dismissed.

—ML

Art Brut: "Formed a Band" 2004

The sheer exuberance of Art Brut's 2004 debut single put the South London quintet mustache-and-shoulders above the stylized moodiness of that year's UK post-punk revival. An ingeniously obvious chorus—"We formed a band!"—didn't hurt either. Charismatic frontman Eddie Argos ranted more than sang, but he wasn't afraid to hit high notes—for example, peace in the Middle East, brokered by "a song as universal as 'Happy Birthday.'"

Implicit throughout "Formed a Band" is a do-it-yourself ethic. In that way, Art Brut stayed truer to the British independent-label movement that spawned post-punk than their haircut-indie contemporaries. Not only didn't Argos worry about selling out, he was equally unconcerned about another post-punk demon, the poseur. Art Brut never played on the British TV show *Top of the Pops* as promised, and wars didn't cease, but "Formed a Band" wasn't irony. Argos's plainspoken lyrics evoked the words of UK punks Desperate Bicycles in 1977: "It was easy. It was cheap. Go and do it."

—MH

Boris: "Farewell" 2005

Tokyo trio Boris put a Nick Drake–pastiche album sleeve on their *Akuma no Uta* LP, paying tribute to the folk singer's *Bryter Layter,* and have parodied Virgin Records' Roger Dean–drawn label-art logo. Even "Boris," the name they lifted off track one of Melvins' *Bullhead,* was as much a send-up as an homage—a way of standing the elder band's grunge-godfather reputation on its head and fanning them out in a deck that included not just Black Sabbath and Blue Cheer, but Cocteau Twins, Merzbow, and Nick Cave.

Despite its misleading title, "Farewell" was actually the first song on *Pink,* the band's 2005 release on metal imprint Southern Lord. This clever sequencing turnaround presaged what was to come: Where "Farewell" envisioned metal as shoegaze—long and swirling, patient and chiming—the rest of the record would be a filthy, garage-rocked suite of short, churning songs. This after a decade of experimentation that took them from grating collaborations with Japanese psych guru Keiji Haino to the resonating calm of 2000's *Flood.* When *Pink* landed on U.S. shores, the liners included a series of squares resembling either Pantone color chips or acid tabs, but the implication was meant to be ambiguous: Whatever you were looking for, you could find here.

—ZB

Mastodon: *"Sleeping Giant"* 2006

Mastodon's take on metal is as queasy and unsettling as it is cathartic. The Atlanta quartet lurches and heaves into new time signatures without warning, piling riffs on top of riffs and never settling into a consistent groove for long. Their 2004 record *Leviathan* might've been a concept album about Moby Dick, but it wasn't a smarter-than-thou lit-crit lecture; it was an LP about a big whale that smashed a lot of shit and killed a lot of people, and it fucking ruled.

"Sleeping Giant" is the first single from the band's follow-up and major-label debut, *Blood Mountain,* but it isn't a pop move by anyone's standards. The song unfolds on its own schedule, opening with an ominous swirl, a lonely acoustic guitar floating through a marsh of heaving sludge. Once it finally snaps into gear, Brent Hinds's strangulated roar burbles up from the depths while his and Bill Kelliher's guitars crash into each other. The lyrics are mythic gibberish, but then again, ambiguous power-fantasy mysticism has always been one of metal's biggest selling points.

—TB

Madvillain: *"America's Most Blunted"* 2003

Empty, flowery rhymes; no bite; no beats. The traditional knock on indie hip-hop has always been that in the course of defining itself in diametric opposition to the mainstream, it unwittingly cut itself off from some of rap's best bits. The result of a joint collaboration between two of the genre's biggest names (Long Island's MF Doom and California's Madlib), Madvillain's 2004 album *Madvillainy* struck

an ideological blow for the indie side by giving it its first classic album in years. With its jokey spoken-word bits, weed references, chugging soul rhythms, false starts, highbrow samples (the intro pinches from a backpacker favorite, Steve Reich's "Come Out"), cartoonist interjections, and pitched-up verses (courtesy of Madlib nom de plume Lord Quasimoto), "America's Most Blunted" is probably as concise a four-minute distillation of the Stones Throw label's contribution to hip-hop as exists, offering up a feature-rich example of how indie rap can thrive on its own terms. In Madvillain's case, it's by tempering indie rap's emo tendencies with an undercurrent of irreverence and by putting particular emphasis on producerly virtuosity with a constantly shifting palette of samples and sounds.

—MP

T.I.: *"What You Know"* 2006

In the context of mainstream rap, the regal synth pattern that forms the backbone of the triumphant "What You Know" sounded unorthodox; but in the context of Southern rap, it sounded downright out of place. Before the emergence of Atlanta's T.I., the South was, for better and for worse, largely constrained to a specific blueprint: Its production was minimal and cavernous, with coarse accents on the high and low ends, leaving lots of empty space for the vocals. T.I.'s ascent to the top of Georgia's rap circuit was a quick one, and by the time he proclaimed himself "King of the South," he'd already established a strong tendency to mess with the blueprint. With its cheery organ lead and junior-choir backing, 2003's David Banner–produced "Rubberband Man" put a fresh spin on the style, while 2004's jubilant "Bring Em Out" combined an unlikely Jay-Z sample with an even more unlikely barrage of lurching rhythms. But neither was as thrilling as this majestic DJ Toomp–produced single, whose baroque, French-house-inspired production beat Daft Punk collaborator and Justice fan Kanye West to the punch.

—MP

Kelly Clarkson: *"Since U Been Gone"* 2004

It's one thing to survive the ridiculously cutthroat dog-and-pony show that is *American Idol*; it's another entirely to survive the music industry. After beating out ten thousand contestants to take top prize during

Selling Advertising: Indie Songs in Commercials Shockah

Tom Waits may be spinning on his barstool, but by now we've all given in to hearing our favorite bands scoring the latest transmissions from our corporate overlords. Sure, shock and indignation was the Pavlovian response that all those years of indie-rock-trination taught us to feel when we first heard the Jam shilling Cadillacs, but that ire couldn't last. Eventually, it became apparent that the flacks working down at the ad agency were twentysomethings raised on *120 Minutes* just like the rest of us, and it was hard to begrudge bands looking to put a couple of extra gallons of fuel in the van for the summer tour. Advertising is the new radio, and we might as well learn to love it, all while drinking Coke Zero and munching on Big Macs.

"Pink Moon," **Nick Drake** (Volkswagen): The godfather of indie-soundtracked commercials, which brilliantly rebranded the VW image from Haight-Ashbury to Park Slope in thirty seconds. Bronze it and put it in the Hall of Fame.

"New Slang," **the Shins** (McDonalds): A melody so sweet it could sell you on the horrors of Filets-O-Fish and McRibs, but they had to have noticed the "dirt in your fries" line, right?

"Wraith Pinned to the Mist (and Other Games)," **Of Montreal** (Outback Steakhouse): Notoriously one of the few to agree to a lyrics change; Kevin Barnes subsequently claimed that selling out is no longer possible.

"Young Folks," **Peter Bjorn and John** (fucking everything): Hey, it's that whistle song! Let's buy a computer/convertible/insurance policy/riding lawnmower/knife set/Nautilus/HeadOn/Fathead of Gilbert Arenas/commemorative plate…

"Seventeen Years," **Ratatat** (Hummer): Few indie-endorsement choices can be considered morally questionable; nobody's shilling Hennessy for Kids (yet). But Ratatat better be all caught up on their carbon offsets. Just sayin'.

"Gravity Rides Everything," **Modest Mouse** (Nissan Quest): Then again, glamorizing four-mpg global-warming machines isn't anywhere near as embarrassing as having your thorny space-rock epic co-opted by a soccer mom's pimp ride.

"Such Great Heights," **The Postal Service** (UPS): True story: The United States Postal Service almost sued the band for infringement, which makes sense; I can't tell you how many times I mistakenly tried to buy stamps from Ben Gibbard.

"Remind Me," **Röyksopp** (Geico): Not sure if it's a compliment or an insult, but this song is an absolute perfect stand-in for the ambient background music of airport terminals. Good counterpoint to scowling cavemen, too.

"1 2 3 4," **Feist** (iPod): 1, 2, 3, 4 times per hour was roughly the rate at which this commercial appeared in the summer of 2007, but Apple is the John Peel of corporations, a guaranteed hitmaker (see also Jet, if you must).

Various songs from *Sky Blue Sky,* Wilco (Volkswagen): And VW takes us full circle, from pursuing the hipster demo with obscure folk singers to pursuing the, well, aging hipster demo with Jeff Tweedy's songs of domestic contentment. Guess which group has more disposable income.
—*RM*

the talent contest's inaugural season in 2002, Texan Kelly Clarkson found herself subjected to a host of contractually obligated indignities, beginning with schlocky debut single "A Moment Like This" and ending with the schlockier *American Idol*–sanctioned film *From Justin to Kelly.* It says volumes about 2004's "Since U Been Gone" that it not only wiped Clarkson's slate clean, but also improbably won over the type of listener who otherwise wouldn't have been caught dead admiring a TV pop star.

It helped that the interlocking guitars and thunderous breakdown of "Since U Been Gone" recalled the Strokes' "Barely Legal" and Yeah Yeah Yeahs' "Maps," respectively; paired with Clarkson's rangy vocal performance, those indie-rooted elements made the song even tougher to discount. Much like Britney Spears' "Toxic" and Justin Timberlake's "My Love," the status of "Since U Been Gone" as pop crossover success story was acknowledged with a handful of loving covers by everyone from Ted Leo to Robyn to Gossip, but it was legitimized as soon as Clarkson belted out *that* chorus.
—MP

Amerie: *"1 Thing"* 2005

The opening clang of "1 Thing"—a harsh, startling shard of guitar and the pulverizing blizzard of drums that follows—are the stuff of modern R&B perfection. They're also a sliver of funk's past. A tight, simple loop from New Orleans funk architects the Meters' "Oh, Calcutta!" comprises the entirety of the song, exhiliratingly mined and chopped by R&B impresario Rich Harrison. But what takes "1 Thing" out of its freewheeling rhythm flurry and into transcendent pop experience is the almost inscrutable siren wail of Amerie Rogers.

Hardly an Aretha Franklin–style belter, Amerie was a little-celebrated coquette, for her looks but never for her clipped, bracing tone—a cheery but tenacious howl. On previous songs, Amerie's tone was jarring—too abrupt to be a balladeer, too girlish to sexually attack a track. "1 Thing" is the perfect convergence of Harrison's ringing, Washington, D.C., go-go-inspired sound and a zoned-in Amerie, yelping, cooing, and whining in key about "this one thing that got me trippin'." Her vocals come hard, fast, and intrepid, the sound of a singer dying to be heard, waiting at your door. Ding dong, ding dong ding.
—SF

Ciara [ft. Ludacris]: *"Oh"* 2004

If crunk, the Southern hip-hop style that dominated the pop-rap landscape in the early 2000s, was all about being wild and in-your-face—you know, getting crunk—then Ciara's "Oh" is its inverse. Although steeped in a crunk pedigree, "Oh" is leisurely and seductive, coy rather than confrontational. The hydraulic lift of producers Dre and Vidal's yawning bass is like a chasm opening and shutting, with synthesizers whistling and sparkling behind Ciara's murmuring. She's not a great singer, but she's a great breather—listen to the way she exhales the title word in the chorus.

In 2005, when "Oh" became Ciara's third Top 5 single from her debut album *Goodies,* it cemented her status as the Princess of Crunk 'n' B—and not just because Ciara's middle name is actually Princess. The song is a club banger and slow jam at once, something to soundtrack both car-humping dance moves and between-the-sheets slinking.
—APh

The Go! Team: *"The Power Is On"* 2004

The indie kids do love the thrift stores. In spite of this, few artists had effectively created an accurate musical representation of resale shops until the Go! Team came along. Documentary filmmaker Ian Parton did the dirty work of searching the dusty shelves and overcrowded racks for the choicest musical debris, coming away with an amalgam of jump-rope chants, show-theme brass, and educational-film soundtracks. All these components are on parade in "The Power Is On," along with the elements that crucially differentiate Parton's sample-driven party-rock from the hundreds of DJs doing similar Dumpster-diving: the sheets of Sonic Youthish noise and a lo-fi basement aesthetic that gives the song a Super-8 grain.

Often such genre grab-bags end up chaotic failures, but Parton collages adeptly, substituting double-dutch girls for MCs, conjuring up a piano thunderstorm, shadowboxing with horn-section blasts, and crusting it all with shrieking guitar abuse. Instead of coasting on empty, nostalgic button-pushing, Parton isolates the warm and unique properties of each sample, reconstituting it as a sun-faded historical document of a musical era that never existed. Anyone can

pull that ironic T-shirt off the thrift-store racks, but it takes a pro to piece together a whole outfit.
—RM

Feist: *"Mushaboom"* 2004

Before she was a star, Leslie Feist logged years as a rhythm guitarist in a line of Canadian indie bands. Despite raising the curtain on her tremendous voice and solo career with 1999's *Monarch,* she wasn't given her due as a frontwoman until three years later, when the Canadian collective Broken Social Scene released *You Forgot It in People.* Emboldened by her memorable on-album performances, Feist's booming voice and hypnotic fitfulness dominated their concerts. Not surprisingly, her next album brimmed with confidence, heart, and style, and the glowing "Mushaboom" was its center.

"Mushaboom" is named after a village about an hour's drive east of Feist's hometown of Halifax, Nova Scotia. The lyrics spin a fantasy about retiring to the countryside, while the song's nursery-rhyme melodies and rich palette of sounds (glockenspiels, horns, backward-looped acoustic guitars, and handclaps) proved accessible enough to cross over to a wider, milder audience. In fact, this vision of pleased domesticity—delivered by a still-hip chanteuse— was the perfect mixed message for the graying indie rockers who embraced her in droves even before her unexpected iPod-commercial-fueled Top 10 single "1 2 3 4" in 2007.
—MP

Arcade Fire:
"Neighborhood #1 (Tunnels)" 2004

First on the teenager fantasy charts has to be the one about the world suffering some sort of huge catastrophe that leaves behind no one but the teenager and the object of his affection. For Arcade Fire, this daydream was prime material for the first installment of *Funeral*'s "Neighborhood" cycle, wherein a snowstorm (they're Canadian, ya know) buries everyone but the narrator and his love, who heroically start civilization anew. But Arcade Fire melodrama is anything but mellow, and "Tunnels" was an early sign of their signature wide-screen scope, a style that helped restore earnest grandeur to the inward irony of indie. Win Butler's quaver suits

the diary-entry lyrics, and the song just keeps upping the ante: the out-of-context disco-punk drums and xylophone, the sawed strings, and the "Chopsticks"-like piano all building to one of their many chorally cathartic finales. It's a formula, sure, but at a time when rock music struggled to find ways to be emotional without being emo, Arcade Fire's all-out live approach was a much-needed alternative to simpering faux intimacy: beating on drums (and fellow band members) with sticks and shouting "WOAH-OH" into megaphones translated the tumult of teenage trauma.
—RM

Wolf Parade: *"I'll Believe in Anything"* 2005

The history of indie rock boasts no lack of comple-mentary, competitive songwriting partnerships: Hüsker Dü's Bob Mould and Grant Hart, the Go-Betweens' Robert Forster and Grant McLennan, Uncle Tupelo's Jay Farrar and Jeff Tweedy. But the Wolf Parade tandem of Dan Boeckner and Spencer Krug seems particularly incompatible. While guitarist Boeckner loaded up the Montreal band's 2005 debut *Apologies to the Queen Mary* with shots of blue-collar bravado ("Shine a Light," "This Heart's on Fire"), keyboardist Krug answered them with twitchy misfit laments—a game of tug-of-war that reached its breaking point with Krug's "I'll Believe in Anything."

On first approach, the song reads as a simple plea for love: "Give me your eyes / I need sunshine," Krug sings, with the prepubescent creak of a nervous teenager asking out his first date. But as the song builds from a martial, organ-grinding stomp into a capsizing surge, there's a creeping sense that Krug isn't singing to a girl but to her ghost. The double-time, victory-lap finale suggests a happy ending, but only because Krug's desperate performance makes you want to believe in one.
—SB

Band of Horses: *"The Funeral"* 2006

When Seattle's Band of Horses released their debut LP, *Everything All the Time,* in early 2006, it was awfully easy to sniff at and dismiss: Vocalist Ben Bridwell sounded a whole lot like My Morning Jacket's Jim James (already channeling Neil Young via Wayne Coyne). Still, Band of Horses' sweeping guitar-rock is huge and lonely, equally well-suited for hurtling down the highway or writhing around on your bedroom floor, and no matter how familiar it may seem on paper, the band's celestial noise is also strange, gripping, and epic.

"The Funeral," the record's first single, is centered around Bridwell's howled assertion that "At every occasion / I'll be ready for the funeral," which—aside from sounding like something Johnny Cash might have mumbled in 1957—describes the experience of watching someone self-destruct. Bridwell's high, tinny pipes stretch for the highest notes, while his bandmates pound on electric guitars, all sopped with reverb. The track is as disorienting as it is stunning, simultaneously fast and slow, bellowing and soft, comforting and completely unsettling.
—AP

The Hold Steady:
"Stuck Between Stations" 2006

The Hold Steady may have earned a reputation as the indie world's best bar band, but the group is less keg-soaked frat boy than literate, stool-bum drunk. "Stuck Between Stations," for instance, kicks off the group's third album, *Boys and Girls in America,* with a thesis statement built from a Jack Kerouac quote ("Boys and girls in America have such a sad time together") and the song's second verse is an account of the Minneapolis suicide of poet John Berryman. That's a pretty hefty syllabus for a four-minute rock song. But the library-card approach works for the Hold Steady, a band whose philosophy is rooted in the kind of profundities that come from chemical-fueled introspection, with characters drinking both to escape and to understand life's static.

Of course, all that pharmaceutical insight comes with a price tag, and "Stuck Between Stations" paints that trade-off vividly, the night's warm feeling vs. the morning's dehydration. But just in case things get too chin-stroking, the Hold Steady haul out classic-rock signifiers like they're going out of style (which they were) to mimic alcohol's ability to inflate every experience. After all, you just can't sing—or in singer/songwriter Craig Finn's case, lecture—early morning epiphany lines like "we drink and we dry up, and then we crumble into dust," without some crunchy power chords and E Street Band piano.
—RM

2007

If any proof were needed that contemporary music stacks up with the best sounds from the Baby Boomer era or earlier, 2007 provided it. From LCD Soundsystem's heartbreaking ruminations on aging to M.I.A.'s 21st-century appropriations of agit-pop to Battles' jaw-dropping and almost inhuman mix of dance dynamics and live playing, many of the year's top artists not only reminded us that pop is as crucial as it ever has been but that much of today's most engaging and rewarding work is a product of our times, music that could only be made in the here and now. Here are 15 future classics that would have competed for spots in our 500 had they been released just one year earlier:

"Fireworks," **Animal Collective:** In 2000, when they were inhabiting a space far left of even indie rock's center, you would have got long odds on Animal Collective becoming one of the most critically loved and, hell, important bands of the 2000s, but here we are. Longtime fans grumbled that AC's *Strawberry Jam* had too many songs and not enough tungs, but even the most protective listeners wouldn't trade the stirring "Fireworks" for a few less jam band and frat dudes at the band's shows.

"Keep the Car Running," **Arcade Fire:** Weirdly maligned in some circles, *Neon Bible* was an earnest adult album rather than an earnest adolescent one (see: *Funeral*). Apparently this reminded people of Bruce Springsteen. Wait, that's supposed to be a bad thing?

"Atlas," **Battles:** Man met machine on this prog-indie stomper, as this mathy supergroup proved that technicical proficiency needn't be missing hooks, melodies, a keen awareness of electronic music, or fun.

"Archangel," **Burial:** Dubstep made deserved waves in 2007, thanks to Burial's addition of vocals—albeit, chopped, screwed, and downright ghostly ones.

"In the City," **Chromatics:** Cold and bleak, the 2000s Italo revival—led by the Italians Do It Better label—was the soundtrack to the train or car ride home from the party rather than the good times themselves. There was still something sleek and sultry about it all, but it came across as if glamour and hedonism were fleeting and empty. Maybe they are.

"Wham City," **Dan Deacon:** This epic theme to a famed Baltimore performance space encapsulated everything great and wonderful about not only the idiosyncratic Deacon, but about the burgeoning electronic and noise underground of the decade. A Day-Glo paean to eschewing cool in favor of fun and individualism, "Wham City" was like a symphony for and by outcasts and geeks, a throwback to 1980s indie, when the point was to be yourself, even if it meant standing out, rather than being someone else and desperately aiming to fit in.

"Rise Above," **Dirty Projectors:** Along with their friends in Vampire Weekend and groups like Celebration and Yeasayer, the Projectors spearheaded a new interest in African music. But conceptual nonsense aside—singer Dave Longstreth insists that *Rise Above* is his interpretation of Black Flag's *Damaged,* played by memory—this album, and particularly its title track, sparked excitement because they're so galvanizing and hopeful.

"1 2 3 4," **Feist:** Even before the Apple ad, Feist had two albums that had sold more than 200,000 copies, but to many she'll still be seen as an overnight sensation. Not that her success isn't deserved: Whether penning her own songs or interpreting those of others ("1 2 3 4" itself was written by New Buffalo), Feist's smooth vocals and grinning persona were endearing from the start.

"D.A.N.C.E.," **Justice:** Blog house, it was called; a decade earlier, it would have been "electronica." Over-compressed, rock-oriented, as subtle as a monster truck—these were selling points to those dipping their toes into Justice and other post-Daft Punk French touch music. Yet on the sunshine playground chant "D.A.N.C.E." even the cognoscenti caved, making it the dance-floor anthem of 2007.

"All My Friends," **LCD Soundsystem:** LCD's James Murphy receives a lot of credit as a sonic archeologist and architect par excellence, but since his first single ("Losing My Edge / "Beat Connection") he's also functioned as an indie scene sociologist. On "All My Friends" he tackled aging, guilt, regret, and doomed expectations with wit and grace.

"Paper Planes (Remix)," **M.I.A. [ft. Bun B and Rich Boy]:** On her second album, *Kala,* this polyglot star shrugged off the "fad" accusations by expanding her worldview to encompass not only London, Kingston, New York, and Sri Lanka, but Bollywood, Africa, and the Dirty South as well. Sampling the Clash's politically charged "Straight to Hell" and appropriating booty anthem "Rump Shaker," M.I.A. here mixed party music and agit-pop into an irresistible blend. The remix with Bun B and Rich Boy improbably improved on the original.

"The Past Is a Grotesque Animal," **Of Montreal:** Elephant 6 vet Kevin Barnes reinvented himself in the 2000s as a glam-pop chameleon, playfully working in character and costume on stage even as he was painfully and pointedly examining himself in song. "We want our film to be beautiful / Not realistic," Barnes admitted, but on this ambitious 12-minute disco-rooted anthem he managed to accomplish both.

"Umbrella," **Rihanna [ft. Jay-Z]:** The Event Pop song of 2007, "Umbrella"—like "Crazy" and "Hey Ya" before it—was not only the car-and-club hit of summer, but crossed over to listeners of all ages and sensibilities, a rare feat in our continually splintered-demo times. At its heart a song of fidelity and durability, Rihanna sold it by famously stretching a few syllables, and the performance cemented her as the R&B princess of the late 2000s. Oh, and Jay-Z has on a verse on it, I think.

"The Underdog," **Spoon:** Few bands make simple look this good: On the face of it, Spoon offer what any number of guitar pop groups are doing, playing traditionally crafted verse-chorus-verse, same as rock ever was. And yet, songs like "The Underdog" boast intricate, charming details polished with a bit of blue-eyed soul. Sometimes the underdog comes out on top.

"Int'l Players Anthem (I Choose You)," **UGK [ft. Outkast]:** The long-suffering UGK stuck together through the incarceration of Pimp C, missed opportunities to capitalize on guest appearances on classic singles "Big Pimpin'" (Jay-Z) and "Sippin' on Some Syrup" (Three 6 Mafia), and record-label interference. So when these Underground Kingz finally landed a number 1 album, and this OutKast-assisted single became a chart smash, it was especially gratifying. By the end of the year, however, Pimp C would be found dead in a hotel room—a tragic ending for of one of hip-hop's most underappreciated groups.
—SP

Beirut: *"Postcards from Italy"* 2006

At nineteen, Zach Condon recorded *Gulag Orkestar* in his Albuquerque bedroom, receiving additional recording help and instrumentation from Neutral Milk Hotel's Jeremy Barnes, among others. Beirut's blend of indie rock and Balkan brass first made waves on mp3 blogs due to Condon's youth, charisma, unique melodic sense, and rich, compelling vocal presence. Befitting Condon's focus on European subjects (songs visit Slovakia, Germany, and Italy) and sounds (he often conjured a Russian man five times his age), the cover of the album featured an image snapped by Russian photographer Sergey Chilikov, which Condon said he found in a German library.

The album's standout, "Postcards from Italy," is a nostalgic, infectious story of love—and perhaps death—accented by majorette drumming, horns, and a ukulele that mixes deftly with Condon's airy singing. Like much of Beirut's output, it sounds like the work of a 1930s crooner. During the rush of accolades and online excitement, Condon relocated to Brooklyn, but he continued to travel musically: After *Gulag,* Condon and his new eight-piece band set much of his second album, *The Flying Club Cup,* in France.
—*BS*

Johnny Boy: *"You Are the Generation That Bought More Shoes and You Get What You Deserve"* 2004

This isn't what protest music is supposed to sound like. Evoking a cut-and-paste aesthetic rather than the one-man-against-the-machine demonstrations of Phil Ochs and Bob Dylan, "You Are the Generation" still proves as righteous as "I Ain't Marching Anymore" and as bitterly sarcastic as "Like a Rolling Stone." Except Liverpool duo Johnny Boy are talking about throwing an entire generation of Hollister shoppers out on their asses.

Johnny Boy shoplift their sounds ambitiously, opening "Generation" with drums straight out of "Be My Baby" and piling on layers of sampled bells, cymbals, chimes, guitars, tympani, and heraldic trumpets. Lolly Hayes sings with no restraint but considerable poise, while choirs recite "oh baby" and "yeah yeah!" like cries

of freedom, as if they've just shed their consumerist shackles and started rioting in the streets. The sound is provocative, deploying warmly familiar elements to express a prickly message. Indeed, on their first try the duo created one of the most exuberant and angry singles of the 2000s. Of course, the self-titled full-length that followed couldn't maintain the magnificence, but "You Are the Generation" remains a spiraling monument to vintage records and direct action.
—*SD*

Love Is All: *"Busy Doing Nothing"* 2005

If Love Is All didn't exist, an mp3 blog would have to invent them. Beyond the enduring pop-cultural cachet of their home country, Sweden, their arrival onto hipster hit lists in 2005 marked a convergence between the two predominant strains of post-millennial indie-rock: corrosive dance-punk and the sort of defiant, group-chorus hysterics that turned Arcade Fire into messiahs. What's more, the compressed, transistor-radio sound quality of Love Is All's debut album, *Nine Times That Same Song,* feels like it was made to be heard through tinny computer speakers, with singer Josephine Olausson's hyperactive shrieks breaking through the distortion.

"Busy Doing Nothing" starts by stopping you dead in your tracks: With a bracing introductory yell of "Five-movie marathon!" the band kicks into a staccato dub-disco that practically induces a strobe-lit seizure. But the song's debt to first-wave post-punk—not unlike the Pop Group's "She Is Beyond Good and Evil"—goes beyond the stylistic to the ideological: What at first sounds like a celebration of indulgence reveals itself as a sly consumerist critique, proving that—contrary to what Gang of Four once told us—the problem of leisure is not a dearth of pleasure, but an excess of it.
—*SB*

Jens Lekman: *"Black Cab"* 2003

Dread, self-loathing, and the vagaries of tram schedules are about to drive Jens Lekman into a vehicle manned by a possible "killer." He gets through the night the only way he knows how: by cranking some classic pop songs. On "Black Cab,"

the Gothenburg, Sweden–based singer/songwriter samples a harpsichord from 1960s baroque-pop group the Left Banke to frame a tale familiar to anyone who depends on public transportation. "Oh no, goddamn / I missed the last tram," Lekman sings between upbeat guitars and lo-fi drums. A snippet of flute from Belle and Sebastian's 1996 track "Mary Jo" sets up the refrain, in which he croons about the song's eponymous transit alternative. Alas, the sensitive maestro's intensely personal relationship with pop pushes him away from more socially accept-able forms of interaction. He'll spend time near the stereo, having already confided that the last time he tried to engage with people, he killed the party. As with doe-eyed Boston proto-punk Jonathan Richman, Lekman does his melancholy so deadpan it's funny and sad at once.
—MH

Christian Falk [ft. Robyn and Ola Salo]:
"Dream On" 2006

When Swedish pop singer Robyn first appeared in the late 1990s, she encapsulated the sunny universality of uncomplicated chart pop. Her return to popular consciousness a decade later took a more perilous route: Still singing pop songs, she self-released them and invested them with a disproportionate, unsettling intensity. "Dream On"—ostensibly a duet with the Ark's barely audible Ola Salo—takes this strategy to its limit, its simple but energetic electro-pop drive offering a platform for Robyn to open her arms to all of life's most unwanted: thugs, bad men, punks, lifers, fucked-up interns, pigs, and snitches.

Robyn's voice, like those of many of her Scandinavian peers, is less world-straddling diva than winsome little sister, but it's precisely this fragility that gives her charged delivery its magnetism. When she tells her unloved congregation, "You won't be backstabbed, double-crossed, face down, teeth knocked out, lying in a gutter somewhere," she sounds aware that she's promising something she likely can't deliver. It's only fair that she turn this risk back on her listeners: If the perfect pop song gives its audience what it didn't know it wanted, "Dream On" simply demands a new audience that can live up to the song's own convictions.
—TF

Peter Bjorn and John:
"Young Folks" 2006

Sweden's Peter Bjorn and John had released two previous albums of smart indie pop before *Writer's Block,* their third and the first to receive wide U.S. distribution, launched a single as immense as the skyscrapers depicted on the cover. The joys of "Young Folks," their surprise hit with former Concretes singer Victoria Bergsman, were atypical in their catalog and included the sublime catchiness of a whistled melody (originally inserted as a placeholder for some other instrument until the trio decided it was perfect as it was), an elastic bongo beat, and the homemade grandeur of chiming guitar crashes. It was soon the province of car commercials, sitcom soundtracks, and mtvU. (Kanye West even rapped over it on a mix CD, with disastrous results.) That "Young Folks" became briefly ubiquitous was ironic, given that the song is an ode to exclusivity, a he-said-she-said duet about a clique of two. Meeting at a party, talking all night, Peter Morén and Bergsman don't care about the old folks' nostalgia or the young folks' impressionability. "All we care about is talking," they sing, safe in each other's company. "Talking, only me and you."
—SD

Justice vs. Simian:
"We Are Your Friends" 2006

When UK psych-pop also-rans Simian released their 2002 single "Never Be Alone," few could've guessed the track would spark a new movement in electronic dance music. It took two young Frenchmen's victory in a radio remix contest to expose the electro house anthem within. Justice duo Gaspard Augé and Xavier de Rosnay bludgeoned "Never Be Alone" with metallic beats and blunt electronic riffs and looped singer Simon Lord's portentous, screamed hook. In the process, they discovered a blueprint for what was termed "the new French touch." The retitled "We Are Your Friends" had become an international club hit. Its iconic status was certified when it seized MTV Europe's "Best Video" honors in 2006—over outraged howls from rap's biggest star, Kanye West.

Championed by Paris labels Ed Banger and Kitsuné, this heavily compressed and hard-rock-tinged sound

looked past house's more insular trends to 1990s electronica—especially original French touch robots Daft Punk. While New York dance-punks and London new-ravers raided disco with guitars, Justice led the opposite charge. Their 2007 debut album, †, used hard-rock distortion and iconography in a dance setting.
—MH

Hot Chip: *"Boy from School"* 2006

Despite looking as gawky as your average tech department, London's Hot Chip have always countered their wobbly synth-driven pop with strangely sensual rhythms and melodies. When done well, the effect can be disarming; listening to some of Hot Chip's best songs can feel like dipping your left hand in cold water and your right hand in hot. Where that kind of counterintuitive hotwiring is concerned, "Boy from School" is their crowning achievement.

With sad, keening vocals that think the song is a ballad and glittery rhythms that move like a dance tune, "Boy from School" pulls off the trick of seeming melancholy without wallowing. Some critics have seized on this alchemy as evidence that Hot Chip are a full-band personification of the mp3 mashup era; but really, they're just musical tourists who know how to finesse their way around different genres. As if to prove that, the ensuing interpretations of "Boy from School" pulled different moods from the source material; Hot Chip's own acoustic version played up the song's strength as a nimble ballad, while Erol Alkan's euphoric remix was the peak-time crowd-pleaser of summer 2006.
—MP

Animal Collective: *"Grass"* 2005

On Animal Collective's *Feels,* the avant-pop choral crew included more structure in their post–*Pet Sounds* psychedelic vocal rounds and yelps. When the group's key members, Avey Tare and Panda Bear, first recorded together in 2000, on the album *Spirit They're Gone, Spirit They've Vanished,* the music was ambient, disconnected, echoed, and spare; interestingly, as they gained members and momentum, and moved to different parts of the world (one left for Portugal, the others stayed in New York and Baltimore), their music grew more cohesive. The band has since described *Feels* as their "love

record," but it retains a slightly warped sound, which came from tuning their instruments to loops from a friend's out-of-tune piano. "Grass," the album's gurgling, percussive, scream-y first single, is exactly three minutes long, offering a great example of how as Animal Collective developed, they managed to shove off-kilter signatures and catchy experimental hooks into smaller, more dynamic structures.
—BS

Black Dice: *"Cone Toaster"* 2003

Brooklyn nu-noisers (or post-hardcore tribal drum-circlers, or fractal mindgaze/New Age/junkyard punks) Black Dice helped break through an invisible barrier on this 2003 single by bringing disco to indie's most dance-resistant masses. Their 2002 *Beaches and Canyons* LP had come somewhat out of left field by trading the band's usual extreme noise for ambient textures and sheer prettiness. Their twelve-inch "Cone Toaster" wasn't pretty, but it was kinetic. (Though it's hard to imagine dancing to this track without hurting yourself, it's nonetheless the kind of meta-quantization that many noise and indie bands applied to their music in the early 2000s.) Several elements of the track would become Black Dice staples (especially the guitar loops and thick vocal reverb), but many insist that the band never topped this song's combination of digitally distorted mayhem and 4/4 pound. Reminiscent of Boredoms' similarly robo-chaotic sounds circa their mid-1990s transitional masterpieces *Chocolate Synthesizer* and *Super Roots 5* the jagged, brittle "Cone Toaster" is an example of what can happen when aggression and release meet head-on.
—DL

Liars: *"The Other Side of Mt. Heart Attack"* 2006

Despite this song's lyrical evocation of stability, noise-rock trio Liars are a thrillingly unstable band. Their 2002 dance-punk debut, *They Threw Us All in a Trench and Stuck a Monument on Top,* was wracked by concussive volleys of noise, foreshadowing the detonated terrain of their murky sophomore album, *They Were Wrong, So We Drowned.* In late 2004, Liars decamped for Berlin to experiment with manipulated ceremonial percussion, droning guitars, and incantatory vocals, producing 2006's spectral *Drum's Not Dead.*

"The Other Side of Mt. Heart Attack" caps the anxious *Drums* on an uncharacteristically relaxed note—although like the album, it seems rooted in nothing solid, just silvery guitar, muted bass drum, loose cymbals, and melting vocal harmonies. Amid this barren expanse, charismatic singer Angus Andrew stands alone, intoning vows of consolation. "Heart Attack" moves like an ice age, each subtle shift a collapsing flow—sensitive singer/songwriter material reborn as a vanishing post-punk hymn.
—*BH*

Panda Bear: *"Bros"* 2006

Little kids like loops: kaleidoscopes, music boxes, chair-o-planes, bicycle wheels, cow buttons on plastic toys that moo on command forever. The experimental folk/rock outfit Animal Collective likes to explore the pain and pleasure that come with being a little kid, and band member Panda Bear (aka Noah Lennox) likes to explore loops. "Bros," the lengthy centerpiece of his solo album *Person Pitch,* is built from a handful of samples that Lennox happily lets spin in place without worrying too much about boredom: There's an acoustic guitar strumming a simple pattern that rotates for minutes on end, a recurring drum roll that lends a vague Latin flavor, another electric guitar picking out a few notes, and a tiny little bass line. Through this merry-go-round of sound swoop both effects—people screaming as if on roller coasters, owls hooting, grown men crying—and the honeyed voice of Lennox, singing lyrics about friendship in a reverb-laden tone reminiscent of *Pet Sounds*–era Beach Boys. Though the source material is vintage and the melody sounds Tin Pan Alley, the repetition and layering—techniques informed by contemporary dance music—keep the music grounded in the present. The tension between these elements results in a track that feels unstuck in time, permanently lodged inside a half-remembered dream that could have been last night or thirty years ago.
—*MR*

Acknowledgments

The co-editors wish to thank Amanda Patten and everyone at Touchstone/Fireside for helping make this project possible. For their invaluable work, dedication, and insight, we thank publisher Chris Kaskie; our editing team of Chris Dahlen, Nitsuh Abebe, Catherine Lewis, and Mark Richardson; and all of our contributing writers. For their help, guidance, and time, we thank Chris Capuozzo, Megan Davey, Rich Orris, Shawn Cooper, Mike Reed, and Jud Laghi. In addition, we wish to thank everyone who has ever helped contribute to making Pitchfork the world's largest and best independent music magazine, particularly our current Pitchfork family, who worked even harder than they already do in order to help us to complete this book. Finally, we wish to thank our wives, Elizabeth Schreiber and Sarah Duston, and our families for their support.

Index